Annual Franchise and Distribution Law Developments 2013

Michael R. Gray
Jeffery S. Haff

Consistent with the disclosure policy of the ABA Forum on Franchising, the reader should be aware of the following:

Michael Gray, or his firm, Gray Plant Mooty, represented the franchisors in: AKC, Inc. v. ServiceMaster Clean, No. 13-CV-388, 2013 U.S. Dist. LEXIS 64361 (N.D. Ohio May 6, 2013); Dunkin' Donuts Franchising LLC v. Oza Bros., Inc., No. 10-13606, 2012 U.S. Dist. LEXIS 140595 (E.D. Mich. Sept. 28, 2012); Live, Inc. v. Domino's Pizza, LLC, No., COA12-930, 2013 N.C. App. LEXIS 84 (N.C. Ct. App. Jan. 15, 2013); Dunkin' Donuts Franchising LLC v. Sai Food Hospitality, LLC, No. 11-CV-1484, 2013 U.S. Dist. LEXIS 55518 (E.D. Mo. Apr. 18, 2013); Motorscope, Inc. v. Precision Tune, Inc., No. 12-1296, 2012 U.S. Dist. LEXIS 143735 (D. Minn. Oct. 4, 2012); Progressive Foods, LLC v. Dunkin' Donuts, Inc., Nos. 11-3296, 11-3335, 2012 U.S. App. LEXIS 16815 (6th Cir. Aug. 9, 2012); Ridgestone Bank v. Dunkin' Donuts Franchising LLC, No 13-CV-3126, 2013 U.S. Dist. LEXIS 60859 (N.D. Ill. April 29, 2013); PSP Franchising v. Dubois, No. 12-CV-11693, 2013 U.S. Dist. LEXIS 28048 (E.D. Mich. Feb. 28, 2013); H&R Block Tax Services, LLC v. Franklin, 691 F.3d 941 (8th Cir. 2012); Precision Franchising, LLC v. Gatej, No. 12-CV-158, 2012 U.S. Dist. LEXIS 175450 (E.D. Va. Dec. 11, 2012).

Jeff Haff, or his firm, Dady & Gardner, was either counsel of record, or, at some time during the proceedings, represented parties in the following matters: Motorscope, Inc. v. Precision Tune, Inc., No. 12-1296, 2012 U.S. Dist. LEXIS 143735 (D. Minn. Oct. 4, 2012); North Star International Trucks, Inc. v. Navistar, Inc., No. A12-0732, 2013 Minn. App. Unpub. LEXIS 294 (Minn. Ct. App. Apr. 8, 2013), North Star International Trucks, Inc. v. Navistar, Inc., 2013 Minn. App. Unpub. LEXIS 447 (Minn. Ct. App. May 30, 2013); Long John Silver's Inc. v. Nickleson, No. 11-CV-93, 2013 U.S. Dist. LEXIS 18391 (W.D. Ky. Feb. 12, 2013); KFC Corporation v. Wagstaff, No. 11-CV-00674, 2013 U.S. Dist. LEXIS 86758 (D. Ky. June 19, 2013); American Dairy Queen Corp. v. Blume, No. 11-358, 2013 U.S. Dist. LEXIS 59394 (D. Minn. Jan. 11, 2013).

Printed in the United States of America.

17 16 15 14 13   5 4 3 2 1

ISBN: 978-1-62722-315-7
ISSN: 1548-9582

Discounts are available for books ordered in bulk. Special consideration is given to state bars, CLE programs, and other bar-related organizations. Inquire at Book Publishing, ABA Publishing, American Bar Association, 321 N. Clark Street, 20th Floor, Chicago, Illinois 60654.

www.ShopABA.org

TABLE OF CONTENTS

ABOUT THE AUTHORS

MICHAEL R. GRAY

Michael R. Gray is a partner in the Minneapolis office of Gray Plant Mooty. He brings 27 years of experience representing franchisors, companies and individuals in trial, arbitration and other civil proceedings throughout the United States. He is lead litigation counsel for several national franchise companies and has litigated all manner of franchise and intellectual property disputes in state and federal courts in over 37 states.

Mike has written many articles and presented materials on franchise and intellectual property topics for The International Franchise Association, The American Bar Association Forum on Franchising, The Franchise Law Journal, The Practising Law Institute, The University of St. Thomas and the Business Law Institute. Mike is a contributing author to the *Franchise Desk Book* (W. Michael Garner, Editor), co-authored *Covenants Not to Compete and Nonsignatories: Enjoining Unfair Conspiracies*, 25-WTR Franchise L.J.107, Winter 2006, co-edited *Covenants against Competition in Franchise Agreements*, ABA Forum on Franchising (3d ed. 2012) and most recently co-authored a chapter on "Intellectual Property Issues in Franchising " for the *Intellectual Property Deskbook for the Business Lawyer* (3rd ed. 2013) published by the ABA.

For several years Mike has been named as one of the "Best Lawyers In America" by Woodward/White, a "Super Lawyer" by *Minnesota Law & Politics,* a "Legal Eagle" by *Franchise Times,* is listed in The International Who's Who of Franchise Lawyers and is a "Certified Franchise Executive" by The International Franchise Association. Mike is admitted to practice in Minnesota and Wisconsin as well as numerous Federal District and Appellate Courts throughout the United States. Mike is a graduate of the University of Wisconsin – Madison and Hamline Law School. When he's not working, Mike enjoys restoring old cars, spending time with his family in northern Wisconsin and being outdoors.

ABOUT THE AUTHORS

JEFFERY S. HAFF

Jeffery Haff is a shareholder at Dady & Gardner, P.A. in Minneapolis Minnesota. Jeff has 24 years of experience as a litigation attorney. Since 1995, Jeff has concentrated his practice on representing franchisees, dealers and distributors throughout the United States.

Jeff has been a regular speaker at the ABA Forum on Franchising, and has often been called upon to provide the franchisee's point of view on various legal matters. Jeff is a contributing author to the Franchise Desk Book (W. Michael Garner, Editor), and to Covenants against Competition in Franchise Agreements, ABA Forum on Franchising (3d ed. 2012).

On multiple occasions, Jeff has been named as one of the "Best Lawyers In America" by Woodward/White, a "Super Lawyer" by Minnesota Law & Politics and a "Legal Eagle" by Franchise Times. Jeff is admitted to practice in Minnesota, as well as numerous Federal District and Appellate Courts throughout the United States.

Raised on a farm in western New York, Jeff was one of 20 Presidential Honors Scholars in his class at the State University of New York at Buffalo, and he graduated with honors from the Duke University School of Law. Jeff enjoys spending time with his wife and three children and has been a season ticket holder for the Minnesota Timberwolves since their inaugural season in 1989.

FOREWORD

Every year, two of our members accept the invitation to be the keynote speakers at one of the Forum's signature events - the Annual Franchise and Distribution Law Developments. While other speakers research and write a paper, the Annual Developments speakers research and write a book. They review hundreds of cases, pore over numerous arbitration opinions, and study statutory and regulatory changes to analyze the trends and developments that have had or will have an impact on our franchise and distribution practices. Basically, these volunteers give up their day jobs for at least ten months to help us better understand our chosen area of law.

It is in that context that I express my sincere thanks to the current authors of this year's Annual Developments – Michael Gray and Jeffery Haff. Many of you know both of these Forum members because of their work on other Forum publications and from their preparation of papers and speeches for the Annual Forum. Mike was one of the co-editors of the recent Covenants Against Competition in Franchise Agreements, Third Edition (2012). Jeff has written for, and spoken at, numerous Annual Meetings, including at Baltimore in 2011 on Differential Treatment of Franchisees in Tough Economic Times. The breadth of what they have undertaken to write about in this book is impressive. They deal with topics ranging from registration and disclosure to termination and renewal to antitrust and international. They have reviewed all of this law and then written thoughtful summaries and insightful analysis about it.

Jim Goniea, one of last year's Annual Developments' speakers, provided these authors invaluable mentoring and guidance throughout this process. My thanks to Jim for a superb job this year.

An organization is only as good as its members. It is a testament to our Forum that we have extraordinary volunteers willing to synthesize this mountain of information and provide us with the excellent scholarship contained in this book. Thank you, Mike and Jeff!

Deborah S. Coldwell
Chair, Forum on Franchising

ACKNOWLEDGMENTS

The authors would like to express their appreciation for the able assistance of Bryan Huntington and Julie Schmit at Dady & Gardner. They spent many hours working hard on case summaries and correcting all of Jeff's errors. Bruce Schaeffer was invaluable in providing updates on developments in the area of taxation.

Several summer law clerks at Gray Plant Mooty spent many hours reviewing and summarizing cases. These individuals included Hallie Goodman, Ashley Bailey, Leah Leyendecker, Wade Hauser, Meg Kelner and Nick De La Cruz. Their assistance was invaluable and made it possible to meet the deadlines established by our task master Jim Goniea, whose periodic phone calls, guidance and editing kept us focused on the task at hand. We also want to thank Andrew Lees at Gray Plant Mooty for his countless hours in assembling the final product, including proofreading, formatting and doing all the things necessary to create the reference tables that make the book user-friendly.

Special thanks go to Peter Snell at Gowlings, Stephen Giles at Norton Rose Fulbright and Mark Abell and Graeme Payne at Bird & Bird for their input and assistance with the International updates for Canada, Australia and Indonesia.

Last, but not least, the authors wish to thank their family members, who gave us the space and time to undertake this project, including several "lost" weekends while we researched, summarized, edited and proofread instead of spending time with them. Their love and support made this possible. We dedicate this book to our spouses, Nancy Gray and Carol Haff.

INTRODUCTION

We were given the task of reviewing the developments in franchise and distribution law for the period of August 1, 2012 through July 31, 2013 (the "Reporting Period") and summarizing the key cases and other developments for your reference. We have chosen to rely upon LEXIS and CCH's Business Franchise Guide for this project. We apologize to those of you who use primarily Westlaw or some other reporting service. We hope that the case names, numbers and summaries will be helpful to you in locating relevant authority. We found that most of the cases were available on Google Scholar within two months of the date of the decision.

We have attempted to provide case summaries that are neither too lengthy nor too brief. Some cases required or warranted a detailed discussion. Other cases merited mere reference. We are certain that there are times when we have summarized either too much or provided unnecessary detail. Hopefully, the majority of the summaries will be "just right." If a case that you were involved with did not make the cut, we apologize as it was probably duplicative of another case on the same point of law.

There were no seismic shifts in franchise and distribution law this year. Cases, for the most part, continued to follow familiar trends. Franchisors generally came out on the winning side of a variety of termination and non-compete disputes. Franchisees continued to struggle to plead and prove good faith and fair dealing claims. Gas station franchisees, auto dealers and equipment dealers continued to enjoy greater statutory protections and rights than most of their franchisee brethren. Both the volume of the cases in those areas and the many favorable results for these franchisees and dealers reflect their increased statutory protections.

Certain cases and trends merit mention:

- The Supreme Court decided two key arbitration cases this year. In *Oxford Health Plans, LLC v. Sutter*, 133 S. Ct. 2064 (2013) the Court left open the possibility that a class arbitration could occur when the parties' agreement is silent on the issue of whether class arbitrations are allowed. Based on Judge Alito's concurrence, this outcome was the result of the parties' decision to allow the

Introduction

arbitrator to decide this "gateway" issue and the court's limited review of the arbitrator's decision under the Federal Arbitration Act. However, shortly thereafter in *American Express Co. vs. Italian Colors Restaurant*, 133 S. Ct. 2304 (2013) the court held that the Federal Arbitration Act does not permit courts to invalidate a contractual class arbitration waiver on the ground that the plaintiff's costs of individually arbitrating a federal statutory claim exceeds the potential recovery. Until the *American Express* case, this was a popular form of attack on class waivers in consumer contracts. This case probably struck the death knell for claims that a "no class arbitration" clause may be avoided. In fact, the *American Express* case forced the Massachusetts Supreme Court to reverse a decision it issued on this subject eight days earlier. See Chapter 9.

- There were a number of cases this year involving the interplay between fraud claims and contract provisions intended to defeat such claims. The rules of law stated by the courts in these cases varied wildly by jurisdiction and governing law. See Chapter 5.

- There continue to be a substantial number of vicarious liability cases brought against franchisors. Plaintiffs include: franchisees claiming to be employees, employees of franchisees claiming to be employees of the franchisor, and injured customers of franchisees who claim that the franchisee was controlled by the franchisor or was the apparent agent of the franchisor. Results were mixed.

- Notwithstanding a variety of excuses and purported defenses asserted by former franchisees, franchisors were universally successful in preventing terminated or expired franchisees from continuing to use or display the franchisor's trademarks. Several decisions included substantial damages and attorney's fees in favor of the franchisor. See Chapter 4.

- With only two unique exceptions, courts were diligent in enforcing choice of venue provisions in franchise agreements – generally requiring litigation in the franchisor's home state. See Chapter 9.

We hope that this book provides a useful reference guide of the developments that have occurred in the past twelve months. We are honored to have been selected to write it for use by our distinguished colleagues.

CHAPTER ❖ 1

Franchise Definitions

I.　　General Analysis – Is It a Franchise?

The title of this book mentions developments in "franchise" law, as well as "distribution" law. To be a "franchise," as defined by certain state or federal laws, the relationship must feature certain definitional elements. While most cases decided annually do not focus on whether these elements are present, cases do arise each year in which the parties dispute whether their relationship really is a "franchise." The Reporting Period featured ten cases addressing these definitional elements.

In *C.N. Wood Co., v. Labrie Environmental Group*, No. 12-11778, 2013 U.S. Dist. LEXIS 78977 (D. Mass. June 5, 2013), the plaintiff, C.N. Wood Company, Inc. ("C.N. Wood"), brought an action in Massachusetts state court after receiving a letter terminating its dealership agreement with the defendant, Labrie Environmental Group ("Labrie"). Since the 1960s (other than a brief time between 2006 and 2008), C.N. Wood had sold and serviced "Leach" refuse collection trucks (now produced by Labrie) in both Massachusetts and Rhode Island. Notwithstanding choice of law and venue clauses calling for application of the law and courts of Quebec, Canada, Wood claimed that Massachusetts and Rhode Island franchise laws applied to the parties' relationship.

Labrie removed the action to federal court and sought to enforce the choice-of-law and forum selection clauses. Wood argued there was a *de facto* franchise between the parties and that the anti-waiver provision in the Massachusetts Motor Vehicle Franchise Act ("MVFA") voided both the choice-of-law clause and the forum-selection clause. The court observed that, in order for there to be a *de facto* franchise relationship, there needed to be a "community of interest" between the parties.

The court consulted numerous definitions of "community of interest." It noted that the Third Circuit looked for specific proof of "certain indicia of control by the supposed franchisor over the supposed franchisee." However, New Jersey courts focused on whether a "symbiotic relationship" exists such that one could say there is "interdependence," normally established by control of the licensor, and economic dependence of the licensee. The court recognized that the Seventh Circuit applied yet another standard, that is, whether the supposed franchisee had made a substantial investment to receive goods and/or skills that would have "minimal utility" outside the parties' relationship. This standard, applied to the Wisconsin Fair Dealership Law, looks at whether the person or entity claiming protection is "subject to exploitation at the hands of a supplier." After considering all of these various approaches, the court settled on an interpretation of the Massachusetts MVFA: "a 'community of interests' ... must reflect the 'potentially oppressive power' of the franchisor over the franchisee[;]" the franchisor must have the franchisee "'over a barrel.'"

C.N. Wood emphasized that, under the parties' agreement, it was obligated to use its best efforts to promote Labrie's products, had to provide sales and service staff, had to have service facilities, tools, a parts inventory, and had to offer regular product demonstrations. C.N. Wood argued that losing the right to sell Labrie products would idle a number of its service bays and would require C.N. Wood to lay off employees. In response, Labrie pointed out that, of C.N. Wood's total annual gross sales, Labrie's products accounted for, at most, 10%. Indeed, C.N. Wood carried multiple product lines, including popular brands that directly compete with Labrie's products. Also, C.N. Wood always retained the right to set its own prices for Labrie products.

The court concluded that there was no "community of interest" under these facts. Important to the court was the fact that Labrie did not have enough economic power over C.N. Wood to place it "over a barrel." Even though the dealer would lose revenue because of termination of the relationship, the court dismissed that fact as not being probative of whether a community of interest existed. A provision in the parties' agreement stipulating the parties had a relationship other than a franchise relationship was treated as irrelevant. The court relegated discussion to this clause to a footnote, dismissed it without authority, and never discussed it directly within the text of the opinion. Accordingly, the court found the contractual choice of law and forum-selection clauses were enforceable, and dismissed the case.

A similar result was reached in *Prim Limited Liability Co. v. Pace-* *Inc.*, No. 10-617, 2012 U.S. Dist. LEXIS 177203 (D. Haw. Dec. 13, 2012), where the court found that Prim, a distributor of electronic gaming equipment, including games such as "Island Fruit," was not a franchisee under the Hawaii Franchise Investment Law because it had no contractual right to use Pace's trademark. The court also found that Prim had not paid any "franchise fee" to enter into or continue in business under the parties' distributor agreement.

While the distributor alleged that it had been charged excessive amounts for game "fills" (an electronic code generated by the putative franchisor that an owner submits to continue operating the machine after a certain number of plays), the court determined that the payment for "fills" did not constitute a franchise fee. The court reasoned that the Hawaii statute did not limit the profit margin a manufacturer could charge for product, and there was no evidence that the "fill" fee was not a cost the distributor could recoup by operating in the ordinary course of business.

Another distributor lost an argument that it was a "franchisee," in *McPeak v. S-L Distribution Co.,* No. 12-00348, 2012 U.S. Dist. LEXIS 179893 (D. N.J. Dec. 19, 2012), McPeak, a New Jersey distributor of Snyder-Lance branded snack products, was terminated despite increasing his sales significantly over a 5-year period. He received a termination notice and then a notice reducing the size of his exclusive territory. At the time the territory was reduced, McPeak and S-L signed a new distributor agreement.

On January 19, 2012, McPeak brought an action alleging that his distributorship had been wrongfully terminated under the New Jersey Franchise Practices Act ("NJFPA"). On March 8, 2012, McPeak sold his distributorship to S-L.

S-L moved to dismiss McPeak's action, stating that (1) he sold his business and therefore lacked standing, and (2) he failed to plead facts sufficient to establish that he was a franchisee under the NJFPA. The court found that McPeak had standing to bring his damages claims for wrongful termination (but not his claims for declaratory or injunctive relief) because his sale of his distributorship did not extinguish his claim that he had lost money as a result of the initial termination notice. The voluntary sale did, however, extinguish his right to be reinstated as a distributor.

However, the court dismissed McPeak's NJFPA claim because he had failed to plead or establish a trademark "license." While McPeak had a right to sell Snyder-Lance branded snack food, the court ruled that the mere right to sell branded product was not a trademark "license" under the NJFPA. The court also gave significant weight to S-L's argument that its distributor agreement (1) specifically prohibited McPeak from using S-L's name, trademarks or trade name, and (2) stated that McPeak was not a franchisee.

Oracle America, Inc. v. Innovative Technology Distributors, LLC, Nos. 11-CV-01043 and 11-CV-02135, 2012 U.S. Dist. LEXIS 134343 (N.D. Cal. Sept. 18, 2012) involved another New Jersey Franchise Practices Act claim, this one by a reseller of Sun Microsystems' products. Innovative Technology Distributors, LLC ("ITD") served as a "value added reseller" of Sun Microsystems' technology products to computer network equipment provider Alcatel-Lucent. Due to its own internal policies, Alcatel-Lucent needed a vendor that was a woman-owned enterprise, and ITD was such an enterprise.

ITD's sales most years were 95% or more attributable to Sun Microsystem' products. When Oracle America, Inc. bought Sun Microsystems in January of 2010, Oracle made an internal decision to eliminate distributors such as ITD and sell directly to end users. Oracle sent ITD a July 1, 2010 termination notice, which was retracted on August 10, 2010. On September 30, 2010, Oracle sent ITD another termination notice. Neither the July 1, 2010 notice nor the September 30, 2010 letter contained any reason for termination. Oracle did not technically enforce either termination notice, and ITD continued in business. On December 29, 2010, Oracle sent an agreement to ITD amending the parties' distributor agreement so that the agreement would be extended for six months and ITD would be limited to selling to three customers. Finally, on April 15, 2011, Oracle sent yet another termination notice to ITD due to ITD's failure to pay over $19 million worth of invoices after receiving the first termination notice on July 1, 2010. ITD failed to pay the $19 million within the 60-day cure period stated in the April 15, 2011 termination notice, and was terminated.

The primary issue before the court on summary judgment was whether the NJFPA applied. The court found that the NJFPA applied despite a California choice–of–law clause in the parties' agreement. The court then proceeded to analyze whether ITD was a "franchisee" under the NJFPA.

The court found that genuine issues of material fact precluded summary judgment on ITD's NJFPA claim. The court found that the franchisee had submitted facts from which a reasonable jury could find that ITD established it had a license to use Sun Microsystems' trademark, there was a community of interest in the marketing of goods or services, and the parties contemplated that ITD would maintain a "place of business" in New Jersey.

While the parties' agreement expressly stated that no franchise license was intended, the court found that the agreement was not dispositive on the issue and the court had to review the parties' actual relationship and course of dealing to determine whether a license existed. The court determined that ITD established: (1) it was allowed to use Sun Microsystems' trademark; (2) customers associated ITD with Sun Microsystems; (3) customers reasonably believed Sun Microsystems "vouched for" ITD and the products sold by ITD; and (4) it had hung a Sun Microsystems banner at its offices. Regarding the "community of interest" prong, the court determined that ITD made substantial franchise-specific investments in excess of $1,000,000 and that nearly all of ITD's business was from Sun Microsystems. This was sufficient to establish a genuine issue of material fact precluding summary judgment.

Finally, ITD had set up an office in Edison, New Jersey where it displayed and marketed Sun Microsystems' products and called upon customers. This fact satisfied New Jersey's "place of business" requirement, particularly given that ITD's sales were not to end users and, therefore, the 2010 amendments to the NJFPA (which expanded the "place of business" definition where a franchisee's sales were not to end users) might apply.

Despite owing over $19,000,000 to Oracle in unpaid invoices, ITD's wrongful termination claim under the NJFPA was allowed to proceed. Although the July 1, 2010 and September 30, 2010 termination letters had been retracted, they effectively terminated the parties' relationship without proper notice, good cause, or opportunity to cure. They were "unequivocal notice" of Oracle's termination decision and the termination decisions were communicated directly to the public, including ITD's customers.

The franchisee in *Chicago Male Medical Clinic, LLC v. Ultimate Management, Inc.*, No. 12 C 5542, 2012 U.S. Dist. LEXIS 183257 (N.D. Ill. Dec. 28, 2012) confidently moved for partial summary judgment seeking a determination that it was a "franchisee" under Illinois law. This case involved an erectile dysfunction clinic run by Chicago Male Medical Clinic, LLC. Defendant Ultimate Management, Inc. licensed and monitored the operation of a nationwide affiliation of clinics that all do business under the name "National Male Medical Clinic." Chicago Male paid UMI a $300,000 "set up fee" and a percentage of gross revenue in return for UMI's assistance in setting up and helping to operate the business.

The business performed poorly, and Chicago Male brought claims for fraud, violation of the Illinois Franchise Disclosure Act, and violations of the Illinois Consumer Fraud Act, alleging it had been sold an unregistered franchise through false and misleading statements and improper earnings claims. Chicago Male brought a motion for partial summary judgment, seeking a determination that it had been sold a "franchise" under Illinois law. The court determined that a genuine issue of material fact existed as to whether a "franchise" relationship existed because the parties' continuing consultation and compensation agreement did not specifically grant the Chicago Male a right to use a trademark and UMI had submitted an affidavit stating that it did not even own a trademark. Accordingly, the court denied Chicago Male's partial summary judgment motion.

Atchley v. Pepperidge Farm, Inc., No. CV-04-452, 2012 U.S. Dist. LEXIS 173974 (E.D. Wash. Dec. 6, 2012) involved a bench trial of a claim by two Pepperidge Farm food distributors, John Atchley and Michael Gilroy. The distributors alleged that they were fraudulently and illegally sold unregistered franchises under the Washington Franchise Investment Protection Act. Atchley and Gilroy had initially lost on summary judgment but prevailed on appeal, with the Ninth Circuit finding that genuine issues of material fact existed as to whether they satisfied the elements of the WFIPA. *See Atchley v. Pepperidge Farm, Inc.*, 379 Fed. Appx. 557 (9th Cir. 2010).

Although a new trial judge was assigned on remand, Atchley and Gilroy fared no better. The trial court, after a bench trial, held that the distributors were not franchisees under the WFIPA because (1) the "pallet fees" and "stale" charges assessed by Pepperidge Farm were ordinary business expenses, not unrecoverable "franchise fees;" (2) there was no "substantial" association between the franchisor's marks and the distributorship; and (3) Pepperidge Farm did not impose a marketing plan upon the distributors. As a result, Pepperidge Farm was granted judgment dismissing all claims against it.

In *GMAC Real Estate, LLC v. Fialkiewicz*, No. 12-60-civ, 506 Fed. Appx. 91 (2d Cir. Dec. 27, 2012), the defendant GMAC Real Estate, LLC appealed the district court's denial of its motion to vacate an arbitration award finding that GMAC violated the Connecticut Business Opportunity Investment Act, Conn. Gen. Stat. § 36b-60, *et seq.*, (the "CBOIA") by selling a real estate franchise to Mr. Fialkiewicz and his related entity, Reality Works, LLC. GMAC's two primary arguments on appeal were (1) the CBOIA did not apply since GMAC fell under a statutory exclusion which excluded "the sale of a marketing program made in conjunction with the licensing of a registered trademark," and (2) the CBOIA did not apply because the franchisee was already in business as a real estate broker before buying the franchise.

The Second Circuit rejected GMAC's first argument, finding that (1) one of the trademarks identified by GMAC was not "federally registered" and (2) the other trademark was not "licensed in conjunction with the franchise agreement." The Second Circuit also rejected GMAC's second argument, finding that the franchisee had changed its accounting and marketing procedures in connection with the franchise agreement. Therefore, the arbitrator had facts before him from which he could possibly find that this was a "new" business and the "existing business rule" did not apply. The Second Circuit affirmed the district court's decision confirming the arbitration award and denying GMAC's motion to vacate the award.

In *Garbinski v. Nationwide Property & Casualty Insurance Co.*, No. 12-3797, 2013 U.S. App. LEXIS 12856 (2d Cir. June 24, 2013), the Second Circuit considered Garbinski's appeal from the district court's grant of summary judgment to Nationwide on wrongful termination claims made by Nationwide's former insurance agent and employee, Garbinski. Garbinski's claims all hinged on the legal argument that he was a "franchisee" protected from termination under the Connecticut Franchise Act, Conn. Gen. Stat. §§ 42-133e to 42-133g.

Garbinski, drunk and on methadone, had held his wife captive at gunpoint while police surrounded his house. Garbinski was terminated as an agent by Nationwide.

The Second Circuit agreed with the district court that, since Garbinski did not buy insurance products from Nationwide, and he did not have to make a specific sales quota, he was basically a commissioned sales representative. Therefore, the Connecticut Franchise Act did not apply to the Nationwide-Garbinski relationship and the district court's decision granting summary judgment to Nationwide was affirmed.

In *Strassle v. Bimbo Foods Bakeries Distributor, Inc.*, No. 12-3313, 2013 U.S. Dist. LEXIS 34560 (D.N.J. Mar. 13, 2013) the court denied Bimbo Foods' motion to dismiss distributor Strassle's claims for wrongful termination under the New Jersey Franchise Practices Act. Strassle and others alleged that they had been terminated as franchisees in violation of the NJFPA when Bimbo Foods refused to supply them with Arnold's, Freihofer's and Thomas's fresh baked bread and roll products. Bimbo Foods contended that the NJFPA did not apply because Strassle operated a bread delivery route and did not have a "place of business" in New Jersey. The court found that the parties' agreement clearly contemplated a "place of business" in New Jersey and, therefore, the NJFPA applied. The court pointed out that, although the distributors did not have an existing "store," the parties' agreement gave the distributors the first right to set up stores and supply bread to customers at the stores if the system evolved to require physical stores where customers would pick up bread products. Therefore, the agreement contemplated a physical place of business in New Jersey.

In *Ocean City Express Co., v. Atlas Van Lines, Inc.*, No. 13-1467, 2013 U.S. Dist. LEXIS 104146 (D. N.J. July 25, 2013), Ocean City Express claimed the defendant, Atlas Van Lines, violated the New Jersey Franchise Protection Act, and breached the implied covenant of good faith and fair dealing. Atlas moved to dismiss on the grounds: (1) the plaintiff did not properly state a NJFPA claim, and (2) Indiana law applied to the parties' contract, and Indiana law does not recognize good faith and fair dealing claims. In the alternative, the defendant sought a venue change.

First considering the NJFPA claim, the court reviewed the threshold statutory requirements: (1) the franchisee will be established or maintained in New Jersey; (2) gross sales of products or services between the franchisee and franchisor exceed $35,000 for the twelve months preceding suit, and (3) more than 20% of the franchisee's gross sales are "intended to be or are derived from such franchise." N.J.S.A. § 56:10-4. While the complaint alleged a franchise had been created, it included no allegation of gross sales created as a result of the franchise relationship, nor did it allude to the percentage of Ocean City Express' sales arising from the franchise relationship. As the plaintiff had failed to correct similar flaws in the first complaint it filed, the court dismissed this claim with prejudice. The court furthermore dismissed the good faith and fair dealing claim pursuant to a choice-of-law clause in the parties' agreement, but did so without prejudice, giving Ocean City Express an opportunity to plead again (if possible) to qualify for Indiana's exception to its "no good faith and fair dealing rule" which permits such a claim where a contract creates an ambiguity.

II.   Franchise Fee

A.   CASES SPECIFICALLY FINDING NO "FRANCHISE FEE"

See Prim Limited Liability Co. v. Pace-O-Matic, Inc., No. 10-617, 2012 U.S. Dist. LEXIS 177203 (D. Haw. Dec. 13, 2012) ("fills" not a franchise fee), as summarized at Chapter 1.I.; *Atchley v. Pepperidge Farm, Inc.*, No. CV-04-452, 2012 U.S. Dist. LEXIS 173974 (E.D. Wash. Dec. 6, 2012) ("pallet fees" and "stale charges" not franchise fees), as summarized at Chapter 1.I. *See also Zentner v. Farmers Group, Inc.*, Bus. Franchise Guide (CCH) ¶ 14,944 (Cal. Ct. App. Nov. 8, 2012) (certain business expenses not franchise fees) summarized at Chapter 1.V.

III. Cases Specifically Analyzing the Issue of "Substantially Associated with the Trademark"

See Prim Limited Liability Co. v. Pace-O-Matic, Inc., No. 10-617, 2012 U.S. Dist. LEXIS 177203 (D. Haw. Dec. 13, 2012), as summarized at Chapter 1.I.; *McPeak v. S-L Distribution Co.*, No. 12-00348, 2012 U.S. Dist. LEXIS 179893 (D. N.J. Dec. 19, 2012), as summarized at Chapter 1.I.; *Chicago Male Med. Clinic, LLC v. Ultimate Mgmt., Inc.*, No. 12 C 5542, 2012 U.S. Dist. LEXIS 183257 (N.D. Ill. Dec. 28, 2012), as summarized at Chapter 1.I.; *Oracle America, Inc. v. Innovative Technology Distributors, LLC*, Nos. 11-CV-01043 and 11-CV-02135, 2012 U.S. Dist. LEXIS 134343 (N.D. Cal. Sept. 18, 2012), as summarized at Chapter 1.I.; *Atchley v. Pepperidge Farm, Inc.*, No. CV-04-452, 2012 U.S. Dist. LEXIS 173974 (E.D. Wash. Dec. 6, 2012), as summarized at Chapter 1.I.

IV. Cases Specifically Analyzing "Community of Interest"

See C.N. Wood Co., v. Labrie Envtl. Grp., No. 12-11778, 2013 U.S. Dist. LEXIS 78977 (D. Mass. June 5, 2013), as summarized at Chapter 1.I.; *Oracle America, Inc. v. Innovative Technology Distributors, LLC*, Nos. 11-CV-01043 and 11-CV-02135, 2012 U.S. Dist. LEXIS 134343 (N.D. Cal. Sept. 18, 2012), as summarized at Chapter 1.I.

V. Cases Specifically Analyzing "Right to Sell or Distribute"

Is a district manager for an insurance company a "franchisee" under the California Franchise Investment Law? The court in *Zentner v. Farmers Group, Inc.*, Bus. Franchise Guide (CCH) ¶ 14,944 (Cal. Ct. App. Nov. 8, 2012) held that he was not, because Zentner, the district manager, did not distribute goods or services to anyone other than to the franchisor and because he did not pay a franchise fee. The court affirmed a summary judgment entered against Zentner by the trial court on the issue.

The court held that, although Zentner performed training and recruitment services for Farmer's Group and received a commission, he was not a franchisee because he only worked for Farmers and not for the general public. While Zentner argued that various business expenses (the cost to attend Farmer's Group conferences, call centers expenses, buying leads) were "franchise fees," the court defined a "franchise fee" as an unrecoverable investment made in return for the right to do business. By contrast, the court found that each of the expenses identified by Zentner were typical business expenses paid in the ordinary course of business.

See also Garbinski v. Nationwide Prop. & Cas. Ins. Co., No. 12-3797, 2013 U.S. App. LEXIS 12856 (2d Cir. June 24, 2013).

CHAPTER ❖ 2

Registration and Disclosure

Federal and state registration and disclosure laws and regulations govern the form, content and manner in which franchisor's must disclose detailed information regarding the franchisor, the nature of the franchise offering, costs, and other information necessary for a prospective franchisee to make an informed decision. As in the recent past, there are relatively few cases addressing alleged violations of the disclosure laws in the franchise context.

I.   Registration and Disclosure Law

A.   EFFECT OF INTEGRATION CLAUSES

See, *Maaco Franchising, Inc. vs. Tainter*, No. 12-5500, 2013 U.S. Dist. Lexis 80790 (E.D. Pa. June 6, 2013), summarized in Chapter 9.A. below, where the court found that the integration clause in the franchise agreement confirmed that the franchisee was not relying on any representations, promises or agreements outside of the franchise agreement regarding venue and choice of law provisions.

B.   FAILURE TO REGISTER

In *Kim v. SUK, Inc.*, No. 12-CV-1557, 2013 U.S. Dist. LEXIS 24703 (S.D. N.Y. Feb. 22, 2013), the plaintiff June-Il Kim ("June") unsuccessfully sought the protection of the New York Franchise Sale Act. June began working as a limousine driver for defendant SUK, Inc. ("SUK") in 2000. June alleged four years later that he was forced to sign the signature page of an unknown document or be terminated. Kim claimed that sometime later he was required to pay SUK $10,000 as a franchise fee, without receiving or reviewing any franchise disclosure documents required by New York or federal law. In 2010, SUK fired June for allegedly engaging in labor-organizing efforts. At that time, June learned that the document that he signed in 2004 was actually a franchise agreement.

June initiated litigation against SUK alleging two claims under the New York Franchise Sales Act. The first was for failure to provide disclosure documents and the second was fraudulent and unlawful practices. SUK filed a motion to dismiss based on the three-year statute of limitations in the New York Act. June alleged that violations took place in 2010 when he "discovered" that the document he signed in 2004 was actually a franchise agreement. The court disagreed stating, "[t]he case law is quite clear that the New York Franchise Sales Act does not incorporate a 'date of discovery' rule for fraud-based claims . . . instead the time on the statute of limitations necessarily starts running at the start of a defendant's violation." Using this rationale, the court found that the violation took place in 2004 when June signed the agreement without being provided the required franchise disclosure documents. Accordingly, the court concluded that his disclosure violation claim was time barred.

June next argued that the statute of limitations should run from the date he paid the $10,000 fee. However, the court found that June's complaint failed to allege that the $10,000 payment was made within the three-year statute of limitations period. Finally, with respect to June's misrepresentation claim, the court found that the alleged misrepresentation took place in 2004, when June signed the agreement without the benefit of the franchise disclosure documents. Because the complaint was filed in 2012, June's misrepresentation claim also was time barred.

In another case involving the failure to register under the New York Franchise Sales Act, *Mangione v. Butler*, No 10-32030, 2012 Bankr. LEXIS 5689 (W.D. N.C. Dec. 10, 2012), the former franchisee, Mangione, sought to recover his initial investment against the owner and managers of the franchisor in their personal capacities. In 2007, Mangione entered into a series of franchise agreements with the franchisor to open and operate up to 20 public relations retail stores in the New York area. Mangione paid the franchisor $714,000 in initial franchise fees. Under the terms of the franchise agreements, the creative work to supply the franchisees was to be performed in Charlotte, North Carolina through a subsidiary of the franchisor owned by the same individuals who owned the franchisor, Mike and Kathy Butler (the "Butlers"). Within a year of purchasing the franchise, Mangione realized that the Butlers were not capable of providing public relations products sufficient to meet his needs. Mangione contacted the New

York State Attorney General and learned that the franchisor had not been registered or authorized to operate in New York at the time it sold the franchises to Mangione in 2007. In August 2009, New York issued a letter advising the Butlers not to sell any further franchises and to escrow all the franchise fees. The letter also advised Mangione that he was entitled to rescind his contracts and get his money back with interest at the rate of 6% from the date of purchase, plus reasonable costs and attorneys' fees. Mangione wrote a rescission letter and demanded the return of his $714,000. When the Butlers failed to respond, Mangione filed a suit in New York State Court to recover his investment. Shortly thereafter, the Butlers dissolved the franchisor and filed personal bankruptcy. Mangione initiated an adversary proceeding in the Bankruptcy Court seeking to recover the $714,000 from the Butlers, jointly and severally, and deeming the debt not dischargeable under 11 U.S.C. § 523(a)(2). Mangione also alleged that the Butlers were liable for fraud or defalcation while acting in a fiduciary capacity for failing to escrow Mangione's initial franchise fees because the franchisor was not authorized to sell franchises at the time Mangione signed his franchise agreements.

The Bankruptcy Court held that the Butlers and the franchisor entity had intentionally allowed its franchise license to lapse in New York and knowingly and willingly sold franchises to Mangione in violation of New York law. Even though the franchisor claimed that an application for reinstatement was in process, the Court found that the application was defective and was filed after negotiations with Mangione began. As a result, the Court found that the Butlers were aware that the franchisor was not entitled to operate or solicit money in New York at the time the agreements were signed and Mangione paid his initial franchise fees.

The Court also found that the Butlers and the franchisor failed to escrow franchise fees as required under New York law following the occurrence of an event requiring an amendment. The Court found that instead of escrowing Mangione's initial $714,000 payment, it was almost immediately dissipated to the Butlers and other employees such that the franchisor was not in a position to refund the fees upon demand by Mangione. As a result of the violations of the New York Franchise Sales Act, the Court found that the Butlers were jointly and severally liable with the franchisor for the unlawful sale of the franchises. Additionally, the Court found that Mangione's claims against the Butlers were not dischargeable in bankruptcy under 11 U.S.C. § 523(a)(2)(A) and (a)(4) because they were monies obtained by "false pretenses, a false representation, or actual fraud" and because the claims arose from the Butlers' defalcation. The Court held that "New York law supplies the trust relationship and fiduciary duties with respect to the escrowing of the franchise fees." The Court found that the Butlers breached this fiduciary duty and were personally liable to Mangione for $714,000 plus 6% interest from the date Mangione signed the franchise agreements, plus attorneys' fees and costs.

C. EARNINGS CLAIMS/FINANCIAL PERFORMANCE REPRESENTATIONS

In *Hanley v. Doctors Express Franchising, LLC*, No. ELH-12-795, 2013 U.S. Dist. LEXIS 25340 (D. Md. Feb. 25, 2013), Raymond Hanley, Marsha Hanley, and Hanley Limited Partners, LLC (collectively, the "Hanleys"), sued Doctors Express Franchising, LLC and its members (collectively "Doctors Express") for violation of, among other things, the Maryland Franchise Registration and Disclosure Law. B.R. §§ 14-201 et seq. The Maryland Franchise Law creates a private right of action for any "person who buys or is granted a franchise" against a "person who sells or grants a franchise," for offering a franchise:

> [b]y means of an untrue statement of a material fact or any omission to state a material fact necessary in order to make the statements made, in light of the circumstances under which they are made, not misleading, if the person who buys or is granted a franchise does not know of the untruth or omission.

B.R. § 14-227(a)(1)(ii).

Doctors Express is a franchisor of urgent care medical centers under the "Doctors Express" or "DRX" brand, and Rhino is a franchise broker that was Doctors Express' agent in marketing DRX franchises. The Hanleys contended that Doctors Express and Rhino made several misleading disclosures and failed to disclose material information in the course of the Hanleys preparation to open a DRX franchise, both before and after execution of the Franchise Agreement. Specifically, the Hanleys claimed that Defendants, through the Franchise Agreement, Franchise Disclosure Agreement, emails, marketing materials, the DRX business model, and oral statements, had provided them with information that Defendants knew was no longer accurate. The alleged misrepresentations and nondisclosures included four categories: (a) the required initial investment; (b) the initial operating capital requirements; (c) the physician credentialing and health insurance reimbursement contracting process; and (d) the projected earnings and financial performance of the DRX franchise. The Hanleys operated their Doctors Express franchise business for approximately 6 months and incurred substantial losses. They also realized that much of the information provided to them by Doctors Express and its agents was inaccurate and outdated. The Hanley's sued Doctors Express, it's individual owners as well as Rhino, the franchise broker seeking over $1.3 million in damages and rescission of their franchise agreement. Doctors Express and Rhino filed motions to dismiss, or alternatively, for summary judgment.

In a lengthy and detailed opinion, the court went to great lengths to outline Maryland law relating to each of the Hanley's claims. For brevity, only Hanley's Maryland Franchise Act claims will be discussed here. Doctors Express advanced two main arguments in support of its motion to dismiss. First, Doctors Express argued that the Hanleys had failed to allege that Doctors Express made any representations of fact, because all of the representations made to the Hanleys were expressly labeled as projections and estimates based on the operations of one affiliate facility and warned prospective franchisees that the projections and estimates could not be relied upon to predict accurately the future performance of a franchise. Doctors Express claimed that it did not misrepresent the actual past performance of their affiliate's location. Therefore, the statements were not actionable under the Maryland Franchise Law. However, the Hanleys argued that Doctors Express overlooked an important caveat articulated in *Jaguar Land Rover North America, LLC. v. Manhattan Imported Cars, Inc.*, 738 F. Supp. 2d 640 (D. Md. 2010) where the court held: "inaccurate projections of . . . future profitability and inaccurate planning volumes could . . . be considered fraudulent if there was evidence that the [defendant] knew they were inaccurate at the time they were made." The Hanleys argued that the detailed allegations in their complaint satisfied the pleading requirement at the 12(b)(6) stage and the court agreed. While the court acknowledged that the evidence may paint a different picture in the future, at the motion to dismiss stage all of the well pleaded allegations in the complaint are accepted as true and reviewed for sufficiency to state a legally cognizable claim. The court held that there was a legally sufficient basis for the Hanley's claims. Furthermore, the court found that even though Doctors Express had no duty to disclose the projected financial performance of a DRX franchise, because Doctors Express did in fact make such a representation, it had a duty to use the information that it knew was accurate at the time it made the representation. The projections it provided to Hanleys were based on financial data from 2007-2008. The Hanley's didn't sign their franchise agreement until 2010. The Hanley's plausibly alleged that the projections were contrary to undisclosed facts within Doctors Express' possession at the time they were made.

Second, Doctors Express argued that the disclaimers in Item 19 of the FDD and in the franchise agreement prevent the Hanley's from alleging reliance on statements outside of the Franchise Agreement and Franchise Disclosure Document, and that therefore any reliance on such claims was unreasonable. The Hanleys argued that the disclaimers were void under the Maryland Franchise Law, which prevents a franchisor from conditioning the sale of a franchise on the prospective franchisee's releasing any person from liability under the act. The court agreed that the disclaimers were legally inoperative to bar the Hanley's Maryland Franchise Law claims, but noted that they remained factually relevant, as a fact finder may find that the Hanleys reliance on the alleged misrepresentations and omissions was unreasonable under the circumstances. Accordingly, the court denied Doctors Express' motion to dismiss.

Similarly, the court denied Rhino's motion to dismiss Maryland Franchise Law claim. The Hanley's alleged that Rhino was an agent of Doctors Express for the purpose of marketing the Doctors Express franchise. Rhino argued that as a franchise broker, it was out of the scope of the Maryland Franchise Law. The court disagreed and found that the language of the statute was sufficiently broad to include franchise brokers. The statute defined "franchisor" as "a person who grants a franchise." As such, the court explained that because the statute created a private right of action against "a person who sells or grants a franchise," that this language was broad enough to apply to agents who participate in selling franchises.

See also Long John Silver's Inc. v. Nickleson, No. 11-CV-93, 2013 U.S. Dist. LEXIS 18391 (W.D. Ky. Feb. 12, 2013) (franchisee allowed to proceed to trial on earnings claims), as summarized at Chapter 5.X.A.

D. OTHER NON-DISCLOSURES

In *Massey, Inc. v. Moe's Southwestern Grill, LLC*, No. 07-CV-741, 2012 U.S. Dist. LEXIS 109081 (N.D. Ga. Aug. 3, 2012), a group of franchisees alleged that Moe's failed to disclose in its FDD, and also misrepresented, the fact that Moe's CEO Martin Sprock received "kickbacks" as a part-owner of an approved supplier of food brokerage services. The court granted summary judgment in favor of Sprock and against the franchisees. The court noted that the franchisees received an FDD accurately disclosing the relationship between Sprock and the supplier and the franchisees failed to bring their claims within a year of discovery, as required by the contractual statute of limitations in the Moe's franchise agreement.

Plaintiffs moved to reconsider, stating that the FDD also disclosed that "we" did not derive any proceeds from approved suppliers, and that it was reasonable for plaintiffs to believe that "we" included Sprock. The court found that this argument could not prevail since the FDD defined "we" to be only "Moe's Southwest Grill, LLC."

See also Mangione v. Butler, No 10-32030, 2012 Bankr. LEXIS 5689 (W.D. N.C. Dec. 10, 2012) summarized in Chapter 2.I.B. above.

II.   Federal and State Regulatory Developments

A.   FEDERAL REGULATORY DEVELOPMENTS

No significant developments.

B.   STATE REGULATORY DEVELOPMENTS

1. Delaware: Effective June 6, 2013, the Delaware legislature amended the Delaware Franchise Security Law to specifically state that "Individuals or entities who are parties to a franchise agreement as set out by the Federal Trade Commission shall not be deemed employees for purposes of Chapter 11 of Title 19 of the Delaware Code." Chapter 11 of title 19 of the Delaware code pertains to the payment of wages for employees and in particular, the A-B-C test for determining whether an individual is an employee or independent contractor.

2. Indiana: Effective July 1, 2013, the Indiana legislature amended the Indiana Dealer Rights Act to prohibit several adverse actions by automobile manufacturers against dealers including: coercing a dealer to change the dealership location, make substantial alterations to the franchise, or make substantial alterations to the dealership premises. The amendment also makes it an unfair practice for a manufacturer or distributor to cancel, terminate or fail to renew an automobile franchise upon expiration without good cause or 90 days' notice or at least 10 days' notice if the franchisee has abandoned the business, is convicted of or pled guilty to a felony, files for bankruptcy or enters into receivership, loses its license or commits fraud. Ind. Code § 9-23-3-23.

3. Montana: Effective April 23, 2013, the Montana Legislature made sweeping changes to the Montana Automobile Dealer Franchise Law, including a clarification that a manufacturer's desire to reduce the number of its franchisees or dealer locations is not good cause for terminating or failing to renew an automobile franchise. For additional changes, see MCA § 61-4-206, 61-4-207 and 61-4-208.

4. New Hampshire passed legislation effective September 25, 2013 which took all dealers previously covered by other New Hampshire dealer protection statutes and gave them all of the same rights held by automobile dealers. *See* N.H. Stat. § 357-C.

5. New Mexico: Effective June 14, 2013, the New Mexico legislature enacted new laws prohibiting automobile manufacturers from requiring a dealer to build a new dealership or relocate an existing dealership unless it is necessary to comply with health and safety laws or the technological requirements of selling certain services. Manufacturers are also prohibited from conditioning their approval of certain purchases on the remodeling or construction of a dealership. See NMSA § 57-16-5

CHAPTER ❖ 3

Relationship, Termination and Renewal

I.   Introduction

With litigation growing more costly every year, many franchise disputes are resolved short of litigation or arbitration.   Termination and non-renewal disputes, however, generally involve an "all or nothing" situation where a final decision has been made which either takes away, or threatens to take away, the business of the dealer, distributor or franchisee. In such instances, litigation often cannot be avoided. There were over a dozen termination or nonrenewal cases decided during the Reporting Period.

II.   Wrongful Termination Claims

A.   GOOD CAUSE FOR ENDING RELATIONSHIP

International House of Pancakes, LLC v. Parsippany Pancake House, Inc., 900 F.Supp.2d 403 (D.N.J. 2012) involves the President of an IHOP franchise who was convicted of sexual assault on a minor. IHOP terminated the franchise agreement and sought injunctive relief to stop the franchisee from operating using IHOP's marks.   The court initially denied IHOP's motion, stating that the New Jersey Franchise Practices Act required 60 days' notice of termination unless the criminal conviction was directly related to the IHOP's business (which, the court concluded, it was not). After the injunction was denied, IHOP waited 60 days and re-filed a motion for an injunction. This time IHOP prevailed. The court found that the crime fell under the lesser contractual standard of "relevant to the operation of the franchise," that IHOP has given proper notice, and that, therefore, IHOP was entitled to a preliminary injunction enjoining the franchisee from continuing to operate the franchise under IHOP's marks.

Mailing and Shipping Systems, Inc. v. Neopost USA, Inc., No. 12-CV-37, 2013 U.S. Dist. LEXIS 44909 (W.D. Tex. Mar. 28, 2013) involved a dealer who sold Neopost's postage meters and mailing machines in New Mexico and Texas.

Mailing and Shipping Systems alleged that the parties' "dealer agreement" consisted of a letter agreement plus various bulletins and manuals provided by Neopost over the years. Mailing and Shipping Systems was terminated on 50 days' notice for failure to meet its sales quotas. Mailing and Shipping Systems sued, alleging that although the letter agreement provided for 30 days' notice of termination, Neopost's dealer manual required 90 days' notice of termination. In addition, Mailing and Shipping Systems alleged that Neopost had failed to prevent other dealers from encroaching upon its exclusive territory.

The court found that the termination was proper because: (1) the parties' "agreement" was the letter agreement which required only 30 days' notice of termination, and (2) the letter agreement contained no language specifically requiring Neopost to prevent encroachment.

In *Dunkin' Donuts Franchising LLC v. Oza Bros., Inc.*, No. 10-13606, 2012 U.S. Dist. LEXIS 140595 (E.D. Mich. Sept. 28, 2012), the court granted summary judgment to Dunkin' Donuts on its claims against Oza Brothers arising out of Oza Brothers' intentional underreporting of sales to both Dunkin' Donuts and to taxing authorities. The court found that Oza Brothers intentionally employed a scheme where it made large wholesale donut sales to auto dealerships and never recorded the sales. The court found this to be a breach of contract which was incurable. Therefore, the court found that Dunkin' Donuts properly terminated the franchise.

Burda v. Wendy's International Inc., No. 08-CV-00246, 2012 U.S. Dist. LEXIS 145447 (S.D. Ohio Oct. 9, 2012), involved a Wendy's franchisee, Burda, with 13 restaurants who failed to make royalty payments and had operational defaults. Burda hired a turnaround consultant named James Taggart who stated that Burda's business was, "completely insolvent" given its debt load. Wendy's terminated Burda. Burda filed a claim against Wendy's alleging antitrust violations associated with Wendy's requirement that Burda buy buns from an affiliate of Wendy's. Wendy's initially lost a motion to dismiss the antitrust claim in 2009. However, Wendy's brought a motion for summary judgment on the issue in 2012.

The court found that Wendy's had good cause to terminate Burda since Burda had not paid and Burda was insolvent. Although Burda claimed that he could not be bound by Taggart's statement regarding insolvency, the court disagreed, and also noted that it was undisputed that (1) Burda's assets were $8,000,000 versus $11,000,000 of secured debt; and (2) Burda had told Taggart that Burda was insolvent. The antitrust claims were dismissed because the party holding those claims had signed a number of general releases in favor of Wendy's. *See* Chapter 5.XIII.

7-Eleven, Inc. v. Upadhyaya, No. 12-5541, 2013 U.S. Dist. LEXIS 29091 (E.D. Pa. Mar. 1, 2013), involved allegations by 7-Eleven that its franchisee was using a variety of means to under-record actual sales and, therefore, deny 7-Eleven its 52% share of the gross profit on those sales. 7-Elven alleged that the franchisees' methods included voiding transactions, keeping cash payments outside of the cash register, and using a "Price Look Up" scan to scan items without recording a sale (but actually taking money from the sale). The franchisee's defense was to concede that mistakes were made, but there was no intentional fraud.

After a four-day hearing, the court concluded that the franchisee had breached the franchise agreement and committed fraud. The court found that the breaches and fraudulent conduct went to the "essence" of the contract and were, therefore, incurable. Accordingly, the court granted 7-Eleven's motion.

Damabeh v. 7-Eleven, Inc., No. 12-CV-1739, 2013 U.S. Dist. LEXIS 66565 (N.D. Cal. May 8, 2013), involved a 7-Eleven store that suffered damage when a nearby store caught fire, causing firefighters to cut a hole in the 7-Eleven's roof to allow smoke to escape from the attic.

A 7-Eleven employee informed the franchisee that the hole in the roof was small and the store could reopen in a week. Shortly thereafter, another 7-Eleven employee visited the premises and removed the money order machine. Less than two weeks later, 7-Eleven convinced the franchisee to travel to Pleasanton, California and advised him that 7-Eleven had changed the locks on the store. The franchisee was handed a termination letter stating that, because the store could not be repaired in 30 days, the franchise was terminated. The franchisee was then told that he could either move to another store or accept a partial refund of his franchise fee.

The franchisee, Damabeh, sued and 7-Eleven moved to dismiss. The court granted 7-Eleven's motion with leave to amend. Damabeh filed an amended complaint, and 7-Eleven moved to dismiss again. The court dismissed the breach of contract claim, finding that all that was necessary to justify the termination was that 7-Eleven determine that the store could not reopen in 90 days and 7-Eleven had, in fact, so determined.

The court was highly critical of Damabeh's sloppy pleading on good faith and fair dealing, stating that he had failed to plead a good faith and fair dealing claim with any particularity. However, the court did in *dicta* take some time to examine what would seem to be the best argument available to Damabeh—that 7-Eleven's determination that the store could not be opened in 30 days was not made in good faith. The court found this argument would be a bridge too far, stating that a court should only limit contractual discretion when to do so would be necessary to avoid an unenforceable and illusory agreement.

The court dismissed Damabeh's complaint without leave to replead.

In an arbitration award confirmed in *Budget Blinds Inc. v. LeClair,* No. 12-1101, 2013 U.S. Dist. LEXIS 7463 (C.D. Cal. Jan. 16, 2013), a franchisor who turned off a franchisee's access to various franchisor services, including the internet portal, franchisee web site and access to customer leads, was found to have constructively terminated the franchisee, in violation of the Wisconsin Fair Dealership Law,

The arbitrator rejected the franchisor's claim that the franchisee sold into a neighboring territory and could be terminated. Accordingly, the arbitrator awarded LeClair over $275,000, which award was confirmed by the court.

Irvin Kahn & Son, Inc. v. Mannington Mills, Inc., No. 11-CV-01135, 2012 U.S. Dist. LEXIS 116308 (S.D. Ind. Aug. 17, 2012) involved interesting arguments by a floor coverings franchisor, Mannington Mills, Inc., that the Indiana Franchise Act did <u>not</u> prohibit <u>actual</u> termination without good cause, but, instead, only prohibited a contract <u>provision</u> permitting termination without good cause. Therefore, Mannington Mills argued that Irvin Kahn & Sons' wrongful termination claim was time barred because it was not brought within two years of signing the illegal contract. (The claim <u>was</u> made within two years of the actual termination.)

The court noted that Mannington Mills' statutory analysis made logical sense, but the Indiana Supreme Court had already found that wrongful termination itself was actionable under the Act in *Continental Basketball Association, Inc. v. Ellestein Enterprises,* 669 N.E.2d 134 (Ind. 1996). The federal court recognized it must follow the law as stated by the Indiana Supreme Court. Therefore, the wrongful termination claim was timely since the claim was brought within two years of termination.

In *H&R Block Tax Services, LLC v. Franklin*, 691 F.3d 941 (8th Cir. 2012) the Eighth Circuit reversed the district court and determined that the franchise agreements between H&R Block and the Franklin defendants, despite specifically stating that they would automatically renew every five years, were terminable at will upon reasonable notice since Missouri law required unequivocal language to create a perpetual contract and no such language was present. The court observed that this result is consistent with *Armstrong Bus. Services, Inc. v. H&R Block*, 96 S.W. 3d 867 (Mo. Ct. App. 2002). Although the district court had distinguished *Armstrong* because the contract in *Armstrong* contained different termination rights than the contract in *Franklin*, the Eighth Circuit found that the rule of law stated in *Armstrong* precluded the *Franklin* claims.

In *Grill Holdings, L.L.C. v. Camellia Grill Holdings, Inc.*, Nos. 2012-CA-1642 and 2012-CA-1643, 2013 La. App. LEXIS 1321 (La. Ct. App. May 8, 2013), the Louisiana Court of Appeals considered an appeal of the trial court's order granting summary judgment to franchisor Camellia Grill Holdings, Inc. ("Camellia") on the wrongful termination claims of franchisee The Grill Holdings, L.L.C. ("The Grill").

Camellia terminated The Grill effective June 1, 2011, alleging that The Grill had altered the franchisor's trademarks, improperly opened sub-licensed locations, failed to pay royalties and failed to provide financial information even after an audit was requested.

Camellia brought an action seeking a declaratory judgment that The Grill had breached the agreement and termination was proper. The Grill argued that (1) Camellia had modified the parties' franchise agreement by routinely accepting late payment; (2) Camellia's allegations were made in bad faith; and (3) The Grill's alleged defaults were not material. The trial court granted Camellia's summary judgment motion.

The Louisiana Court of Appeal reviewed the parties' franchise agreement in detail and found that The Grill had clearly breached the agreement. Therefore, Camellia was entitled to terminate the agreement, and the agreement itself stated that it could not be "amended, modified or supplemented except by a written agreement executed by all the Parties."

The court of appeal affirmed the grant of summary judgment and allowed Camellia to recover an additional $3,222.00 for its attorneys' fees on appeal.

In *Lift Truck Lease & Service, Inc. v. Nissan Forklift Corp., North America.*, No. 12-CV-153, 2013 U.S. Dist. LEXIS 87391 (E.D. Mo. June 21, 2013), Missouri and Illinois dealer Lift Truck, in connection with a wrongful termination action, proposed an expert witness to testify regarding "good cause" to terminate. The dealer's expert was prepared to testify that (1) Lift Truck substantially achieved its sales goals; (2) Nissan treated Lift Truck differently than similarly situated dealers; and (3) Nissan's termination of Lift Truck did not conform to forklift industry custom and practice. Nissan moved to exclude the testimony under the rule set forth in *Daubert v. Merrill Dow Pharmaceuticals, Inc.*, 509 U.S. 579 (1993).

The court denied Nissan's motion in part and granted it in part, concluding that (1) the expert could testify regarding whether Lift Truck "substantially complied with" certain market share requirements; (2) the expert could testify that Nissan treated Lift Truck differently than similarly-situated dealers; but (3) the expert could not testify that the termination did not comply with "forklift industry custom and practice."

The Eighth Circuit's opinion in *Lauzon v. Senco Products, Inc.*, 270 F.3d 681, 686 (8th Cir. 2001) required that (1) an expert's opinion must be relevant to the case; (2) the expert must be qualified to assist the finder of fact; and (3) the expert must have reliably applied principles and methods to the facts of the case. Applying this rule, the court found that the expert's 38 years of experience in the forklift industry qualified him to testify regarding the first two matters, which clearly involved legal standards to be applied in the case under the relevant dealer protection statutes. However, the proposed opinion on "custom and practice" relied upon outdated information and was opining on a legal concept (custom and practice) mentioned nowhere in the applicable statute.

B.   STATE FRANCHISE PROTECTION STATUTES

Cases involving state franchise protection statutes are summarized throughout the text. *See* cases set forth in Chapter 1.I. and Chapter II.A.

International House of Pancakes, LLC v. Parsippany Pancake House, Inc., 900 F.Supp.2d 403 (D.N.J. 2012) and *Budget Blinds Inc. v. LeClair,* No. 12-1101, 2013 U.S. Dist. LEXIS 7463 (C.D. Cal. Jan. 16, 2013), summarized above, both applied state "franchise" acts (not dealer acts) and addressed the issue of whether statutory "good cause" existed.

C.   OTHER TERMINATION ISSUES

Oracle America, Inc. v. Innovative Technology Distributors, LLC, Nos. 11-CV-01043 and 11-CV-02135, 2012 U.S. Dist. LEXIS 134343 (N.D. Cal. Sept. 18, 2012), previously summarized in Chapter 1.I., found that the New

Jersey Franchise Practices Act might protect from termination a "value added distributor," even though it owed over $19 million in unpaid invoices.

JOC Inc. v. ExxonMobil Oil Corp., 507 Fed. Unpub. Appx. 208 (3rd Cir. Dec. 18, 2012), involved a dispute between ExxonMobile and a gas station franchisee, JOC. JOC moved for an injunction against a threatened franchise termination and the district court granted a preliminary injunction against the threatened termination, but not against a termination by ExxonMobile for future misconduct. Both parties appealed. While the appeal was pending, ExxonMobile terminated JOC.

The Third Circuit dismissed the appeal as moot, stating that no franchise existed due to the termination, and, even if there had been no termination, the franchise would have expired by its own terms in February of 2012. Therefore, the court stated, "Because there is no longer any franchise to terminate or to save, we cannot grant either party effective relief."

In *Royal Dispatch Services, Inc. v. UBS Financial Services, Inc.*, No. 12-CV-2032, 2013 U.S. Dist. LEXIS 107672 (E.D. N.Y. July 31, 2013), the court found that UBS's decision to terminate the parties' transportation services contract on 60 days' notice was not a breach of contract, but the "wholesale dismantling of UBS of the means by which its employees hired Royal . . . during the 60-day notice period would constitute a breach of contract." However, the court denied either party to the contract summary judgment since Royal did, in fact, receive a fair amount of business during the 60-day period. *See* summary of court's ruling on damages in Chapter 5.VIII.B.

In *ERA Franchise Systems, LLC v. Hoppens Realty, Inc.*, summarized in Chapter 5.VI., the court refused to dismiss a Wisconsin Fair Dealership Law claim, stating that, although success seemed doubtful, at the motion to dismiss stage the terminated franchisee's claims was "facially plausible."

III.   Renewal

Some prospective franchisees are able to obtain contract language in their initial franchise agreements that protect them from the imposition of less favorable contract terms by the franchisor upon renewal. The franchisee in *Home Instead, Inc. v. Florance*, No. 12-CV-264, 2012 U.S. Dist. LEXIS 134554 (D. Neb. Sept. 20, 2012) believed that its initial franchise agreement contained such terms. Florance's renewal agreement stated that he could maintain his territorial exclusivity if he met certain billing quotas, including a $30,000 per month billing quota "from the end of the fifth year of operation of the Franchised Business through the end of the term of this Agreement or any renewal terms of a renewal Franchise Agreement." Upon renewal, Home Instead, Inc., attempted to impose a $70,000 billing quota. Florance argued that the $30,000 quota by its terms applied to all renewals.

The trial court found that Florance had no likelihood of success on its claims and denied Florance's motion for preliminary injunction against nonrenewal, finding that Florance had agreed to sign the "then current" Franchise Agreement upon any renewal and, that, because the new franchise agreement provided for a $70,000 sales quota, it was permissible for Home Instead to impose that term upon Florance upon renewal. The court found that the "$30,000 quota" language was merely a <u>floor</u> that set forth the <u>lowest</u> quota Florance could achieve and maintain exclusivity. However, the court concluded that Home Instead was permitted to raise the quota level above $30,000 if it chose to do so.

The trial court's denial of the franchisee's request for a preliminary injunction was reversed by the Eighth Circuit in *Home Instead, Inc. v. Florance*, No. 12-3521, 2013 U.S. App. LEXIS 14336 (8th Cir. July 16, 2013). While each party at the trial court had argued that the written franchise agreement unambiguously favored its position, the Eighth Circuit found that the franchise agreement was ambiguous on the issue of whether the $30,000 quota was a floor or a ceiling, so the trial court made an error of law when it found that the franchisee had no likelihood of success of the merits. The Eighth Circuit remanded the matter, directing the trial court to conduct a full analysis of the preliminary injunction motion under the Eighth Circuit's four-part balancing test.

IV. Transfers

Dealers and franchisees often attempt to transfer their businesses to entities which the manufacturer or franchisor find objectionable. These attempted transfers often occur when the dealer or franchisee is struggling and may face termination if it cannot sell the franchise or dealership. There were a few cases during the Reporting Period involving attempted transfers.

Indiana dealer law requires a manufacturer or supplier to accept or reject a proposed dealer transfer by certified mail within 60 days of receiving certain statutorily-defined information regarding the transfer of motor vehicles. *See* Ind. Code § 9-23-3-22. In *Utility Trailers of Indianapolis, Inc. v. Utility Trailer Manufacturing Co.*, 11-CV-01597, 2013 U.S. Dist. LEXIS 36721 (S.D. Ind. Mar. 18, 2013), the selling dealer claimed that the manufacturer failed to specifically reject a proposed dealer transfer (and provide the reasons for its rejection) by certified mail within 60 days, and, therefore, the transfer had been approved as a matter of law.

The manufacturer did not dispute that it never gave specific written reasons for rejecting the transfer and never met the 60 day deadline, but countered that (1) the dealer was told by phone and email why the sale was rejected; and (2) the dealer did not provide the statutorily-required information to start the 60-day clock running.

The parties filed cross-motions for summary judgment. The court granted the manufacturer summary judgment, finding that the application provided by the dealer was incomplete, had items left blank, and failed to attach key documents. Thus, the court concluded, the 60-day clock never started ticking and the dealer's statutory claim that the manufacturer had failed to timely reject the transfer was without merit.

In *Paccar, Inc. v. Elliot Wilson Capitol Trucks, LLC*, 905 F.Supp. 2d 675 (D. Md. 2012), a dispute arose between truck manufacturer Paccar, Inc. and its Maryland based dealer of "Peterbilt" trucks, Elliot Wilson Capitol Trucks. Elliott Wilson had attempted to sell its dealership, and been rejected by Paccar. Paccar also sent Elliot Wilson a termination notice. Even after receiving the termination notice, Elliot Wilson forged ahead and signed another letter of intent to sell. Paccar then withdrew its termination notice and exercised its right of first refusal to buy the dealership. Paccar brought a declaratory judgment action, seeking a determination that it had acted properly under the parties' dealer agreement and the Maryland Vehicle Dealer Act. Elliot Wilson counterclaimed, alleging violations of the Maryland Vehicle Dealer Act and the parties' agreement. Paccar moved to dismiss a number of the claims made by Elliot Wilson, including the Maryland Vehicle Dealer Act and breach of contract claims based upon Paccar's refusal to approve the proposed transfer.

The court denied Paccar's motion to dismiss on the transfer-related claims, stating that Elliot Wilson had plausibly alleged that Paccar had (1) acted in bad faith by refusing to approve the transfer request; (2) acted improperly in attempting to coerce Elliot Wilson into selling only to Paccar or Paccar's preferred buyer; and (3) discriminated against Elliot Wilson and its proposed buyer because they carried lines other than Peterbilt. Therefore, the Maryland Vehicle Dealer Act claims all stated a plausible claim upon which relief could be granted.

The Paccar-Elliot Wilson dealer agreement contained a clause requiring Paccar to use its "best efforts to conditionally approve potential buyers to facilitate DEALER's negotiations." Peterbilt argued that this clause did not require any efforts by Peterbilt to actually work toward approving a buyer. The court disagreed, finding that, because the Maryland Vehicle Dealer Act prevented Paccar from unreasonably withholding its consent to a transfer, Peterbilt had an obligation to use at least reasonable efforts "to not unreasonably reject a transfer." Therefore, Elliot Wilson stated a claim by alleging that Paccar had a plan to only allow certain buyers and Paccar would not consider the buyer presented by Elliot Wilson.

As the case progressed, in *Paccar, Inc. v. Elliot Wilson Capitol Trucks, LLC*, No. 11-2016, 2013 U.S. Dist. LEXIS 21004 (D. Md. Feb. 8, 2013) Elliot Wilson argued that Peterbilt had failed to act in a timely manner and could not, therefore (1) exercise the right of first refusal, or (2) deny the dealer's transfer request. The court agreed that exercise of the right of first refusal was untimely, but found that denial of the transfer request was proper as a matter of law because the two rights were unrelated. The court analyzed the facts in great detail.

In August 2011, dealer Elliott Wilson Capitol Trucks advised Peterbilt that it was transferring its dealership to Norris Automotive Group. Peterbilt refused to approve transfer on the basis that Peterbilt had been involved with Norris Automotive Group in the past and did not want to deal with Norris Automotive Group any longer. In October of 2011, EWCT told Peterbilt that, despite Peterbilt's rejection of the proposed transfer, EWCT and Norris desired to proceed anyway. EWCT's lawyer on October 5, 2011 outlined the terms of the deal.

On November 3, 2011, Peterbilt responded, stating that it did not understand the deal and that certain deal terms were missing. Peterbilt, however, did not ask for more information. Instead, Peterbilt stated that the proposal was so insufficient that it did not comply with the notice requirements under the parties' dealer agreement.

After various discussions back and forth and legal maneuvering by the parties, on February 1, 2012, Peterbilt provided notice of its intention to exercise its right of first refusal. EWCT rejected this, stating that Peterbilt has missed its 30 days window to exercise the right.

The parties filed cross-motions for summary judgment. The court ruled that Peterbilt had sufficient information about the proposed sale before January 2, 2012, and, therefore, it had missed its 30-day window to exercise its right of first refusal. The court further found that a party holding such a right who is provided with information concerning a proposed transfer must affirmatively inquire about missing or confusing terms. If it fails to inquire, the party cannot rely upon minor deficiencies in the notice of proposed sale.

The court found that Peterbilt could have inquired, but it chose, instead, to criticize and reject the notice of proposed sale.

Nevertheless, the court found that Peterbilt's right to reject the transfer was unrelated to its untimely exercise of its right of first refusal. Therefore, Peterbilt could reject the transaction if it acted reasonably. The court found that it was reasonable as a matter of law for Peterbilt to reject a buyer with whom it had had contentious litigation in the past. The court granted summary judgment in favor of Peterbilt on the issue of the proprietary of Peterbilt's refusal to approve the transfer.

In *Mt. Clemens Auto Center, Inc. v. Hyundai Motor America*, 897 F. Supp. 2d 570 (D. Mich. 2012), the court granted the defendant's motion to dismiss. Plaintiff Mt. Clemens Auto Center ("Mt. Clemens") brought a claim against Hyundai Motor America ("Hyundai") alleging that Hyundai breached the dealer agreement and violated Michigan law when it would not allow it to transfer the dealer agreement to another entity. The agreement required Mt. Clemens to have a floor plan credit source. When Mt. Clemens lost its floor plan credit source, Hyundai terminated the agreement. Mt. Clemens then tried to transfer the agreement to another dealer. However, Hyundai denied it could consent to such an action because the agreement already had been terminated.

Mt. Clemens claimed that Hyundai unreasonably withheld consent of the transfer in violation of Michigan law. The Michigan statute provided that a dealer should have 180 days after notice to remedy the situation. Mt. Clemens claimed that the proposed transfer would have cured the failure to perform and would have taken place within the 180-day period. However, Hyundai argued that the failure to have floor plan financing was not a mere failure to perform under the sales provisions of the franchise agreement, but rather a breach under a completely separate provision of the franchise agreement and only provided for 90 days' notice and opportunity to cure. Therefore, as a breach, Mt. Clemens was entitled only to 90 days' notice of termination under the Michigan statute. Even if the breach was curable, Hyundai also argued that a transfer to a third party would not be a sufficient cure.

Examining whether the failure to maintain floor plan financing was a failure to perform under the sales provisions or a breach under the termination provisions, the court applied the rules of contract construction and statutory interpretation. Under the plain language of the agreement, the court found that failure to maintain financing was an independent breach of the contract. It reached this conclusion because the provision was separate from the sales provisions and the ability to cure a failed performance was limited in the sections on sales. Therefore, the court found that the agreement treated sales and financing separately.

Finding that a failure to maintain floor plan financing was a breach, the court considered if Hyundai had provided proper notice under the Michigan statute. The court found that the proper 90-day notice had been given, and that there was no evidence that the notice had been altered or withdrawn. Mt. Clemens' proposed transfer occurred six days before the expiration of the 90-day period. The court observed that the Michigan statute allowed a manufacturer 60 days to respond to a proposal to transfer. However, the termination became effective before the 60 days were over and Hyundai no longer had any further obligations. Examining both the agreement and Michigan law, therefore, the court found that plaintiff had not stated a claim upon which relief could be granted and dismissed the complaint.

V.   Non-Compete Agreements And Restrictive Covenants

The courts were clogged with dozens of non-compete disputes this year, many of which resulted in written opinions which generally (but not always) enforced the covenants not to compete.

A.   NON-COMPETE NOT ENFORCED

The court in *Allegra Network, LLC v. Ruth (In re: Ruth)*, No. 10-50184, 2013 Bankr. LEXIS 133 (Bankr. E.D. Tex., Jan. 10, 2013), determined that a Michigan choice-of-law clause contained in a 2006 Renewal Addendum to the parties' 1984 Franchise Agreement rendered the covenant not to compete void under an obsolete Michigan statute disfavoring non-compete agreements. The court found that although the Michigan statute disfavoring non-compete agreements had been repealed in 1985, the 1984 Franchise Agreement still had contained an illegal term at the time of its consummation. The subsequent repeal of the statute did not suddenly render the illegal term legal. The court also determined that the non-compete was a "claim" that could be discharged in bankruptcy.

Tutor Time Learning Centers, LLC v. Kog Industries, No. 12-CV-4129, 2012 U.S. Dist. LEXIS 162124 (E.D. N.Y. Nov. 13, 2012), involved a franchisee who closed two Tutor Time franchises in Queens and Staten Island and rebranded them as "Ivy League Learning Academy." Tutor Time sought an injunction to enforce its non-compete provisions.

The Eastern District of New York denied the motion, finding no irreparable harm. The court found: (1) irreparable harm could not be presumed; (2) a franchise agreement term stating irreparable harm would occur was not dispositive; (3) there was no public confusion because customers knew the locations were no longer affiliated with Tutor Time; (4) Tutor Time could not claim "loss of business" because it was not registered to sell new franchises and had never tried to recruit the customers being lost due to the franchise termination; (5) the claim that existing franchisees would be harmed created no "irreparable harm" to Tutor Time; and (6) the Staten Island location had been allowed to operate without a signed franchise agreement for two years.

Having found no irreparable harm, the court denied the injunction.

In *Curves International, Inc. v. Shape Fitness, LLC*, No. 13-11859, 2013 U.S. Dist. LEXIS 60441 (E.D. Mich. April 29, 2013), the Curves system proved to be a victim of its own success. When Curves terminated its Essexville, Michigan franchisee for non-payment of fees, the franchisee immediately opened a competing club.

The court denied Curve's motion for a temporary restraining order, stating that it was highly unlikely that Curves, the "world's largest fitness franchise," would suffer any irreparable harm due to competition with its former franchisee for a few days in "Essexville, Michigan – a town of fewer than 4,000." The court found that any harm that could occur before a preliminary injunction hearing could be scheduled would be fully compensated for by money damages.

The distinction between the "termination" and "expiration" of a franchise agreement was relied upon by a franchisee of a car painting and dent repair franchisee to avoid a non-compete obligation in *Hamden v. Total Car Franchising Corp.*, No. 12-CV-0003, 2012 U.S. Dist. LEXIS 111432 (W.D. Va. Aug. 7, 2012). Hamden owned 30 Total Car franchises. All 30 of Hamden's franchises were governed by a single franchise agreement which expired on May 9, 2011. Neither party recognized this fact until October 12, 2011, when Total Car Franchising advised Hamden that he needed to renew his Franchise Agreement.

Hamden advised Total Car Franchising on November 30, 2011 that he would not renew, and he ceased all franchised operations on December 1, 2011. Hamden's post-contract non-compete and confidentiality obligations only applied in the event that Total Car Franchising terminated the franchise. Hamden alleged that, because Total Car Franchising allowed the agreement to expire, none of the post-contract covenants applied and he could compete. The court agreed, holding that the non-competes only applied upon termination and there had been no termination. Therefore, Hamden had no non-compete obligations.

B. NON-COMPETE "BLUE PENCILED"

In *Novus Franchising, Inc. v. Superior Entrance Systems, Inc.*, No. 12-CV-204, 2012 U.S. Dist. LEXIS 182460 (W.D. Wis. Dec. 28, 2012), the court, applying Minnesota law, "blue penciled" the two-year and ten-mile covenant not to compete contained in the franchise agreement. As "blue penciled," the covenant applied only to preclude the franchisee's guarantor's interest in a competing glass business to the extent that he was working in concert with the corporate franchisee. The court found that the franchisee's guarantor had no involvement in the franchised business and received no confidential information. Accordingly, the court concluded that a non-compete could be enforced against him only if he acted in concert with the corporate entity who had, in fact, received the confidential information.

In *Cottman Transmission Systems, LLC v. Gano*, No. 12-CV-05223, 2013 U.S. Dist. LEXIS 31195 (E.D. Pa. Mar. 7, 2013), the court, considering Cottman's request for an injunction enforcing the terms of the franchise agreement's non-competition provision, expressed the rule of law in Pennsylvania as follows: "Pennsylvania law permits the equitable enforcement of a covenant not to compete included in a franchise agreement where the restrictions are reasonably necessary for the protection of the franchisor without imposing undue hardship on the franchisee and the restrictions are reasonably limited as to duration of time and geographical extent."

Under this standard, the court enforced a two-year non-compete restriction within 10 miles of the franchisee's center and within 3 miles of any Cottman center located in the "Greater Pittsburgh Area." The court refused to enforce the portion of the non-compete prohibiting competition within 3 miles of any Cottman center anywhere in the world. The court blue penciled the non-compete accordingly.

In *Golden Krust Patties, Inc. v. Bullock*, No. 13-CV-2241, 2013 U.S. Dist. LEXIS 99184 (E.D. N.Y. July 16, 2013), the court considered the franchisor's motion for a preliminary injunction enforcing a 2-year post-termination non-compete that prohibited Bullock from owning or operating any restaurant within (a) 10 miles of its franchised location or (b) 5 miles of any other existing Golden Krust location.

The court found that the non-competes are generally enforceable under New York law if they protect the franchisor's good will or customer relationships. Since the franchisee had taken certain actions that endangered both the goodwill of Golden Krust and its customer relationships (for example, using the franchisor's logos, trademarks and trade dress), the court found that a preliminary injunction was necessary to avoid irreparable harm.

The court, however, found the non-compete to be overbroad and blue-penciled it. Even though Golden Krust itself in its motion papers had limited the scope of the non-compete to only the operations of a "Caribbean-themed" restaurant, the court found the 10-mile and 5-mile geographic limitations to be overbroad in light of the densely-populated New York City trade area and the admission of Gold Krust's counsel that few customers in New York would ever "travel ten miles – or even five miles – to a fast-food establishment." The court blue penciled the non-compete to apply only to a Caribbean-themed restaurant or food service business to be operated within 4 miles of the franchisee's former location or within 2.5 miles of any other existing Golden Krust restaurant.

C.   NON-COMPETE ENFORCED AS WRITTEN

In *Stanley Steemer International, Inc. v. Hurley*, No. 2:13-CV-005, 2013 U.S. Dist. LEXIS 10631 (S.D. Ohio Jan. 18, 2013), the court granted a temporary restraining order enjoining Hurley from operating a competing cleaning business if she (1) used Stanley Steemer's distinctive color, (2) used phone numbers advertised under Stanley Steemer's marks, (3) held herself out as a current or former Stanley Steemer franchisee, or (4) advertised any "method, procedure or technique" associated with Stanley Steemer. The court ordered immediate transfer of the business phone number and only required Stanley Steemer to post a $1,000 bond.

Tantopia Franchising, Co., LLC v. West Coast Tans of PA, LLC, No. 12-6700, 2013 U.S. Dist. LEXIS 8266 (E.D. Pa. Jan. 22, 2013), resulted in a complete franchisor victory at the preliminary injunction stage. Tantopia sought to enforce a 2-year non-compete with a territorial scope that included: (1) the franchisee's territory; (2) the franchisee's county; (3) five miles from the franchisee's location; or (4) ten miles from any Tantopia location.

The court found that the defendants, owners of the failed franchisee, through a straw-man owner/operator, had set up a competing tanning business less than 10 miles from two Tantopia locations. As a result, the court found that the defendants had violated their non-compete. In addition, the court found that Tantopia had demonstrated a reasonable likelihood of success on the merits and that an injunction was necessary to prevent "irreparable harm," which the court identified as (1) use of the franchisor's good will, and (2) the message to other franchisees that they could leave the system with impunity.

The Western District of North Carolina took a favorable view of a 1 year, 20-mile non-compete in *Econo-Lube N' Tune, Inc. v. Orange Racing, LLC*, No. 12-CV-449, 2012 U.S. Dist. LEXIS 129219 (W.D.N.C. Sept. 10, 2012). A car care franchisee abandoned its Econ-Lube N' Tune location and opened a competing location one mile away. Econo-Lube N' Tune moved for a preliminary injunction enforcing the non-compete. Although the franchisee failed to appear to contest the motion, the court, nevertheless, wrote an extensive opinion enforcing the non-compete, finding that the provision (1) was reasonable in time and territory covered; (2) was not broader than necessary to protect the franchisor and its franchisee from unfair competition; and (3) was necessary to enable the franchisor to re-franchise the territory.

In another default matter, *Novus Franchising, Inc. v. AZ Glassworks, LLC*, No. 12-CV-1771, 2013 U.S. Dist. LEXIS 36830 (D. Minn. Mar. 18, 2013), while initially indicating some hesitancy to enforce a 2-year non-compete applicable within 10 miles of any Novus location, the court nonetheless found that since the case law was mixed and defendant failed to present any defense, the court would enforce the covenant.

In *AAMCO Transmissions, Inc. v. Singh*, No. 12-2209, 2012 U.S. Dist. LEXIS 141764 (E.D. Pa. Oct. 1, 2012), the court granted a preliminary injunction enforcing a post-termination non-compete that prohibited Singh from operating a transmission repair business for 2 years within 10 miles of his former AAMCO center or any other AAMCO center. The court found that, if AAMCO could not enforce the covenant, the franchisor also risked losing the remainder of the franchisees who could violate their agreements and leave the system.

Then in *AAMCO Transmissions, Inc. v. Singh*, No. 12-2209, 2012 U.S. Dist. LEXIS 163930 (E.D. Pa. Nov. 16, 2012), the franchisee sought reconsideration of the order. In support of the motion for reconsideration, the franchisee relied upon a 2011 case in which another judge in the Eastern District of Pennsylvania found AAMCO's non-compete to be overbroad.

The court rejected the motion for reconsideration, stating that (1) the 2011 case was not binding authority and (2) there was no compelling argument by Singh establishing that the covenant was clearly unreasonable.

In *Allegra Network, LLC v. Cormack*, No. 11-13087, 2012 U.S. Dist. LEXIS 178822 (E.D. Mich. Dec. 3, 2012), the Cormacks attempted to overturn a preliminary injunction against post-termination competition by arguing (1) the franchise agreement listed them as operating in Waterbury, Connecticut instead of their actual location of Fayetteville, Arkansas, so their continued operation in Arkansas was not within 10 miles of Waterbury, Connecticut; and (2) they never intended to sign the Franchise Agreement individually.

The court found that the Connecticut reference was clearly a typo and created no real ambiguity in the document (which in another place also contained the correct Arkansas address). In addition, the court found the defendants' contention that they did not intend to sign as individuals made no difference – the Cormacks clearly, in fact, had signed as individuals and therefore, the noncompetition covenant was enforceable against them individually.

In *Lawn Doctor, Inc. v. Rizzo,* Bus. Franchise Guide (CCH) ¶ 14,950 (D. N.J. Dec. 11, 2012), Rizzo and Lawn Doctor disagreed on the scope of the non-compete written into a settlement agreement between the parties. Rizzo argued that he could irrigate lawns because the settlement agreement did not specifically preclude irrigation services and Rizzo had never sold such services as a Lawn Doctor franchisee or obtained any training or information from Lawn Doctor on such services. The court disagreed, finding that Rizzo had agreed to not perform services involving "care and condition of lawns or other vegetation or related or ancillary services . . .." In the court's opinion, this language clearly included irrigating lawns. The court found Lawn Doctor's need to protect its customer base outweighed any hardship to Rizzo in not performing irrigation services.

Jackson Hewitt's 2011 victories in a non-compete case against its former franchisee DJSG Utah Tax Service were challenged twice during the Reporting Period. In *Jackson Hewitt, Inc. v. DJSG Utah Tax Service, LLC,* No. 10-CV-5330, 2012 U.S. Dist. LEXIS 111389 (D. N.J., Aug. 8, 2012) the court upheld its prior preliminary injunction, stating that the motion for reconsideration was untimely and offered no new arguments. In *Jackson Hewitt, Inc. v. DJSG Utah Tax Service, LLC,* No. 10-CV-5330, 2013 U.S. Dist. LEXIS 79556 (D. N.J., June 6, 2013), the court denied a Rule 60(b)(6) motion for relief from its final judgment granting Jackson Hewitt a permanent injunction for two years after the date of the order (not two years after the termination of the franchise agreement). The court found that its decision was justified by DJSG's competition immediately after the termination of the franchise agreement. As an alternative holding, the court denied the Rule 60(b)(6) motion as improperly brought because the judgment at issue had already been appealed.

In *Victory Lane Quick Oil Change, Inc. v. Darwich,* No. 11-11786, 2013 U.S. Dist. LEXIS 12877 (E.D. Mich. Jan. 31, 2013), the franchisor, Victory Lane Quick Oil Change, sought to enforce its two year and 25 mile post-termination non-compete against franchisee Darwich Brothers and certain guarantors. Certain defendants settled and Victory Lane moved for summary judgment against the two remaining defendants.

The defendants argued that they were not violating the non-compete because all they had done was sublease the property at issue to family members who were running "Saline Quick Lube." The court disagreed. The non-compete prevented the defendants from being "connected with," having an "interest in," or "assisting" any person engaged in a competitive business. The court found that acting as the sub-landlord for the property violated the non-compete. Therefore, Victory Lane was granted summary judgment on its breach of contract claim and enforced the non-compete.

The parties in *Astral Health & Beauty, Inc. v. Aloette of Mid-Mississippi, Inc.*, No. 12-CV-1904, 2012 U.S. Dist. LEXIS 146671 (N.D. Ga. Oct. 1, 2012), permitted their skincare and beauty products franchise agreements to expire in 2001 and 2004, but continued to do business with each other. When franchisee Aloette began competing by selling other beauty products, franchisor Astral sought to enforce the non-compete and confidentiality provisions of the franchise agreements. Aloette responded that the agreements had long ago expired and the post-expiration non-compete had elapsed.

The court found that Georgia law was not well developed on the issue of "holding over" after expired agreements, so the court would permit the parties to conduct discovery so that a ruling could be made on a better record. The court also found that Aloette's declaratory judgment claims asking for a declaration that it could compete, while duplicative of its defenses, could be sustained at the early stages of the proceeding.

See also Curves International, Inc. v. Fox, No. 12-12250, 2013 U.S. Dist. LEXIS 66235 (D. Mass. May 9, 2013) (one year non-compete within 10 miles of any Curves is reasonable under Massachusetts law).

VI.   Industry-Specific Statutes

There are state and federal laws that protect dealers, distributors and sales representatives of any number of products, including gasoline, beer, liquor, automobiles, farm equipment and construction equipment. These statutes gave rise to a large number of cases during the Reporting Period.

A.   PETROLEUM MARKETING PRACTICES ACT ("PMPA")

Gas station franchisees generally enjoy statutory protection from a variety of unfair or inequitable practices under the Petroleum Marketing Practices Act,

15 U.S.C. §2801 *et seq.* This Reporting Period featured a large number of reported opinions involving the PMPA and state equivalents.

1.   Termination

In *Jimico Enterprises, Inc. v. Lehigh Gas Corp.*, 708 F.3d 106 (2d Cir. 2013), the Second Circuit affirmed the trial court's judgment awarding $141,892.79 in compensatory damages, and $30,000 in punitive damages, plus attorneys' fees, costs and pre-judgment and post-judgment interest to two terminated gas station franchisees who operated gas stations along the New York State Thruway in upstate New York.

Lehigh Gas alleged that the plaintiffs were merely "trial franchisees" operating on one-year contracts and, therefore, they were not protected by the PMPA from non-renewal without good cause. In contrast, the plaintiffs argued that, while they were entitled to 90 days' notice of termination under the PMPA, they instead, had been terminated without any notice.

The trial court agreed with the plaintiffs that the PMPA applied, granted the franchisees summary judgment on liability, and entered a monetary judgment after an evidentiary hearing on damages.

On appeal, Lehigh Gas argued that the PMPA had no private right of action for failure to give 90 days' notice, and, even if it did, trial franchisees were not entitled to any such notice. The Second Circuit quickly disposed of these arguments, stating that a violation of 15 U.S.C. §2802 clearly gave rise to a private right of action under 15 U.S.C. § 2805, and failure to give proper notice under 15 U.S.C. § 2804 was a violation of 15 U.S.C. § 2802.

Accordingly, the Second Circuit affirmed the trial court's order and granted the franchisees the right to seek their fees and costs related to the appeal from the district court on remand.

A California Shell gas station franchisee did not fare as well on its PMPA claim in *BSD, Inc. v. Equilon Enterprises, LLC*, No. 05223, 2013 U.S. Dist. LEXIS 33426 (N.D. Cal., Mar. 11, 2013). The gas station franchisor, Equilon, sold its gas station to Anabi Oil Corporation and had to provide the existing franchisee, BSD, with a statutory right of first refusal to buy the station. In September of 2010, BSD exercised the right of first refusal "under protest."

Equilon subsequently determined that, while it <u>thought</u> it had sold its rights as a landlord to Anabi, it had not. Therefore, Equilon still was the property's landlord and still was entitled to rent payments from BSD (BSD stepped into Anabi's shoes by exercising its statutory right of first refusal). As a result, BSD was supposed to pay Equilon rent, but had paid no rent at all for months. BSD owed Equilon $115,000 in back rent. Equilon eventually advised BSD that it would be terminated as a franchisee if it failed to pay back rent in full by March 2, 2011 and that BSD would also forfeit its right of first refusal.

BSD never paid and was to be terminated as a franchisee on June 30, 2011, but instead surrendered the station to Equilon on June 17, 2011. BSD sued for wrongful termination.

The court found that failure to pay rent was a proper basis for a PMPA termination. The court further found that Equilon had provided sufficient notice (approximately 94 days) of its intention to terminate for failure to pay rent. Accordingly, the court granted Equilon's motion for summary judgment on its breach of contract claim.

Equilon, for some unknown reason, decided not to submit the actual right of first refusal document to the court. As a result, Equilon's summary judgment motion on Equilon's termination of BSD's right of first refusal was denied.

After Equilon filed the right of first refusal document with the court and moved for partial summary judgment, the court granted the motion, finding that termination of the right of first refusal was proper. *See BSD, Inc. v. Equilon Enterprises, LLC*, No. 10-05223, 2013 U.S. Dist. LEXIS 105941 (N.D. Cal. July 20, 2013).

Evans Group, Inc. v. Foti, No. 11-274, 2012 Vt. LEXIS 75 (Vt. Sept. 14, 2012), involved Foti Fuels, Inc., a jobber who sold Citgo gasoline to Quick Stop gas stations. Foti Fuels got its gasoline from a larger jobber, Evans Group, Inc., who, in turn, had purchased the gasoline from a huge Citgo fuel depot in Albany, New York.

In 2008, Foti Fuels came under new management and began to balk at the idea of paying Evans Group for the gasoline. Due to various delivery issues and business disputes, Quick Stop stopped buying Citgo gas from Foti Fuels and began buying from Evans Group directly. On April 21, 2009, Evans terminated the Evans/Foti agreement and informed Foti Fuels that it owed Evans $68,864. Evans sued, and Foti Fuels counterclaimed, alleging improper termination under the PMPA.

The trial court found that Foti Fuels was not a franchisee under the PMPA because it had no control over the Citgo trademark. Even though the Evans/Foti relationship was a distributor-to-distributor relationship that might otherwise qualify as a franchise relationship under the PMPA, the court found that Foti Fuels did not qualify for PMPA protection. On appeal, the Vermont Supreme Court affirmed this finding as not clearly erroneous.

In *Joseph v. Sasafrasnet, LLC*, No. 11-CV-402, 2012 U.S. Dist. LEXIS 182442 (N.D. Ill. Dec. 28, 2012), the fuel distributor terminated its relationship with Joseph due to Joseph bouncing payments for fuel purchases. The court rejected Joseph's argument that its NSF payments to its BP franchisor were "beyond its control" or "technical and unimportant." Of the three NSF checks at issue, the court found that checks 1 and 3 were the fault of Joseph, and, therefore, proper grounds for termination. The court also found that, under Seventh Circuit precedent, it need not determine whether a payment term of an agreement was "reasonable," since failure to pay in a timely manner was a specific grounds for termination listed in the PMPA. The court went on to find that repeated failures to pay in excess of $50,000 were not a "technical or unimportant failure" under 15 U.S.C. § 2801(13)(A) since they "constituted significant breaches of an important part of the agreement."

PC Puerto Rico, LLC v. El Smaili, No. 12-1973, 2013 U.S. Dist. LEXIS 28701 (D.P.R. Feb. 28, 2013), involved El Smaili, a Puerto Rico dealer of Texaco products, who had the right to buy and resell these products under sublease agreements and two supply agreements with PC Puerto Rico. El Smaili stopped paying for his gasoline and his agreements were terminated. El Smaili continued to operate and use the Texaco trademarks after termination. After an evidentiary hearing, the court ordered that a preliminary injunction prohibiting El Smaili from using the Texaco marks be issued since he had clearly violated the parties' agreements and federal and Puerto Rico trademark law.

In *Gun Hill Road Service Station, Inc. v. ExxonMobil Oil Corp.*, No. 08 CV 7956, 2013 U.S. Dist. LEXIS 14199 (S.D.N.Y. Feb. 1, 2013), the plaintiffs asserted several contract and tort claims against the defendant–franchisor and alleged that the defendant's termination of the franchise agreement violated the Petroleum Marketing Practices Act. Finding no oral modification of the contract, breach of the express terms, or breach of the implied covenant of good faith and fair dealing, the court largely granted the defendant's motion for summary judgment.

See also Gles, Inc. v. MK Real Estate Developer & Trade Co., No. 11-2438, 511 Fed. Appx. 189 (3d Cir. 2013) (affirming judgment made after a bench trial that a BP franchisee had failed to pay and could be terminated).

2. Right of First Refusal

Caputo v. BP West Coast Products, LLC, No. S-1-722, 2012 U.S. Dist. LEXIS 138702 (E.D. Cal. Sept. 26, 2012), involved the PMPA's statutory right of first refusal. The franchisee, Caputo, exercised his right of first refusal under the PMPA, paying $1.12 million "under protest" for a gas station in Sacramento. After buying the assets, Caputo sued, alleging that the sale he was forced to match: (1) was made in bad faith; (2) had bidding irregularities; (3) exceeded fair market value; (4) was not a bona fide offer; (5) did not involve a buyer who was "ready, willing and able," since the buyer had not secured financing; and (6) involved incomplete disclosures by the franchisor.

The court found no genuine issues of material fact with respect to any of these allegations and granted BP summary judgment.

3. Other Issues/State Law Equivalents

SSS Enterprises, Inc. v. Nova Petroleum Suppliers, LLC., No. 1:11-CV-1134, 2012 U.S. Dist. LEXIS 126225 (E.D. Va. Aug. 30, 2012), involved a variety of claims by 18 gasoline dealers in northern Virginia against distributors of Shell and Exxon branded motor fuels. The distributors brought motions for partial summary judgment on a number of claims, including the dealers' PMPA claims for bad faith termination. The court granted all of the summary judgment motions, concluding that the PMPA claims had to be dismissed because termination for failure to make payments on time was *per se* a proper ground for termination and a distributor's motive for such a termination was irrelevant.

Almasi v. Equilon Enterprises, LLC, No. 10-CV-03458, 2012 U.S. Dist. LEXIS 128623 (N.D. Cal. Sept. 10, 2012), involved Equilon's efforts to sell 250 Shell-branded gas stations in Northern California. Equilon wanted to withdraw from the market, so it solicited bids for its stations in "clusters" based upon location. "Cluster 7" involved gas stations in San Mateo and Santa Clara counties. These Cluster 7 stations were sold to a bidder named Nakash.

As required by Cal. Bus. & Prof. Code § 20999.25(a), Equilon then took Nakash's winning bid and offered the plaintiffs, who had been leasing those stations, a right of first refusal to buy on the same terms as Nakash. The plaintiffs exercised their statutory right of first refusal "under protest" and then sued for damages caused by Equilon submitting Nakash's "commercially unreasonable" offer to them.

The court denied Equilon's motion for summary judgment, stating genuine issues of material fact existed on whether Nakash's offer was "commercially reasonable." If the offer was found to be commercially unreasonably, Equilon had violated Cal. Bus. & Prof. Code § 20999.25(a), and, by extension, California's Unfair Competition Law, Cal. Bus. & Prof. Code § 17200.

B.   AUTOMOBILE/MOTOR VEHICLE DEALER LAWS

Few entities in the United States enjoy the level of statutory protection enjoyed by automobile dealers. As a result, dealers bring a lot of cases before courts and state motor vehicle boards, and the dealers often win disputes. This Reporting Period was no different. There were a number of reported cases, and dealers obtained either a positive or a mixed result in over half of them.

1.   Dealer Wins

In *LaFontaine Saline Inc., v. Chrysler Group LLC*, No. 307148, 2012 Mich. App. LEXIS 2378 (Mich. Ct. App. Nov. 27, 2012), the Michigan Court of Appeals considered a 2010 statutory amendment that extended the protected territory around a Michigan dealer from a six-mile radius to a nine-mile radius. In *Lafontaine*, the court was faced with a situation in which Chrysler had decided to place a new dealer more than six miles, but less than nine miles, away from Lafontaine. In addition, Chrysler had entered into a letter of intent with the new dealer and given notice of the proposed dealership addition prior to the 2010 Amendment being passed. But Chrysler had not entered into an actual dealer agreement with the new dealer until after the 2010 Amendment was passed. Chrysler took the position that it was not required to give any notice of protest rights to Lafontaine. Lafontaine disagreed and demanded a letter from Chrysler providing it with its protest rights. Chrysler refused. Lafontaine sued, asserting that, since the dealer agreement with the new dealer was not signed until after the 2010 Amendment, that the "nine mile rule" applied rather than then the "six mile rule."

The trial court disagreed, stating that the letter of intent triggered this statutory protest right and, therefore, the six mile rule applied. Thus, Lafontaine had no valid protest rights. The Michigan Court of Appeals reversed, stating that the letter of intent was not a "dealer agreement" because it did not establish the rights of the parties with respect to the manufacturer/dealer relationship. Therefore, the date when the dealer's protest rights vested was after the 2010 Amendment came into effect. Therefore, Lafontaine did, in fact, have protest rights triggered under the nine-mile rule, and the matter was reversed and remanded to the trial court for further proceedings.

In *North Star International Trucks, Inc. v. Navistar, Inc.*, No. A12-0732, 2013 Minn. App. Unpub. LEXIS 294 (Minn. Ct. App. Apr. 8, 2013), dealer North Star International Truck, Inc. lost an appeal of a trial court decision based upon a combined jury trial and bench trial of various statutory and common law claims by North Star against Navistar. The court of appeals found that the jury's determinations of good cause for termination and the jury's findings of waiver of certain claims by the dealer, were supported by sufficient evidence and, therefore, the court and jury had committed no error in finding that Navistar could legally remove 51 zip codes from North Star's area of responsibility and give them to another dealer without any liability to North Star.

However, all did not go so well for Navistar. After the jury and trial court determined that Navistar had good cause to terminate or substantially change the competitive circumstance of North Star's truck dealership, Navistar sent a termination letter to North Star. This termination letter caused North Star to commence another action in Minnesota state court, alleging wrongful termination under two Minnesota dealer statutes. Navistar moved to dismiss these claims based on the fact that a jury had already found that Navistar had good cause to terminate North Star. Therefore, the new claims of North Star were barred by principles of *res judicata* and collateral estoppel.

The trial court granted Navistar's motion to dismiss and motion for summary judgment on North Star's claims, agreeing that they were barred by principles of *res judicata* and collateral estoppel. Unfortunately for Navistar, the Minnesota Court of Appeals reversed. In *North Star International Trucks, Inc. v. Navistar, Inc.*, 2013 Minn. App. Unpub. LEXIS 447 (Minn. Ct. App. May 30, 2013), the Minnesota Court of Appeals ruled that the claims tried in the first jury trial and the claims brought by Navistar in 2012 were different claims and that the 2009 claims and 2012 claims were based upon different sets of operable facts and might require that a different legal standard or burden of proof be applied to the claims. Therefore, *res judicata* and collateral estoppel did not apply. The court of appeals reversed and remanded the case to the trial court.

Audi of Smithtown, Inc. v. Volkswagen of America, Inc., 100 A.D.3d 669 (N.Y. App. Div. 2012), was the rare case this year in which a dealer was granted summary judgment on its claims against a manufacturer. Audi conducted two programs which benefited new Audi dealers more than existing Audi dealers (the CPO Purchase Bonus Program and the Keep It Audi Program). As a result of these programs, new franchised dealers obtained greater rebates and, therefore, cheaper cars than could dealers who had not been newly franchised. Audi of Smithtown sued for improper price discrimination under New York's Franchised Motor Vehicle Dealer Act (Vehicle and Traffic Law § 460, *et seq.*). The trial court found that Audi of

Smithtown had proved its claim of price discrimination and was entitled to summary judgment. The appellate division agreed, stating that, since newly franchised dealers automatically qualified for a higher level in the program, and deposition testimony confirmed that fact, Audi of Smithtown had proved its case as a matter of law and Audi had violated New York law. The matter was remanded to the trial court for further proceedings.

As part of the continuing saga between Chrysler and former Chrysler dealers who had been terminated during Chrysler's bankruptcy, *Chrysler Group LLC v. South Holland Dodge, Inc.*, Nos. 10-12984, 10-13290, and 10-13908, 2013 U.S. Dist. LEXIS 52123 (E.D. Mich. Apr. 11, 2013), involved the continuing efforts of Chrysler dealers who has won their arbitration under Section 747 of the Consolidated Appropriations Act of 2010, Pub. L. No. 111-117 to regain their Chrysler dealerships. The Eastern District of Michigan had already previously determined that Chrysler was under no obligation to give the dealers back their dealership but, instead, only had to provide them with the "customary and usual [l]etter of [i]ntent" that new Chrysler (*i.e.*, post-bankruptcy Chrysler) was providing to its dealers. Faced with a motion for summary judgment from both the dealers and Chrysler, the trial court determined that a bench trial was necessary to determine whether the letter of intent that Chrysler was offering the dealers at issue was a "usual and customary" letter of intent.

Strike Four, LLC v. Nissan North America, Inc., No. 2012-193, 2013 N.H. LEXIS 37 (N.H. Apr. 12, 2013), involved a settlement agreement between a dealer and Nissan through which the dealer agreed either to meet certain minimal sales requirements or be terminated. The dealer argued that such a settlement agreement itself is a violation of New Hampshire's Regulation of Business Practices Between Motor Vehicle Manufacturers, Distributors and Dealers Act, N.H. Rev. Stat. Ann. Chapter 357-C.

In July of 2005, Nissan had issued Strike Four a notice of termination, which Strike Four had protested to the New Hampshire Motor Vehicle Industry Board. Rather than proceeding with the termination, the parties agreed to stay the Board proceeding while they worked out a settlement agreement. This settlement agreement took two years to complete, but on October 15, 2007, the parties entered into a settlement agreement under which Nissan and Strike Four would execute a new two-year term dealer agreement and Strike Four would withdraw its protest. The settlement agreement provided Strike Four with this two-year term agreement expressly upon the condition that Strike Four had to meet certain performance criteria. In 2008 and 2009, Strike Four failed to meets its criteria, but the term agreement continued to be extended, nevertheless, with new requirements each year for Strike Four to meet.

In the extensions, Strike Four always agreed that if it failed to meet the new sales requirements by the revised dates that it would sell its dealership to a qualified buyer within one year thereafter. On November 12, 2010, Nissan advised Strike Four that it was highly unlikely that Strike Four would be able to meet its sales obligations and, therefore, suggested that Strike Four begin looking for a new buyer to sell the business to within six months.

Rather than performing under its agreement, Strike Four stated that the sales performance obligations under the various agreements were unreasonable and filed a protest with the New Hampshire Motor Vehicle Industry Board, asking that the termination be enjoined. Nissan filed a counter-protest with the Board, alleging that Strike Four's actions constituted bad faith conduct in violation of N.H. Rev. Stat. 357-C:3, I (2009). The New Hampshire Board found the settlement agreement between the parties to be enforceable and not in violation of New Hampshire statutes. Therefore, the Board granted Nissan's protest and dismissed Strike Four's protest.

Strike Four appealed to the superior court. The superior court reversed the Board and stated that the settlement agreement between the parties was void under New Hampshire law, and that, therefore, Strike Four did have the right to protest the termination and challenge the reasonableness of the termination and challenge the reasonableness of the stated requirements.

The matter was then appealed to the New Hampshire Supreme Court. The New Hampshire Supreme Court ruled that the parties' settlement agreement was, in fact, invalid under New Hampshire law and that it did not comply with New Hampshire Rev. Stat. Chapter 357-C's requirements.

Under that statute, the court held, the only way for a dealer and a manufacturer to settle a dispute was to agree that the dealer would dismiss Board proceedings or stipulate to the dismissal of Board proceedings. According to the New Hampshire Supreme Court, "the only way for a dealer to be terminated was for the Motor Vehicle Board to find good cause for termination or for the dealer to specifically acquiesce to termination prior to the discontinuance of the dealer-manufacturer relationship."

Nissan had argued that virtually every dealer law in the nation permits a party protected by the dealer law to waive its dealer rights through a settlement agreement bargained for with the assistance of counsel. The New Hampshire Supreme Court found no merit to this argument, stating that New Hampshire's law did not permit any such waiver, and that the waiver would be ineffective "notwithstanding the terms or provisions of any waiver." The court went on to state that any settlement agreement that effectively creates a "refusal to do business timeline" is void.

Surprisingly, the court then went on to state that Nissan was entitled to bring a claim under the New Hampshire Dealer Act that Strike Four had acted in bad faith in failing to follow the parties' settlement agreement. The court found that, while the parties' agreement was illegal and unenforceable, the conduct of Strike Four outside of the four corners of the agreement (leading Nissan to believe that Strike Four would actually comply with the settlement agreement), could constitute "bad faith," which was actionable under the New Hampshire Dealer Act.

Legend Autorama, Ltd. v. Audi of America, Inc., 954 N.Y.S.2d 141 (N.Y. App. Div. Nov. 14, 2012), was another case in the Northeast area involving Audi of America, Inc. This time, the Volkswagen division was involved. Legend Autorama, Ltd. filed an action against Audi alleging violations of the covenant of good faith and fair dealing and breach of fiduciary duty involving Audi's decision to place a competing dealer within 13 miles of Legend Autorama, Ltd. The trial court denied Audi's motion for summary judgment.

The appellate court affirmed, stating that while the parties' dealer agreement did permit Audi to add new dealers and provided no exclusive territory to Legend Autorama, the covenant of good faith and fair dealing still stated that the discretion to add new dealers had to be exercised in good faith so as not to frustrate the rights of the other party to the contract. In addition, the Appellate Division also agreed with the trial court that Audi failed to prove a right to summary judgment on the dealer's claim that Audi failed to "actively assist dealer in all aspects of dealer's operations through such means as Audi considers appropriate." The dealer had obtained deposition testimony from Audi executives stating that the general practice of Audi was to discuss underperformance issues with dealers and give them time to fix their underperformance prior to opening a new dealership nearby to the underperforming dealer. Although that was Audi's policy, Audi had not done so in connection with Legend Autorama and the new dealer appointed 13 miles from Legend Autorama. Therefore, summary judgment was inappropriate.

The Appellate Division, however, granted Audi one victory, reversing the trial court's decision not to grant summary judgment to Audi on Legend Autorama's fiduciary duty claim. The court found that generally automobile dealers and manufacturers are not fiduciaries and that Legend Autorama had produced no evidence to establish that its case was one of the "rare instances" in which the terms of the franchise agreement or the nature of the relationship created a fiduciary duty.

In *Lou Bachrodt Chevrolet Co. v. General Motors, LLC*, No. 12-CV-7998, 2013 U.S. Dist. LEXIS 98870 (N.D. Ill. July 15, 2013), GM had filed removal papers and sought to avoid a proceeding before the Illinois Motor Vehicle Review Board on the basis that (1) GM had previously filed for bankruptcy protection, and (2) GM had then been forced into arbitration with Lou Bachrodt Chevrolet by Section 747 of the Consolidated Appropriations Act of 2010. Lou Bachrodt Chevrolet replied that its rights were governed not by bankruptcy law or Section 747, but by a settlement agreement entered into by GM that resolved the Section 747 arbitration voluntarily. Therefore, the dealer argued, the matter should be remanded to the Illinois Motor Vehicle Review Board.

The Northern District of Illinois agreed with the dealer – GM had voluntarily entered into a private contract with an auto dealer and that contract was subject to the jurisdiction of the Illinois Motor Vehicle Review Board. Therefore, the court remanded the matter to the Board.

2.   *Manufacturer Wins*

In *WMW, Inc. v. American Honda Company, Inc.*, No. S11G1828, 2012 Ga. LEXIS 777 (Ga. Oct. 15, 2012), the Georgia Supreme Court considered the issue of what "8-mile circle" of statutory protection belonged to a dealer who sold Hondas in Roswell, Georgia and had a service center in Alpharetta, Georgia. Honda sought to add a new Honda dealer in Cumming, Georgia – less than 8 miles from the Alpharetta service facility, but more than 8 miles from the Roswell sales facility. WMW protested, saying it was statutorily entitled to 8-mile circles of protection around both Alpharetta and Roswell.

The trial court rejected WMW's argument, finding that WMW lacked standing. The Georgia Court of Appeals found that WMW had only one protected circle – around its "principal place of business" in Roswell. Accordingly, it affirmed the dismissal for lack of standing. WMW appealed.

The Georgia Supreme Court affirmed on different grounds, stating that WMW could be a "dealer" under the Georgia Act in only one of two ways: (1) by selling new cars; or (2) by <u>exclusively</u> servicing cars. Since WMW sold new cars, it was a dealer under factor number 1, so WMW's 8-mile circle of protection was measured from any location where it <u>sold</u> new cars (not from the Alpharetta facility where it only serviced cars). The proposed Cumming facility was over 8 miles away from anywhere that WMW sold new cars, therefore, WNW lacked standing to protest the proposed facility.

In *Bergstrom Imports Milwaukee, Inc. v. Chrysler Group LLC*, NO. 12-CV-603, 2012 U.S. Dist. LEXIS 155902 (E.D. Wis. Oct. 31, 2012), the court granted Chrysler Group LLC's motion to dismiss a dealer's claims under the Wisconsin Motor Vehicle Dealer Law, Wis. Stat. § 218.0116 (2009-10). The owner of Bergstrom Imports claimed that Fiat (owned by Chrysler) had promised him that he would have the exclusive right to sell Fiat vehicles in Wisconsin outside the City of Kenosha, Wisconsin. Bergstrom operated a dealership in Milwaukee. After the roll out of the Fiat brand in Wisconsin and throughout the nation was a horrible disaster, Fiat's CEO Sergio Marchionne conceded in an interview that the Fiat launch had been botched and that Fiat had not supported its dealers during the roll out. As a result of Fiat's botched rollout, Bergstrom struggled financially.

While Bergstrom was struggling, Fiat agreed with a dealer to open a Fiat location in Madison, Wisconsin, 90 miles away from Bergstom's facility. Bergstrom viewed this as a violation of his alleged state-wide exclusivity for the Fiat brand.

Bergstrom sued Fiat, alleging that Fiat had violated the Wisconsin Motor Vehicle Dealer Law by acting in an "arbitrary and unconscionable manner." The trial court dismissed Bergstrom's claims, stating that while Fiat had done a terrible job of rolling out the Fiat brand nationwide, it was merely negligent. Its negligent conduct did not rise to the level of "arbitrary or unconscionable." The court also found that the failure to adequately roll out of the Fiat brand was not a violation of the covenant of good faith and fair dealing because Fiat was, again, merely negligent, and no one suggested that Fiat was treating Bergstrom unfairly or dealing with him in bad faith.

Bergstrom also brought a claim against Fiat based upon his alleged exclusivity in the State of Wisconsin. The dealer entity, Bergstrom Imports Milwaukee, Inc., had its claims dismissed based on its written contract with Chrysler, which did not include Wisconsin as its exclusive territory. The parent corporation, Bergstrom Corporation, had its claim dismissed because there was no evidence that any of the alleged oral representations regarding exclusivity were made to Bergstrom Corporation. Bergstrom Corporation had never done any business with Chrysler, and there was no evidence that Chrysler understood that, when talking to John Bergstrom, they were talking to Bergstrom Corporation rather than the dealer entity, Bergstrom Imports Milwaukee, Inc.

In addition, the court found that any claims by Bergstrom Corporation would also be barred because it could not reasonably rely upon a promise of Wisconsin exclusivity when the contract signed by Bergstrom Imports Milwaukee, Inc. did not include any representations regarding such exclusivity.

In *Abington Auto World, LP v. Bureau of Professional & Occupational Affairs*, Nos. 374 C.D. 2012 and 377 C.D. 2012, 2013 Pa. Commw. LEXIS 73 (Pa. Commw. Ct. Mar. 19, 2013), the issue for the court was whether Chrysler had properly taken advantage of a provision in the Pennsylvania Board of Vehicles Act, 63 P.S. § 818.27(B)(2), which stated that Chrysler could add a new dealer without protest by existing dealers if the new dealer was added within two miles of a location at which a former licensed vehicle dealer for the same line make of vehicle had ceased operating within the previous two years. This "two-year two-mile" rule was invoked by Chrysler.

Abington Auto World sued, stating that, while Chrysler had given notice of intent to add the new dealer within two years of the old dealer going out of business, no dealer agreement had been signed within two years and the proposed new dealer had not applied for a dealer license until after more than two years had expired. The Pennsylvania State Board of Vehicle Manufacturers, Dealers & Sales Persons ruled in favor of the dealer, stating that the two years had run before the dealer license application had been filed.

The commonwealth court reversed, stating that "based upon a review of the statutory language, the right of protest and any exemptions thereto are triggered simply by a manufacturer's notice to the Board of its intent to establish a new dealer." The court found that all Chrysler was required to do was to give notice to the Board within two years after the old dealer had gone out of business. Chrysler had done so, and, therefore, Abington Auto World had no right to protest as its right to protest was barred by the "two-year and two-mile" rule of 63 P.S. § 818.27(B)(2).

In *B.A. Wackerli, Co. v. Volkswagen of America, Inc.,* No. 12-CV-00373, 2012 U.S. Dist. LEXIS 115369 (D. Idaho Aug. 13, 2012), a dealer in Idaho Falls, Idaho was in danger of being terminated by Subaru. As a means of avoiding the Subaru termination, the dealer agreed to build a separate facility for his Volkswagen and Audi lines and make the existing facility Subaru only. Despite making this agreement with Subaru, Volkswagen, and Audi, the dealer made very little progress towards ever constructing the new Volkswagen and Audi facility. As a result, Volkswagen and Audi threatened to terminate B.A. Wackerli, Co. and B.A. Wackerli petitioned an administrative board for relief from the termination. The hearing officer ruled against B.A. Wackerli, Co., which then appealed to the Director of the Idaho Transportation Department. The hearing officer at that level also found that Volkswagen and Audi had good cause to terminate the dealer.

Wackerli filed an emergency motion for an injunction against termination in Idaho state court. The Idaho state court granted the TRO. Audi and Volkswagen removed the matter to federal court, and asked that the TRO be dissolved in light of the Transportation Department's final order. Wackerli asked that the Department's order be overturned or, in the alternative, that the court enjoin Audi and Volkswagen from terminating the dealer agreement. While the Idaho federal district court stated that it was deferring to the rulings of the Idaho Transportation Department, it also added that it agreed with the findings of the Idaho Transportation Department that the dealer had failed to comply with the requirements to build the separate facility and there was no evidence that either Volkswagen or Audi had attempted to coerce the agreement out the dealer. As a result, the court found that Wackerli had not established a reasonable likelihood of success on the merits, and, therefore, the final decision of the Idaho Transportation Department should take effect without further delay.

In *Kia Motors America, Inc. v. Glassman Oldsmobile Saab Hyundai, Inc.,* 706 F.3d 733 (6th Cir. 2013), the issue to be determined was whether the 2010 Amendment to the Michigan Motor Dealers Act, which gave dealers protest rights within a nine mile territory (versus the six mile territory that they had under the old Act), applied to Kia's efforts to add a new dealer in Troy, Michigan, approximately seven miles from Glassman's Southfield, Michigan location. While Kia's notice of the new dealer point preceded the 2010 Amendment to the statute, Glassman argued that the amendment was merely procedural and that it should be applied retroactively to the proposed Troy, Michigan location.

The district court found that the parties did not agree to comply with the 2010 Amendment and that the 2010 Amendment could not be applied retroactively. On appeal, the Sixth Circuit affirmed the district court and stated that the 2010 Amendment was substantive because it impacted significantly the rights of the parties. Therefore, the amendment should not be interpreted as being retroactive but, instead, should only apply to actions taken by manufacturers after the date of the amendment. As a result, Glassman had no protest right and Glassman's suit was dismissed.

Metro Ford Truck Sales v. Department of Motor Vehicles, No. 12-CV-00411, 2013 Tex. App. LEXIS 2495 (Tex. App. Mar. 13, 2013), involved a bankruptcy court's decision that Ford Motor Company, Freightliner Corporation and Sterling Truck Corporation had no further obligation to provide any vehicles to dealer Metro Ford Truck Sales. The dispute between Metro and Ford, Freightliner, and Sterling had been the subject of at least five published opinions prior to this March 13, 2013 opinion. Never one to give up, Metro sued the Texas Department of Motor Vehicles for a determination that (1) the Board could not permit the termination of Metro's franchise, and (2) the Board's order permitting the termination of the franchise was not supported by substantial evidence.

The Texas Court of Appeals found the agency not only was within its authority, in addition, it was required to issue the orders that it did, permitting termination. The court of appeals stated, "It was issuing the orders required by this Court's prior opinions and mandates. The ordering paragraphs include legal conclusions that follow directly from this Court's previous rulings. The referenced opinion of this Court and the Bankruptcy Court provide the background and the basis for the agency's orders."

In *Alliance of Automobile Manufacturers, Inc. v. Jones*, No. 08-CV-555, 2012 U.S. Dist. LEXIS 136660 (N.D. Fla. Sept. 20, 2012), a trade group of auto manufacturers brought an action against Julie Jones, in her capacity as the Executive Director of the Department of Highway Safety and Motor Vehicles in the State of Florida, alleging that various amendments to Florida Statute Chapter 320 were unconstitutional under either the Commerce Clause or the Contracts Clause of the United States Constitution, or under the Florida Constitution. Jones moved to dismiss, stating that the trade group failed to state a claim upon which relief may be granted. The court denied Jones' motion, finding that the manufacturers had standing and that they had pled enough to survive a motion to dismiss on their due process claims, Contracts Clause claim and Commerce Clause claims.

First United, Inc. v. General Motors LLC, No. D061563, 2013 Cal. App. Unpub. LEXIS 2518 (Cal. Ct. App. Apr. 9, 2013), involved General Motors' refusal to allow the transfer and relocation of a dealership from Poway, California to El Cajon, California. Dealer First United put on a great deal of evidence, including extensive expert witness testimony, that GM had acted unreasonably in refusing to permit the move from Poway to El Cajon, that GM's actions were inconsistent with its prior actions and other cases, and that the move was in everyone's best interest. The court, however, granted summary judgment to General Motors, finding that the parties' dealer agreement, Article 4.4.2, allowed GM to consider any such requests for change of location or premises and make a "final decision in light of dealer network planning considerations." The dealer agreement also stated that "no change in location or in the use of the premises, including addition of other vehicle lines, will be made without GM's prior written authorization pursuant to its business judgment."

The extensive testimony of dealer expert Ted Stockton that GM's refusal to permit the relocation was contrary to GM's own policies and made no reasonable business sense, was rejected completely by the trial court, which stated that all GM was required to do was make a reasonable inquiry and follow ordinary procedures to review the matter. The court found that no evidence had been submitted by the plaintiff that GM was acting through pretext, improper motive or inadequate investigation and, therefore, GM's business judgment (as defined in the agreement) could not be challenged. Summary judgment was affirmed on the same grounds by the court of appeals.

W&D Imports, Inc. v. Lia, No. 11-CV-4144, 2013 U.S. Dist. LEXIS 58651 (E.D. N.Y. Apr. 22, 2013), involved a claim by W&D Imports, Inc. that it should have been given a dealership in Hamilton, New Jersey. When W&D Imports did not get the dealership, it sued American Honda Motor Company in New Jersey under the New Jersey Franchise Practices Act and lost. After having lost at both the trial court and appellate level in New Jersey, W&D Imports, Inc. turned to the New York federal court system and sued Honda and the dealers who did obtain the dealership for a variety of claims, including state and federal racketeering claims, tortious interference and equitable estoppel. W&D Imports fared no better in New York court than it had in New Jersey court. The New York court granted the defendants' motions to dismiss in full.

The RICO claims brought by W&D Imports were improperly pled and failed to satisfy the various significant pleading requirements of a RICO claim, including failure to allege an open-ended pattern of racketeering. Even if the claims had been properly pled, the court found that since they involved the same issues of fact as those raised in the New Jersey action, that any claims against American Honda under the RICO statute would have been barred by the doctrine of collateral estoppel.

In *Giuffre Hyundai, Ltd. v. Hyundai Motor America*, No. 13-CV-0520, 2013 U.S. Dist. LEXIS 67795 (E.D.N.Y. May 10, 2013), Hyundai terminated Giuffre Hyundai without notice or opportunity to cure after the New York Attorney General's Office prosecuted Giuffre for various fraudulent and illegal business activities. Giuffre sued to get its dealership back. The court ruled against Giuffre at the summary judgment stage, finding that Hyundai had both due cause and good faith in terminating the dealership and that the law does not require a "second chance" for such a serious deviation from the stated obligations of the franchisee. The court found this to be true, in particular, where the breach of duty involves fraudulent and illegal practices.

An unremarkable trademark infringement victory for General Motors, LLC ("GM") was scored in the case of *General Motors, LLC v. Rapp Chevrolet,*

Inc., No. 12-4209, 2013 U.S. Dist. LEXIS 74234 (D.S.D. May 21, 2013). GM entered into a dealer agreement with Rapp Chevrolet, Inc. ("Rapp") in 2005. Years later, when GM entered bankruptcy, GM offered Rapp the opportunity to execute a wind-down agreement, which would phase out the dealership. Rapp refused. Following this refusal, the bankruptcy court authorized GM to reject disagreeable dealerships' agreements, and further stated in an order that dealers like Rapp were "'no longer authorized to ... display, distribute or otherwise use any signage, promotional or other materials bearing or containing'" either old or new GM trademarks, trade names, or service names except to the same extent allowed by law as a nondealer would be able to use them. The parties' dealer agreement further restricted Rapp from using GM's marks following termination, in part, in a manner "likely to cause confusion or mistake[.]"

Notwithstanding the bankruptcy court's order, and the contractual prohibition on continued improper use of the marks, Rapp used the name "Rapp Chevrolet" on its website (which was www.rappchevrolet.com), on its subsequently created Facebook page, and on its premises. This name usage continued for over a year, during which time GM sent numerous cease and desist letters. Rapp even sent one letter in which it stated it would continue using the name Rapp Chevrolet. In another letter, Rapp's president, on letterhead marked "Rapp Chevrolet," which advertised Rapp's website, and which was contained in an envelope marked "Rapp Chevrolet," wrote that Rapp was "not presently using and ha[d] not used General Motors trademarks[.]" GM filed suit. The court granted GM's motion for summary judgment on its claims for (1) trademark infringement, (2) breach of contract, (3) trademark dilution, and (4) entry of a permanent injunction.

Greater New York Automobile Dealers Association v. Department of Motor Vehicles, No. 5685-12, 2013 N.Y. Misc. LEXIS 2650 (N.Y. Sup. Ct. April 10, 2013), the Greater New York Automobile Dealers Association sought to keep Tesla Motors, Inc. from operating its electric car sales outlets in New York through its affiliate, Tesla Motors New York. The dealers in New York, and elsewhere in the nation, were upset that Tesla would operate through affiliates, not through independent third-party dealers.

The court dismissed the dealers' claims made under the New York State Franchise Dealer Act, stating that (1) Tesla Motors, Inc. had no contractual relationship with any of the complaining dealers or their association, and (2) none of the complaining dealers competed with the Tesla Motors New York for Tesla products or sales of Tesla products. Therefore, the dealers and their association also had no standing to sue. The motion to dismiss was granted and the motion of the New York State Automobile Dealers Association to intervene was denied.

In *Chrysler Group LLC v. South Holland Dodge, Inc.*, No. 10-12984, 2013 U.S. Dist. LEXIS 102570 (E.D. Mich. July 23, 2013), the court finally determined, after a bench trial, whether the letters of intent offered to Chrysler dealers who won arbitrations under § 747 of the Consolidated Appropriations Act of 2009 were "customary and usual" letters of intent. Chrysler in bankruptcy had received approval to reject 789 dealer agreements; only 32 dealers were successful in arbitrations taking place under the federal statute. The statute provided as a remedy that winning dealers would be provided "a customary and usual letter of intent to enter into a sales and service agreement."

The court found that the proper way to determine whether the letters of intent sent to the dealers in this case were "customary and usual" was to compare them to the "relevant universe" of such letters issued by Chrysler following the bankruptcy to new dealers, from the time Chrysler began operating after bankruptcy until the time the last letter of intent was issued to a dealer in the action. The court decided Chrysler used the same process in issuing letters of intent to old dealers as it used to issue them to new dealers, that all such letters were created using a similar template, and that the letters were "substantially the same." Therefore, the dealers had received all the relief they were entitled to under the statute and had to take or leave the letters of intent in the form presented. The court dismissed the case.

3. Mixed Results

Ford Motor Co. v. Ghreiwati Auto, No. 12-14313, 2013 U.S. Dist. LEXIS 68924 (E.D. Mich. May 15, 2013), involved agreements between Ford and Ghreiwati and one other dealership to sell Ford vehicles in Syria and Iraq. After dealerships were set up in Syria and Iraq, on August 22, 2011, Ford sent a letter to two dealerships explaining that President Obama's Executive Order of August 18, 2011 prohibited the exportation, re-exportation, sale, or supply, direct or directly, from the United States, or by a United States person, wherever located, of any services to Syria. Ford also sent a letter to its Baghdad territory dealer, indicating that it was being terminated for selling vehicles outside of Baghdad. Ford also stated that the Baghdad dealership had made an unauthorized transfer without Ford's approval. The dealer alleged that both of these claimed reasons for termination were pretextual.

Ford filed suit against the two dealers in the Eastern District of Michigan, seeking a declaration that Ford had no obligation to arbitrate with these dealers and a declaration that the dealers had to stop using the Ford trademark in their operations. The dealers counterclaimed for wrongful termination under the Michigan dealer act and various common law claims. The court granted Ford's motion to dismiss the Michigan Dealer Act claim, stating that the Michigan Dealer Act did not apply to dealerships located outside the State of Michigan and, since the dealers were located outside the State of Michigan, they could make no claim under the Michigan Dealer Act, despite a Michigan choice of law clause. The court also found that Ford was not a fiduciary to the dealers and that Ford had not taken any trade secrets or corporate opportunities from the dealers.

The court, however, refused to dismiss the dealers' unjust enrichment and promissory estoppel claims. While Ford had argued that these claims were barred by the parties' written agreements, the court found that since Ford's performance under the contracts at issue may have been excused by the defense of impracticability, if the contracts were voided, then the dealers would have the right to bring equitable claims, such as unjust enrichment and promissory estoppel.

Foulke Management Corp. v. Audi of America, Inc., No. A-4717-11T2, 2012 N.J. Super. Unpub. LEXIS 2763 (N.J. Sup. Ct. App. Div. Dec. 18, 2012), involved the termination of an Audi dealer in New Jersey. The Audi dealer alleged that it had failed to meet certain sales criteria set by Audi only because Audi had not given the dealer sufficient cars to meet the requirements of what Audi said an average dealer would do (approximately 150 to 170 cars per year). The appellate court granted Foulke an injunction against termination and, as a means of preventing a future termination, ordered Audi to provide at least 170 cars to Foulke in calendar year 2012 at a rate of at least 14 cars per month. Audi appealed. The New Jersey Superior Court Appellate Division found that a mandatory injunction requiring Audi to provide 170 cars per year to the dealer was unnecessary and unwarranted by the conflicting affidavits presented at the trial court level. The court expressed grave concerns as to whether such an order was consistent with the "turn and earn" system of inventory allocation that Audi generally used. The court stated that it would be unfair to provide Foulke with 170 cars that it did not "earn" while not providing the same level of inventory to other dealers throughout the nation and throughout the world. This portion of the district court's ruling was reversed.

A Massachusetts federal district court decided in *Aston Martin Lagonda of North America, Inc., v. Lotus Motorsports, Inc.*, No. 13-11213, 2013 U.S. Dist. LEXIS 79678 (D. Mass. June 6, 2013), that the defendant, Lotus Motorsports, Inc. ("Lotus"), was not entitled to a preliminary injunction against the plaintiff, Aston Martin Lagonda of North America, Inc. ("Aston Martin"), enjoining Aston Martin from opening a new dealership in an area Lotus claimed was its exclusive territory. In considering whether irreparable harm would be done to Lotus, the court noted that Aston Martin had expressly voiced its intent not to appoint a competing dealership while the litigation was pending. The dealer could point to no evidence indicating Aston Martin actually would appoint a new dealership until the litigation was concluded. At bottom, the court reasoned there was no need for an injunction to maintain the status quo, as it appeared the status quo would remain absent the court order, at least until the court had the opportunity to consider the merits of the case. The court found that Lotus had made an insufficient showing on the irreparable harm factor, so no further analysis was necessary and the preliminary injunction motion was denied.

Sims v. Nissan North America, Inc., Nos. 12AP-833 and 12AP-835, 2013 Ohio App. LEXIS 2642 (Ohio Ct. App. June 25, 2013), involved an appeal of an Ohio Motor Vehicle Dealers Board decision finding that (1) Sims could not be terminated for alleged poor market share and (2) Sims was entitled to attorneys' fees in an amount far less than he requested. Nissan appealed the first finding, Sims the second. The trial court affirmed the Board on the termination issue and remanded for further fact finding on the attorneys' fees issue. Both parties appealed.

The Ohio Court of Appeals found that the trial court had not abused its discretion by finding that good cause did not exist for termination. While Sims' market share performance was poor, Sims had claimed that this was because a GM factory was located nearby and most of his potential customers were loyal to GM. The Board had accepted this fact and found that Nissan failed to account for this local factor in its termination decision.

On the attorneys' fees issue, Sims argued that his fee recovery should be over $400,000, plus expert fees of $57,700, and costs of almost $14,000. The Board awarded Sims $175,324.99 total.

The court of appeals found that contrary to both the Board and the district court, the Ohio statute at issue <u>did</u> allow for recovery of expert witness fees. It remanded the case to the Board for a review of the reasonableness of those fees, plus the additional fees incurred in arguing for the expert witness fees. The court also rejected Sims' argument that he should recover twice the "lodestar" figure (hours x hourly rate) because the statute never contemplated such a double recovery. The matter was remanded to the trial court for further proceedings.

In *General Motors Corp. v. Motor Vehicle Review Bd.*, No. 4-08-0893, 2013 Ill. App. Unpub. LEXIS 1465 (Ill. App. Ct. June 26, 2013), the Illinois

Appellate Court reversed a $1,033,607 attorneys' fees award in favor of four Chicago-area dealers who had prevailed many times in a 12-year battle involving GM's efforts to add two new encroaching dealer points in the Chicago area.

The case began in 2001. The dealers prevailed at the State of Illinois Motor Vehicle Review Board, and at the Illinois Appellate Court (in 2005) and Illinois Supreme Court (in 2007). The matter was remanded to the Board. The dealers were awarded $1,033.607 by the Board (in March of 2008) and prevailed on an appeal by GM to the Illinois Circuit Court. GM refused to surrender, and on June 26, 2013, the entire award of attorneys' fees was vacated.

The Illinois court of appeals found that, while the dealers had won, they had <u>not</u> substantially prevailed under Section 13 of the Franchise Act, 815 ILCS 710/13 (West 2010), which requires that a dealer prove that the manufacturer has engaged in an unfair method of competition or a deceptive or unfair act or practice.

The dealers argued that all they were required to do to recover attorneys' fees is prevail on any claim under the statute. The court disagreed, finding that to "substantially prevail" under Section 13, the dealer needed to establish unfair or deceptive acts or practices. Since the dealers never even accused GM of such misconduct, there was no need for remand, the dealers could not prevail.

Brockman v. American Suzuki Motor Corp., No. 6:11-3381, 2012 U.S. Dist. LEXIS 112424 (D.S.C. Aug. 10, 2012) involved a novel claim by a Suzuki dealer claiming the Suzuki dealer's business had been ruined by a corrupt Suzuki dealer named Joe Gibson who operated a bogus "Drive a Suzuki" or "Drive for Life" program, which misled customers into believing that they could always trade in their Suzuki vehicles purchased from Joe Gibson at the current loan value. In fact, the promotional "Drive for Life" and "Drive a Suzuki" programs were scams. The customers only were permitted a ten month to one-year period under the program and then had to reapply at that time. Customers regularly failed to "qualify" at the end of the initial period, and then were required to make full payments on the vehicles, sometimes at a rate as high as $700 per month.

Plaintiff Brockman alleged that the corrupt program run by Joe Gibson and authorized by American Suzuki Motor Corp. had ruined the value of his dealership and, therefore, he was entitled to recover damages from American Suzuki Motor Corp. (Gibson had filed for bankruptcy protection).

Since Brockman had not been a dealer when the corrupt programs were going on, American Suzuki moved to dismiss on the basis of lack of standing. The district court found that the Motor Vehicle Dealer Act specifically provided standing to "any person" who is injured by reason of any action forbidden by the Act. Therefore, since the statute did not solely limit its potential plaintiffs to "only franchisees," and it could have done so, the court found that Brockman had standing to make a claim under the South Carolina Motor Vehicle Statute due to the damage caused by Gibson's improper advertising scheme.

The remainder of Brockman's claims were not as successful. The court dismissed Brockman's claims that Suzuki had treated him in an "arbitrary" or "bad faith" or "unconscionable" manner since Suzuki had done nothing to actually damage Brockman. The court also doubted that Brockman had any damages and dismissed these claims against Suzuki subject to Brockman's right to replead how he had been damaged by Suzuki.

Similarly, Brockman's unfair competition claim failed because he did not allege that Joe Gibson's dealership was owned, operated or controlled by Suzuki. Brockman's claim for wrongful termination failed because he sold his dealership prior to ever being actually terminated. Therefore, since Brockman sold, he had never actually been terminated, and he could not make a wrongful termination claim under the statute.

In *Franklin Park Lincoln-Mercury, Inc. v. Ford Motor Co.*, No. 11-4375, 2013 U.S. App. LEXIS 15291 (6th Cir. July 24, 2013), the plaintiff, Franklin Park Lincoln-Mercury, Inc. ("Franklin Park"), an auto dealer selling vehicles manufactured by Ford Motor Company, sued the manufacturer alleging it knowingly allowed another dealer to merge with an existing dealer in the plaintiff's area. The plaintiff brought claims under the Ohio Motor Vehicle Dealers Act, the Automobile Dealers' Day in Court Act, and a common law breach of fiduciary duty claim. On appeal, the Sixth Circuit was considering the district court's dismissal of Franklin Park's state law claims.

Franklin Park had two sales and service agreements ("SSAs") in place with Ford, which allowed it to sell Lincoln and Mercury vehicles. Before 2008, two other dealerships were located close to Franklin Park, the first a Lincoln-Mercury dealer, Rouen Lincoln-Mercury ("Rouen") in Maumee, Ohio, and the second being Brondes Ford Maumee, Ltd. ("Brondes Ford"), in Rouen, Ohio. The plaintiff had voiced its view to its manufacturer since 2002 that its market could not support more than one dealership. Ford itself commissioned a market study in 2005 which revealed one dealership was optimal, but that two dealerships could possibly better serve customer convenience. At some point in late 2007 or early 2008, Rouen and Brondes Ford began negotiating for Brondes Ford to purchase the Rouen dealership. After plaintiff received notice of the ownership change following a final sale agreement, the plaintiff sought relief with the Ohio Motor Vehicle Dealers Board. While the plaintiff pursued state court relief, it brought suit in federal court.

The court considered Franklin Park's Ohio Dealers Act predatory practices claim. Ohio Rev. Code § 4517.59(A)(15) forbids a manufacturer from "engag[ing] in any predatory practice or discriminat[ing] against any new motor vehicle dealer including discriminating against a franchisee ... with regard to" a variety of practices. Franklin Park's contention was that Ford made a conscious decision to favor Brondes Ford over it. While this statute listed a variety of practices, dealership transfers were not among them, and the court affirmed judgment against the dealer on this claim.

Franklin Park also claimed that Ford violated § 4517.59(A) of the Ohio Motor Vehicle Dealers Act, which requires franchisors to act in good faith when "acting or purporting to act under the terms, provisions, or conditions of a franchise or in terminating, canceling, or failing to renew[.]" In particular, the dealer asserted Ford did not act in good faith by structuring the Brondes transaction in a way that would avoid a protest and by agreeing to a second Lincoln/Mercury dealership in a market it knew could only support one Lincoln/Mercury dealership. The district court had dismissed this claim out of hand, as, in its view, there was no allegation Ford was acting pursuant to the "'terms, provisions, or conditions of the franchise agreement.'" The appellate court reversed, as the plaintiff only had to show the dealer was acting "under" the terms/provisions/conditions of the franchise agreement. Since Franklin Park had alleged bad faith in Ford's alleged active concealment of the dealership transfer, the Sixth Circuit reversed the district court's dismissal of the dealer's claim under Ohio Rev. Code § 4517.59(A).

C.   OTHER INDUSTRY SPECIFIC STATUTES

As reflected in the various state "Relationship and Termination Laws" section of the CCH Business Franchise Guide, there are numerous statutes throughout the nation that protect certain entities other than (1) true "franchisees" or (2) gas station franchisees or (3) car dealers, from certain actions including wrongful termination or nonrenewal. There were a few such reported cases this year.

Beverage Distributors, Inc. v. Miller Brewing Co., No. 11-3484, 2012 U.S. App. LEXIS 17186 (6th Cir. Aug. 16, 2012), involved five beer distributors who, as of July 1, 2008, were either Miller beer distributors or Coors beer distributors in Ohio. In 2007 and 2008, through a variety of transactions, Miller and Coors created a joint venture – MillerCoors, LLC – which eventually came to hold all of the U.S. assets of Miller Brewing Company and Coors Brewing Company.

Between August 19, 2008 and September 4, 2008, MillerCoors notified the five distributors that it intended to terminate their beer distributorships, and it had the right to do so as a "successor manufacturer" under Ohio Rev. Code § 1333.85(D). This code section permits a successor manufacturer to terminate all existing distributors without statutory "good cause" if the successor manufacturer sends out notices of termination within 90 days of buying all of the stock or assets of a particular manufacturer.

The trial court found MillerCoors was not a successor manufacturers and granted summary judgment to the distributors. MillerCoors appealed.

The Sixth Circuit affirmed, stating that the Ohio statute specifically prohibited termination due to a brewer's transfer to an entity over whom it exercised control. *See* Ohio Rev. Code § 1333.85(b)(4). Miller and Coors both exercised control over MillerCoors through funding of the entity, various voting rights in MillerCoors, and the right to appoint directors of MillerCoors. Therefore, neither Miller, Coors or MillerCoors could terminate the distributors without statutory "good cause." Since the distributors were terminated without good cause, they were entitled to summary judgment.

A.D. Lift Truck Lease and Service, Inc. v. Nissan Forklift Corp., No. 12-CV-153, 2012 U.S. Dist. LEXIS 127138 (E.D. Mo. Sept. 7, 2012), involved a St. Louis area dealer of Nissan forklifts and Barrett Industrial Trucks. Nissan gave notice on January 10, 2012 that Nissan was not renewing its dealer agreement on February 1, 2012, but that Nissan was also providing 90 days' notice that Lift Truck would no longer be a dealer as of April 15, 2012. Lift Truck sued under the Missouri Franchise Act, Mo. Rev. Stat. § 407.405, and the Illinois Franchise Disclosure Act, Ill. Comp. Stat. § 705/1.

Nissan moved to dismiss both counts. The court granted Nissan's motion to dismiss the Illinois claim because Lift Truck failed to even allege that it paid a franchise fee. The court, however, denied the motion to dismiss the Missouri claim, stating that, even though Lift Truck was protected by a dealer statute, it might also be protected by the Missouri Franchise Act.

The court also found that Lift Truck had adequately pled a claim for termination without good cause under the Missouri Power Equipment Act, Mo. Rev. Stat. § 407.753.

Subsequently, in *A.D. Lift Truck Lease and Service, Inc. v. Nissan Forklift Corp.*, No 12-CV-153, 2013 U.S. Dist. LEXIS 82313 (E.D. Mo. June 12,

2013), the court considered Nissan's summary judgment motion claiming that it had "good cause" to terminate.

Nissan moved for summary judgment on the two statutory claims, stating that (1) it had given 90 days' notice as required by the Missouri Franchise Act and (2) it had "good cause" to terminate or not renew the relationship as required by the Missouri Power Equipment Act. The court granted Nissan summary judgment on the Missouri Franchise Act claim, finding that Nissan had twice given at least 90 days' notice. However, the court denied Nissan's motion on the Missouri Power Equipment Act claim, finding that genuine issues of material fact existed on whether Nissan's reasons for termination/non-renewal constituted "good cause."

Fact issues existed, for example, on whether Lift Truck "consistently failed" to meet "essential" and "reasonable" requirements that were uniformly applied to "similarly situated" dealers.

In *Interstate Equipment Co. v. Esco Corp.*, No. 11-CV-51, 2012 U.S. Dist. LEXIS 150105 (W.D. N.C. Oct. 18, 2012), the trial judge denied an equipment manufacturer's summary judgment motion on the issue of whether it had to buy back certain inventory and parts upon a dealer termination under N.C. Gen. Stat. § 66-183, *et seq.* The court found that material facts existed on the age and condition of the equipment, whether it was encumbered, and whether the parts had been properly tendered in the 90 days window established by statute.

CHAPTER ❖ 4

Intellectual Property

I. Introduction

As in years past, franchisors have been almost universally successful in preventing unauthorized use of their trademarks. In most situations, the infringer is a former franchisee who continues to use the Mark in some form after expiration or termination of the franchise agreement. A collection of these "run-of-the-mill" cases is gathered at the end of section 4. I. A. below. A discussion of more interesting cases where the fact patterns are somewhat different include Two Men and a Truck, Putt Putt and Accor Franchising, each faced with a situation where someone who has never been a franchisee is using their mark. Section B. includes cases where former franchisees used the mark, but raised issues requiring the court's analysis. Finally, this chapter includes cases dealing with motions for contempt, as well as requests by franchisors for protection of alleged trade secrets and trade dress.

II.   Lanham Act

A.   INFRINGEMENT CLAIMS AGAINST NON-FRANCHISEES

In *Two Men and a Truck, Inc. v. Lee*, No. 12-CV-340, 2012 U.S. Dist. LEXIS 159554 (D. Neb. Nov. 7, 2012), the franchisor, Two Men and a Truck, sought to enjoin the defendants from operating a directly competitive businesses called "Two Men and Two Trucks." The defendants were not, and never had been, Two Men and a Truck franchisees and had no affiliation with the franchisor. The franchisor initiated litigation against the defendants seeking to prevent them from using the confusingly similar name. In support of their motion, the franchisor produced evidence of four separate instances of actual confusion when customers hired the defendants believing that they were hiring a business associated with the franchisor. Several of the customers received unsatisfactory service and complained to the franchisor, believing that the franchisor's businesses had provided their services. As further proof of the defendants' shoddy work, the franchisor introduced evidence that the defendants had received a grade of "F" from the local Better Business Bureau and had been ordered by the Nebraska Public Service Commission to cease performing moving services without insurance and motor carrier authorization.

The court found that the franchisor had a high degree of likelihood of success on the merits based on the actual confusion, the strength of the franchisor's mark, similarity and competitive proximity. The court also noted that the defendants' workers, on at least one occasion, wore a hat bearing the "Two Men and a Truck" official registered trademark. On more than one occasion the defendants held themselves out to be official Two Men and a Truck franchisees. The court found the defendants intended to confuse customers and actual confusion ensued. The court also found the threat of irreparable harm to the franchisor and that the balance of hardships tipped in its favor because of the possible damage to the franchisor's reputation and good will. Accordingly, the court granted the franchisor's motion for a preliminary injunction and ordered the defendants to completely remove all vestiges of the franchisor's marks and surrender control of its website URL and telephone numbers to the franchisor.

In *Accor Franchising North America, LLC v. Hi Hotel Group, LLC*, No. 11-CV-02176 (M.D. Pa. June 14, 2013), franchisor Motel 6 sought a temporary restraining order enjoining the defendant purchaser of real property upon which a Motel 6 franchise operated. The defendant purchased the property from the former franchisee and continued to operate it as a Motel 6, despite lack of authority to conduct business using Motel 6's registered trademarks. Motel 6 sued the defendant under the Lanham Act and sought a restraining order forbidding the defendant from selling, refinancing or encumbering the property to protect the money damages Motel 6 expected to recover from the defendants at the conclusion of the lawsuit.

The court found that Motel 6 was likely to succeed on the merits of its Lanham Act claim because the defendant was operating the property using Motel 6's trademarks in a manner that was likely to cause confusion. However, Motel 6 did not fare as well with respect to the issue of irreparable harm. Because Motel 6 sought injunctive relief to prevent the defendant from selling, refinancing or otherwise encumbering the property in order to protect its anticipated future recovery, the court held that Motel 6 must show not only that it is likely to become entitled to the encumbered funds upon judgment, but also that Motel 6 would probably be unable to recover those funds without a preliminary injunction. Motel 6 argued that they would suffer irreparable harm if defendant sold the property because the difference between the property's value and the mortgage represented equity that could satisfy a judgment in their trademark infringement action against the defendant. The court found, however, that the purported differential in value was based upon unsworn statements made by defendant's former counsel in an email to plaintiff's counsel a month earlier. The court noted that defense counsel had withdrawn and was not in communication with the defendant's employees. In other words, Motel 6's irreparable injury argument rested on defense counsel's belief that his client was attempting to refinance or sell the property and that the funds would be the only means by which the defendant could satisfy judgment in the case. The court held that Motel 6 failed to allege facts sufficient to support a finding of irreparable injury. Accordingly, the court denied the motion for a preliminary injunction.

In *Putt Putt, LLC v. 416 Constant Friendship, LLC*, No. 12-CV-03018, 2013 U.S. Dist. LEXIS 49833 (D. Md. April 5, 2013), the franchisor, Putt Putt, brought suit against a defendant who continued to use Putt Putt's name and marks after acquiring a former franchisee's "family fun establishment" through foreclosure. After the former franchisee's agreement was terminated, the defendant came into possession of the property and continued to operate it using all vestiges of the former "Putt Putt Fun Center" franchise. To make things worse, the new entity filed an application with United States Patent and Trademark Office (PTO) seeking to register the mark "Putt Putt Fun Center" for amusement arcade services and amusement centers. The franchisor had filed for the exact same mark one month earlier. The PTO issued a non-final office action refusing the defendant's registration due to the likelihood of confusion with the Putt Putt's long-standing trademark registrations going back to the mid-50s. Because the defendant refused to cease operating as a "Putt Putt Fun Center," the franchisor initiated litigation and sought injunctive relief and compensatory damages. The court granted the franchisor's request. The court found that Putt Putt had valid and incontestable marks going back to 1955 and that the marks were strong and recognizable by the public based on six decades of nationwide use and promotion. The court also found that Putt Putt's primary mark was not generic, as alleged by the defendant. Because the defendant continued to use an identical mark at the facility that was once a former authorized Putt Putt franchise, the court found there was a significant likelihood of customer confusion. The court also found that since the facility was once an authorized Putt Putt franchise, the defendant's intent was to get a "free ride on Putt Putt's good will." Accordingly, the court granted Putt Putt's motion for summary judgment on its federal trademark infringement claim.

In *Ford Motor Co. v. Heritage Management Group*, 911 F. Supp. 2d 616 (E.D. Tenn. 2012), the court granted Ford's motion for summary judgment against Heritage Management Group et al. and its owner for trademark infringement, false designation of origin and trademark dilution. The defendants purchased auto parts on eBay, created packaging and labels designed to look like Ford's own labels and sold the parts to Ford dealerships. Ford discovered this practice and filed suit seeking damages and an injunction. The defendants contended the parts were genuine Ford products.

First, the court considered Ford's trademark infringement claim. To demonstrate trademark infringement, a plaintiff must satisfy three elements: 1) the plaintiff must own a valid trademark, 2) the defendant must use the mark in commerce without the plaintiff's consent, and 3) the use must create a likelihood of consumer confusion. Here, the defendants only contested the third prong. Generally, courts apply an eight-factor test when determining likelihood of confusion. However, the court held this analysis is unnecessary where, as here, the defendants misappropriated precise counterfeits of Ford's trademarks and used them to compete with Ford's own goods. In such cases, a likelihood of confusion is presumed when the defendant intentionally copies a trademark design with the intent to benefit from the trademark owner's reputation.

The defendants attempted to avoid the likelihood-of-confusion conclusion by focusing on the "first sale doctrine." The first sale doctrine provides that it does not constitute trademark infringement for a first purchaser to resell a trademarked item. However, if the purchaser repackages the item, the purchaser must provide notice of the repackaging and a disclaimer that the reseller does not have an affiliation with the original manufacturer. The defendants failed to include the required notice and disclaimer here.

Ford also argued that the defendants infringed Ford's trademarks by selling non-genuine products. Ford contended that the defendants' products were not genuine because they were not subject to Ford's quality control standards. The court held that Ford need not prove that the products were counterfeit or defective. It was sufficient that the products defendants sold risked injury to Ford. The defendants' products jeopardized Ford's reputation because the defendants' packaging would confuse customers and cause them to believe that Ford authorized the sale and subjected the products to its quality control standards.

With respect to Ford's false designation of origin claim, the court's conclusion that there was a likelihood of confusion was dispositive. Accordingly, for the same reasons the court found defendants engaged in trademark infringement, the court concluded that Ford has established its claim of false designation of origin.

Finally, the court addressed Ford's claim of trademark dilution. Although the court articulated a multipronged test, the primary issue was whether the defendants' conduct diluted the "distinctive quality of Ford's mark." Because the defendant admitted that the mark he used on his packaging was identical to Ford's mark, the court presumes there was dilution. Accordingly, the court granted Ford's motion for summary judgment and for a permanent injunction.

1. Standing to Allege Infringement

In a case with potential implications for franchisors that do not directly own the trademarks under which they operate, in *Aceto Corp. v. TherapeuticsMD, Inc.*, No. 12-CV-81253, 2013 U.S. Dist. LEXIS 100605 (S.D. Fla. July 16, 2013), the court reviewed whether a patent and trademark licensee had standing to sue an infringer under the Lanham Act. Gnosis S.P.A. licensed the exclusive right to sell, offer for sale, buy, use, and import its patented Quatrefolic Products to plaintiff Aceto. Aceto, as the exclusive licensee, sued TherapeuticsMD for allegedly violating the trademark and patent. TherapeuticsMD moved to dismiss Aceto's federal and state claims for lack of standing, alleging that Aceto, as the licensee and not the trademark holder, had no standing to sue for infringement under the Lanham Act. The district court agreed, and dismissed Aceto's claims for lack of standing under Section 43(a) of the Lanham Act. The court noted that a trademark assignment and license are fundamentally different. Under the Lanham Act Section 32(1), only the "registrant of record," an assignee, or an exclusive licensee with all substantial rights in the trademark have the right to sue and seek remedies. Therefore, Aceto lacked standing to sue TherapeuticsMD under the Lanham Act.

The court also reviewed whether Fed. R. Civ. P. 19(a) requires that a licensee must join the trademark-owner to its claim. Under FRCP 19(a), the plaintiff must join a person in whose absence the court could not accord "complete relief among the existing parties," or a person whose interest in the matter is such that disposing of the action in that person's absence would leave an existing party subject to a substantial risk of incurring "inconsistent obligations" because of the absent party's interest.

Here, Gnosis licensed the Quatrefolic Product trademark to Aceto. When Aceto sued TherapeuticsMD for infringement under the Lanham Act, Aceto did not join Gnosis in the suit. Aceto believed that as an exclusive licensee, it did not need to join Gnosis. The court disagreed. The court ruled that unless Aceto could demonstrate it was the assignee, or a legal equivalent of a trademark assignee, Aceto must join Gnosis as the owner of the Quatrefolic trademark. If Aceto failed to join Gnosis, Gnosis could theoretically sue TherapeuticsMD separately for the same claims. Gnosis' possible claim would violate Rule 19(a)(1)(b) by exposing TherapeuticsMD to multiple, "inconsistent obligations" for the same actions. The court dismissed Aceto's claims without prejudice for lack of standing.

B.   UNAUTHORIZED USE FOLLOWING TERMINATION

In *Choice Hotels Int'l, Inc. v. Bhakta*, No. 11-CV-00411, 2013 U.S. Dist. LEXIS 49863 (S.D. Texas Apr. 5, 2013), the franchisor Choice Hotels ("Choice") sought injunctive relief and damages for a former franchisee's continued use of the franchisor's trademarks after termination. The franchisee countered that the franchise agreement was wrongfully terminated and that Choice acquiesced in the franchisee's continued use of the marks during a period of time in which the franchisee was attempting to cure the defaults. The court granted Choice's motion for summary judgment finding that the franchise agreement had been properly terminated for failure to pass inspections and pay franchise fees. The court granted Choice's motion for an injunction preventing the franchisee from continued use of the marks, citing customer complaints as compelling and uncontroverted evidence that the franchisee's continued usage of the marks was causing actual confusion and harm. The court found that notwithstanding a lengthy series of letters back and forth between the parties, once Choice gave notice of termination that included a demand to cease and desist using the trademark, the acquiescence defense was no longer available and the franchisee's continued use of the marks after that date was at its own peril.

Although it took two attempts and a supplemental notice of default, the franchisor in *International House of Pancakes, LLC v. Parsippany Pancake House, Inc.*, 900 F.Supp.2d 403 (D.N.J. 2012), ultimately prevailed in terminating the franchise agreement and enjoining the terminated franchisee from continuing to use its marks. The owner and president of the franchisee admitted to sexually assaulting a minor and pled guilty to a charge of endangering the welfare of a child. IHOP thereafter terminated the franchise agreement, effective immediately, based on a franchise agreement provision allowing immediate termination of the franchise based on franchisee's conviction of a felony or other criminal misconduct "which is relevant to the operation of the franchise." Shortly thereafter, IHOP sought a preliminary injunction preventing the franchisee from continuing to use the marks in the operation of its restaurant. The court denied the motion finding that IHOP had failed to demonstrate that it was likely to ultimately succeed on its trademark infringement claim, which required proof that the franchise agreement was properly terminated. The court's concern was based on the fact that IHOP had terminated the franchise agreement without notice and an opportunity to cure, which potentially violated the New Jersey Franchise Practicing Act. ("NJFPA") The court also noticed that there was nothing to suggest that the crime occurred at the franchisee's location or that IHOP had received any adverse publicity as a result of the conviction. The court also questioned whether there was any direct factual nexus between the franchisee's conviction and whether it was "directly related" to the business conducted pursuant to the franchise and the franchise agreement.

Shortly after the court denied IHOP's first motion for injunctive relief, IHOP served the franchisee with an amended notice of termination advising the franchisee that the agreement would terminate 60 days later for substantially the same reasons as the initial notice of termination. When the opportunity to cure expired, IHOP again filed a motion for preliminary injunction to enjoin the franchisee from continuing to use IHOP's marks. The only substantive difference between the first motion and the second motion was the fact that IHOP had given the franchisee 60 days' notice before terminating the franchise . The court found that because IHOP had now satisfied the notice provisions of the NJFPA, the only issue was whether IHOP had good cause to terminate the agreement under the NJFPA, which defined "good cause" as the "failure by the franchisee to substantially comply with the requirements imposed upon him by the franchise." N.J.S.A. § 56:10-5. The court found that the franchisee admitted to sexually assaulting a minor resulting in a guilty plea and the requirement that the franchisee register as a sex offender. The court also found that while imprisoned, the franchisee would be unable to actively participate in the day-to-day operation of the franchise, which the franchise agreement required. On these facts, the court held that IHOP had demonstrated it was likely to prevail on the claim that the franchisee's conviction was "relevant to the operation of the franchise" and that, therefore, IHOP had the right to terminate the agreement. Because the agreement had been properly terminated, the court enjoined the franchisee from using IHOP's trademarks.

CHAPTER 4

In *7-Eleven, Inc. v. Dhaliwal*, No. 12-CV-02276, 2012 U.S. Dist. LEXIS 166691 (E.D. Cal. Nov. 21, 2012), the franchisor 7-Eleven sought a preliminary injunction against a terminated franchisee's continued operation of a 7-Eleven store in northern California. The lessor of the franchisee's location declined to renew the lease resulting in a premature termination of the franchise. Pursuant to the terms of the franchise agreement, the franchisee could transfer his franchise, without paying a new franchise fee, to any other 7-Eleven store which was available for purchase that had been open for business at least one year. The franchisee was told that there were no corporate 7- Eleven stores available for purchase in northern California. The franchisee also expressed an unwillingness to pay the purchase price that independent 7-Eleven franchise owners were requesting for their stores in northern California. As a result, the franchisee entered into a new franchise agreement with 7-Eleven to operate a new store in Rocklin, California. The new store did not meet expectations and the franchisee was soon in financial default for failing to maintain net worth of at least $15,000 at all times. After several notices of breach for failing to maintain net worth standards, 7-Eleven terminated the franchise agreement in the summer of 2012. However, notwithstanding the termination, the franchisee continued to operate as a 7-Eleven displaying 7-Eleven marks and offering 7-Eleven products. 7-Eleven initiated litigation to obtain injunctive relief.

In opposing the motion, the former franchisee argued that 7-Eleven could not prove that it was likely to succeed on the merits because the franchisee's failure to maintain net worth resulted from 7-Eleven's refusal to let him transfer his franchise to the Rocklin store without paying a transfer fee and that this constituted a breach of his original franchise agreement. Although the court expressed sympathy for the former franchisee's position, it held that 7-Eleven did not breach the original franchise agreement and had no obligation to allow the former franchisee to transfer his franchise to a new store without paying a new franchise fee. The court also noted that 7-Eleven made stores available outside the franchisee's desired territory and the former franchisee admitted he could not afford to pay the purchase price for existing franchises in his territory. Therefore, the court found that 7-Eleven was likely to succeed on the merits of its claim for breach of the franchise agreement. Because the court found that the franchise agreement had been properly terminated, 7-Eleven's motion for preliminary injunction to prevent post-termination infringement was easily decided. The court discussed *E-Bay, Inc. v. Merc Exchange, LLC*, 547 U.S. 388, 394, 126 S. Ct. 1837 (2006) and noted that the Ninth Circuit stated in a recent opinion that presuming irreparable harm was inappropriate under *E-Bay* when considering a preliminary injunction in the copyright infringement context.

With no presumption of irreparable harm, the court held that 7-Eleven must produce evidence that it would suffer irreparable harm if the defendant continued to display the 7-Eleven marks at the Rocklin store. However, the court found that 7-Eleven's "loss of control" over its trademarks due to the former franchisee's unauthorized use was sufficient to demonstrate irreparable harm. The court found that 7-Eleven had the right to maintain control over its trademarks to prevent customer confusion. Accordingly, the court granted 7-Eleven's motion and ordered the former franchisee to surrender possession of the premises and refrain from using any of 7-Eleven's trademarks.

In *Wyndham Hotels and Resorts, LLC v. North Star Mt. Olive, LLC*, No. 10-2583, 2013 U.S. Dist. LEXIS 44468 (D. N.J. Mar. 28, 2013), the court grappled with the franchisor Wyndham's request for injunctive relief preventing a former franchisee's post termination infringement in the face of the franchisee's allegation of a putative pre-existing breach of the franchise agreement by Wyndham. The case involved a Wyndham Hotel in Mount Olive, New Jersey. The franchisee negotiated a provision whereby Wyndham guaranteed a certain level of revenue if the franchisee converted one of the hotel meeting rooms into a training facility with computers and amenities necessary for corporate meetings. It was undisputed that Wyndham did not fulfill its conditional obligations under the revenue guaranty clause. Also undisputed was the fact that the franchisee failed to pay recurring fees due under the franchise agreement. Wyndham terminated the franchise agreement for failure to pay the recurring fees and thereafter sought an injunction to prevent the former franchisee from continuing to operate as a Wyndham hotel. The franchisee counterclaimed for breach of contract, wrongful termination and other related claims. With respect to Wyndham's request for an injunction enjoining trademark infringement, the franchisee argued that it stopped making recurring franchise payments because, among other things, Wyndham had already breached its obligations under the agreement with respect to the revenue guaranty. Wyndham countered by invoking the holding in *S&R Corp. v. Jiffy Lube Int'l., Inc.*, 968 F.2d 371 (3d Cir. 1992) wherein the court held that a franchisor's right to terminate a franchise agreement exists independently of any claim the franchisee might have against the franchisor. The *Jiffy Lube* court also held that under no circumstances may the non-breaching party stop performance and continue to take advantage of the contract's benefits. *Id.* at 376. After reviewing several cases construing the *Jiffy Lube* decision, the court concluded that Wyndham was entitled to summary judgment on the question of the franchisee's breach. It was undisputed that the franchisee did not pay recurring fees to Wyndham even as it continued to operate as a Wyndham franchise. Therefore, the franchisee was barred from asserting Wyndham's alleged breach of the franchise agreement as an affirmative defense to infringement liability. The court declined to determine the issue of damages given the franchisee's pending counterclaim against Wyndham. It did, however, enjoin the former franchisee from continuing to use Wyndham's trademarks.

In *You Fit, Inc. v. Pleasanton Fitness, LLC,* No. 12-CV-1917, 2013 U.S. Dist. LEXIS 18106 (M.D. Fla. Feb. 11, 2013), the district court reviewed a magistrate's report and recommendation granting the franchisor, You Fit, a preliminary injunction preventing a former franchisee from continuing to operate as "Fit U." The former franchisee challenged the magistrate's report and recommendation claiming that the franchisor's marks were merely descriptive, weak or invalid and that there was no likelihood of confusion. The former franchisee also alleged that the magistrate judge failed to consider whether the franchisor demonstrated that the former franchisee was using a confusingly similar mark "in the same trade area."

The franchisor's marks included "You Fit," "It's Where You Fit In" and "Fit Begins with You." The former franchisee contended that these marks were descriptive and weak. The court disagreed. It found that due to the multiple meanings of the word "fit," an imaginative leap is required to associate the franchisor's marks with a health club. Therefore, the franchisor was more likely to be able to prove that their marks are suggestive and accorded a heightened level of protection. However, with respect to the commonality of the marks, the court was less generous to the franchisor. The former franchisee submitted evidence of 11 similar trade names using the words "you" and "fit" for health services available in Florida and ten trade names for services available in California. The court found that because the franchisor's marks use words that are both general and common in the fitness market, it militated in favor of finding that the franchise marks were weak, even though suggestive. The court found persuasive evidence of actual confusion in the form of online postings where customers were actually confused by the two different fitness operations. While not conclusive evidence of actual confusion, the court found that the evidence was indicative of potential consumer confusion. The court also found that the marks were similar and were used for similar services and advertised in a similar manner. In summary, four of the seven "likelihood of confusion" factors weighed in favor of the franchisor, including the most important factor: actual confusion. Balancing the factors, the court found that indications of actual confusion and the close similarities of the marks and services created a likelihood of confusion supporting the franchisor's request for injunctive relief. Finally, the court rejected the former franchisee's "zone of natural expansion" argument, finding that the franchisor's marks were federally registered and, thus, entitled to exclusive use. Accordingly, the court adopted the magistrate's report and recommendation and entered injunctive relief in favor of the franchisor.

In another case involving a former franchisee's continued use of marks after termination, the franchisor was successful in obtaining injunctive relief, but fact issues precluded summary judgment on its claim for damages. In *Choice Hotels Int'l, Inc. v. Patel*, No. 12-CV-00023, 2013 U.S. Dist. LEXIS 55345 (S.D. Tex. Apr. 16, 2013), the franchisee operated a Choice Hotel in Victoria, Texas for 15 years. Choice elected not to renew the franchise agreement on the 15th anniversary date in 2009. Although the former franchisee made extensive efforts to remove the Comfort Inn names and marks from the hotel, he did not initially remove or paint over the 30 foot exterior sign or the smaller entrance and exit signs because he claimed that he planned to use them at a new Comfort Inn to be built elsewhere. He eventually put tarps over the signs, but they sagged or fell off repeatedly. Over two years after termination, the former franchisee finally had the exterior signs painted black. Even then, the former franchisee continued to use the Comfort Inn name on credit card receipts and the Hotel's wireless internet service. Choice initiated litigation to seek permanent injunctive relief as well as damages for trademark infringement. In its motion for summary judgment, the court had little trouble finding that the former franchisee continued to use the franchisor's marks after termination. The court also found a likelihood of confusion as a matter of law. As a result, the court granted Choice's summary judgment establishing the defendant's liability for infringement and entered a permanent injunction preventing the defendant from further infringement.

For additional cases where the franchisor obtained injunctive relief against former franchisees in relatively routine fashion, see *Dunkin' Donuts Franchised Restaurants, LLC v. Springhill Realty, Inc.*, No 12-2010, 2013 U.S. Dist. LEXIS 70025 (E.D. Penn. May 17, 2013) (franchisor granted injunction preventing terminated franchisee from continuing to use and display franchisor's marks and ordered to turn over franchise premises within 48 hours); *Cottman Transmission Systems, LLC v. Gano*, No. 12-CV-05223, 2013 U.S. Dist. LEXIS 31195 (E.D. Pa. Mar. 7, 2013) (franchisor obtained a permanent injunction preventing terminated franchisee from continuing to use or display "Cottman" trademarks after termination); *7-Eleven, Inc. v. Upadhyaya*, No. 12-5541, 2013 U.S. Dist. LEXIS 29091

(E.D. Pa. Mar. 1, 2013) (franchisor granted permanent injunction preventing franchisee from continuing to use marks post termination and compelling surrender of premises); *Curves International, Inc. v. Fox*, No. 12-12250, 2013 U.S. Dist. LEXIS 66235 (D. Mass. May 9, 2013) (franchisor granted injunction preventing former franchisee from continuing to use or display Curves trademarks after expiration of the franchise agreement); *Mr. Electric Corp. v. Khalil*, No. 06-2414, 2013 U.S. Dist. LEXIS 15723 (D. Kan. Feb. 6, 2013) (franchisor granted summary judgment finding former franchisees liable for trademark infringement and federal unfair competition for continued use of franchisor's trademarks after termination); *Century 21 Real Estate, LLC v. All Professional Realty, Inc.*, 889 F. Supp. 2d 1198 (E.D. Ca. 2012) (former franchisee's continued use of franchisor's marks after termination deemed willful resulting in treble damages based on minimum royalty during period of infringement); *DFO, LLC v. Hammoud*, No. 12-CV-900 (W.D. Tex. June 17, 2013) (franchisor Denny's granted preliminary injunction preventing former franchisee from continuing to use trademark after expiration of extension of time granted to sell a restaurant pursuant to settlement agreement); *Novus Franchising, Inc. v. AZ Glassworks, LLC*, No. 12-CV-1771, 2013 U.S. Dist. LEXIS 36830 (D. Minn. Mar. 18, 2013) (franchisor Novus granted permanent injunction preventing former franchisee from using Novus marks and awarding Novus attorneys' fees, costs and disbursements as an "exceptional" case).

C.   INTERNET USE – KEYWORDS

Although not a franchise case, in an important case dealing with the common practice of purchasing keywords to advance results in Google Internet searches, in *1-800-Contacts, Inc. v. Lens.com, Inc.*, No. 11-4114, 11-4204, 12-4022, 2013 U.S. App. LEXIS 14368 (10th Cir. July 16, 2013) the court was asked to resolve whether it was a violation of the Lanham act to purchase advertiser's use of keywords on Google that resembled a competitor's trademark. Google sells an advertising program whereby a client's paid advertisement appears onscreen whenever a designated term, known as a "keyword", is used in a Google search. In this case, 1-800-Contacts (1-800) discovered that searches on Google for "1-800 contacts," "1800Contacts," and "1-800-Contacts" (and six additional mis-spelled versions of 800-contacts) yielded sponsored advertisements for Lens.com, a competitor. 1-800 filed suit under §32 of the Lanham Act alleging that Lens.com infringed 1-800's trademark by purchasing keywords resembling the mark. 1-800 also alleged that third-party marketers hired by Lens.com, known as affiliates, also purchased keywords resembling the Mark. 1-800 sought to hold Lens.com secondarily liable for its affiliate's conduct. The district court awarded summary judgment to Lens.com and dismissed all claims. It ruled that 1-800 created no genuine factual issue regarding whether Lens.com's keyword use was likely to cause confusion. 1-800 appealed to the Tenth Circuit Court of Appeals.

In order to demonstrate infringement, the plaintiff must show: (1) that the plaintiff has a protectable interest in the mark, (2) the defendant used an identical or similar mark in commerce, and (3) that the alleged infringer's use of the mark is likely to confuse consumers. The appellate court focused on the only contested element-likelihood of confusion. 1-800's theory of confusion was "initial interest confusion" which results when a consumer seeks a particular trademark holder's product and instead is lured to the product of a competitor by the competitor's use of the same or similar trademark. 1-800 attempted to support their initial interest confusion theory by introducing data regarding how often consumers really were lured in such a fashion. According to a report by Lens.com's expert, only 1.5% of individuals who entered one of the nine challenged 1-800 keywords clicked on the advertisement for Lens.com. Even then, there was no data as to how many of these individuals actually made a purchase from Lens.com. The court held that this number could not support an inference that Lens.com's keyword activity was likely to lure consumers away from 1-800. As such, 1-800 failed to demonstrate one of the key elements of infringement to hold Lens.com directly liable.

However, the court of appeals did reverse the district court's summary judgment on the contributory infringement claim. The court reasoned that a reasonable jury could find that Lens.com knew that one or more of its affiliates was using 1-800's trademark, but failed to take reasonable steps to stop the practice. Lens.com argued that it had no literal knowledge which of its affiliates was using a 1-800 trademark. However, the court noted that Lens.com had the ability to e-mail all of affiliates to notify them that some among them were infringing 1-800's marks and request that they stop. The court ruled that Lens.com's failure to take action to stop affiliates' use of 1-800's marks in their advertising content after learning that one of its affiliates had used 1-800's mark could amount to contributory infringement under the Lanham Act.

D.   POST-INJUNCTION CONTEMPT

In *Allegra Network, LLC v. Cormack*, No. 11-13087, 2012 U.S. Dist. LEXIS 181640 (E.D. Mich. Nov. 2, 2012), the franchisor filed a motion for an order to show cause for the former franchisee's failure to comply with an injunction order enforcing the post-termination noncompete agreement in the parties' former franchise agreement. The franchisor, Allegra, had obtained an injunction preventing the former franchisees from owning, operating, or having any direct or indirect interest in any competitive business within ten miles of their former Insty-Prints' location in Fayetteville, Arkansas. Approximately three weeks after the date of the injunction, the franchisor hired a private investigator who observed that the front door of the former business identified it as "Hog Country Media" and the former franchisees appeared to be operating their business in the same manner as they did prior to the injunction. In response to the show cause motion, the former franchisee (preceding *pro se*) filed an affidavit stating that he and his wife had retained a real estate company to locate another building in excess of ten miles from their former location and assured the court that neither he nor his current business, "Hog Country Media, LLC" identified themselves as a current or former Insty-Prints center or as a current or former Allegra franchisee. In a subsequent affidavit, the former franchisee claimed that they sold their ownership interest in Hog Country Media to another individual who was a long-time employee and was leasing the building to this individual until they could locate another building. Based on the statements made in the former franchisee's affidavit, the court found that, at best, the former franchisee had an indirect interest in the competitive business. At worst, the former franchisee that purchased the business was nothing more than the former franchisee's nominee, and the arrangement a sham. The court held both "any way, the defendants are in violation of both the letter and spirit of the preliminary injunction." The court ordered that the defendants appear and show cause why they should not be held in contempt and impose a conditional fine of $100 per day, increasing to $500 per day if the defendants failed to comply within 28 days. The court also awarded the franchisor its reasonable costs and attorneys' fees.

In *Rossi Ventures, Inc. v. Pasquini Franchising, LLC*, No. 11-CV-02838, 2012 U.S. Dist. LEXIS 168925 (D. Colo. Nov. 28, 2012), the court considered a motion for contempt of an injunction entered two months earlier. The plaintiff owned the rights to use the name "Pasquini's Pizzeria." However, she acquiesced to the defendant's use of the Pasquini Pizzeria mark in connection with stores distant from her exclusive area. When the defendant exceeded the scope of the consent, plaintiff sought and obtained an injunction preventing the defendant from using the "Pasquini's Pizzeria" name, or any variation thereof, in connection with the operation of a restaurant located on Milwaukee Street in Denver. The defendant then changed the name of the restaurant to "Tony P's." However, in connection with promoting Tony P's, the defendant engaged in a marketing campaign using the tagline "Restaurants by Tony Pasquini." The court found that the defendant's use of the name "Pasquini" in the defendant's marketing campaign was "overwhelming" and constituted a prohibited use of the Pasquini's trademark in connection with the operation of Tony P's. The court noted that a screen shot of the "Restaurants by Tony Pasquini" homepage showed the name "Pasquini" appearing in logo form seven times and word "Pasquini" appeared 28 times. By contrast, the name "Tony P's" only appeared five times. The court observed that "a clearer example of defendant's promoting Tony P's through the use of the Pasquini's name would be difficult to imagine." Based on this evidence, the magistrate issued a report and recommendation that "[t]he restaurants by Tony Pasquini's marketing campaign obviously and blatantly violates the preliminary injunction, and the Pasquini defendant's interpretation of the preliminary injunction is unreasonable." The court adopted the magistrate's report and recommendation and held that the defendants had failed to show either that they complied with the injunction or that they could not do so. The court held the defendants in contempt and ordered them to comply with the injunction and awarded the plaintiff costs and attorneys' fees.

In *American Honda Motor Company, Inc. v. V.M. Paolozzi Imports, Inc.*, No. 10-CV-955, 2013 U.S. Dist. LEXIS 41852 (N.D. N.Y. Mar. 26, 2013), the court found a former Honda dealer in contempt for failing to cease using Honda's trademarks after termination of the defendant's dealer agreement. The injunction was issued in February 2012. In March 2012, Honda filed a motion to hold the defendants in contempt and impose sanctions because they continue to display Honda trademarks on their dealership properties. In September 2012, the court granted Honda's motion and ordered defendants to show cause why they should not be held in contempt. In response to the show cause order, defendants claimed that they removed, destroyed, and disposed of all Honda trademarks except for a trademark sign on the exterior of one of the dealership buildings. As justification for their noncompliance, the defendants claimed lack of funds, their inability to make building design alterations and lack of consent from the mortgage holder on the dealership building not to make any material alterations to the building. The court rejected these claimed justifications for noncompliance. First, the court noted that the defendants had not filed for bankruptcy or offered sufficient documentation supporting their alleged financial inability to comply with the order. Defendants submitted the affidavit of their own employee and simply stated that the defendants had no money or cash liquidity, operated at an annual loss in 2010 and had not filed federal tax returns since 2007. The court found it significant that the affidavit did not state that the defendants were insolvent or lacked assets against which they could borrow. In short, the court was not convinced and held that "[d]efendants have squandered their opportunity to show cause why the court should not hold them in contempt and impose sanctions." Noting that the purpose of sanctions is to coerce the contemptor into complying in the future with the court's order or to compensate the complainant for losses resulting from the contemptor's noncompliance, the court imposed a per diem sanction of $2,000 to accrue daily beginning ten days from the date of the order until defendants complied in full with the previous injunction. With respect to costs and attorneys' fees, the plaintiff submitted a request for $21,030.50 in costs and attorneys' fees based on New York City hourly rates. The court reviewed the submission and determined that reasonable rates in the Northern District of New York were $250 for experienced attorneys, $150 for junior associates and $80 for paralegals. Based on the hours submitted by plaintiffs' counsel, the court awarded plaintiffs a total of $8,754 in attorneys' fees.

See also *Otiogiakhi v. Aamco Transmissions, Inc.*, No. 11-4620, 2002 U.S. Dist. LEXIS 129302 (D. N.J. Aug. 23, 2012) (former franchisee held in contempt of injunction preventing trademark infringement and enforcing noncompete and awarding Aamco the amount of $750 per day for each day of noncompliance); *Allegra Network, LLC v. Iiames*, No. 12-CV-11152, 2002 U.S. Dist. LEXIS 173052 (E.D. Mich. Dec. 6. 2012) (former franchisee held in contempt for failing to comply with post-termination noncompete agreement with a civil penalty of $100 per day for 28 days and $500 per day thereafter and potential incarceration for failure to comply).

E. TRADE SECRET / TRADE DRESS

In *Little Caesar Enterprises, Inc. v. Sioux Falls Pizza Company Inc.*, No. 12-CV-4111, 2012 U.S. Dist. LEXIS 108828 (D. S.D. Aug. 3, 2012), Little Caesar was unsuccessful in establishing that its "Hot-N-Ready" operating system was a trade secret entitling it to an injunction preventing a former franchisee from using an allegedly similar all day, every day, ready for pick up pizza system.

When the former franchisee's franchise agreements expired in 2012, he converted one of his locations to a "Pizza Patrol" but continued to sell all day, every day, ready for pick up pizza, as well as other menu items not sold by Little Caesar. Little Caesar initiated litigation alleging misappropriation of trade secrets and trade dress and moved for injunctive relief. With respect to the trade secret claim, Little Caesar argued that its trade secret consisted of a system that determines what franchisees must prepare on a daily and hourly basis and how to prepare each product on an hour-by-hour basis. Little Caesar also alleged that the system included a methodology for calculating specific preparation requirements as well as methods for preparation, storing and cooking products inherent to the "Hot-N-Ready" system. The former franchisee argued that he had gone to great lengths to differentiate himself from the Little Caesar's system and to make his Pizza Patrol a completely distinct business. He also alleged that Little Caesar failed to describe its alleged trade secret with sufficient detail and that he was doing nothing more than what every other pizza proprietor in the restaurant business was doing.

The court found that Little Caesar failed to produce sufficient proof that its "Hot-N-Ready" system could be the type of information that is a method, technique, process or program under a broad view of the definition of a trade secret. First, Little Caesar did not make a clear showing of what information within its system is "not generally known." Nor did Little Caesar provide sufficient evidence of economic value above and beyond the generic knowledge of how to run a restaurant that provides ready-made pizza. The court found that, at the preliminary injunction stage of the litigation, Little Caesar's description of what makes up its "Hot-N-Ready" system was too generic or general to amount to a trade secret based on the evidence presented. With respect to Little Caesar' efforts to maintain secrecy, the court found fault with the fact that Little Caesar did not require that its franchisee's employees sign any form of confidentiality agreement, yet they had the most detailed knowledge because they were actually preparing the pizzas as part of the "Hot-N-Ready" system. Because Little Caesar did not establish what specifically was its trade secret beyond what appeared to be a common method for making pizza that was generally known in the restaurant business, the court found that it was not likely to succeed on the merits of its trade secret claim and denied its injunctive relief.

With respect to Little Caesar' trade dress claim, the court found that Little Caesar failed to offer evidence of specific trade dress requirements mandated by Little Caesar that were either typical or required in each Little Caesar's stores. The former franchisee claimed that he removed all Little Caesar's signs, point of purchase materials, menu boards, paper goods, and other marks, and remodeled the exterior and interior of the store to alter it from a Little Caesars store to a Pizza Patrol. At the time of the hearing, Little Caesar was only able to argue about wall and floor tile color, the general layout of the store, and other minute details. Under the circumstances, the court ruled that Little Caesar did not carry its burden to show that it was likely to succeed on the merits of its trade dress claim and denied injunctive relief.

The franchisor was unsuccessful in obtaining injunctive relief based on a trade dress claim in *Happy's Pizza Franchise, LLC v. Papa's Pizza, Inc.*, No. 10-15174, 2013 U.S. Dist. LEXIS 10130 (E.D. Mich. Jan. 25, 2013). The franchisor Happy's Pizza operated a fast food pizza restaurant since 1996. The defendant Papa's Pizza incorporated in August 2005 and was owned by Phil Almaki. Later that year, Almaki invested in a Happy's Pizza location as a shareholder. In the process, he signed a noncompete agreement prohibiting him from opening a pizza restaurant within five miles of any Happy's Pizza restaurant for two years after his departure from Happy's Pizza. He also disclosed that he owned two pizza restaurants before he signed the noncompete agreement. In 2007, Almaki sold his shares in the Happy's Pizza's store and opened up numerous Papa's Pizza restaurants in close proximity to Happy's Pizza restaurants. Happy's Pizza initiated litigation alleging infringement of trade dress and unfair competition. Notwithstanding the noncompete agreement, Happy's Pizza's primary claim was that Papa's Pizza copied the design of its restaurants and use of its expansive menu.

With respect to the trade dress claim, Happy's Pizza alleged that it employed unique décor protocols that distinguished it from other restaurants, including granite countertops, ceramic tile walls and faux venetian plaster, neon lighting, backlit menus, black industrial style rugs, backlit pictures of menu items, stainless steel shelving, stacks of prefolded pizza boxes and large coin operated candy and bubble gum dispensers. Happy's Pizza claimed that this created a uniform look and feel which customers associated with Happy's Pizza restaurants. Referring to *Two Pesos, Inc. v. Taco Cabana, Inc.*, 505 U.S. 763, 112 S. Ct. 2753 (1992), the court stated that in order for Happy's Pizza to succeed, it must prove that its trade dress is distinctive in the marketplace, thereby indicating the source of the goods it dresses, that the trade dress is primarily nonfunctional and that the trade dress of the competing goods is confusingly similar. Happy's Pizza offered one theory of distinctiveness: their trade dress was inherently distinctive based on their arbitrary use of each element constituting the décor. The court disagreed, finding Happy's Pizza failed to provide evidence that each Happy's Pizza restaurant uses a specific uniform theme, that other fast food restaurants do not use these elements, that customers exclusively associate these elements and menu items with Happy's Pizza, that other restaurants do not offer similar food combinations and that all of Papa's restaurants use these elements. There was no evidence that Happy's Pizza combination of elements was original in design and there were no menu items that were trademarked. The court held that Happy's Pizza use of generic elements to create a fast food restaurant setting was indistinguishable from many others. In fact, without the use of Happy's Pizza name and logo within the design or on the menu, there was nothing that would alert the average consumer that they were in a Happy's Pizza restaurant. Thus, the court found Happy's Pizza trade dress was generic and not subject to protection and denied its motion for preliminary injunction.

CHAPTER ❖ 5

Common Law

Most franchise and distribution law disputes, even if they involve statutory issues, also involve common law claims such as breach of contract, fraud, and other tort claims. Courts are also asked to opine upon a variety of damages issues. This year saw dozens of reported cases on a large variety of issues, all of which are summarized in the roughly sixty pages set forth below.

I. Contract Formation

In *Gold's Gym Franchising LLC v. Brewer*, No. 11-CV-00699, 2013 Tex. App. LEXIS 4959 (Tex. App. Apr. 22, 2013), putative guarantor Brewer disputed he had ever signed a guaranty dated in 2008 and submitted to the court an affidavit of forgery. The franchisor disputed the claim of forgery and also argued that Brewer, by his conduct, had "ratified" the guaranty by, among other things, operating the franchise and paying royalties. Since the franchise agreement required executed guaranties, Brewer's performance under the franchise agreement also "ratified" that agreement's personal guaranty requirements.

The Texas Court of Appeals ruled that, under Texas law, a party may not "ratify" a contract to which it is not a party. Therefore, since Brewer was not a party to the franchise agreement, he could not "ratify" the franchise agreement or any of its terms no matter what he did. With respect to the guaranty documents, Brewer had consistently denied any liability and he, obviously, had never "ratified" the guaranties.

The trial court's grant of summary judgment on these issues was affirmed. The court, however, found genuine issues of fact on (1) the guaranty "forgery" defense and (2) the franchisor's claim based upon a 2005 guaranty that Brewer admitted to signing. (Brewer alleged that the 2005 guaranty has been terminated in 2008.) The matter was remanded to the trial court to resolve those two issues.

In *Andy Mohr Truck Center, Inc. v. Volvo Trucks North America*, No. 12-CV-701, 2012 U.S. Dist. LEXIS 145057 (S.D. Ind. Oct. 9, 2012), Volvo allegedly promised car dealer Andy Mohr both the Volvo truck line and the Mack truck line in an oral promise. Volvo followed through and signed a written dealer agreement on the Volvo truck line, but reneged on the oral promise to award a Mack dealership.

Volvo moved to dismiss the oral contract claim on the grounds that the contract allegations were too vague to state a cause of action. The court disagreed, holding that Andy Mohr alleged specific promises provided by specific Volvo employees on a specific date and facts sufficient to demonstrate mutual assent to the agreement.

Under Indiana law, to establish the existence of a contract, a party must show: (1) offer, (2) acceptance, (3) consideration; and (4) manifestation of mutual assent. Volvo, allegedly, had offered to give Andy Mohr both lines (the "offer"); Andy Mohr had accepted the offer both verbally and by taking on the Volvo line (the "acceptance"). There was consideration given by Andy Mohr (agreeing to act as a dealer) and manifestation of mutual assent (when Andy Mohr asked about the Mack truck line, a Volvo employee told Andy Mohr that Volvo was "making progress" toward that end and it was just a "matter of time" until Andy Mohr got the Mack line). Volvo's motion to dismiss was denied.

The battle between Volvo and Andy Mohr Truck Center continued in *Volvo Trucks North America v. Andy Mohr Truck Center*, No. 12-CV-448, 2013 U.S. Dist. LEXIS 83835 (S.D. Ind. June 14, 2013). After Mohr succeeded in dismissing three of Volvo's initial claims, all that remained were claims for declaratory judgment, violation of the Indiana Franchise Disclosure Act, and breach of contract. Mohr moved for judgment on the pleadings as to these three remaining claims.

Volvo listed 14 representations made by Mohr to induce Volvo to enter into the dealer agreement. The court dismissed Volvo's breach of contract claim because it was based upon Mohr's 14 representations and his failure to perform any of the 14. The court found that the parties had a fully integrated contract and none of Mohr's 14 promises was in the contract. Similarly, the court dismissed the Indiana Franchise Disclosure Act claim on the basis that Volvo could not have reasonably relied on any of the 14 representations.

The court, however, denied Mohr's motion for judgment on the pleadings on one Volvo claim. Volvo requested a declaration that it had "good cause" to terminate Mohr because Mohr made misrepresentations of material fact in connection with his dealer application for the Volvo line. The court found that Mohr had made certain statements of fact and that Volvo had pled that the statements were material and false. Since Mohr was seeking judgment on the pleadings, Volvo's allegations had to be accepted as true for purposes of the motion and Mohr's motion was denied.

Last Time Beverage Corp. v. F & V Distribution Co., Nos. 2010-03438 and 2010-09092, 2012 N.Y. App. Div. LEXIS 6092 (N.Y. App. Div. Sept. 12, 2012), involved former Coke and Pepsi distributors in New York City who claimed that they had been awarded contracts (one written, one verbal) to be the exclusive distributors of Royal Crown soft drinks and other soft drinks in the area where they used to distribute Coke and Pepsi.

F&V and the distributor had disputes regarding distribution rights, and eventually the distributors sued, alleging that F&V was reducing or eliminating their exclusive territory rights, selling directly into their territories, and unreasonably withholding consent to transfers of their distributorships. After 40 days of trial held over 17 months, the referee recommended judgment in favor of the distributors. The New York state trial court confirmed the referee's report, and F&V appealed.

The New York Appellate Division affirmed, finding that, although the one written distributor agreement was far from clear, it could be explained by evidence of custom and practice in the industry. Considering this evidence, the referee found that the custom and practice in the industry gave the distributors the exclusive right to distribute new beverages in their territory "once a franchisor placed a new beverage on the distributor's truck." Therefore, the referee's ruling was affirmed.

With respect to the distributor who operated under an oral argument, that distributor claimed it had it had the same rights provided in writing to Last Time Beverage. F&V argued that such a claim was barred by the statute of frauds. The appellate division disagreed, stating that the oral contract was taken outside of the statute of frauds by partial performance of the contract by the distributor. The rulings in favor of the distributor claiming an oral contract were also affirmed. The Appellate Division also found that the distributor's performance gave rise to proper claims for promissory estoppel and unjust enrichment.

Reidlinger v. Steam Bros., Inc., 826 N.W.2d 340 (N.D. 2013), involved franchisees' allegations that under 1991 and 1996 license agreements with Steam Brothers (1) they were not required to provide Steam Brothers with any business information regarding franchisee operations, and (2) they had a "lifelong" license agreement that could only be terminated with the franchisees' mutual consent. The trial court granted the franchisees summary judgment, stating that the franchisor had previously had certain rights under old franchise agreements to terminate a franchisee and demand certain documents, but those provisions were removed from the 1991 and 1996 agreements.

The North Dakota Supreme Court reversed, stating that there were certain terms remaining in the 1991 and 1996 agreements which implied that (1) the franchisor needed information necessary to protect its trademarks; and (2) the franchisor retained some right to terminate the agreement for good cause. Stating that "rational arguments can be made for both parties' interpretation of the license agreements," the court reversed and remanded for further proceedings.

II.   Standing to Bring Breach of Contract Claims

In *Meade v. Kiddie Academy Domestic Franchising, LLC*, No. 12-2147, 2012 U.S. App. LEXIS 21283 (3rd Cir. Oct. 15, 2012), the Third Circuit affirmed the lower court's dismissal of an action brought by the president and principal shareholder of a franchisee in his individual capacity. Meade alleged, primarily, that illegal earnings claims were made and that Kiddie Academy failed to provide services as promised.

The Third Circuit found that Meade had no standing to bring claims in his own name since all of his claims alleged injury to his corporation and alleged no "direct individual injury."

III.   Breach of Express Contract Terms

A.   VICTORIES FOR FRANCHISEES AND SIMILAR PARTIES

In *Service Source, Inc. v. DHL Express (USA), Inc.*, No. 301013, 2013 Mich. App. LEXIS 1206 (Mich. Ct. App. July 11, 2013), DHL had decided that its domestic shipping market was unprofitable and announced on November 10, 2008 that it was ending domestic shipping on January 30, 2009.

Plaintiffs The Service Source, Inc. ("TSS") and The Service Source Franchise, LLC ("TSSF") had contracts with DHL and sued on February 10, 2009, alleging that DHL had repudiated the agreement. Plaintiffs stopped paying DHL and eventually ran up over $500,000 in unpaid DHL invoices. DHL terminated plaintiffs' agreements for non-payment on March 5, 2009. (The contracts were set to expire in July of 2013).

The trial court found that the parties' contracts required DHL to provide domestic service. Since no one disputed that DHL failed to provide domestic service, the trial court granted summary judgment on liability and held a trial on damages. After a bench trial, the court granted judgment to each plaintiff - $3,546,789 to TSS and $287,522 to TSSF. DHL appealed.

The Michigan Court of Appeals affirmed on the issue of wrongful termination, finding that the contract, read as a whole, required DHL to provide domestic service (for example, the contract's title itself included a reference to domestic service).

The court of appeals affirmed the damages judgment, except it found that the judgment should be reduced by the salary expenses of the two owners who took salaries. Since these salaries totaled as much at $400,000 a year, the reduction in damages could be substantial.

One other damages issue addressed by the court was whether TSSF, which was never profitable, could recover any damages. The court found that TSSF had "reliance" damages and could recover those out of pocket expenditures, regardless of whether TSSF ever made a profit.

B.   VICTORIES FOR FRANCHISORS AND SIMILAR PARTIES

In *Century 21 Real Estate LLC v. All Professional Realty, Inc.*, Nos. 10-2751, 10-2846, and 11-2497, 2012 U.S. Dist. LEXIS 111744 (E.D. Cal. Aug. 8, 2012), Century 21 had terminated the franchise agreements of All Professional Realty and other franchisees for non-payment of fees, but All Professional and the other franchisees continued to use the Century 21 trademarks post-termination.   After bringing a successful temporary injunction motion, Century 21 moved for summary judgment on its own claims and the franchisees' various claims regarding breach of contract and wrongful termination.

The court granted summary judgment against the franchisees on all counts.   The franchisees claims that (1) other franchisees stole the franchisees' employees; (2) the franchisor allowed non-franchisees to use similar trademarks; (3) the franchisor failed to provide "tools and systems;" and (4) the franchisor, in bad faith, prevented a cure of the franchisees' defaults.

The court found no such obligations in the plain language of the franchise agreement and, therefore, no breach of contract. Further, the court found that if Century 21 had the right to terminate the franchise agreement (the court felt Century 21 did; the franchisees had not paid royalties), then its motive in terminating was irrelevant.

In *Leisure Systems, Inc. v. Roundup* [*see* Chapter 5.VIII.E. *infra*.], the court found that since the franchisee had been given a five day cure period and yet had failed to cure, termination was proper. Leisure Systems was granted summary judgment on its breach of contract claim.

In *Sayles v. G & G Hotels, Inc.*, No. A 2926-11T1, 2013 N.J. Super LEXIS 5 (N.J. Super. Ct. App. Div. Jan. 16, 2013), Sayles, a hotel guest, fell through a third floor window at a Howard Johnson's hotel along with his friend O'Neill. Sayles died. O'Neill was seriously injured. Sayles' estate sued both franchisee G&G Hotels and franchisor Howard Johnson's International. Howard Johnson moved for summary judgment against G&G, stating that G&G was required by the parties' franchise agreement to indemnify Howard Johnson's, even if Howard Johnson's was itself negligent.

The trial court ruled for Howard Johnson's and awarded Howard Johnson's $13,402 in attorneys' fees. G&G appealed. The Appellate Division affirmed, stating that the franchise agreement required indemnification "including when the active or passive negligence of [Howard Johnson's] is alleged or proven." The court rejected G&G's contract interpretation argument and found that the express language of the agreement required indemnification.

In *Eureka Water Co. v. Nestle Waters North America, Inc.*, 690 F.3d 1139 (10th Cir. 2012), the Tenth Circuit rejected the contract claim that the distributor had the right to distribute Nestlé's "Ozarka Spring Water" when the contract language covered only "purified water and/or drinking water made from OZARKA drinking water concentrates." The court found that there was no ambiguity in the parties' agreement and therefore, no evidence should have been received as to what the contract meant. The jury's breach of contract verdict was reversed.

Eureka, however, was allowed to prevail on its tortious interference and promissory estoppel claims. *See* Chapters 5.IV. and 5.XII.

As discussed in Chapter 3.II.A., *H&R Block Tax Services, LLC v. Franklin*, 691 F.3d 941 (8th Cir. 2012), involved the interpretation of a franchise agreement calling for unlimited five year renewals. Since Missouri law disfavors perpetual contracts, the court interpreted this "unlimited five year renewal" contract as not providing for unlimited five year renewals. The franchisor could choose not to renew the agreement at any five-year interval, with or without "good cause."

In *Dunkin' Donuts Franchising LLC v. Oza Bros., Inc.*, No. 10-13606, 2012 U.S. Dist. LEXIS 140595 (E.D. Mich. Sept. 28, 2012), as discussed previously at Chapter 3.II.A., the court granted summary judgment to Dunkin' Donuts on its claims against Oza Brothers arising out of Oza Brothers intentionally underreporting sales to both Dunkin' Donuts and to the taxing authorities. The court found that Oza Brothers intentionally employed a scheme where it made huge wholesale sales to auto dealerships and never recorded the sales. The court found this to be a breach of contract which was incurable. Therefore, the court found that Dunkin' Donuts properly terminated the franchise.

In *Sullivan v. Jani-King of New York, Inc.*, No. 11-CV-01546, 2013 Tex. App. LEXIS 8640 (Tex. App. July 11, 2013), the Texas Court of Appeals affirmed a breach of contract jury verdict in favor of Jani-King and against its former franchisee Sullivan in the amount of $223,075 plus $80,000 in attorneys' fees.

Sullivan and Jani-King had been involved in litigation previously. During the course of that litigation, Jani-King found that Sullivan was operating a competing business without paying royalties. The parties settled their dispute, and Sullivan agreed to immediately cease his competing business. He did not. Jani-King sued Sullivan again and obtained a jury verdict in its favor.

The Texas Court of Appeals affirmed all aspects of the jury verdict, including the jury's rejection of Sullivan's fraud claim. The court found that Sullivan had agreed to pay royalties and other fees for the full term of the franchise agreement, and, thus, he could not complain that the jury appeared to award all of the royalties and fees sought by Jani-King (the jury was asked one broad-form damages question).

One unusual occurrence in the case was Jani-King presenting an expert witness on attorneys' fees. The expert opined that reasonable fees for the case would be $150,000 to $175,000. The expert had not reviewed any actual legal bills. The jury awarded only $80,000, and the court of appeals affirmed, finding the award supported by "more than a scintilla" of evidence.

C.   CONTRACT DEFENSES

Arguments of impossibility, impracticability, frustration of purpose and *force majeure* were all raised and rejected in *Howard Johnson International, Inc. v. M.D.1., LLC*, No. 11-CV-2593, 2012 U.S. Dist. LEXIS 151223 (N.D. Ill. Oct. 19, 2012). Doctors who were failed Howard Johnson's franchisees were sued for unpaid franchise fees. They defended on the basis that they had been wrongfully accused of running a Ponzi scheme by a bankruptcy trustee in a separate matter, which caused their hotel financing options to dry up.

The court granted Howard Johnson's motion for summary judgment, stating that failure to obtain financing is a "foreseeable" event and does not give rise to a defense of impossibility or commercial impracticability. The doctrine of "frustration of purpose" requires the destruction of the entire purpose of the transaction for both parties (here, the purpose was the operation of a hotel). Nothing about the alleged defamation actually prevented the operation of a hotel, so there was no valid "frustration of purpose" defense.

While the franchise agreement contained a *force majeure* clause, none of the language found in the clause came anywhere close to excusing performance due to failure to obtain financing. The franchisor was granted summary judgment.

IV.   Unjust Enrichment

Last Time Beverage Corp. v. F & V Distribution Co., Nos. 2010-03438 and 2010-09092, 2012 N.Y. App. Div. LEXIS 6092 (N.Y. App. Div. Sept. 12, 2012), as summarized above in Chapter 5.I., involved former Coke and Pepsi distributors in New York City who claimed that they had been awarded contracts (one written, one verbal) to be the exclusive distributors of Royal Crown soft drinks and other soft drinks in the area where they used to distribute Coke and Pepsi. The appellate court found a breach of contract and also found that the distributor's performance also gave rise to proper claims for promissory estoppel and unjust enrichment.

In *Huddle House, Inc. v. Two Views, Inc.*, No. 12-CV-03239, 2013 U.S. Dist. LEXIS 48754 (N.D. Ga. April 4, 2013), a Huddle House franchisee was terminated for selling unapproved product, opened a restaurant called "The Gravy Boat," and was sued by Huddle House for damages and enforcement of the post-termination non-compete.

In an odd twist, the franchisee took the offensive and moved to dismiss certain of Huddle House's ancillary claims, including unjust enrichment. The court granted the franchisee's motion, stating that a party in Georgia may not even plead an unjust enrichment claim where the party's pleading also states that a written contract governs the parties' relationship.

In *Better Homes and Gardens Real Estate LLC v. Mary Holder Agency, Inc.*, No. 11-34280, 2012 Bankr. LEXIS 3774 (Bankr. D.N.J. Aug. 9, 2012), the Mary Holder Agency, a Better Homes and Gardens real estate franchisee, was terminated for alleged failure to pay royalties. Mary Holder Agency then, allegedly, terminated all of its real estate listings so that they would all go to competitor SCS Realty Investment Group, rather than Better Homes and Gardens.

Mary Holder Agency and Mary Holder personally filed for bankruptcy protection. Better Homes and Gardens continued to pursue Mary Holder, alleging non-dischargeable tortious conduct, and also sued SCS for *inter alia*, tortious interference with contract conversion and unjust enrichment. Mary Holder and SCS moved for summary judgment.

The court denied the motions for summary judgment. On the issue of tortious interference, the court found issues of material fact as to whether SCS interfered with BH&G's contractual right to the listings of MHA prior to the termination of the franchise agreement.

The court also refused to dismiss the unjust enrichment claim against SCS, finding that <u>if</u> BH&G was entitled to MHA's real estate listing then SCS <u>could</u> be liable to BH&G for taking the listings under a theory of unjust enrichment under New Jersey law.

In *Eureka Water Co. v. Nestle Waters North America, Inc.*, 690 F.3d 1139 (10th Cir. 2012), previously summarized in Chapter 5.III.B., the court affirmed the district court's dismissal of an unjust enrichment claim based upon Nestle not paying Eureka for sales of spring water that Nestle made in Eureka's territory. Since Eureka had no license to sell spring water, it was entitled to no recovery whatsoever, under any legal or equitable theory, for sales of spring water made into its territory.

In *Ford Motor Co. v. Ghreiwati Auto*, No. 12-14313, 2013 U.S. Dist. LEXIS 68924 (E.D. Mich. May 15, 2013), as summarized in Chapter 3.VI.B., the court refused to dismiss the dealers' unjust enrichment claims. While Ford had argued that these claims were barred by the parties' written agreements, the court found that, since Ford's performance under the contracts at issue may have been excused by the defense of impracticability, if the contracts were voided, then the dealers would have the right to bring equitable claims, such as unjust enrichment.

In *ERA Franchise Systems, LLC v. Hoppens Realty, Inc.*, No. 12-CV-594, 2013 U.S. Dist. LEXIS 107078 (W.D. Wis. July 31, 2013), summarized in Chapter 5.VI., the court permitted the terminated franchisee's case to proceed on its unjust enrichment claim (that ERA received certain payments for no value), noting that, at the motion to dismiss stage, the court had to assume that the unjust enrichment allegations were true. At trial, however, the terminated franchisee would need to decide which theory to pursue, as it could not pursue both a breach of contract claim and an unjust enrichment claim.

V.   Promissory Estoppel And Equitable Estoppel

In *Ford Motor Co. v. Ghreiwati Auto*, No. 12-14313, 2013 U.S. Dist. LEXIS 68924 (E.D. Mich. May 15, 2013), as summarized in Chapter 3.VI.B., the court refused to dismiss the dealers' promissory estoppel claims. While Ford had argued that these claims were barred by the parties' written agreements, the court found that since Ford's performance under the contracts at issue may have been excused by the defense of impracticability, if the contracts were voided, then the dealers would have the right to bring equitable claims, such as promissory estoppel.

In *Last Time Beverage Corp. v. F & V Distribution Co.*, Nos. 2010-03438 and 2010-09092, 2012 N.Y. App. Div. LEXIS 6092 (N.Y. App. Div. Sept. 12, 2012), as summarized in Chapter 5.I., the distributors' performance also gave rise to proper claims for promissory estoppel.

In *Volvo Trucks North America v. Andy Mohr Truck Center*, No. 12-CV-448, 2012 U.S. Dist. LEXIS 145054 (S.D. Ind. Oct. 9, 2012), summarized at Chapter 5.I.1., a claim of promissory estoppel was barred by the existence of a written contract, and a claim of constructive fraud by Volvo's failure to plead a special relationship between the parties. Volvo's claim for equitable estoppel was dismissed as not a valid legal claim under Indiana law. Under Indiana law, equitable estoppel is only recognized as a defense based upon fraud, which Volvo could not prove in any event.

VI.   Integration Clauses

In *ERA Franchise Systems, LLC v. Hoppens Realty, Inc.*, No. 12-CV-594, 2013 U.S. Dist. LEXIS 107078 (W.D. Wis. July 31, 2013), the court refused to dismiss a breach of contract claim based upon oral promises of franchisor support at the pleading stage, but cautioned that such claims are generally barred by application of the franchise agreement's integration clause.

VII.   Damages, Other Remedies

The ability to establish and defeat claims for monetary damages is a key skill that all litigation attorneys should possess. Given the emphasis in commercial litigation practice on motions to dismiss and motions for summary judgment, damages issues are often given little attention. But this Reporting Period featured numerous cases involving the sufficiency of damages proof under applicable law.

A.   COMPENSATORY DAMAGES

In *Alaska Rent-A-Car, Inc. v. Avis Budget Group, Inc.*, Nos. 10-35137 and 10-35615, 2013 U.S. App. LEXIS 4566 (9th Cir. Mar. 6, 2013), summarized in greater detail in Chapter 5.VIII.D., the court found that the "new business rule" did not preclude a $16,000,000 recovery for the franchisee because the franchisee already was operating a profitable business. The court also found that it was proper for the expert witness on damages to calculate damages based upon a comparison of what the franchisee actually did with competition from "Budget-helped-by-Avis" and what hypothetically the franchisee would have done had Budget emerged from bankruptcy without the help of Avis. The court also affirmed a jury award of almost $1.5 million in pre-judgment interest, finding that New York law clearly called for such an award in a lost profits case.

On June 19, 2013, the 9th Circuit amended its prior decision by finding that the trial court had incorrectly awarded $57,739.51 in pre-judgment interest from the date of the verdict to the date of the judgment. Since this "post-verdict interest" was already counted once in "pre-judgment interest," awarding the $57,739.51 in this manner was "double counting." The court otherwise affirmed its earlier decision. *See Alaska Rent-A-Car, Inc. v. Avis Budget Group, Inc.*, Nos. 10-35137 and 10-35615, 2013 U.S. App. LEXIS 12709 (9th Cir. June 19, 2013).

In *Progressive Foods, LLC v. Dunkin' Donuts, Inc.*, Nos. 11-3296, 11-3335, 2012 U.S. App. LEXIS 16815 (6th Cir. Aug. 9, 2012), a Dunkin's Donuts franchisee won $336,000 at trial but lost on appeal due to a contractual statute of limitations. The trial court found that Dunkin' Donuts had failed to assist franchisee Progressive in opening three stores, awarded Progressive $336,000 in damages, and permitted Progressive three years to develop the three at issue locations.

Unfortunately for Progressive, it sued on October 3, 2007 and stated in its complaint that it had provided Dunkin' Donuts with notice of its claims "on or about August 4, 2005[.]" Therefore, the Sixth Circuit found that Progressive's entire claim was barred by a two year contractual statute of limitation. Dunkin' Donuts was awarded $92,000 in unpaid franchise fees.

The court in *Dunkin' Donuts Franchising, LLC v. Sai Food Hospitality, LLC*, No. 11-CV-1484, 2013 U.S. Dist. LEXIS 98912 (E.D. Mo. July 16, 2013), found that if the franchisee could prove wrongful termination of his franchise that he could claim "reliance damages" equal to the difference between (1) his investment in the franchised business and (2) the current value of the business. The franchisee would also be required to reduce his damages by any profits made during the time he was a franchisee.

Service Source, Inc. v. DHL Express (USA), Inc., No. 301013, 2013 Mich. App. LEXIS 1206 (Mich. Ct. App. July 11, 2013), as summarized in Chapter

5.III.A., the court of appeals affirmed the damages judgments in favor of the franchisees for over $3,000,000, except it found that the judgment should be reduced by the salary expenses of the two owners who took salaries. Since these salaries totaled as much as $400,000 a year, the reduction in damages could be substantial.

One other damages issue addressed by the court was whether TSSF, which was never profitable, could recover <u>any</u> damages. The court found that TSSF had "reliance" damages and could recover those out of pocket expenditures, regardless of whether TSSF ever made a profit.

In response to a motion brought by Nissan under the *Daubert* rule, a court found that a dealer's damages witness was not an expert witness at all, but, rather, a lay witness testifying under Rule 701 of the Federal Rules of Evidence. The court found that, while the witness made a number of errors in his analysis of damages, his testimony might be helpful to the trier of fact, particularly where the statute at issue broadly permitted recovery of "damages sustained . . . as a consequence of the violation." *A.D. Lift Truck Lease and Service, Inc. v. Nissan Forklift Corp.*, No. 12-CV-153, 2013 U.S. Dist. LEXIS 85183 (E.D. Mo. June 18, 2013).

The court also found that Nissan's "no damages" clause was unenforceable because it limited the protections of the Missouri Power Equipment Act. The Power Equipment Act expressed the fundamental public policy of Missouri and could not be waived.

Red Roof Franchising LLC, Inc. v. AA Hospitality Northshore, LLC, Nos. 10-CV-4065 and 10-CV-4120, 2013 U.S. Dist. LEXIS 44046 (D.N.J. Mar. 28, 2013), involved two Red Roof Inn hotels, one in New Jersey and one in Minnesota. The New Jersey franchise was terminated for failure to pay royalties and other fees. The Minnesota franchise was terminated after the franchisee changed brands to "America's Best Value Inn." Red Roof brought a New Jersey action and a Minnesota action, which were later consolidated. In the consolidated action, Red Roof Franchising sued for breach of contract, was granted summary judgment on liability, and then was ordered to submit more detailed damages proof.

In addressing the New Jersey portion of the action, after first disposing of the franchisees' motion for reconsideration as being both procedurally and substantively insufficient, the court considered Red Roof Franchising's submissions on unpaid fees, liquidated damages, interest, and attorneys' fees.

The court reviewed a variety of fees charged by Red Roof Franchising and found that most were authorized by the franchise agreements at issue, but one was not. The court also found one uncredited $5,081.65 payment made by the franchisee.

The court authorized a $75,000 liquidated damages recovery, but found that late fees and interest could not be applied to the liquidated damages calculation. The court also awarded $66,103.01 in attorneys' fees, finding that since the defendants failed to object to the reasonableness of the amount, Third Circuit precedent prohibited the court from reducing the fee award *sua sponte*.

The analysis under the Minnesota portion of the action was similar. Since the Minnesota Franchise Act bars liquidated damages, Red Roof Franchising sought, instead $82,419.44 of "lost profits," based upon 24 months of lost royalties. The court awarded the entire amount sought as "reasonably certain lost profits."

While the court was highly critical of Plaintiff's counsel for billing $30,478.63 for work that was basically just cut and pasting from the New Jersey portion of the action, the court found that it had to award the entire amount sought because the franchisees failed to object to the reasonableness of the fees.

In *Portugues–Santana v. Rekomdiv International, Inc.*, No. 12-1178, 2013 U.S. App. LEXIS 15331 (1st Cir. July 29, 2013), the First Circuit affirmed a jury verdict of $625,000, plus restitution, in favor of Portugues-Santana, who had been misled into believing that he would receive a Victoria's Secret franchise if he paid the Venable Law Firm $400,000 and a business broker named Rekomdiv $225,000. The jury found for Portugues-Santana on claims of breach of contract and "dolo" (fraud). The trial court then found that the $625,000 damages judgment against Rekomdiv and its employee could not be offset by a settlement payment previously made by Venable. The court noted that Portugues -Santana had sought $2,000,000 in damages plus restitution. Since Portugues-Santana prevailed on a "dolo" claim, he was entitled to restitution as a matter of law (even through the jury had not awarded restitution).

Despite the fact that the "damages" award was exactly the same amount paid to the wrongdoers ($625,000), Portugues-Santana was entitled to the $625,000 plus restitution. The settlement payment had already reduced the amount of the restitution available to Portugues-Santana, so to reduce the damages verdict by that amount would be improper. The jury had been presented with admissible evidence to establish $2,000,000 in damages, therefore, they were entitled to award any lesser amount, including $625,000. The jury's reason for awarding $625,000 as damages was not relevant.

B.   PROSPECTIVE DAMAGES

When American Suzuki Motor Corporation filed for Chapter 11 bankruptcy protection, it informed roughly 220 automobile dealers that they had two choices: (1) have their entire dealer agreement rejected in bankruptcy, or (2) sign a release of claims and stay on as parts and service dealers for 8 years. Almost all 220 chose option 2, but Florida dealer South Motors Suzuki, Inc. did not. The court in *In re American Suzuki Motor Corp.*, No. 12-BK-22808, 2013 Bankr. LEXIS 2276 (Bankr. C.D. Cal. June 4, 2013), awarded South Motors only $21,461 in past lost profits, denied all claims for lost future profits, and awarded American Suzuki its attorneys' fees. The court rejected South Motors' claim for $1,595,601 plus attorneys' fees and costs based primarily upon Florida's dealer protection statute.

The court found that the 2009 Florida statute at issue (which greatly expanded dealers' ability to recover termination damages) was not intended to apply retroactively to a 1995 dealer agreement. Even if the statute were applied retroactively, it would then be preempted by the Bankruptcy Code. While the dealer protection statute claimed to award "damages," the amounts awarded were actually statutory penalties skewed unfairly in favor of dealers. The bankruptcy court was bound to apply general state damages law, not penalties of this sort.

The court rejected the argument that the contractual "buy back" of parts and inventory requirement of the contract needed to be enforced, determining that clause was, in effect, a liquidated damages clause.

The court would, instead, award only actual breach of contract damages, which the court found to be $21,461.00.

Adding insult to the dealer's injury, the court rejected the dealer's own $200,000 claim for attorneys' fees and determined that American Suzuki was the prevailing party under California law (the law chosen in the dealer agreement). The court ordered American Suzuki to submit declarations to the court on the amount of the claimed fees and costs.

The ultimate result was that a dealer who claimed to make roughly $70,000 to $90,000 per year in profit was terminated without good cause, had to pay its own attorney $200,000, and will likely end up owing its supplier around $200,000, all to "recover" roughly $21,000 in damages.

In *Royal Dispatch Services, Inc. v. UBS Financial Services, Inc.*, No. 12-CV-2032, 2013 U.S. Dist. LEXIS 107672 (E.D. N.Y. July 31, 2013), summarized in Chapter 3.II.C., the court granted UBS summary judgment because the parties' agreement contained a clause in which Royal agreed that UBS would not be liable to Royal for damages. Royal argued that such an exculpatory clause was unenforceable since UBS had breached the contract by acting in bad faith. The court found that UBS had not acted in bad faith, so the clause was enforceable and Royal could claim no damages.

See also Precision Franchising, LLC v. Gatej, No. 12-CV-158, 2012 U.S. Dist. LEXIS 175450 (E.D. Va. Dec. 11, 2012) (franchisor awarding $64,980 in unpaid advertising payments and $183,511 in lost profits due to early franchisee termination); *Novus Franchising, Inc. v. AZ Glassworks, LLC*, No. 12-CV-1771, 2013 U.S. Dist. LEXIS 36830 (D. Minn. Mar. 18, 2013) (franchisor awarded $18,654.66 for past due amounts and $68,040 for lost future profits).

C. LANHAM ACT DAMAGES

Franchisors were generally successful this year in recovering Lanham Act damages.

In *Choice Hotels Int'l, Inc. v. Bhakta*, No. 11-CV-00411, 2013 U.S. Dist. LEXIS 49863 (S.D. Texas Apr. 5, 2013), the franchisor Choice Hotels ("Choice") sought injunctive relief and damages for a former franchisee's continued use of the franchisor's trademarks after termination. The court awarded Choice damages in the amount of the franchisee's "profits" as permitted by 15 U.S.C. § 1117(a). Using the franchisee's monthly profit and loss statements, Choice claimed damages based on the franchisee's "net income." Choice did not deduct from net income those months in which the hotel actually operated at a loss. The court approved this procedure and awarded Choice $105,453.29 based on the franchisee's net income for the 15 months that it continued to display the marks after termination. The court also awarded Choice damages in the form of lost royalties based on the percentage contained in the franchise agreement. With respect to Choice's request for treble damages and attorneys' fees under 15 U.S.C. § 1117(b), the court found that the franchisee continued to use the trademarks after repeated cease and desist letters and warnings from Choice. Consequently, the court exercised its discretion in adding an additional $75,000 in damages, but declined to designate the case as "exceptional" for attorney's fees purposes because there was no evidence that the franchisee acted in a malicious, fraudulent or willful manner.

However, Choice was not as fortunate in *Choice Hotels Int'l, Inc. v. Patel*, No. 12-CV-00023, 2013 U.S. Dist. LEXIS 55345 (S.D. Tex. Apr. 16, 2013) where the court declined to grant Choice's damages request for an award of profits during the period of infringement, finding that genuine issues of material fact regarding the willfulness of the defendant's breach precluded a ruling on summary judgment. The court found that given the former franchisee's efforts to remove the Comfort Inn name from the hotel, a reasonable jury could find that the defendant did not intend to confuse or deceive the public. The court also noted that Choice failed to present evidence explaining how its sales were diverted to the defendant based on the limited use and display of the trademarks. Significantly, the court noted that questions remained about how much of the defendant's income was attributable to using the trademarks, as opposed to the oil shale induced economic boom in Victoria, Texas where the former franchisee operated. Given these unanswered questions, the court concluded that Choice had not proven that an award of profits was appropriate at that stage of the litigation. The court was equally skeptical of Choice's request for damages in the form of royalties. Because Choice had not presented sufficient evidence calculating the purported damage to its goodwill or the defendant's unjust enrichment from unlawfully using the Comfort marks, the court declined to enter summary judgment awarding Choice royalty damages.

A rare victory for a trademark infringer was fashioned by the court in *Carpet Cops, Inc. v. Carpet Cops, LLC*, No. 11-CV-00561, 2012 U.S. Dist. LEXIS 127239 (D. Nev. Sept. 6, 2012). Plaintiff had owned the trademark "Carpet Cops" since 2002. In 2011, Plaintiff became aware that Defendant advertised in Nevada using the mark "The Carpet Cops." Plaintiff sued and was awarded default judgment. However, the court found that since Defendant had stopped using the mark at issue, that Plaintiff was only entitled to $2,500 in statutory damages plus $4,396.75 in fees and costs. (Plaintiff had sought $2,000,000 for willful infringement.)

See also Century 21 Real Estate LLC v. All Professional Realty, Inc., Nos. 10-2751, 10-2846, and 11-2497, 2012 U.S. Dist. LEXIS 111744 (E.D. Cal. Aug. 8, 2012) (infringement was willful, treble damages under 15 U.S.C. § 1117(a) equals $86,022); *Ramada Worldwide, Inc. v. Petersburg Regency, LLC*, No. 10-CV-4092, 2012 U.S. Dist. LEXIS 142172 (D.N.J. Oct. 1, 2012) (infringement was willful, treble damages equal $265,545.18).

D.   ATTORNEYS' FEES AND PUNITIVE DAMAGES

1.   Attorneys' Fees After Dismissal

This past year had a bevy of opinions regarding the propriety of attorneys' fees awards. Attorneys who handle cases nationwide will find some rather useful, and sometimes surprising, attorneys' fees findings.

In *Alboyacian v. BP Products N. Am., Inc.*, Bus. Franchise Guide (CCH) ¶ 14,894 (D. N.J. Sept. 5, 2012), a group of BP franchisees who had been granted summary judgment on their wrongful nonrenewal claims under the New Jersey Franchise Practices Act, but who had had all of their remaining claims dismissed, settled their one final claim with BP by agreeing to file a voluntary dismissal pursuant to Fed. R. Civ. P. 41. The parties could not agree as to which side should be awarded legal fees.

The franchisees maintained that they were entitled to legal fees and costs by virtue of their having successfully sued to prevent a violation of the NJFPA. BP, meanwhile, asked that the court condition the voluntary dismissal upon an award of attorney fees to BP because BP had been forced to defend against that meritless claim. In the alternative, BP requested attorney fees for the time that its counsel had expended in briefing the pending motion to dismiss. The court held that only the franchisees were entitled to attorneys' fees and costs.

BP argued that since the franchisees had only stopped a threatened violation of the NJFPA, they had not proved an actual NJFPA violation and could not recover fees. The court called BP's argument a "fundamental misreading of the statute," and found that the franchisees could recover fees for preventing a violation of the Act. The court observed that other franchisees had been awarded fees in actions seeking injunctions to prevent violations from occurring under the NJFPA, and those results made common sense.

The court, however, limited the attorney fees awardable to the franchisees under the NJFPA to the time spent on their one successful claim and not on the nine claims that had been dismissed or the one remaining claim that had been settled. The court directed the franchisees to submit revised documents that included only those fees, costs, and expenses relating to the winning claim.

The court rejected BP's argument to recover its fees, stating that BP had never answered or filed a motion for summary judgment, so the plaintiffs could dismiss the claims under Rule 41 without BP's permission or input and without a court order. While the court conceded that it may have equitable jurisdiction to award fees after a Rule 41 dismissal, there was no equitable reason to award BP its fees.

The issue in *Eaddy v. Precision Franchising LLC*, No. A12A2545, 2013 Ga. App. LEXIS 130 (Ga. Ct. App. Mar. 5, 2013), was whether franchisor Precision Franchising could take advantage of a Georgia statute which authorized a party to recover attorneys' fees if it made an offer of judgment in excess of the plaintiff's ultimate recovery. Ms. Eaddy had sued a

Precision Tune franchisee and Precision Tune for injuries she received due to an altercation at the franchisee's premises. Precision Franchising offered $1,000 pursuant to OGCA § 9-11-68. Precision Franchising was found to have no liability at the summary judgment stage. Eaddy appealed. Eaddy then settled for $200,000 with the franchisee and dismissed her appeal against the franchisor. Precision Franchising pounced, claiming $28,656.37 in attorneys' fees were owed because it offered $1,000 on a claim that netted $0. The trial court awarded the fees, and Eaddy appealed.

The Georgia Court of Appeals affirmed, finding that the $1,000 offer was made in good faith and exceeded the $0 recovered. While the various parties and insurer in the case had made different settlements, none impacted the OCGA § 9-11-68 claim by Precision Franchising against Eaddy.

2. Attorneys' Fees as a Sanction

See *JTH Tax, Inc. v. Noor*, No. 11-CV-22, 2012 U.S. Dist. LEXIS 138657 (E.D. Va. Sept. 26, 2012) (court awarded attorneys' fees as a penalty after a violation of court order) and *Bletas v. Deluca*, No. 11-CV-1777, 2013 U.S. Dist. LEXIS 103592 (S.D. N.Y. July 18, 2013)(the count granted the defendants' motion for sanctions and attorneys' fees).

Rule 11 of the Federal Rules of Civil Procedure continues to have significant potency, as evidenced by *Bletas v. Deluca*, No. 11-CV-1777, 2013 U.S. Dist. LEXIS 103592 (S.D. N.Y. July 18, 2013). In *Bletas*, pro se plaintiffs sued a long list of defendants, including a federal district court judge, asserting a panoply of claims and seeking over one billion dollars in damages. The court dismissed the amended complaint in its entirety, and granted a motion for sanctions (including attorneys' fees) against the plaintiffs. The Second Circuit affirmed as against one *pro se* plaintiff who was found to be engaging in the unauthorized practice of law. When the case was sent back down to the trial court, the defendants submitted a memorandum claiming over $19,000 in attorneys' fees in bringing the motion. The court awarded the defendants the full amount of their claimed attorneys' fees in their entirety.

3. Auto Manufacturer Recovers Fees For Defeating a Claim Under a Dealer Protection Statute

Gray v. Toyota Motor Sales, U.S.A., Inc., No. 10-CV-03081, 2012 U.S. Dist. LEXIS 133284 (E.D. N.Y. Sept. 17, 2012) (New York Vehicle and Traffic Law § 469 permits award of fees "to any party" and does not require a showing that dealer's claim was frivolous).

4.   *"Reasonableness" of Attorney Rates and Hours*

The reasonable rate in the Eastern District of New York is $100 to $200 per hour for junior associates, $200 to $300 per hour for senior associates and $300 to $450 per hour for partners. Therefore, rates of $600 to $675 per hour charged by counsel were 40% too high and would be reduced accordingly. *Six Continents Hotels, Inc. v. CPJFK, LLC*, No. 09-CV-2021, 2012 U.S. Dist. LEXIS 131675 (E.D. N.Y. Sept. 11, 2012) ($100 to $150 per hour for junior associates, $200 to $250 for senior associates, $200 to $350 per hour for partners, $80 per hour for law student interns). The court also found 92.7 hours expended in obtaining a default judgment to be excessive, particularly where most of the work was done by a senior partner. ($25,747.50 request denied and reduced to $15,000).

Faring better in connection with a default judgment win were Novus's lawyers in *Novus Franchising, Inc. v. AZ Glassworks, LLC*, No. 12-CV-1771, 2013 U.S. Dist. LEXIS 36830 (D. Minn. Mar. 18, 2013) (almost $43,000 award where law was unclear and issues were complex).

A summary judgment win on a franchise dispute involving a terminated 7-Eleven franchisee was worth $233,706.91 in fees and costs to the prevailing franchisor in *7-Eleven, Inc. v. Spear*, No. 10-CV-6697, 2013 U.S. Dist. LEXIS 59392 (N.D. Ill. April 25, 2013). The court found that 7-Eleven had prevailed completely, and the most important factor in determining the amount of a fee award was "the degree of success obtained." The franchisor in *Spear* was also awarded an injunction and roughly $116,000 in damages.

By contrast, an in-house counsel who successfully obtained injunctive relief against a franchisee in *AAMCO Transmissions, Inc. v. Singh*, No. 12-2209, 2013 U.S. Dist. LEXIS 82921 (E.D. Pa. June 12, 2013) was not awarded a requested $21,000 fee award, and his fee award was reduced to $7,500 on the basis that "70 hours spent on such was excessive." The court found 25 hours to be reasonable, stating that the fee award was reduced, in part, because the attorney was in-house counsel.

In *Cicero v. Richard L. Rosen Law Firm, PLLC*, No. 08-CV-026272, 2012 N.Y. Misc. LEXIS 4292 (N.Y. Civ. Ct. Aug. 17, 2012), a billing dispute resulted in a malpractice claim against the Rosen Firm by Mr. Cicero. The Rosen Firm billed Cicero $33,414.25 to assist in vacating a settlement in connection with a gas station dispute. Cicero made a claim of malpractice and "abusive" overbilling. The Rosen Firm counterclaimed for approximately $18,000 in unpaid fees.

The court conducted a bench trial and made various findings: (1) there was no malpractice because nothing The Rosen Firm did caused Cicero any damages; (2) because there was no malpractice, The Rosen Firm was entitled to recover reasonable attorneys' fees; (3) work done before being retained was recoverable under the theory of *quantum meruit*; (4) the lack of a fee letter does not *per se* bar a fee recovery; (5) $450 per hour is a reasonable hourly rate for an attorney of Richard Rosen's expertise; (6) there would be no recovery for work done by an associate and later re-done or edited by a partner; (7) there would be no double recovery for a client meeting where two lawyers were present; (8) certain of the partner-level work done was not recoverable.

The court found $20,000 to be a fair and reasonable billing amount. Since the Rosen Firm had been paid a $15,000 retainer, judgment was entered for $5,000.

On January 13, 2013, the Eastern District of Michigan determined that $195 per hour was a reasonable hourly rate in the Sixth Circuit, and that "a few" billing entries with a rate of $310 to $400 per hour were "within the realm of reasonableness." The court also found that 27.65 hours was a reasonable amount of time to spend on a petition and motion to compel arbitration. The court awarded all $4,764.66 sought. *Allegra Network, LLC v. Horvath Co.*, No. 12-12683, 2013 U.S. Dist. LEXIS 10151 (E.D. Mich. Jan. 25, 2013).

The winner for "attorneys' fee award of the year" came in the franchisee's $16,000,000 encroachment victory in *Alaska Rent-A-Car, Inc. v. Avis Budget Group, Inc.*, Nos. 10-35137 and 10-35615, 2013 U.S. App. LEXIS 4566 (9th Cir. Mar. 6, 2013). A 1997 settlement between Avis and its franchisees obligated Avis not to use its assets to market for, or provide other services to, any rental car companies purchased by Avis in the future. In 2002, Avis purchased Budget Rent-A-Car out of bankruptcy. The franchisees sued.

The franchisee's expert testified that lost past and future profits from Avis's breach of contract were $16,000,000. Avis presented no contrary figure from an expert witness. The jury awarded $16,000,000, which was upheld on appeal.

Alaska Rent-A-Car then sought attorneys' fees under Alaska's "English Rule," which awards attorneys' fees to the prevailing party and Rule 82 of the Alaska Rules of Civil Procedure. The district court awarded $1,605,500, and the Ninth Circuit affirmed, stating that Alaska's law on attorneys' fees was "procedural," and, therefore, the District of Alaska was required to apply this Alaska law (not the New York law chosen by the parties' agreement). A fee equal to roughly 10% of the ultimate recovery was found to be reasonable under Alaska law.

In *Atchley v. Pepperidge Farm, Inc.*, No. 04-CV-452, 2012 U.S. Dist. LEXIS 173974 (E.D. Wash. Dec. 6, 2012), as summarized in Chapter 1.I.

Pepperidge Farm was granted judgment in its favor and directed to submit documents supporting its claims for attorneys' fees and costs.

In *Red Roof Franchising LLC, Inc. v. AA Hospitality Northshore, LLC*, Nos. 10-CV-4065 and 10-CV-4120, 2013 U.S. Dist. LEXIS 44046 (D.N.J. Mar. 28, 2013), as summarized in Chapter 5.VIII.A., while the court was highly critical of Plaintiff's counsel for billing $30,478.63 for work that was basically just cutting and pasting from a related action, the court found that it had to award the entire amount sought because the franchisees failed to object to the reasonableness of the fees.

Sims v. Nissan North America, Inc., Nos. 12AP-833 and 12AP-835, 2013 Ohio App. LEXIS 2642 (Ohio Ct. App. June 25, 2013), involved an appeal of an Ohio Motor Vehicle Dealers Board decision finding that (1) Sims could not be terminated for poor market share and (2) Sims was entitled to attorneys' fees in an amount far less than he requested. Nissan appealed the first finding, Sims the second.

On the attorneys' fees issue, Sims argued that his fee recovery should be over $400,000, plus expert fees of $57,700, and cost of almost $14,000. The Board awarded Sims $175,324.99 total.

The court of appeals found that contrary to both the Board and the district court, the Ohio statute at issue did allow for recovery of expert witness fees. It remanded the case to the Board for a review of the reasonableness of those fees, plus the additional fees incurred in arguing for the expert witness fees. The court also rejected Sims' argument that he should recover twice the "lodestar" figure (hours worked x hourly rate) because the statute never contemplated such a double recovery. The matter was remanded to the trial court for further proceedings.

In *General Motors Corp. v. Motor Vehicle Review Bd.*, No. 4-08-0893, 2013 Ill. App. Unpub. LEXIS 1465 (Ill. App. Ct. June 26, 2013), the Illinois Court of Appeals reversed a $1,033,607 attorneys' fees award in favor of four Chicago-area dealers who had prevailed many times in a 12-year battle involving GM's efforts to add two new encroaching dealer points in the Chicago area. *See* summary at Chapter 3.VI.B.

In *Sullivan v. Jani-King of New York, Inc.*, No. 11-CV-01546, 2013 Tex. App. LEXIS 8640 (Tex. App. July 11, 2013), the Texas Court of Appeals affirmed a jury verdict in favor of Jani-King and against its former franchisee Sullivan in the amount of $223,075 plus $80,000 in attorneys' fees. *See* summary at Chapter 5.III.B.

One unusual occurrence in the case was Jani-King presenting an expert witness on attorneys' fees. The expert opined that reasonable fees for the case would be $150,000 to $175,000. The expert had not reviewed any actual legal bills. The jury awarded only $80,000, and the court of appeals affirmed, finding the award supported by "more than a scintilla" of evidence.

In *Victory Lane Quick Oil Change, Inc. v. Darwich*, Bus. Franchise Guide (CCH) ¶ 15,049 (E.D. Mich. May 8, 2013), the court awarded the franchisor $44,823.25 in attorneys' fees and $4,336.86 in expenses and obtaining a preliminary injunction and summary judgment on its claims against former franchisee Darwich. (*See* summary at Chapter 3.V.C.). The franchisee claimed that the franchisor was overly aggressive in pursuing litigation, but the court disagreed, finding that the franchisee had fought the franchisor every step of the way and forced the franchisor to enforce its rights in court.

In *Gray v. Toyota Motor Sales, U.S.A., Inc.*, No. 10-CV-3081, 2013 U.S. Dist. LEXIS 99113 (E.D. N.Y., July 16, 2013), Toyota prevailed in a dealer dispute and sought $253,980.75 in attorneys' fees and less than $2,000 in costs. The court reviewed Toyota's fee petition and reduced the requested fee to $150,050 but awarded all requested costs.

The court found that counsel's hourly rate exceeded the maximum hourly rates recognized as reasonable in the district. The court set the reasonable rates for the work done at $450/hour for the partners, $300/hour for a senior associate and $200/hour for junior associates. The court found that all hours were reasonable for which recovery was sought. Doing the math, it appears that the hourly rates permitted by the court were roughly 60% of the actual rates charged to Toyota.

In *Volvo Construction Equipment Rents, Inc. v. NRL Rentals, LLC*, No. 09-CV-32, 2013 U.S. Dist. LEXIS 103734 (D. Nev. July 23, 2013), the court considered whether a construction equipment rental franchisor, Volvo Rents, was liable for attorneys' fees under Nevada law when the franchisor had judgment as a matter of law entered against it at a bench trial. The franchisor brought suit against two franchisees, NRL Rentals in Las Vegas, Nevada, and NRL San Antonio in New Braunfels, Texas, after running an audit and finding the franchisees consistently failed to meet certain loan obligations. The franchisees were granted judgment after the franchisor put on its case, and the franchisees subsequently asserted the franchisor was liable for their attorneys' fees under state law. Nevada law provided for attorneys' fees to the prevailing party where a litigant engaged in frivolous litigation. NRS § 18.010(2)(b) provides that, "[i]t is the intent of the Legislature that the court award attorney's fees pursuant to this paragraph and impose sanctions … in all appropriate situations to punish for and deter frivolous or vexatious claims and defenses[.]"

After considering the six justifications for bringing suit offered by the franchisor, the court determined that its claims were "not frivolous or vexatious." The court stated that simply losing as a matter of law did not necessarily mean that the franchisor had violated § NRS 18.010(2)(b).

In *Curves International, Inc. v. Nash*, No.11-CV-0425, 2013 U.S. Dist. LEXIS 104095 (N.D. N.Y. July 25, 2013), Curves International, Inc. ("Curves") sued franchisee defendants on a number of grounds and obtained a partial default judgment. When Curves sought attorneys' fees, the court granted the request, partially on the basis the parties' franchise agreement provided for them, and partly because the court found this was an exceptional misuse of proprietary marks. The franchisees had used the Curves marks in marketing their own business similar to Curves. This convinced the court the franchisees were willful violators and therefore Curves' Lanham Act claims also merited an award of attorneys' fees.

The court first recognized that courts in the Second Circuit calculate attorneys' fees by use of the lodestar method. The court noted that, as early as 2008, a court in the Northern District of New York awarded fees in this manner: $210 for an experienced attorney, $150 for an attorney with more than four years of experience, $120 for an attorney with less than four years of experience, and $80 an hour for a paralegal. The court noted that "courts have recently found higher rates to be appropriate[,]" citing a case that allowed $275 an hour for experienced attorneys, $200 for attorneys with more than four years of experience, $170 for attorneys with less than four years of experience, and $90 an hour for a paralegal. The most generous award recognized by the court was $585 an hour for a partner.

Here Curves had retained out-of-district counsel, counsel that requested an award higher than the recognized reasonable fee amount. The Second Circuit employed a presumption against higher awards when sought by out-of-district attorneys absent evidence a "'reasonable client would have selected out-of-district counsel because doing so would likely (not just possibly) produce a substantially better net result.'" As the plaintiff brought forth no evidence why higher rates were appropriate, the court refused to award rates higher than those recently found appropriate.

See also Alboyacian v. BP Products N. Am., Inc., Bus. Franchise Guide (CCH) ¶ 14,894 (D. N.J. Sept. 5, 2012), summarized at Chapter 5.VIII.D.

5.   Punitive Damages

Fullington v. Equilon Enterprises, LLC, 210 Cal. App. 4th 667 (Cal. Ct. App. 2012) involved Keith Fullington, a Shell gas station franchisee who had already been part of a consolidated action against Shell/Equilon for failure to allow Fullington the opportunity to buy his station. Fullington recovered damages in that consolidated action. Subsequently, Fullington became part of another group action alleging: (1) Equilon unreasonably refused to allow Fullington to transfer his franchise; and (2) Equilon would on occasion reduce rent, but Equilon lied to Fullington and told him there was nothing it could do about reducing his rent.

The damages issue in *Fullington* was whether Mr. Fullington could bring a fraud claim when all of his fraud damages had been recovered in the prior action. The trial court found that Mr. Fullington could not continue to seek punitive damages, because he had recovered his compensatory damages. The California Court of Appeal disagreed, stating that, although Fullington could <u>recover</u> no more compensatory damages, he could <u>prove</u> compensatory damages for his fraud claim and, therefore, he could prove all elements of fraud and seek punitive damages.

In *Huddle House, Inc. v. Two Views, Inc.*, (*see* Chapter 5.IV. *supra*), the court dismissed a franchisor's claim for punitive damages, finding that the claims pled by the franchisor (breach of contract, negligence, Lanham Act violation) did not support a claim for punitive damages.

E.   LIQUIDATED DAMAGES

A claim for what the court viewed to be a whopping $25,500,000 in "liquidated damages" was considered in *Dow Chemical Canada Inc. v. HRD Corp.*, 909 F. Supp. 2d 350 (D. Del. 2012). Dow Chemical Canada, Inc. ("Dow"), the plaintiff, brought an action against HRD Corporation ("HRD"), for HRD's breach of a joint development agreement and a supply agreement. The agreement revolved around the parties' joint development of polyethylene wax products. Dow was to manufacture and supply wax products from a Dow plant, made specifically for the manufacture of the wax product. The parties' agreement contained a number of express conditions centered on the achievement of certain points in the development and supply cycle before there would be a right to payment. After Dow had begun manufacturing wax, and had actually shipped two railcars full of product, triggering Dow's right to payment, HRD requested, on July 30, 2004, that Dow halt production, alleging the wax did not meet HRD's requirements. Dow did not inform HRD that the supply agreement was terminated until January 18, 2005.

The supply agreement provided for a number of separate payments to Dow. The first type of payment, the Annual Operating Payment ("AOP"), was an annual fee of $16,500,000 (in Canadian currency) to be invoiced in monthly installments. This AOP was intended to reimburse Dow for the operation of its plant. In practice, this payment required that HRD would have to pay Dow for the unpaid AOP balance for the remainder of the year. The second type of payment, the annual capacity termination payment, was meant to compensate Dow for a three year period following a potential breach by HRD of the supply agreement.

Dow's first argument was that HRD was liable for the entire 2005 AOP payment because Dow did not terminate until after December 31, 2004. HRD replied by invoking the constructive termination doctrine, stating that Dow had made it clear through its conduct that the parties' business relationship was terminated in 2004. HRD relied on evidence from Dow employees suggesting Dow had begun closing the plant in 2004, and evidence revealing that Dow employees had consciously decided to delay giving notice of termination until after the end of 2004. Dow, on the other hand, relied on a contract provision which required Dow's written notice in order to terminate the supply agreement. Dow also proved that the earliest it could terminate the agreement was December 4, 2004. The court held the constructive termination doctrine had no application to this dispute.

Nonetheless, the court considered whether subjecting HRD to a full year's payment of the AOP would amount to an unenforceable penalty under the commonly applied liquidated damages two-prong test, requiring an analysis of whether damages could be foreseen with reasonable certainty, and whether the liquidated amount was reasonable. On the first prong, the court accepted Dow's argument the supply agreement was executed before the product or plant had been designed, and two years before production, making it difficult to predict damages with certainty. On the second prong, the court agreed with HRD that the AOP's arbitrary award of the remainder of a year's payment based solely on the date of termination did not relate to a rational estimation of Dow's likely damages at the time of contracting. Thus, the court struck down this provision as a penalty. Instead, the court stated that it would give Dow a later opportunity to prove its actual damages.

Dow was, however, successful on its second liquidated damages claim. Dow alleged that under the contract it was owed $.05 per pound of wax multiplied by three times the annual capacity of Dow's plant. Dow argued this payment was meant to compensate Dow for its lost opportunity, as the parties' agreement prohibited Dow from selling the manufactured wax for three years after delivery of a certain amount of conforming wax. The court noted this symmetry between the damages provision and the restriction on Dow's ability to sell as supporting the clause's validity. Not only would it have been hard to speculate Dow's losses, as it could not be predicted what demand would be for the wax during the three years following a breach, but it also established a rational relationship to Dow's losses. Therefore, the court ordered HRD to pay Dow $9,000,000 for the capacity termination payment.

In *Ramada Worldwide, Inc. v. Petersburg Regency, LLC*, No. 10-CV-4092, 2012 U.S. Dist. LEXIS 142172 (D.N.J. Oct. 1, 2012), hotel franchisor Ramada Worldwide was granted summary judgment enforcing its liquidated damages provision in a franchise agreement that was terminated eight years. early by franchisee Petersburg Regency, LLC.

The liquidated damages provision at issue calculated liquidated damages at $1,000 for each guest room the franchisee was licensed to operate at the time of termination. The court held that the agreement tied the amount of liquidated damages to the royalties and fees the franchisor would lose due to premature termination and the amount of actual damages that would result from the breach would be extremely difficult to estimate, given the fluctuations in room rates and occupancy levels.

The court found that New Jersey law permitted recovery of liquidated damages if the damage sustained by the non-breaching party would be difficult to ascertain and the amount is a reasonable forecast of the loss sustained. The court concluded that Ramada was entitled to $192,000 in liquidated damages but the court did not award any pre-judgment interest on the liquidated damages since the liquidated damages provision did not call for interest, and the provision also made no reference to another clause of the agreement, on recurring fees, which did provide for the recovery of interest under certain circumstances.

In *Six Continents Hotels, Inc. v. CPJFK, LLC*, No. 09-CV-2021, 2012 U.S. Dist. LEXIS 131675 (E.D. N.Y. Sept. 11, 2012), the court granted summary judgment to Six Continents in the amount of $326,719.73 in unpaid fees; $1,973,689.37 in liquidated damages; $703,931.39 in prejudgment interest; and $114,658.17 in attorneys' fees and costs. The court found that the contract term calling for recovery of 36 months' worth of royalties was an enforceable liquidated damages provision under Ga. Code Ann. § 13-6-7, and that the liquidated damages bore interest from the date they were unpaid until paid in full. The court awarded pre-judgment interest at the contract rate of 18% per annum.

Former "Jellystone Park" franchisees located in Michigan, Indiana and Ohio were terminated in June of 2011 due to non-payment of fees. The franchisor, Leisure Systems, Inc., sued in Ohio federal court, seeking unpaid fees and liquidated damages. The franchisees counterclaims for breach of contract, tortious interference and defamation. The parties made cross-motions for summary judgment and the court issued its opinion in *Leisure Systems, Inc. v. Roundup LLC*, No. 11-CV-384, 2012 U.S. Dist. LEXIS 155948 (S.D. Ohio Oct. 31, 2012). After finding that notice of termination was proper and the franchisees had failed to pay as agreed, the court awarded Leisure Systems its past-due fees and turned to the issue of liquidated damages.

The court found that liquidated damages clauses are generally enforceable, if freely entered into, where (1) damages are uncertain as to amount and difficult to prove; (2) the contract as a whole is not unconscionable; and (3) the contract is consistent with the conclusion that it was the intention of the parties that damages in the amount stated should follow the breach thereof. The court approved the liquidated damages provision under factors 1 and 2, but not factor 3.

The defect in Leisure Systems' liquidated damages provision was that it called for liquidated damages in an amount equal to (a) all sums due and owing, plus (b) the average monthly royalty payment for the 36 months prior to termination, times (c) the number of months remaining on the franchise agreement. (A + B) x C = "Total Amount." The "Total Amount" would then be reduced to present value. By using the "all sums due and owing" figure (Figure "A") in this manner, the resulting liquidated damages were grossly inflated versus the likely actual damages for wrongful termination. Therefore, the liquidated damages provision was unenforceable under both Ohio and Indiana law.

The franchisees were granted summary judgment on this issue, and the franchisor was required to prove actual damages at trial.

There were numerous cases that were decided in the past 12 months in which liquidated damages provisions were upheld and liquidated damages awarded.

See Baymont Fran. Sys., Inc. v. Raj, No. 11-3777, 2013 U.S. Dist. LEXIS 8588 (D. N.J. Jan. 22, 2013) (summary judgment under New Jersey law); *Century 21 Real Estate LLC v. All Professional Realty, Inc.*, Nos. 10-2751, 10-2846, and 11-2497, 2012 U.S. Dist. LEXIS 111744 (E.D. Cal. Aug. 8,

2012) (summary judgment under New Jersey law, over $575,000 awarded); *Choice Hotels Int'l, Inc. v. Cherokee Hospitality, LLC*, No. 11-2095, 2012 U.S. Dist. LEXIS 169793 (D. Md. Nov. 29, 2012) (arbitrator award under Maryland law upheld, over $35,000 in liquidated damages); *Choice Hotels Int'l, Inc. v. Jai Shree Navdurga, LLC*, No. 11-2893, 2012 U.S. Dist. LEXIS 169283 (D. Md. Nov. 29, 2012) (same, $75,000 in liquidated damages); *Choice Hotels Int'l, Inc. v. Yami, Inc.*, No. 11-2354, 2012 U.S. Dist. LEXIS 169796 (D. Md. Nov. 29, 2012) (same, $57,962.67 in liquidated damages); *Days Inn Worldwide, Inc. v. Hazard Mgmt. Grp., Inc.*, No. 10-CV-7545, 2012 U.S. Dist. LEXIS 163489 (S.D. N.Y. Nov. 13, 2012) (New York law, summary judgment granted, hearing to determine exact amounts due for all damages); *Days Inn Worldwide, Inc. v. May & Young Hotel – New Orleans, LLC*, No. 11-CV-01546, 2012 U.S. Dist. LEXIS 179344 (D. N.J. Dec. 19, 2012) (chosen law not mentioned, one day bench trial, over $214,000 in liquidated damages plus almost $98,000 in interest on the liquidated damages); *Howard Johnson International, Inc. v. Kim*, No. 11-3438, 2012 U.S. Dist. LEXIS 178026 (D.N.J. Dec. 17, 2012) (New Jersey law, over $85,000 in liquidated damages plus over $26,000 in prejudgment interest); *Six Continents Hotels, Inc. v. CPJFK, LLC*, No. 09-CV-2021, 2012 U.S. Dist. LEXIS 131675 (E.D. N.Y. Sept. 11, 2012) (Georgia statute permits liquidated damages "unless the agreement violates some principle of law;" awarding $1,973,689.37 plus interest); *Ramada Worldwide, Inc. v. Petersburg Regency, LLC*, No. 10-CV-4092, 2012 U.S. Dist. LEXIS 142172 (D.N.J. Oct. 1, 2012) (New Jersey law, $192,000 awarded).

As stated by the *Ramada Worldwide v. Petersburg Regency* court, the general rule of law is that liquidated damages are enforceable where (1) the damage sustained by the non-breaching party would be difficult to ascertain, and (2) the amount is a reasonable forecast of the loss sustained. The burden is on the breaching party to offer proof of contractually acceptable excuses to avoid the liquidated damages clause.

F.   INTEREST

In *Tricon Energy Ltd. v. Vinmar International, Ltd..*, 718 F.3d 448 (5th Cir. 2013), arbitrators had awarded post-award interest to the party initiating arbitration proceedings, Tricon Energy, Ltd ("Tricon"), at a rate of 8.5%. When Tricon sought to confirm the award, the court rejected the 8.5% interest rate Tricon had been awarded and instead awarded the federal rate provided by 28 U.S.C. § 1961. The district court ruled against Tricon because it was convinced that arbitrators could not award post-judgment interest at a rate other than the federal rate.

The Fifth Circuit stated that whether parties could contract for a rate other than the federal statutory rate was a question of first impression in the circuit. Following case law from the Tenth Circuit, the Fifth Circuit noted that arbitrators could decide as a matter of contract interpretation whether the arbitration provision allowed the arbitrators to set post judgment interest, and the court concluded a provision relegating to the arbitrators "'[a]ny and all differences and disputes of whatsoever nature arising out of this Agreement" included issues regarding post judgment interest. The Fifth Circuit did not believe, however, that the arbitration award, which granted post-award, and not post judgment, interest, clearly referred to post judgment interest. Since the arbitrators only awarded "post-award" interest, interest after judgment was entered would be awarded at the federal statutory rate, not at the 8.5%.

In *Six Continents Hotels, Inc. v. CPJFK, LLC*, No. 09-CV-2021, 2012 U.S. Dist. LEXIS 131675 (E.D. N.Y. Sept. 11, 2012), the court granted summary judgment to Six Continents in the amount of $326,719.73 in unpaid fees; $1,973,689.37 in liquidated damages; $703,931.39 in prejudgment interest; and $114,658.17 in attorneys' fees and costs. The court held that liquidated damages bore interest from the date they were unpaid until paid in full. The court awarded the contract rate of 18% per annum.

In *Alaska Rent-A-Car, Inc. v. Avis Budget Group, Inc.*, Nos. 10-35137 and 10-35615, 2013 U.S. App. LEXIS 4566 (9th Cir. Mar. 6, 2013), summarized in Chapter 5.VIII.D., the court affirmed a jury award of almost $1.5 million in pre-judgment interest, finding that New York law clearly called for such an award in a lost profits case.

G.   INJUNCTIONS

In *Curves International, Inc. v. Negron*, No. 11-CV-2986, 2012 U.S. Dist. LEXIS 142055 (E.D. N.Y. Aug. 31, 2012), the court denied Curves' request for a permanent injunction against defendant Derrick Negron precluding him from competing with Curves in a business called the "Ultimate Sweat Zone." Curves had sued, and settled with, Derrick Negron's wife, Wendy. Curves had stated in court papers that Curves had no reason to believe that Derrick Negron was involved in the Ultimate Sweat Zone. Therefore, the court found that Curves had no reasonable likelihood of success on the merits.

In *Noya v. Frontier Adjusters, Inc.*, No. 13-0965, 2013 U.S. Dist. LEXIS 80672 (D. Md. June 7, 2013) a franchisee of an insurance franchise sued, complaining about a program known as "FANRCP," which was a national and regional accounts program which Frontier claimed was necessary to grow the business, but which Noya said would devastate his business.

Noya sought a preliminary injunction in early 2013 against the institution of FANRCP and against efforts by Frontier to terminate or non-renew his franchises. The court denied Noya's motion, stating that he had known from the date he signed his agreement for his primary franchise (this franchise brought in 60% of his total business) that it expired 10 years later. Noya also knew about FANRCP for three or four years, but had never previously sought injunctive relief. The court also noted that Noya had sold or was selling the franchise threatened with non-renewal to another franchisee, and Noya had 12 remaining franchises. In light of all of these facts, Noya's motion for a preliminary injunction was denied.

In *Live, Inc. v. Domino's Pizza, LLC*, No., COA12-930, 2013 N.C. App. LEXIS 84 (N.C. Ct. App. Jan. 15, 2013), a Domino's Pizza franchisee obtained a preliminary injunction against termination and Domino's appealed. The court dismissed Domino's appeal, finding that keeping one pizza franchisee in operation posed no threat of ongoing "irreparable harm" to Domino's overall business.

The court compared Domino's situation to that of a bar owner prohibited from offering topless dancing. Just as the bar owner could serve alcohol and offer non-topless dancing, so could Domino's operate the rest of its entire system while this one franchisee continued in business.

In *Novus Franchising, Inc. v. AZ Glassworks, LLC*, No. 12-CV-1771, 2012 U.S. Dist. LEXIS 186996 (D. Minn. Sept. 27, 2012), Novus sought injunctive relief (1) against trademark infringement by an affiliate of the terminated franchisee and (2) enforcing a covenant not to compete against the franchisee entity. The court granted injunctive relief against trademark infringement, but denied the request for covenant not to compete relief, stating that it was unclear as to whether the entity in question ever signed a non-compete. In any event, the court added that since the entity in question was not actually competing, there was no "irreparable harm" necessary for injunctive relief.

The District of Colorado court granted a preliminary injunction against a former Play It Again Sports franchisee who continued to display certain of Winmark's trademarks post-termination. The court found both a substantial likelihood of success on the Lanham Act claim and irreparable harm through use of the marks. *Winmark Corp. v. Schneeberger*, No. 13-CV-0274, 2013 U.S. Dist. LEXIS 37804 (D. Col. Mar. 19, 2013). The court failed to address Winmark's arguments under its post-termination non-competition provisions.

Stuller, Inc. v. Steak N Shake Enterprises, Inc., 695 F.3d 676 (7th Cir. 2012), involved a demand by the franchisor that Stuller sell all items at his Steak N Shake franchise at the price dictated by Steak N Shake. The franchisee sought and obtained a preliminary injunction at the trial court against complying with this pricing requirement. The franchisor appealed, stating that Stuller had caused its own harm by non-compliance and, therefore, under Seventh Circuit precedent, could not obtain injunctive relief. The Seventh Circuit disagreed, finding that the "self-inflicted harm" rule was not a blanket prohibition on obtaining injunctive relief, and holding that Stuller would suffer irreparable harm because if it changed its prices it would have great difficulty changing them back, and this substantial harm could not be remedied by a final judgment on the merits.

In *Dunkin' Donuts Franchising LLC v. Oza Bros., Inc.*, No. 10-13606, 2012 U.S. Dist. LEXIS 140595 (E.D. Mich. Sept. 28, 2012), as summarized in Chapter 3 II.A., the court granted Dunkin' Donuts preliminary injunction motion against a franchisee who was properly terminated for intentional underreporting of sales and tax evasion, but nevertheless, continued to use the Dunkin' trademarks post-termination.

In *7-Eleven, Inc. v. Upadhyaya*, No. 12-5541, 2013 U.S. Dist. LEXIS 29091 (E.D. Pa. Mar. 1, 2013) (*see also* Chapter 3.II.A.), 7-Eleven was granted a permanent injunction ordering the franchisee to surrender his store and leave the premises. *See* summary at Chapter 3.II.A.

VIII.   Implied Covenant Of Good Faith And Fair Dealing

Franchisees continued to struggle again this year to properly plead a prove good faith and fair dealing claims. Of the half dozen reported cases this Reporting Period, only one favored the franchisee.

A.   CASES GRANTING MOTION TO DISMISS THE IMPLIED COVENANT CLAIM

Damabeh v. 7-Eleven, Inc., No. 12-CV-1739, 2013 U.S. Dist. LEXIS 66565 (N.D. Cal. May 8, 2013), summarized in Chapter 3.II.A., involved many issues, including a poorly-pled good faith and fair dealing claim.

The court was highly critical of Damabeh's sloppy pleading on good faith and fair dealing. However, the court did take time to examine what would seem to be the crux of Damabeh's complaint – that 7-Eleven's determination that the store could not be opened in 30 days had to be exercised in good faith. The court found this argument was a bridge too far, stating that a court should only limit contractual discretion when to do so would be necessary to avoid an unenforceable and illusory agreement.

The court dismissed Damabeh's complaint without leave to replead.

B. CASES DENYING MOTION TO DISMISS THE IMPLIED COVENANT CLAIM

No such cases were reported this year.

C. CASES GRANTING SUMMARY JUDGMENT TO DISMISS IMPLIED COVENANT CLAIM

Texas courts' general disdain for the implied covenant of good faith and fair dealing was evident again this year. In *Mailing and Shipping Systems, Inc. v. Neopost USA, Inc.*, No. 12-CV-37, 2013 U.S. Dist. LEXIS 44909 (W.D. Tex. Mar. 28, 2013), summarized in Chapter 3.II.A., a dealer of postage meters and mailing machines complained that it had an exclusive territory. The franchisor had a policy against such encroachment, but did nothing to protect the dealer from the encroaching dealers.

The dealer fell behind on its sales quota and received a 30-day notice of termination. The Operations Manual had stated dealers would receive 90 days' notice of termination. The court found no "special relationship" between the parties and, therefore, no common law covenant of good faith and fair dealing under Texas law. The court mused briefly about whether the Texas Uniform Commercial Code's covenant of good faith and fair dealing might apply.

The court then determined that even if such a covenant might apply, the two claimed breaches (not policing encroachment and not giving proper notice) could not give rise to a good faith and fair dealing claim since nothing in the contract required 90 days' notice or the policy of franchisee encroachment. The franchisor was granted summary judgment.

Watkins, Inc. v. Chilkoot Distributing, Inc., 719 F.3d 987 (8th Cir. 2013), involved a dispute between Watkins, a Minnesota manufacturer of personal care, household and organic products and Chilkoot Distributing, a Canadian distributor, over whether Watkins properly terminated the parties' business relationship.

Watkins and Chilkoot signed two different agreements – a 1988 "Dealer Agreement" and a 2006 "International Associate Agreement." There was a dispute between the parties as to whether the 2006 agreement was intended to supersede and replace the 1988 agreement. Watkins believed that only the 2006 agreement governed the parties' relationship, but Chilkoot believed that certain portions of the relationship was still governed by the 1988 agreement.

Chilkoot had successfully recruited a sales associate named the Lambert Group to help sell Watkins' insect repellent products in Quebec. The Lambert Group was wildly successful in selling insect repellent, and Chilkoot received commissions from these sales. Due to the Lambert Group's impressive sales volume, Chilkoot, under its contract(s), also received lower wholesale pricing from Watkins.

By late 2008, Watkins determined that the Chilkoot-Lambert Group relationship was hurting Watkins' bottom line. Watkins was paying Chilkoot too much in commissions, and Chilkoot's earned discount on product was too high. Watkins informed Chilkoot and the Lambert Group that the parties needed to negotiate an arrangement that was more profitable to Watkins. They never did.

In January 2009, Watkins reclassified Chilkoot as a "manufacturer's representative," and Watkins dealt directly with the Lambert Group. This change eliminated Chilkoot's commission on the Lambert Group's sales. As an accommodation, Watkins offered Chilkoot a fifty percent lower commission on the Lambert Group's sales for the remainder of 2009. Chilkoot accepted these payments.

Chilkoot's attorney sent Watkins a letter in May of 2009 alleging that the reclassification breached the parties' agreements. Watkins quickly filed suit in Minnesota, asking for a declaratory judgment that it had the right to do what it had done. Chilkoot counterclaimed. In 2009 and 2010, the case made its way through the court system for the first time. The parties cross-moved for summary judgment and the district court granted Watkins summary judgment based upon its right under the 2006 agreement. On appeal, the Eighth Circuit stated that the genuine issues of material fact existed on whether the 2006 agreement superseded the 1988 agreement, and the matter was remanded. *Watkins, Inc. v. Chilkoot Distributing, Inc.*, 655 F.3d 802 (8th Cir. 2011).

Chilkoot fared no better on remand. The district court found the second time around that, under either the 1988 agreement or the 2006 agreement, Watkins had the right to reclassify Chilkoot. The court granted Watkins summary judgment again. Chilkoot appealed again.

This time, the Eighth Circuit affirmed, finding that nothing in the parties' agreements or the implied covenant of good faith and fair dealing precluded Watkins from "reclassifying a sales associate as a manufacturing [*sic*] representative." While the district court had also noted that the Lambert Group's sales efforts had technically violated Watkins' stated corporate policies (so the change was justified due to this breach of agreement), the Eighth Circuit affirmed only on the basis that the 1988 and 2006 agreements did not prohibit the reclassification of Chilkoot.

With respect to Chilkoot's argument under the covenant of good faith and fair dealing, the Eighth Circuit took the position that, since Watkins had no express contractual obligation not to reclassify Chilkoot, the covenant had no express contract term to which it could attach. Therefore, the Eighth Circuit affirmed the grant of summary judgment on this issue as well. The Eighth Circuit also found that Chilkoot's equitable claims were barred by an unambiguous written agreement, since the parties had a clear agreement on compensation, the court could not award Chilkoot equitable compensation.

In *Royal Dispatch Services, Inc. v. UBS Financial Services, Inc.*, summarized in Chapter 3.II.C., the court found that Royal Dispatch's good faith and fair dealing claim was based upon the same facts that the court had already found would support a straight breach of contract claim. Therefore, the good faith and fair dealing claim was duplicative and would be dismissed.

See also Grill Holdings, L.L.C. v. Camellia Grill Holdings, Inc., Nos. 2012-CA-1642 and 2012-CA-1643, 2013 La. App. LEXIS 1321 (La. Ct. App. May 8, 2013), previously summarized in Chapter 3.II.A.

D.   RULINGS ON THE IMPLIED COVENANT CLAIM FOLLOWING TRIAL

In *BMW Financial Services, NA, LLC v. Rio Grande Valley Motors, Inc.*, No. 11-2192, 2012 U.S. Dist. LEXIS 142440 (S.D. Tex. Oct. 1, 2012), one issue was whether BMW's financing arm enforced its floorplan financing contract in good faith. The court found that the car dealer/financing company arrangement was <u>not</u> a "special relationship" and no covenant of good faith and fair dealing attached.

In *Stuller, Inc. v. Steak N Shake Enterprises, Inc.*, 695 F.3d 676 (7th Cir. 2012) (*see* Chapter 5.VII.B supra), the Seventh Circuit affirmed a preliminary injunction in favor of a franchisee where the primary underlying claim was a violation of a covenant of good faith and fair dealing by the franchisor through its decision to set all of the franchisee's prices.

IX.   Fraud

As is the case most years, franchisees, dealers and distributors brought a number of common law fraud claims in the past 12 months, enjoying mixed results. Different jurisdictions issued vastly different decisions, particularly in the area of disclaimers and "reasonable reliance."

A.   PLEADING FRAUD WITH PARTICULARITY

In *WW, LLC v. The Coffee Beanery, Ltd.*, No. 05-3360, 2012 U.S. Dist. LEXIS 121347 (D. Md. Aug. 27, 2012), the court determined that the plaintiff franchisee had not adequately pled common law fraud against two individual defendants. Therefore, that claim was dismissed. The remainder of the case continued.

Approximately eleven months later, after what the court described as "extensive discovery," both parties moved for summary judgment – the defendant on all of the plaintiffs' remaining claims and the plaintiff on only certain of its claims. The court denied plaintiff's motion. The court granted in part, and denied in part, defendant's motion for summary judgment. *See WW, LLC v. The Coffee Beanery, Ltd.*, No. 05-3360, 2013 U.S. Dist. LEXIS 100673 (D. Md. July 17, 2013).

WW had brought claims based upon seven misrepresentations or omissions in the UFOC it had been provided. The court stated:

> This is a case of buyers' remorse. The question presented by the parties' pending cross-motions for summary judgment is whether Plaintiffs have produced sufficient evidence that their remorse is the result of misrepresentations by Defendants, to take their claim to trial. Based on the substantial record developed through extensive discovery, the Court now determines that they have.

Volvo Trucks North America v. Andy Mohr Truck Center, No. 12-CV-448, 2012 U.S. Dist. LEXIS 145054 (S.D. Ind. Oct. 9, 2012), as summarized in Chapter 5.V., involved the very unusual claim made by a truck manufacturer that it was defrauded into a dealer agreement by the false representations of a dealer and its promises/guarantees on how it would perform as a dealer.

The court dismissed all of Volvo's claims based upon the alleged fraud, finding that all of the promises/guarantees were promises of future conduct, not actionable as fraud.

In *Chicago Male Medical Clinic, LLC v. Ultimate Management, Inc.*, No. 12-CV-5542, 2012 U.S. Dist. LEXIS 183257 (N.D. Ill. Dec. 28, 2012), summarized in Chapter 1.I., the court found that Chicago Male had failed to plead common law or statutory fraud with particularity, and had failed to establish a right to sue under the Illinois Consumer Fraud Act.

See also Accor Franchising N. Am., LLC v. Gemini Hotels, Inc., No. 12-CV-541, 2012 U.S. Dist. LEXIS 152988 (E.D. Mo. Oct. 23, 2012) (franchisee failed to allege specific persons, statements, timing, circumstances and how franchisee was injured; fraud claim dismissed under Rule 9(b)).

B.   STANDING TO SUE

In *Meade v. Kiddie Academy Domestic Franchising, LLC*, No. 12-2147, 2012 U.S. App. LEXIS 21283 (3d Cir. Oct. 15, 2012), the Third Circuit affirmed the lower court's dismissal of an action brought by the president and principal shareholder of a franchisee in his individual capacity. Meade alleged, primarily, that illegal earnings claims were made and that Kiddie Academy failed to provide services as promised.

The Third Circuit found that Meade had no standing to bring claims in his own name since all of his claims alleged injury to his corporation and alleged no "direct individual injury."

C.   RELIANCE

1.   Actual Reliance

In *ABC Seamless Siding & Windows, Inc. v. Ward*, 398 S.W.3d 27 (Mo. Ct. App. 2013), a Missouri-based ABC Seamless franchisee, Martin, sued a local insurance agent, Ward, for representing that Martin would not need workers' compensation insurance to operate his franchise.

Martin checked with the State of Missouri and was told he needed to file for an exemption from the workers' compensation law. Martin did so. Martin then obtained a project and hired a subcontractor who falsely stated that he had workers' compensation coverage. The subcontractor's employee cut off his fingertip and sued the subcontractor and Martin. Martin paid the injured party $35,000 and sued Ward for fraud for falsely stating that Martin did not need workers' compensation insurance.

The trial court granted Ward summary judgment and Martin appealed. The Missouri Court of Appeals affirmed, finding that Martin had not, in fact, relied upon Ward's statements since Martin had checked the statements with the State of Missouri. As a result, there was no "justifiable reliance" by Martin on Ward's statements and no fraud.

Another iteration of *Damabeh v. 7-Eleven, Inc.*, No. 12-CV-1739, 2012 U.S. Dist. LEXIS 130333 (N.D. Cal. Sept. 12, 2012), summarized in Chapter 3.II.A, involved a claim for fraud based upon 7-Eleven's statement that Damabeh's store could reopen in a week. The court found that Damabeh may have identified a false statement, but he never relied upon the statement or suffered any monetary loss as a result of the statement. Therefore, the fraud claim was dismissed.

2.   *Reasonable Reliance*

A major battlefield in franchise law is whether contractual disclaimers, no representations clauses, checklists and integration clauses render reliance upon oral misrepresentations unreasonable. The cases came to vastly different conclusions this year.

a.   Contract Clauses Don't Preclude Fraud Claim

Hanley v. Doctors Express Franchising, LLC, No. 12-CV-95, 2013 U.S. Dist. LEXIS 25340 (D. Md. Feb. 25, 2013), more fully summarized at Chapter 2.I.C, involved common law and statutory fraud claims brought by failed Doctors Express franchisees alleging false representations by Doctors Express with respect to initial investment, initial capital requirements, credentialing and contracting, projected earnings and financial performance. Doctors Express moved to dismiss or, alternatively, for summary judgment.

The court denied the motion to dismiss, finding that Hanley had adequately pled false and misleading statements and omissions and that reliance on those statements and omissions were not overcome by the various disclaimers in the FDD and franchise agreement. At best, the disclaimers presented a fact issue on reasonable reliance that the jury could address at trial.

One case cited and relied upon by the *Hanley* court was a case decided only 13 days earlier in the Western District of Kentucky, *Long John Silver's Inc. v. Nickleson*, No. 11-CV-93, 2013 U.S. Dist. LEXIS 18391 (W.D. Ky. Feb. 12, 2013). In 2008, A&W sought to convince Nickleson to build a new, more expensive type of drive-in franchise in Inver Grove Heights, Minnesota. Nickleson alleged that A&W eventually induced him to purchase the franchise through false and misleading financial projections and statements such as "Wisconsin and Florida drive-in franchises are doing great" when, in fact, they were failing miserably. After opening, Nickleson's drive-in failed miserably, forcing Nickleson to tap equity in the other three franchises, and eventually driving all four franchises into bankruptcy.

A&W sued Nickleson in Kentucky, successfully denying Nickleson a Minnesota venue. Nickleson counterclaimed for common law fraud and violations of the Minnesota Franchise Act. With respect to the statutory and common law fraud claims, A&W moved for summary judgment, stating that the claims were barred by contractual disclaimers which negated reasonable reliance as a matter of law. The court rejected this argument and found that an individual franchisee's reliance was a question of fact and the existence of a disclaimer did not negate reliance as a matter of law. The court also refused to find the disclaimers completely void.

On the Kentucky common law fraud claim, the court found that while disclaimers are enforceable if they specifically negate alleged representations, the disclaimers relied upon by A&W were so broad that they could not negate (and did not specifically negate) the very specific misrepresentations alleged by Nickleson.

The court did dismiss Nickleson's material omission claim, finding A&W owed no special duty to Nickleson and that the franchise agreement encouraged Nickleson to do his own due diligence.

Another blow to disclaimers came in *C&M Hardware, LLC v. True Value Co.*, No. 211AP1047, 2013 Wis. App. LEXIS 404 (Wis. Ct. App. May 9, 2013), where C&M alleged fraud in the inducement by True Value. True Value relied upon two broad and general "disclaimer" clauses. One was a broad "no representations" clause, and the other was an integration clause. The court found that neither clause could defeat C&M's fraud claim under Wisconsin law, because neither clause specifically set forth the torts that True Value was trying to disclaim. Since the disclaimers did not mention "fraud" or "misrepresentation," the disclaimers were ineffective. Therefore, the trial court's grant of summary judgment to True Value was reversed and remanded.

b. Contract Clauses Do Preclude Fraud Claims

In *Wingate Inns International v. Swindall*, No. 12-248, 2012 U.S. Dist. LEXIS 152608 (D.N.J. Oct. 22, 2012) the District of New Jersey held that a franchise agreement's integration clause barred a terminated franchisee's counterclaim for fraudulent inducement, because it prevented her from establishing that she reasonably relied on the franchisor's representations in deciding to enter into the franchise relationship.

Franchisor Wingate Inns International (Wingate) alleged that the franchisee transferred control of the hotel without the franchisor's consent. Wingate then terminated the franchise agreement and sought an accounting of revenues earned and recovery of outstanding fees. Defendant asserted, among other things, counterclaims based on fraud in the inducement and violation of the New Jersey Consumer Fraud Act (NJCFA).

The counterclaim for fraudulent inducement alleged that before the franchisee purchased a franchise, Wingate's sales personnel falsely assured Ms. Swindall that the hotel would be "an extremely profitable business" and that if she built a 116-room hotel, she would receive "extra marketing dollars." Wingate argued that the franchisee's fraudulent inducement claim must fail because she could not establish the required element of reasonable reliance on a false representation, in light of the express terms of the franchise agreement.

The agreement contained numerous acknowledgements that the franchisee relied on no promise made by the franchisor or its representatives that was not included in the franchise agreement, which constituted the entire agreement among the parties. Based on these provisions, the court concluded, the franchisee's reliance on alleged prior representations by Wingate or its representatives was not reasonable.

The franchisee also alleged that Wingate violated the NJCFA, which prohibits any unconscionable commercial practice, deception, fraud, false pretense, false promise, and misrepresentation with the intent that others rely upon it in connection with the sale of merchandise. The court found that the NJCFA was intended to protect consumers who purchased "goods or services generally sold to the public at large," that the franchisee was not a consumer, and that a franchise is not merchandise. Even though franchises and distributorships may be available to the public at large for purchase, the court reasoned, they are businesses, not consumer goods and services, and thus they are not covered by the NJCFA.

A strong legal rule in favor of disclaimers was applied in *Ayu's Global Tire, LLC v. Big O Tires, LLC*, No. B236930, 2013 Cal. App. Unpub. LEXIS 3721 (Cal. Ct. App. May 24, 2013). Despite making a plethora of fraud and misrepresentation claims against Big O Tires on everything from Big O's expertise, to the statement that Ayu's needed no experience to succeed, to the false offer of training, to the false claims of franchisee profitability, to Big O guaranteeing a supply of tires, Ayu's Global lost at the summary judgment stage at the trial court. Ayu's Global appealed.

Ayu's Global fared no better with the California Court of Appeals. The panel found that Colorado law applied and all of the fraud claims were barred by a combination of the FDD and Franchise Agreement disclosures and Colorado's general common law rule that a purchaser on "inquiry notice" must seek out facts which would lead him to discovery of a seller's fraud. Given this "buyer beware" attitude expressed in Colorado law, the court had no trouble finding that all of the various FDD and Franchise Agreement language and disclaimers put the franchisee on "inquiry notice" and he thus could not reasonably rely upon the alleged statements made by the franchisor. The franchisee needed to conduct its own inquiry and had not done so. Summary judgment was affirmed.

In *Palermo Gelato, LLC v. Pine Gelato, Inc.*, No. 12-CV-00931, 2013 U.S. Dist. LEXIS 85925 (W.D. Pa. June 19, 2013), the court granted licensor Pine Gelato's motion to dismiss a fraud in the inducement claim based upon the integration clause in the parties' license agreement.

, Franchisee Palermo Gelato signed up as a Pittsburgh-area licensee of Pine Gelato in 2008 and signed a license agreement which stated that it contained the parties' agreement and superseded "any prior understandings between or among any of [the parties]."

Palermo alleged that Pine induced Palermo into the relationship by representing orally and in writing that Pine was the owner and/or originator of a top-shelf special gelato recipe. Around September of 2011, Palermo discovered that Pine did not own any recipe for small-batch crafted gelato and, instead, purchased its gelato in bulk from G.S. Gelato. G.S. Gelato product could be purchased on a wholesale basis by anyone through G.S. Gelato's website.

Palermo sued Pine, alleging fraud in the inducement. Pine moved to dismiss under Rule 12(b)(6), arguing that Palermo's claims were barred by the integration clause of the parties' license agreement. After reviewing Pennsylvania Supreme Court precedent, the court determined that, since Palermo's allegations of fraud dealt with the gelato recipe and the manufacturing and supply of gelato, they dealt with the "same subject matter" as the license agreement. Therefore, Palermo's "understanding" as to the source of the gelato was barred by the parol evidence rule.

The court went one step further and noted that, under Pennsylvania law, a misrepresentation claim is barred even if the alleged representations are not contrary to the parties' written agreement. All that is required under Pennsylvania law to bar the claim is the fact that the agreement deals with the same subject matter as the alleged representations, and the alleged representations are not specifically contained in the parties' agreement.

The California Supreme Court overturned the nearly 70 year old precedent, *Bank of America etc. Association v. Pendergrass*, 48 P.2d 659 (Cal. 1935)

("Pendergrass") in its January 2013 decision, *Riverisland Cold Storage, Inc. v. Fresno-Madera Production Credit Association*, 55 Cal.4th 1169 (Cal. 2013). *Pendergrass* required a party alleging fraud in the inducement to prove the fraud "tend[ed] to establish some independent fact or representation, some fraud in the procurement of the instrument or some breach of confidence concerning its use, and not a promise directly at variance with the promise of the writing." The plaintiffs in *Riverisland*, Lance and Pamela Workman (the "Workmans"), fell behind on loan payments to the defendant, Fresno-Madera Production Credit Association ("FMPC"). The Workmans entered into a debt restructuring agreement that, on paper, provided for a three month extension for the Workmans to bring current their delinquency and had the Workmans pledge eight pieces of property as collateral.

The Workmans alleged that the FMPC's Vice President told them two weeks before entering into the restructuring agreement that the extension would be for two years and that the plaintiffs would be pledging two pieces of property as collateral. According to the Workmans, these promises were repeated at the time the plaintiffs signed the extension agreement (the plaintiffs admitted they did not read the agreement). The Workmans sued, alleging fraud, and the defendant invoked the rule of *Pendergrass*. The trial court granted summary judgment to the defendants, holding the promises contradicted the writing. The California Court of Appeal then reversed the trial court, holding that the alleged fraud was not a promise that contradicted the writing but, instead, a misrepresentation of fact about the writing's contents.

In ruling that the parol evidence rule would not bar this alleged fraud, the California Supreme Court focused upon California Code of Civil Procedure Section 1856, subdivision (f), which establishes a broad exception to the operation of the parol evidence rule. The provision reads: "[w]here the validity of the agreement is the fact in dispute, this section does not exclude evidence relevant to that issue." In deciding to overrule its precedent, the court recognized that there were no restrictions upon proving fraud under the Restatements, that the treatises generally recognized a pure fraud exception to the parol evidence rule, and that the majority view does not place a limitation on the fraud exception to the parol evidence rule. The supreme court affirmed the court of appeals, stating that "it was never intended that the parol evidence rule should be used as a shield to prevent the proof of fraud."

The California Court of Appeal fleshed out the meaning of the California Supreme Court's *Riverisland Cold Storage* decision in *Julius Castle*

Restaurant, Inc. v. Payne, 216 Cal.App.4th 1423 (Cal. Ct. App. 2013). The case arose out of the purchase of assets for a restaurant by the buyers, Julius Castle Restaurant, Inc. ("JCRI"), Charles Stinson, and John Bonjean (collectively "Plaintiffs"), from the sellers, James Payne and Top of the Rock Castle, LLC. The buyers had purchased Julius Castle, both a restaurant and an official historical landmark in the City and County of San Francisco. In 2007, Stinson and Bonjean, through JCRI, entered into a long-term lease with the defendants. The lease included an independent investigation clause and purported to void any extra-contractual representations made by the landlord to the tenant.

In their first amended complaint, Plaintiffs alleged defendant Payne had made substantial improvements to the building without obtaining proper permits, had misrepresented the building was in good condition, and falsely told Plaintiffs he would make good on defects in the building or equipment if they were not in good condition. Payne denied that he had represented he would fix any equipment or defect on the premises.

Considering whether the alleged guarantee of the restaurant's equipment was parol evidence, the California Court of Appeal determined such a guarantee would directly contradict the independent investigation clause, as well as the lease's waiver of statutes requiring Payne to maintain or repair the property, or allowing JCRI to make repairs and deduct the cost. Thus, the evidence offered by Plaintiffs was parol evidence (and Plaintiffs could not use the evidence to prove a breach of contract). Nonetheless, the appeals court recognized it should admit the evidence in relation to plaintiffs' fraudulent inducement claim following *Riverisland Cold Storage*. In an effort to distinguish that case, Defendants argued the parties in *Julius Castle Restaurant* were sophisticated and therefore Plaintiffs could not claim fraud, and that there had been no showing of disproportionate bargaining power. However, given the unambiguous holding of *Riverisland Cold Storage*, the appeals court refused to create exceptions to the fraud parol evidence exception.

c. Mixed Result

Appearing to strike a middle ground on the disclaimer issue is *Beaver v. Inkmart, LLC*, No. 12-60028, 2012 U.S. Dist. LEXIS 125051 (S.D. Fla. Sept. 4, 2012) which found that FDD and franchise agreement disclaimers were sufficient to bar Beaver's common law, fraud claim, earnings claim, damages claim and Florida Franchise Act claim, but not sufficient to bar Beaver's claims related to FDD non-disclosures under the legal theories of (1) violation of the Florida Deceptive and Unfair Trade Practices Act, or (2) common law fraud, or (3) common law rescission.

The court also found that reasonable reliance is <u>not</u> necessary for a rescission claim, so Inkmart's fraudulent promises of support, while contradicted by the franchise agreement, could still form the basis of a rescission claim. Similarly, "no representation" and "integration" clause had no impact on a statutory non-disclosure claim under the FDUTPA.

D.   ECONOMIC LOSS RULE

Applying Arizona law, a federal court found that a franchise trainer, Biz Card, could bring a fraud in the inducement claim against a corporation specializing in franchise start-up and expansion. In *International Franchise Solutions, LLC v. BizCard Xpress, LLC*, No.13-CV-0086, 2013 U.S. Dist. LEXIS 69600 (D. Ariz. May 16, 2013). The court held that, while the "economic loss doctrine" barred negligence claims, negligent misrepresentation claims, and fraud claims seeking recovery of damages, the economic loss rule did <u>not</u> preclude a rescission claim based upon fraud in the inducement.

Similarly, in *Beaver v. Inkmart, LLC*, No. 12-60028, 2012 U.S. Dist. LEXIS 125051 (S.D. Fla. Sept. 4, 2012) (*see* Chapter 5.X.C.), the court concluded that promissory fraud claims addressing issues addressed in the franchise agreement would be barred by the economic loss rule, but claims based upon FDD omissions would not.

While not a case involving a fraud claim, *Huddle House, Inc. v. Two Views, Inc.*, (*see* Chapter 5.IV *supra*) found that a franchisor's negligence claim was barred by the parties' franchise agreement and the economic loss rule. The franchisor's remedy was in contract, not tort, despite its claim that the franchisee was "damaging" its "trademarked property."

In *ERA Franchise Systems, LLC v. Hoppens Realty, Inc.*, summarized in Chapter 5.VI., the terminated franchisee sued for conversion based upon facts related to ERA's alleged breach of contract. The court found that, under New Jersey law, the economic loss doctrine barred tort claims for damages arising out of the contractual relationship. Therefore, the conversion claim was dismissed.

E.   SUFFICIENT EVIDENCE OF FRAUD

In *Tufail v. Midwest Hospitality, LLC*, 833 N.W.2d 586 (Wis. 2013), the Wisconsin Supreme Court, reversing a Wisconsin Court of Appeals ruling, found that a franchisee <u>could</u> legally operate a Church's Chicken restaurant in Milwaukee and, therefore, the landlord's representation that no ordinances prevented the operation of a Church's Chicken restaurant was <u>not</u> false. Therefore, the trial court's judgment in favor of the landlord was affirmed.

The landlord knew that the City of Milwaukee was upset with his operation of his "New York Chicken" restaurant and its drive-thru window because the restaurant attracted a late-night crowd that led to crime problems and litter that blew around the neighborhood. Nevertheless, the landlord represented that there were no ordinances that prevented the tenant's intended use as a Church's Chicken.

When the Church's franchisee applied for a special use permit, the City of Milwaukee granted a one-year permit with no renewal option conditioned upon (1) the restaurant closing at 9:00 p.m., and (2) the franchisee picking up all garbage on the ground within one block of the premises. The franchisee found these provisions prohibitively expensive and advised the landlord that it would no longer pay rent. The landlord sued for breach of contract.

The Wisconsin Supreme Court found that the franchisee could, in fact, operate a Church's Chicken restaurant at the premises and nothing stated by the landlord was false. While the franchisee might not <u>like</u> the early closing time and garbage pick-up restrictions, the restrictions did not <u>prevent</u> the franchisee from operating. The franchisee could have bargained for lease terms that better protected it from unreasonable use restrictions, but did not do so.

In a blunt and straightforward opinion, the bankruptcy court in *Eldredge v. Crusberg*, No. 11-33205, 2013 Bankr. LEXIS 2874 (Bankr. S.D. Tex. July 17, 2013) rejected an investor's claim that he had been defrauded into investing into a Blimpie's franchise by false earnings claims. The court found that a representation of a $6,522 monthly cash flow was not materially different than the actual $5,110.04 monthly cash flow.

X.   Vicarious Liability

Spurred in part by recent Massachusetts opinion dictating that janitorial franchisees may actually be employees of the franchisor, there were a large number of vicarious liability opinions this year, including claims brought by customers, guests and employees. Results were mixed, and courts continue to struggle with the analysis of how much "control" is necessary for a franchisor to be liable for a franchisee's actions or inactions.

A. "OUTSIDE THE SCOPE OF EMPLOYMENT" DEFENSE

Franchisors sometimes defend against vicarious liability claims by first arguing the franchisee's employee's conduct was outside the scope of employment. This argument won the day for Domino's Pizza LLC ("Domino's") in *Holt v. Torino*, No. 2012 CA 1579, 2013 La. App. LEXIS 832 (La. Ct. App. Apr. 26, 2013). The plaintiff, Milton Holt, was injured in an auto accident when an employee, Tammy Torino, of a Domino's franchisee, RPM Pizza, strayed across the center line and struck the plaintiff's vehicle head on. Torino was driving home from RPM Pizza at the time of the accident. The plaintiff brought claims, amongst others, against RPM Pizza for negligence, and against Domino's on the theory of vicarious liability. RPM Pizza and Domino's subsequently moved for summary judgment, asserting Torino was not within the scope of employment, and Torino was not a Domino's employee. The trial court granted summary judgment for both defendants on the ground the plaintiff was not acting within the course of employment, and plaintiff appealed.

Relying upon the fact that defendant Torino was driving home from RPM Pizza at the time of the accident, the court of appeals determined she was not within the course of employment and affirmed the trial court's grant of summary judgment for both franchisee and franchisor. The court determined that three prerequisites must exist for an act to be within the course of employment, the act: (1) must be "'of the kind that he is employed to perform;'" (2) must occur "'substantially within the authorized limits of time and space;'" and (3) must be "'activated at least in part by a purpose to serve the employer.'" Additionally, the court pointed out four separate considerations that would guide its inquiry of whether, based on time, place, and causation, the employee's conduct could be considered a fairly attributable risk to the employer's business. The factors include whether the act was "primarily employment rooted: reasonably incidental to performance of employment duties; occurred during working hours and was on the employer's premises." The court stated the general rule that an employee's travel to and from work is not considered an employment function.

The plaintiff attempted to avoid the general rule by relying upon evidence that Torino's manager, at the time Torino was leaving work, was aware that she was "'too impaired to drive'" and, further, that the manager had given Torino specific instructions to drive herself home in case she would be needed at work later. The manager neither recalled telling Torino to drive herself home in case she would need to return later nor recalled Torino looking sleepy. The court concluded RPM Pizza and Domino's had demonstrated Torino was not on RPM Pizza's premises at the time of the act, was not then engaged in work activities, and was not doing anything "reasonably incidental" to performing employment duties while driving home. The court also relied upon the fact Torino was thirty years old at the time of the accident as evidence the defendants did not have responsibility for her actions in driving home. As the court determined Torino was not acting within the scope of employment with RPM Pizza, the court held there was no evidence of negligence on the part of Domino's.

B.   CASES FOCUSING ON "AGENCY"

In *Linke v. Heritage New London, LLC*, No. 116009956S, 2013 Conn. Super. LEXIS 635 (Conn. Super. Ct. Mar. 21, 2013), the plaintiff, Norma Linke, tripped on a carpet located in the restaurant and lounge of the Holiday Inn in which she was staying. Included in the plaintiff's six-count complaint was a claim against Intercontinental Hotels Corporation ("IHC"). IHC was the licensor of Holiday Hospitality Franchising Inc. ("HHF"), the entity responsible for exercising direct management control over the hotel. When IHC brought a motion for summary judgment, it included, amongst other things, a copy of the IHC licensing agreement.

IHC relied upon two primary arguments in moving for summary judgment: first, IHC owed the plaintiff no duty as it was not a party to the licensing agreement because its agent did not have capacity to bind it; and, second, even if it was a franchisor, it did not exercise control over the hotel. The court rejected the first argument. IHC's own motion stated it was including a copy of the IHC/HHF licensing agreement, and the capacity issue was a question of fact. The court ultimately found the second argument persuasive. In so doing, the court stated two general propositions: first, "'absent exceptional circumstances a franchisee is an independent contractor of the franchisor[,]'" and second, "'the franchisor is not liable as an agent for the torts committed by a franchisee.'" For there to be liability based upon this relationship, the court said, the level of control must rise to the level of a principal-agent relationship. The court recognized it needed to survey both the parties' relationship and also the control retained by IHC. Based on certain clauses in the license agreement, such as an independent contractor clause and an indemnity clause, the court determined this was a franchise relationship. The court found no evidence the franchisor exercised control over the rug on which the plaintiff tripped; nor did it find evidence of the franchisor's control of the premises going beyond its general rights as a franchisor. For these reasons, the court granted IHC's summary judgment motion.

Applebee's Inc., was able to avoid vicarious liability where its franchisee, Southern River Restaurants, LLC, served part of a human finger along with a patron's salad in *Chambers-Johnson v. Applebee's Restaurant, Inc.*, No. 12-CA-98, 2012 La. App. LEXIS 1130 (La. Ct. App. Sept. 11, 2012). Along with its summary judgment motion, Applebee's filed an affidavit by the area developer of Southern River that indicated Southern River employed all restaurant workers, had sole responsibility to train, supervise, and monitor its employees, and was responsible for obtaining, and safeguarding, food. The patron, May Deal Chambers-Johnson, opposed the motion by presenting the franchise agreement, which included procedures for food preparation, and demonstrated that the franchisor was responsible for training the franchisee's general and assistant managers and kitchen manager. The court found uniformity and standardization of procedures was a legitimate franchisor goal, and was advanced by the franchisee's promises to "'adhere strictly to [Applebee's] standards and specifications relating to the selection, purchase, storage, preparation, packaging, service and sale of all food and beverage products being sold at the [r]estaurant.'" As Southern River still had control of its daily restaurant operations, there was no agency. Therefore, summary judgment was affirmed.

Another decision that should make franchisors consider the potential of signage and advertising requirements to expose them to claims of apparent agency is *Ford v. Palmden Restaurants, LLC*, No. E053195, 2012 Cal. App. Unpub. LEXIS 5596 (Cal. Ct. App. July 31, 2012). This case involved a Denny's franchise, operated by Palmden Restaurants, LLC ("Palmden"). Every Saturday night for two years, at 2 a.m. in the morning, the Denny's was overtaken by members of the Gateway Posse Crips ("Crips"). Whenever the gang members would arrive, ordinary customers fled. The Crips' table-hopping and profanity were ubiquitous, and alcohol and drug use was rampant in the parking lot. In Mar. of 2003, at the initiation of a Crips member, a melee ensued at the restaurant. In a separate incident over a year later, 10 to 30 Crips members began beating a single man outside the restaurant. The plaintiff, Terrelle Ford, a patron, initially stayed inside the restaurant. However, when a number of Ford's friends attempted to stop the violence, Ford went through an emergency exit to assist them (the restaurant's main door had been locked). Ford was then severely beaten, leading to a broken upper jaw, a broken nose, and severe head trauma.

Ford brought claims against both Palmden, and against numerous related franchisor entities, including DFO, LLC, Denny's Corporation, Denny's Holdings, Inc., Denny's Inc., and Denny's Realty, Inc. (collectively referred to as "Denny's"). Ford ostensibly claimed these franchisor entities could be held liable both under theories of actual control, as well as apparent control. First, in considering the underlying liability of the franchisee, the court noted, under California law, the burden was on the plaintiff to show the injury was "actually caused by the failure to provide greater measures." That is, while proving the franchisee's knowledge of the dangerous condition, the plaintiff points to safety measures that the franchisee failed to adopt as evidence of the franchisee's negligence in protecting the plaintiff. Here, police officers recommended to the franchisee that: (1) more light be added to the parking lot; (2) the franchisee purchase "No Loitering" signs; (3) video surveillance be installed; and (4) the franchisee contract with off-duty police officers to act as security guards. Taking these security measures under consideration, the court doubted that adding signs, lighting, or security cameras would have deterred the gang members, and further doubted that a measure called for by an expert proffered by Ford, that the franchisee should have installed a panic button, would have been more effective than a 911 call. As for contracting with security guards, the court stated it was speculative as to whether guards would have deterred Ford's injuries. The court was convinced, however, one option open to the franchisee—closing down at a certain time during the night—may have been required under the circumstances.

Concluding the franchisee may potentially be liable, the court considered the liability of the Denny's franchisor entities. While the franchise agreements included an independent contractor clause, it also gave the franchisor control of franchisees' business practices, including vendors, uniforms, menus, signs, and advertising, and also required the franchisee keep the restaurant open 24 hours a day, seven days a week, unless the franchisee could demonstrate above-normal criminal activity. Franchisees could, but did not have to, post signs stating the restaurant was owned independently. The court thought the plaintiff's claim of ignorance of the restaurant's independently owned status was reasonable, as: (1) the fact some Denny's restaurants are corporate owned, and others are franchisee-operated, meant it was not common knowledge that all Denny's are by necessity franchises; (2) no signs indicated the restaurant was a franchise; and (3) Ford testified corporate advertisements promoted that Denny's was a "family style restaurant" and that a meal could be enjoyed in a "safe, and secure environment." The franchisor's public policy argument—that imposing liability here would either entice franchisors to go out of business or require them to impose higher fees—was given little weight, as Denny's "'could have easily protected itself by requiring that its licensee inform the public of his [franchisee] status in more effective ways.'"

In *Ross v. Choice Hotels International, Inc.*, No. 10-CV-1098, 2012 U.S. Dist. LEXIS 107101 (S.D. Ohio Aug. 1, 2012), the plaintiffs, Candice Ross and Tiffany Gray, sought to rent a room that would serve as a gathering place, and then place of overnight accommodation, for Shaun Ross-Mitchell, who was celebrating his birthday. Plaintiffs first went to the hotel, operated by Shree Nathaji Hospitality, Inc., and owned by GNA Properties, LLC ("GNA"), and paid for it without issue, but later that evening, upon returning with a total of five persons, the same clerk who had originally sold plaintiffs the room told them of the hotel's "no party" policy. Supposedly, the policy limited the number of persons per room to five. Plaintiffs sought a refund, but were refused; instead, the clerk called the police. Shortly thereafter, the clerk revealed the hotel, in fact, did not have a five person room limitation. The plaintiffs brought suit under 42 U.S.C. § 1981 and a state statute prohibiting public accommodation discrimination. At this stage of the proceedings, the court was considering Choice's summary judgment motion on vicarious liability.

Choice first presented an affidavit prepared by its senior counsel which sought to establish Choice in no way operates, rents, or offers public accommodations to anyone. This argument was intended to defeat the second element of the plaintiff's § 1981 claim, which requires a § 1981 plaintiff "sought to make or enforce a contract for services ordinarily provided by the defendant." However, the plaintiff recognized that it could satisfy § 1981's requirements by establishing Choice was the apparent owner of the hotel. In support of this, the plaintiffs pointed to Choice's franchise agreement and rules, which required GNA to use Comfort Suites signage and logos in and around the hotel and, furthermore, Choice's directory and website both list the hotel as a Comfort Suites hotel. The court disregarded some of this evidence, as plaintiffs had only demonstrated they saw signs and logos at the hotel (there was no evidence they relied upon the directory or website listing). Plaintiffs averred they went to the hotel because they saw a road sign bearing the Comfort Suites logo, believed the hotel was owned and operated by Comfort Suites, that the sales clerk was wearing a Comfort Suites uniform and that the receipt they received bore the Comfort Suites insignia. Notwithstanding the fact the court found contradictory testimony in the record conflicting with the plaintiffs' claims of reliance on the Comfort Suites brand, the court held there was a genuine issue of material fact on the issue of apparent agency. Further still, and perhaps of more concern to franchisors, the court said it agreed there was a "genuine issue of material fact over the degree of control exercised by Choice Hotels over GNA." Thus, the court denied the summary judgment motion.

CHAPTER 5

C.   CASES ADDRESSING "CONTROL" BY FRANCHISOR

1.   Franchisor Wins

In *Courtland v. GCEP – Surprise, LLC*, No. 12-CV-00349, 2013 U.S. Dist. LEXIS 105780 (D. Ariz. July 29, 2013), Buffalo Wild Wings was granted summary judgment finding that it had no liability for the actions of franchisee's bartender in sexually harassing bartender/waitress Angela Courtland.

The District of Arizona stated that the appropriate rule of law was that a franchisor could be vicariously liable for a franchisee's misconduct if the franchisor "controls or has the right to control the daily conduct or operation of the particular instrumentality or aspect of the franchisee's business that is alleged to have caused the harm." In the sexual harassment context, that meant the franchisor could be liable if it controlled the daily hiring, firing and supervision of franchisee employees.

Buffalo Wild Wings did not have a contractual right to control these sorts of matters and, in fact, did not exercise any such control. The sole guidance to franchisees on sexual harassment was to tell Franchisees to follow the law. In light of the undisputed facts, Buffalo Wild Wings was found to be not vicariously liable as a matter of law.

Courtland's subjective belief that she was employed by Buffalo Wild Wings was found to be (1) not objectively reasonable, and (2) not based upon Buffalo Wild Wings' manifestations. Therefore, her claim under an "apparent authority" theory was also rejected.

A case involving the control retained by car dispatch delivery service franchisors was *Leach v. Kaykov*, No. 07-CV-4060, 2013 U.S. Dist. LEXIS 8046 (E.D. N.Y. Jan. 20, 2013). In this case, defendant J. Fletcher Creamer, Inc. ("JFC"), made a contribution claim against a car dispatch franchisor, Royal Dispatch Services ("Royal"). The underlying case went to trial and, after the plaintiffs' case-in-chief and following Royal's sole fact witness, Royal moved for judgment as a matter of law. The court was required to determine whether a reasonable juror could conclude there was sufficient evidence of control between Royal and its franchisees to qualify under New Jersey's independent contractor control exception. This exception applies where the employer retains control of the "manner and means" of the contractor's work.

The court first reviewed the franchise agreement between the driver/franchisee and Royal and found that franchisees were required to either purchase and install, or lease, equipment allowing the franchisee to receive calls from the franchisor. If the franchisee leased from Royal, they would have to pay a deposit, but that, along with the franchise fee, would be returned upon termination of the franchise agreement. The franchisor collected commissions of between 18% and 24%. Additionally, the franchisee was required to attend and pass a training course. While the franchise agreement required the franchisee to comply with regulations contained in a rule book, which were in practice very specific, the court did not to see this as evidence of franchisor control, as the rulebook was "developed and implemented by a [f]ranchisee [b]oard comprised of franchisees elected by the franchisees themselves." The board could discipline drivers, as well as periodically inspect the vehicles for cleanliness. Also weighing in favor of insufficient control was the fact that franchisees were allowed to accept jobs from other dispatch companies as well as from Royal customers not dispatched through Royal. Lack of control was also shown through the franchisees' ability to hire drivers to operate their vehicles (subject to franchisor approval).

The court decided that Royal franchisees were independent and could exercise self-determination. The court saw this as was a "complete lack of control" by the franchisor, and awarded the franchisor judgment as a matter of law.

The question of a franchisor's vicarious liability for physical injury where the franchisor selected the equipment causing the injury, and set standards relating to health and employee training, was decided in favor of the franchisor in *Calvasina v. Wal-Mart Real Estate Business Trust*, No. SA-09-CA-1024, 2012 U.S. Dist. LEXIS 158735 (W.D. Tex. Nov. 5, 2012). Plaintiff Peter Calvasina, was a Service Writer/Greeter working in the Tire Lube Express ("TLE") of a Wal-Mart store located in San Antonio, Texas. He fell from a platform while working on the upper level of a tire rack system. At the time of the incident, the plaintiff was throwing or dropping a tire down from the platform. Generally, Wal-Mart employees like Mr. Calvasina are employed by Wal-Mart Associates, Inc., and this corporation leases employees to other Wal-Mart entities such as the franchisee operating this store, Wal-Mart Texas. Wal-Mart Texas operated the store pursuant to a franchise agreement with Wal-Mart Stores, Inc. Wal-Mart, Inc. was named as a defendant on the ground it exercised control over the tire rack. The court considered the franchisor's motion for summary judgment.

The posture of this case demonstrates the potential for plaintiffs and franchisors to rely on inconsistent positions at different stages of the litigation. Here, the plaintiff, in order to avoid the workers' compensation statute's exclusive remedy bar, had argued that Wal-Mart, Inc. was not his employer because the entity did not exercise control over the details of the work giving rise to the injury. Conversely, Wal-Mart, Inc. argued it was the plaintiff's employer. By contrast, in the summary judgment motion, the franchisor argued that the standard employed in determining whether there is sufficient control to establish vicarious liability is identical under Texas law to the standard which determines whether an entity is the plaintiff's employer for purposes of the workers' compensation statute. The court rejected this argument, concluding Wal-Mart, Inc.'s relationship to Mr. Calvasina was akin to that of a general contractor and sub-contractor, and therefore Wal-Mart Inc. could still owe the plaintiff a duty.

This duty could be established by proving Wal-Mart, Inc. retained the right to supervise in a manner such that the plaintiff was unable to do the work in his own way, such as by directing the order in which work is done, or forbidding the work from being done in a dangerous manner. To prevail, plaintiff either demonstrate contractual assignment of control to Wal-Mart, Inc., or Wal-Mart's actual exercise of control.

Arguing there was contractual evidence of control, the plaintiff emphasized the franchise agreement's establishing a "continuing advisory relationship" such that the franchisor would provide operating manuals with the "'standards, specifications, procedures, and techniques of the franchise system.'" Furthermore, the franchisee was required to maintain its premises, including equipment and fixtures, so as to "'conform with [the franchisor's] standards of health, cleanliness, and neatness.'" The franchisee was also required to train its employees in accord with the franchisor's training aids.

Nonetheless, the court found it dispositive that the franchise agreement did not expressly assign workplace safety to the franchisor, and indeed assigned "health standards" to Wal-Mart Texas. The court stated that the general rule of law was that a general contractor may recommend how to operate in a safe manner without establishing control. As for training, the court stated that, absent evidence either (1) Wal-Mart, Inc. knew its franchisee "routinely failed" to train its leased employees, and that Wal-Mart, Inc. had an express contractual right to correct this failure; or (2) the franchisor's materials and training requirement made the risk of injury greater for Mr. Calvasina, merely requiring the franchisee to train employees did not create liability for the franchisor.

The plaintiff also sought to rely upon the fact the franchisor selected the tire rack, and required the franchisee use the tire rack in its TLE. The court, however, required the plaintiff to prove the additional fact that the franchisor knew or should have known the tire rack was defective or dangerous. Despite numerous flaws in the installation of the tire rack, Mr. Calvasina did not present evidence the franchisor controlled installation, and thus these errors did not aid the plaintiff's claim. Furthermore, though the franchisor had the right to inspect the TLE, that fact alone was insufficient to create an issue of fact on the vicarious liability claim. Since the plaintiff did not present a convincing argument demonstrating control, the court granted summary judgment to Wal-Mart, Inc.

Summary judgment was affirmed in favor of McDonald's Corporation ("McDonald's") where a franchisee's employee beat a customer with a spatula inside a McDonald's restaurant in *Parmenter v. J & B Enterprises., Inc.*, 99 So. 3d. 207 (Miss. Ct. App. 2012). The plaintiff, Parmenter, entered the restaurant to check on the status of her drive-through order and an argument ensued with the cashier. Following this argument, the cashier returned to the kitchen, picked up a spatula, and delivered blows to the plaintiff's cheek, head, and arm. The plaintiff sued, naming McDonald's as a defendant. McDonald's submitted an affidavit of senior counsel of the franchisor that, *inter alia*, stated McDonald's "'does not, nor does it have the right to, control the day-to-day activities necessary to carrying on the business operations of the restaurant[.].'" The trial court gave heavy weight to this affidavit, determining McDonald's concern was with the result of its franchisees' efforts, and not the details of their work. On appeal, the plaintiff pointed to the McDonald's logo on the building and on employees' uniforms, the franchise agreement, and McDonald's reputation for providing good food, but cited no relevant authority that the franchisor could be vicariously liable under Mississippi law. Therefore, the court ruled the plaintiff was procedurally barred from arguing vicarious liability. The court stated as an alternative holding that the franchisor could not be held vicariously liable.

In another victory for McDonalds, in *Bracken v. McDonald's Corp.*, No. 13-CV-00697, 2013 U.S. Dist. LEXIS 94481 (D. Or. July 2, 2013), the court granted Defendant McDonald's Corp.'s motion to dismiss after concluding that Plaintiff Bracken failed to state a claim against the franchisor. Plaintiff commenced the action against the franchisor after a franchisee's employee allegedly violated the American with Disabilities Act (ADA) at one of the restaurants in which Plaintiff was a customer.

In July 2012, Plaintiff brought his dog into a McDonald's franchise in Salem, Oregon. While he was eating, a franchise employee approached him and asked for certification to indicate that his dog was a service animal according to Oregon State law. Plaintiff explained that his dog was a service animal and that no certification was required. Plaintiff also quoted the Department of Human Services website, which states that it is illegal under the ADA to deny an individual public accommodation simply because the service dog lacks proper documentation. The employee responded that she was only asking the dog, and not the Plaintiff, to leave for potential health code violations. The employee later apologized and offered to refund Plaintiff's money or prepare a new meal, but Plaintiff left.

In December 2012, Plaintiff brought a pro se claim against McDonalds, alleging a violation of his rights. In May 2013, McDonalds moved to dismiss the action. The court evaluated the claim under Rule 12(b)(6) of the Federal Rules of Civil Procedure, giving greater deference to the pro se Plaintiff. The court determined that Plaintiff had a legally cognizable claim; specifically, that he was denied admission with a service animal to a public place in violation of the ADA and state law. However, neither the complaint nor plaintiff's response brief recited the elements of a state or federal disability discrimination claim, or set forth sufficient factual allegations in support of such a claim. The complaint also failed to link McDonalds to the franchisees' employee's conduct. In other words, without allegations that McDonalds had a right to control the franchise location in which the events took place, Plaintiff could not establish the requisite agency relationship to give rise to vicarious liability. Accordingly, Plaintiff's complaint was dismissed for failure to state a claim upon which relief can be granted.

2. Franchisor Possibly Vicariously Liable Under "Control Test"

In *People v. JTH Tax, Inc.*, 212 Cal. App. 4th 1219 (Cal. Ct. App. 2013) the franchisor, JTH Tax, Inc. ("JTH"), doing business as Liberty Tax Services ("Liberty"), sought to avoid vicarious liability for the unlawful advertising of its franchisees on numerous grounds—including, that the mere right to control, and not actual control, was required under California law for the imposition of vicarious liability against franchisors, and that Liberty's extensive control of its franchisees' advertising was only to protect its own trademarks and goodwill. Liberty's arguments were all rejected. Liberty, a Delaware corporation with its headquarters in Virginia, has a system that assists with tax preparation and related loan services throughout the country. Liberty had more than 2,000 stores, franchise and company-owned, 195 of which were located in California, at the time of trial. Of significance in this case, Liberty offered "refund anticipation loans" ("RALs") and "electronic refund checks" ("ERCs"). In February of 2007, the Attorney General of California sued Liberty, claiming that advertising (both advertising run by Liberty and by Liberty's franchisees) regarding Liberty's offering of RAL and ERC services violated both federal and state law. The trial court concluded Liberty's franchisees acted as its agents, and ordered the franchisor to pay civil penalties of $50,000 for their advertisements.

The trial court recognized Liberty could exercise control to advance its own legitimate interests, but could not exercise control beyond that. The lower court focused on Liberty's operations manual as evidence of the franchisor's regulating beyond its legitimate interests, such as the franchisor's: (1) selecting which banks franchisees could offer RALs and ERCs through; (2) prohibiting franchisees from offering products/services without the franchisor's permission; (3) regulating miscellaneous details of daily operation, such as minimum operating hours, which computers could be used, and how to properly clean bathrooms; (4) reserving the right to intervene in customer disputes; (5) requiring franchisee commitment to the franchisor's filing system; (6) controlling franchisee discounting; and (7) retaining the unilateral right to modify the operations manual at any time. Moreover, the court found the franchisor exercised a "particularly extensive" right of control over franchisee advertising, such as by providing detailed instructions, mandating extensive preapproval, and setting out a "host of marketing and advertising methods." Liberty appealed.

The court of appeal refused to allow Liberty to escape liability because, among other things, it did not train, hire, fire, or supervise franchisees' employees. Nor was the court willing to accept that vicarious liability in the franchise context required application of a standard other than the "right of complete or substantial control" test previously applied by California courts. Of potentially major significance on the agency impact of unilateral modification clauses, the appellate court reasoned that "Liberty 'retained an open-ended right to modify the operations manual without consent of the franchisees. This right of essentially complete control over franchisee operations, and specifically advertising operations, exceeded what liberty reasonably needed to protect its trademark and goodwill.'" Moreover, evidence in the record that Liberty used its advertising approval power to advance its own business strategies and tactics, such as its directing what discounts could be offered at what time of year, supported a conclusion of agency. Liberty itself admitted that an e-mail sent by a Liberty agent rejecting a proposed franchisee advertisement did so partially because it was "good for business[.]" As this supported the view the franchisor had the right to exercise control outside of its legitimate interests, the court affirmed the trial court's finding of agency and penalty imposition.

In *Depianti v. Jan-Pro Franchising International, Inc.*, 990 N.E.2d 1054 (Mass. 2013), the Massachusetts Supreme Court answered three questions certified to it pursuant to S.J.C. Rule 1:03: (1) Were janitorial franchisees (who claimed they were actually employees) required to exhaust all administrative remedies before they could sue Jan-Pro; (2) Whether and how to apply the "right to control test" for vicarious liability to the franchisor-franchisee relationship; and (3) Whether a defendant may be liable for employee misclassification under Massachusetts law where there was no contract for services between the plaintiff and the defendant.

The court first decided that the franchisees could sue without exhausting administrative remedies. The court did not rule that a plaintiff making this sort of claim never had to pursue its administrative remedies, but, instead, found that since the plaintiffs had advised the Attorney General of their claims and had timely brought the claims, they did not need to exhaust their administrative remedies.

With respect to the second question, the Supreme Court directed the federal court to apply the "right of control" test to review vicarious liability claims related to the franchisor-franchisee relationship. The issue in *Depianti* was whether franchisor, Jan-Pro, could be held liable for the actions of its master franchisee, Bradley Marketing Enterprises. Bradley was alleged to have (1) made false representations to franchisees, and (2) committed "systemic" breaches of contract. The Supreme Court directed the federal court to review the alleged misconduct of Bradley and determine whether Jan-Pro "controls or has a right to control the specific policy or practice resulting in the harm to the plaintiff."

With respect to the final question, Jan-Pro argued that it could not, as a matter of law, be liable as the employer of the janitorial franchisees because Jan-Pro had no contract for services with the franchisees. The Supreme Court disagreed, stating that, if an employer could simply avoid Massachusetts' employment statutes by working through a "middle man" entity, the purposes of the statute would be defeated entirely. If Jan-Pro were, in fact, Depianti's employer, the fact that Jan-Pro set up Bradley as a middle man would not allow Jan-Pro to escape liability.

In *Licari v. Best Western International, Inc.*, No. 11-CV-603, 2013 U.S. Dist. LEXIS 97725 (D. Utah July 12, 2013), Mr. and Mrs. Licari sued Best Western and a Utah franchisee due to Mr. Licari allegedly catching Legionnaire's Disease in the franchisee's hotel due to poor maintenance of the hotel's water system. Best Western moved for summary judgment, asserting that it had no ownership of the hotel, no duty of care to the Licaris, and could not be held liable under a "vicarious liability" theory or an "apparent authority" theory.

The court agreed that Best Western had no direct liability to the Licaris and owed them no direct duty of care. Therefore, it granted Best Western's summary judgment motion on this legal theory.

The court, however, denied the remainder of Best Western's summary judgment motion. The court found that genuine issues of material fact existed on the issues of (1) the degree of control that Best Western exercised over the franchisee, and (2) whether the Licaris reasonably believed the franchisee was merely an agent acting on behalf of Best Western.

The court stated that since Legionnaire's Disease was caused by a long-term neglect of the water system, there was an issue of fact as to whether Best Western controlled the upkeep of the water system through Best Western's regular inspections of the hotel and its very detailed "Rules and Regulations" regarding hotel upkeep.

With respect to the "apparent authority" theory, although the franchisee had a sign stating that it was independently owned and operated, the Licaris stated that they only relied upon the "Best Western" sign visible from the road and assumed that Best Western owned the hotel. The court found that the Licaris affidavits on this issue created a genuine issue of material fact.

3.   *Mixed Results*

In *Wilkerson v. McDonald's Corp.*, No. 12-10775, 2013 U.S. Dist. LEXIS 105727 (D. Mass. July 29, 2013), the franchisor moved for summary judgment at a time where the only evidence before the court was the parties' franchise agreement. The court found that, given the uncertain status of the law on vicarious liability, that summary judgment was improper without hearing the evidence regarding the franchisor's actual exercise of control.

D.   FRANCHISEE LIABLE FOR FRANCHISOR EMPLOYEE'S MISCONDUCT

The court considered the question of a franchisee's liability for the actions of a franchisor's employee, stationed and granted some level of authority at the franchisee's location, in the case of *Magallon v. Wireless Unlimited, Inc.*, No. CL-2012-03867, 2012 Va. Cir. LEXIS 98 (Va. Cir. Ct. Oct. 23, 2012). In *Magallon*, the plaintiff alleged that an account manager for Cricket Communications, Inc. ("Cricket"), the franchisor of Wireless Unlimited, Inc. ("Wireless Unlimited"), the plaintiff's employer, sexually assaulted and defamed her. Specifically, the sexual assault was alleged to have occurred while the account manager was driving the plaintiff home after a mandatory meeting and a dinner in which the plaintiff was pressured to attend by supervisors. Wireless Unlimited operates several cell phone and wireless equipment stores in Virginia. Cricket is a national wireless service provider. The account manager defendant was a personal friend of the franchisee operator and was assigned to the franchisee's store in Vienna, Virginia. In part, the plaintiff sought to hold the franchisee vicariously responsible for the sexual assault. Wireless Unlimited moved to dismiss the plaintiff's claims against it on a number of bases, including (1) there was no principal-agent relationship between the franchisee and the franchisor's employee, and (2) the sexual battery occurred outside the scope of employment. The court rejected both of these arguments.

Considering the first argument, the court acknowledged that Virginia law requires four "elements" to be weighed in order for someone to be an "employee:" (1) selection and engagement of the servant; (2) payment of wages; (3) power of dismissal; and (4) power to control the servant's actions. Although there was no evidence the account manager was an official employee of Wireless Unlimited, there was evidence the franchisee had ceded ability to control the franchisee's employees to him. In particular, he participated in operational and management decisions, enforced sales quotas, ordered the plaintiff to take pictures of a store marketing effort, and had threatened the plaintiff with termination. The court, in concluding the franchisee could be held liable, proffered that "[t]he management of employees may be considered a business's most essential duty and Wireless Unlimited should not be able to absolve itself of liability by surrendering this duty to others."

As for the scope of employment action, having determined a principal-agent relationship existed, the court placed the burden on the defendant to show the act was outside the scope of employment. The court determined the defendant did not rebut the presumption for purposes of the motion and stated the issue should be decided by the fact finder.

XI.   Tortious Interference

Tortious interference case discussions this year generally featured "throw in" claims for tortious interference which were quickly disposed of without much analysis. There were a few exceptions.

In *G.L.M. Security & Sound, Inc. v. Lojack Corp.* (summarized in Chapter 8), the court found that Lojack's fraudulent conduct was directed at G.L.M. and not "directed at G.L.M.'s customers," so the tortious interference claim was dismissed.

In *Damabeh v. 7-Eleven, Inc.*, (previously summarized in Chapter 5.IV.C) the franchisee brought claims against 7-Eleven for negligent and interference and intentional interference with prospective business advantage for terminating Damabeh's 7-Eleven franchise and removing merchandise from the store. The court dismissed this claim, stating that Damabeh had established no wrongful conduct, and, even if he could do so, he had not pled the identity of any specific customer with whom 7-Eleven had interfered.

In *Eureka Water Co. v. Nestle Waters North America, Inc.*, 690 F.3d 1139 (10th Cir. 2012), previously summarized in Chapter 5.III.B, Tenth Circuit affirmed the dismissal of a tortious interference claim based upon an alleged unfair price increase, stating that Nestle had the undisputed right to raise customer prices if it so chose, so its interference, if any, was legally justified.

Leisure Systems, Inc. v. Roundup LLC, No. 11-CV-384, 2012 U.S. Dist. LEXIS 155948 (S.D. Ohio Oct. 31, 2012), previously summarized in Chapter 5.VIII.E, involved a post-termination letter sent by Leisure Systems' Vice President of Operations to a customer of Roundup LLC. The Vice President implied that Roundup LLC had been terminated for poor operating conditions at its campgrounds when it had, in fact, been terminated for failure to pay royalties. The court found this letter to be potentially defamatory but, nonetheless, dismissed Roundup LLC's tortious interference claim.

The court found that, while the letter was possibly defamatory, Roundup LLC had produced no evidence that it lost any specific customers or specific business as a result of the letter. Therefore, Leisure Systems was granted summary judgment on this claim.

Oracle America, Inc. v. CedarCrestone, Inc., No. 12-CV-04626, 2013 U.S. Dist. LEXIS 89986 (N.D. Cal., June 26, 2013), involved a tortious interference claim by Oracle that one of its former product support providers, Cedar Crestone, misappropriated Oracle's intellectual property related to its PeopleSoft branded software and sold infringing software updates to Oracle's customer base. Cedar Crestone moved to dismiss.

The court reviewed Oracle's allegations and found them sufficient to overcome a motion to dismiss. First, Oracle pled that it had specific relationships with specific PeopleSoft customers who needed regular software updates and support. Second, Oracle alleged that Cedar Crestone targeted and obtained certain specific customers and used improper means (selling infringing products) to compete. Finally, Oracle alleged certain specific damages related to the tortious interference. While Cedar Crestone alleged that Oracle simply had poor products that customers were fleeing, the court found such arguments inappropriate at the motion to dismiss stage of the proceedings.

In *Better Homes and Gardens Real Estate LLC v. Mary Holder Agency, Inc.*, No. 11-34280, 2012 Bankr. LEXIS 3774 (Bankr. D.N.J. Aug. 9, 2012), discussed previously at Chapter 5.IV., the court denied various motions for summary judgment. On the issue of tortious interference, the court found issues of material fact as to whether SCS interfered with BH&G's contractual right to the listings of MHA prior to the termination of the franchise agreement.

XII.   Settlement And Release

At times, a settlement (or what people thought was a settlement) can spin off additional motion practice or full-scale litigation. There were a few such cases this year.

The court in *Burda v. Wendy's Int'l, Inc.*, summarized in Chapter 3.II.A, found that Burda's counterclaims were barred by releases he had signed in 1996, 2000, 2001, 2002, 2003, 2004 and 2006. Burda's arguments of lack of bargaining power and failure to realize what he was releasing were both rejected, as was his claim that public policy forbids the release of antitrust claims.

KFC Corp. v. Kazi, No. 11-CV-00475, 2013 U.S. Dist. LEXIS 72258 (W.D. Ky. May 22, 2013) involved a KFC extension agreement which permitted Kazi to remain a franchisee at three stores only if he successfully remodeled any two within six months. Before the deadline, Kazi requested, and was granted, a three-week extension. Despite the extension, Kazi never even began remodeling any store. KFC terminated all three stores and sued to enforce Kazi's agreement to shut down if he failed to remodel.

Kazi argued that he had been the victim of a "permit delay" and would have remodeled but for the delay. Unfortunately for Kazi, the settlement agreement specifically dealt with "permit delays" and allowed an extension of time if Kazi requested a building permit within one week of KFC approving his plans. Kazi had waited over a month before making any request. Therefore, Kazi had no defense and was required to shut down. This case officially dealt only with the closure of two stores, the third store was also ordered closed in *KFC Corp. v. Kazi*, No. 11-CV-00475, 2013 U.S. Dist. LEXIS 69004 (W.D. Ky. May 15, 2013).

Similarly, in *KFC v. Sahadevan*, No. 10-CV-00612, 2013 U.S. Dist. LEXIS 78203 (W.D. Ky. June 4, 2013), the franchisee entered into an Agreed Judgment whereby the franchisee would execute a $50,000 promissory note and retain his franchise so long as he paid the note on time. The franchisee failed to pay, and the court enforced the settlement, terminating the franchise and ordering judgment against the maker of the note and the guarantor.

Interestingly, the court found that generally a federal court lacks jurisdiction to enforce the terms of a Lanham Act settlement agreement because the settlement no longer is related to the Lanham Act (it is just a private contract made under state law). However, an exception to this general rule exists when the court (1) specifically retains jurisdiction, or (2) incorporates the settlement into an Order. The court found both factors to be present, so it determined that it had jurisdiction to enforce the settlement.

In *Kreisler v. McDonald's Corp.*, No. 09-CV- 9358, 2013 U.S. Dist. LEXIS 92864 (S.D. N.Y. June 27, 2013), the court reviewed a settlement agreement between a McDonald's franchisee and a disabled individual, Mr. Kreisler. The franchisee, per Mr. Kreisler, had agreed to build an entrance to his McDonald's accessible to the disabled. All agreed that the franchisee had not done so, and Kreisler moved to enforce the settlement agreement.

The court denied Kreisler's motion, finding that the franchisee's actual agreement was to build an accessible entrance or, if precluded from doing so, advise Kreisler of why he was being delayed. The franchisee was delayed due to his inability to get a permit without significantly renovating the premises. The franchisee had informed Kreisler that the renovations would begin in July of 2013. Therefore, the franchisee was not in violation of the settlement agreement. Kreisler's motion was denied.

A McDonald's employee's efforts to void two releases of claims was unsuccessful in *Nelson v. Lattner Enterprises of N.Y.*, No. 515927, 2013 N.Y. App. Div. LEXIS 5277 (N.Y.A.D. July 18, 2013). Ms. Nelson claimed sexual harassment and threatened to sue both her franchisee employer and McDonald's. She subsequently settled for $18,688.10 plus medical benefits, signing two separate releases.

Nelson then tried to pursue a Human Rights claim. State and federal authorities informed her that her claims had been waived by the releases she signed. She then sued. The trial court dismissed her claims, and she appealed. She fared no better at the Appellate Division, which also found the releases enforceable. Nelson's primary defense to the releases was "duress." The duress defense was barred because (1) the second release permitted her to void it within 21 days and she never did (even if she was under duress, the duress did not last 21 days), and (2) she accepted the money and benefits and, therefore, ratified the release by her conduct.

A preliminary agreement settling a trademark dispute was found unenforceable in *Strong College Students Moving, Inc. v. CHHJ Franchising, LLC*, No. 12-CV-01156, 2013 U.S. Dist. LEXIS 105739 (D. Ariz. July 29, 2013). The court found that, while the parties had reached an agreement on all material settlement terms, the ancillary terms were important to the parties, as was a written agreement. The court also noted that parties had previously informed the court that (1) they had a "preliminary" agreement, and later (2) "there is no settlement at this time."

In *Grayson v. 7-Eleven, Inc.*, No. 09-CV-1353, 2013 U.S. Dist. LEXIS 40462 (S.D. Cal. Mar. 21, 2013), the court considered whether prior release agreements signed by the class action Plaintiffs barred recovery for their claims. Plaintiffs Grayson and McKenzie ("Plaintiffs"), former 7-Eleven franchisees, executed "Release of Claims and Termination" agreements relating to prior claims. Plaintiffs' stores had sold pre-paid long-distance telephone cards that were subject to federal excise taxes, half of which Plaintiffs were responsible for paying. However, when the tax was repealed, 7-Eleven did not inform its former franchisees about the refund. Plaintiffs brought a nationwide class action against the franchisor 7-Eleven seeking to recover federal excise tax refunds issued to 7-Eleven. Plaintiffs asserted three causes of action: conversion; money had and received; and implied breach of contract. Both parties moved for summary judgment.

The court found that the "Release of Claims and Termination" agreements signed by Plaintiffs barred recovery for all three claims. Plaintiffs argued that California Civil Code section 1668, which invalidates the release of liability for future wrongdoing and prohibits contractual releases of simple negligence claims when the public interest is involved, prevented the release agreements from excusing the Defendant's intentional wrongdoing. The court first addressed the conversion claim. Absent a public interest, section 1668 does not invalidate strict liability claims. As such, the court found that because the conversion claim had no public interest involved and was a strict liability tort, section 1668 did not invalidate the release agreements. The court next addressed the money had and received claim, and found that the releases were not barred by section 1668 because proving money had and received did not require any showing of intentional wrongdoing or gross negligence. Finally, the court addressed the breach of implied contract claim, and found that the releases were not barred by section 1668 because the contract claim did not involve an intentional tort. Accordingly, the court granted 7-Eleven's Motion for Summary Judgment and dismissed the Plaintiffs' claims.

See also Lawn Doctor, Inc. v. Rizzo, Bus. Franchise Guide (CCH) ¶ 14,950 (D. N.J. Dec. 11, 2012), as summarized at Chapter 3.V.C.

XIII. Fiduciary Duty

In *Legend Autorama, Ltd. v. Audi of America, Inc.*, 954 N.Y.S.2d 141 (N.Y. App. Div. Nov. 14, 2012), summarized in Chapter 3.VI.B.1., the court reversed the trial court's decision not to grant summary judgment to Audi on Legend Autorama's fiduciary duty claim. The court found that generally automobile dealers and manufacturers are not fiduciaries and Legend Autorama had produced no evidence to establish that its case was one of the "rare instances" in which the terms of the franchise agreement or the nature of the relationship created a fiduciary duty.

In *Franklin Park Lincoln-Mercury, Inc. v. Ford Motor Co.*, No. 11-4375, 2013 U.S. App. LEXIS 15291 (6th Cir. July 24, 2013), the Sixth Circuit decided that Ford was not a fiduciary to its dealer. In reviewing the district court's dismissal of the plaintiff's breach of fiduciary duty claim, the appellate court reviewed the three proffered bases for a fiduciary relationship: (1) Ford's position of dominance over Franklin Park; (2) Ford's requiring Franklin Park to disclose confidential and proprietary information; and finally (3) Ford's making Franklin Park economically dependent on it for survival. The plaintiff relied principally upon *Manhattan Motorcars, Inc. v. Automobili Lamborghini*, 244 F.R.D. 204 (S.D. N.Y. 2007), where the court stated: "Generally, where parties deal at arms-length in a commercial transaction, no relation of confidence or trust sufficient to find the existence of a fiduciary relationship will arise absent extraordinary circumstances. Nevertheless, a distributorship agreement may, in some rare instances, create a confidential relationship out of which a duty of fiduciary care arises." Amongst other things, the dealer pointed to its SSAs, which, it alleged, imposed conditions upon it that gave Ford extreme control.

The manufacturer answered that Franklin Park continued to have exclusive control over its human resource decisions and advertising, and that no prospective customer information had to be shared with Ford. The court agreed with Ford, relying upon the SSAs grant of authority to Franklin Park to make advertising and staffing decisions, and discretion to decide on the purchase and sale of used cars and the ability to sell cars outside of its market area. Finding no facts making this an extraordinary circumstance creating a fiduciary relationship, the court affirmed summary judgment on this claim.

CHAPTER ❖ 6

Antitrust

I.   Introduction

As in the recent past, antitrust cases in the franchise space are few and far between. In both cases reported below, the franchisor/manufacturer prevailed.

A.   TYING CLAIMS

In *Dunkin' Donuts Franchising LLC v. Sai Food Hospitality, LLC*, No. 11-CV-1484, 2013 U.S. Dist. LEXIS 55518 (E.D. Mo. Apr. 18, 2013), the court considered plaintiffs Dunkin' Donuts' motion to partially dismiss franchisee defendants third amended counterclaim. Dunkin' Donuts franchised the Dunkin' Donuts system, which involved the production, merchandising and sale of donuts and other products using special equipment and management programs, and proprietary marks. Among other agreements, franchisee defendants owned two Dunkin' Donuts franchises. Following uncertainty surrounding the ownership of the two franchises, Dunkin' Donuts sued franchisee defendants alleging breach of certain agreements, trademark infringement, trade dress infringement, and unfair competition. In their third amended counterclaim, franchisee defendants asserted claims against Dunkin' Donuts, Dunkin' Brands Group Inc. ("DGBI"), and Dunkin Brands Inc. ("DBI") for violation of the Sherman Act, the Clayton Act and state anti-trust law, due to unlawfully tying the sale of the donut franchises/quick-serve donut-coffee restaurant franchises (the tying product) to the purchase of equipment needed to operate the franchise stores (the tied product).

Dunkin' Donuts argued that "donut franchises" did not constitute a viable market for purposes of establishing an illegal tying arrangement under

144

the Sherman Act or state antitrust law. Specifically, Dunkin' Donuts argued that the relevant section of the Clayton Act did not apply to franchisees. Further, Dunkin' Donuts argued that because DGBI and DBI were not parties to the contracts or negotiations at issue and constituted separate legal entities, the franchisee defendants had no basis to bring any claims against either DGBI or DBI. Franchisee defendants however, argued that "donut franchises" are a relevant market for tying purposes because there is no reasonably interchangeable substitute for a donut. Further, franchisee defendants argued that they sufficiently pled that DGBI and DBI, along with Dunkin' Donuts, had the market power to restrain trade in the related equipment market.

The court concluded that the franchisee defendants had failed to state antitrust claims that were plausible on their face. The court relied on guidance from the Supreme Court's decision in *Illinois Tool Works, Inc. v. Independent Ink, Inc.*, 547 U.S. 28 (2006) where the Supreme Court explained that, "the essential characteristic of an invalid tying arrangement lies in the seller's exploitation of its control over the tying product to force the buyer into the purchase of a tied product that the buyer . . . might have preferred to purchase elsewhere on different terms." Further, the Supreme Court concluded that many "tying arrangements . . . are fully consistent with a free, competitive market." Relying on the Supreme Court's holding, the district court explained that "while tying arrangements that 'are the product of a true monopoly' are still unlawful, 'that conclusion must be supported by proof of power in the relevant market rather than by a mere presumption thereof.'" Further, the court explained that the "claimant has the burden of defining a relevant market in which the defendant's power can be assessed." The court noted that such purported markets are usually rejected in antitrust claims, and concluded that the franchisee defendants' antitrust claims were not plausible on their face. Accordingly, the court granted the motion for partial dismissal with respect to the antitrust claims and dismissed DGBI and DBI from the action.

Further, in *Dunkin' Donuts Franchising LLC v. Sai Food Hospitality, LLC*, Bus. Franchise Guide (CCH) ¶ 15,071 (E.D. Missouri, May 15, 2013), the court considered Dunkin' Donuts' motion for summary judgment dismissing franchisee defendants' third amended counterclaim. The court noted that even assuming that the anti-trust claims should not have been previously dismissed in Dunkin' Donuts' motion for partial dismissal, the claims would not have survived summary judgment for the same reasons as described in the motion for partial dismissal.

CHAPTER 6

In *Witt Company v. Riso, Inc.*, Bus. Franchise Guide (CCH) ¶ 15,079 (D. Or. June 7, 2013), the court considered defendant RISO, Inc.'s ("RISO") motion to dismiss plaintiff Witt Company's ("Witt") claims under the Sherman and Clayton Acts alleging an unlawful tying arrangement. Witt, a provider of office technology products and related services, was an authorized dealer of RISO digital duplicators and other related products. As such, Witt entered into several RISO Domestic Dealer Agreements ("Dealer Agreements"). Witt alleged that in 2011, RISO informed Witt that it would have to execute a new Dealer Agreement in connection with a different transaction between the parties. Witt found the new Dealer Agreement to be overly restrictive, and objected to a provision that would deny Witt the right to purchase and sell RISO digital duplicators unless it also agreed to exclusively purchase RISO brand supplies for use in RISO equipment, and not use any competitive supplies. According to Witt, RISO then informed Witt that to maintain its status as an authorized dealer, it would have to sign the new Dealer Agreement with the offending provision. Further, Witt alleged that after its termination as a RISO dealer, RISO prohibited Witt from purchasing RISO parts to service and maintain duplicators that Witt had previously sold unless Witt also continued to purchase only RISO supplies.

Witt sued alleging that digital duplicators and supplies used in digital duplicators constituted two separate and distinct products, and that tying the purchase of RISO supplies to the purchase of RISO digital duplicators violated antitrust laws. Further, Witt alleged that RISO possessed economic power in the digital duplicator market sufficient to coerce its authorized dealers to agree to purchase only RISO applies, and that this coercion had "reasonably restrained competition in the relevant market." RISO moved to dismiss the claim on the basis that it was barred by the statute of limitations, or, alternatively, that the claim failed to state a claim.

The court found that there was no existing operative Dealer Agreement in place under which RISO was allegedly enforcing the illegal provision. Therefore, the claim was barred by the four year statute of limitations. Further, the court noted that there were no continuing violations that would have triggered a new statute of limitations period. The court also considered Witt's argument that the antitrust claim was based on RISO's threat to terminate Witt's authorized dealer status if Witt did not sign the new Dealer Agreement. The court found that this was insufficient to state an antitrust claim because the Supreme Court held in *United States v. Colgate*, 250 U.S. 300 (1919), that "a manufacturer's unilateral refusal to deal with distributors did not violate antitrust laws." The court also found that Witt had failed to state a claim because Witt had not sufficiently pled market power. Witt had the burden of alleging that there were significant barriers to entering the relevant market and that existing competitors lacked the capacity to increase their output. The court found that Witt's allegation that RISO possessed 65% of the market was insufficient to establish barriers to entry or that RISO's conduct precluded competitors from increasing their output. Accordingly, the court granted RISO's motion to dismiss.

See also, Burda v. Wendy's Int'l, Inc., summarized in Chapter 3.II.A. (antitrust claims barred by general releases)

CHAPTER ❖ 7

Other Federal Issues

I.   Bankruptcy

A.   DISCHARGEABLE DEBT

In re: Man Soo Yun., No. 11-1595, 2012 Bank. LEXIS 3793 (Bankr. App. Panel 9th Cir. Aug. 14, 2012) involved an appeal by the California Corporation Commissioner ("Commissioner") from a bankruptcy court's order limiting the Commissioner to only seeking injunctive relief in a state court proceeding against the debtor for violation of the California Franchise Investment Law (CFIL).

Man Soo Yun ("Yun") was the president and chief operating officer of Green On Blue, Inc. ("GOBI"). Yun and GOBI were the master franchisors for Yogurberry frozen yogurt outlets in the United States. The California Corporations Commission ("Commission") approved GOBI's registration to sell Yogurberry franchises in California for the time periods December 21, 2006 through April 21, 2008 after reviewing and approving GOBI's Uniform Franchise Offering Circular ("UFOC").

After receiving a number of complaints, the Commissioner investigated. The Commissioner discovered that Jun and GOBI sold franchises in California prior to registering and without providing prospective franchisees with a UFOC and by means of written or oral communications containing untrue statements or omissions of material fact, all violations of the CFIL. The Commissioner issued a "Citation & Desist and Refrain Order" on January 7, 2010. The order included an administrative penalty in the amount of $42,500 and an order to pay $2,339,400 for restitution, out-of-pocket expenses and for rescission of franchise fees, royalty fees and other fees paid to Yun and GOBI by nine "victims/franchisees". Yun and GOBI failed to request a hearing on the Commissioner's Order within 60 days and the Order became final on June 9, 2010. Yun filed Chapter 7 bankruptcy on July 2, 2010. The notice of commencement of bankruptcy case set a deadline of October 1, 2010 for creditors to object to the discharge of Yun's debts. Yun listing the California Department of Corporations as a creditor with a claim in the amount of $2,384,400 based upon his personal liability on a business judgment. The address Yun used for the Corporations Department was accurate, but it did not include the name of the individual assigned to enforce the Commissioner's Order. Although three Yogurberry franchisees filed nondischargeability complaints against Yun, the Commissioner did not.

The Commissioner claimed he did not receive actual notice of Yun's bankruptcy until June 27, 2011 – nearly a year after Yun's case was filed. The Commissioner filed a motion for exception and/or relief from an automatic stay to pursue a money judgment against Yun in the state court proceeding based on the Commissioner's previous Order. Yun claimed that the Commissioner was served with notification of the proceedings and had opportunity to file a timely nondischargeability complaint. The bankruptcy court terminated the automatic stay only to permit the Commissioner to "obtain a judgment for nonmonetary relief and to enforce such nonmonetary judgment." The Commissioner appealed.

As an initial matter, the appellate panel took the Commissioner to task for failing to include a transcript of the bankruptcy court's hearing on the Commissioner's motion for relief from stay. The bankruptcy court's Order included no factual findings or legal conclusions, thus hampering appellate review. Regardless, the court considered whether the Commissioner's failure to file a nondischargeability complaint in the bankruptcy court precluded him from pursuing a monetary judgment against Yun in the state court. Unfortunately, without a record of the proceedings in the bankruptcy court, the appellate court could not review what facts, if any, the bankruptcy court considered in connection with the timeliness of pursuing a nondischargeability determination. The appellate court could not say that the bankruptcy court's findings were clearly erroneous because they didn't know what they were. Interestingly, the appellate court opinion indicates that the Commissioner suggested at oral argument that the court should remand with instructions to the bankruptcy court to make findings of fact. This suggestion was rebuked: "However, in the absence of the transcript, we cannot know that the bankruptcy court did not make the requisite findings upon which to base its Order. Because the Commissioner did not provide a transcript of the hearing for our review, we may presume that nothing that happened at the hearing would aid his case on appeal." The court affirmed the bankruptcy court order.

In *Pu v. Mitsopoulos (In re Mitsopoulos)*, No. 11-41911, 2013 Bankr. LEXIS 930 (Bank. E.D. N.Y. Mar. 8, 2013), the court denied the debtor, a Medicine Shoppe franchisee, discharge under 11 U.S.C. § 727(a) due to the franchisee's failure to keep records during the period of time between the close of his business and when he filed for bankruptcy. After two years of litigation with its franchisor, the franchisee filed for bankruptcy and left his attorney unpaid. The franchisee sought to discharge his debt to the attorney in bankruptcy. The attorney initiated an adversary proceeding seeking a judgment denying the debtor discharge under section 727.

The statute at issue, 11 U.S.C. § 727(a)(3), reads that a "court shall grant the debtor a discharge unless the debtor has concealed, destroyed, mutilated, falsified, or failed to keep or preserve any recorded information, including books, documents, records, and papers from which the debtor's financial condition or business transactions might be ascertained, unless such act or failure was justified under all of the circumstances of the case." The core purpose underlying the statute is to ensure that the trustee and creditors have sufficient information to enable them to trace the debtor's financial history and reconstruct the debtor's business transactions. *Helms v. Gangemi*, 291 B.R. 242, 246 (E.D. N.Y. 2003). If the debtors fail to produce the records under 727(a)(3), the court must deny his discharge. *Id.*

Mitsopoulos attempted to justify his lack of records because: 1) his accountant approved of his record-keeping; 2) he believed he was not obligated to maintain additional records for a defunct corporation, and; 3) his landlord or the subsequent tenant disposed of the records before Mitsopoulos could retrieve them. The court rejected the franchisee's attempted justifications. First, the court found no facts supported the debtor's assertions that his accountant approved of his record-keeping. Next, the court said a debtor's honest belief that he had no duty to maintain records after closing his business is no defense for inadequate recordkeeping under 727(a)(3). Finally, the court disagreed that the landlord or next tenant's disposal of the records excused Mitsopoulos because he waited two months before returning to the space, and admitted that nothing left in the space "was necessary to the determine the [franchisee's] financial condition." Accordingly, Mitsopoulos was denied a discharge of his debts.

In *ETRG Investments v. Hardee (In re Hardee)*, No. 11-60242, 2013 Bankr. LEXIS 949, (Bankr. E.D. Tex. Mar. 14, 2013), the court considered whether James Hardee, a manager of ETRG Investments LLC ("LLC"), an LLC that held Zaxby franchises, could discharge his debts in a Chapter 7 bankruptcy proceeding. The creditors, members of the LLC that Hardee mismanaged, sought to recover their investments in the LLC that Hardee allegedly obtained through actual fraud or by false representations under 11 U.S.C. § 523(a)(2)(A), and sought to recover taxes Hardee failed to pay the IRS as a defalcation of a fiduciary duty under § 523(a)(4).

Hardee was the manager of LLC, a company that members, Dan Tomlin and Mark Scott, created to operate Zaxby's franchises. Hardee used LLC money to wrongfully pay his mortgage, car payments, and personal credit card debts. Hardee created false financial documents for LLC members to obscure the misappropriation. Hardee also failed to pay the required tax payments to the IRS on behalf of the LLC.

The court denied Tomlin and Scott's claim to recover their initial investment in the LLC under § 523(a)(2)(A). Under § 523(a)(2)(A), a § 727 discharge does not discharge a debtor from any debt to the extent that he obtained the money by a false representation or actual fraud. The bankruptcy court distinguished false representation and fraud. False representation is an express statement intended to create a false impression depicting current or past events. However, a party cannot falsely represent what they will do in the future. The court found that Tomlin and Scott invested in the LLC relying on Hardee's representations about his future conduct, therefore the court barred recovery for "false representations" under § 523(a)(2)(A). The court also denied that Hardee committed actual fraud, because when Hardee breached his duties as manager, he breached the terms of the Member Control Agreement for the LLC and did not commit a tort. Contract debts are dischargeable.

However, the court granted Tomlin and Scott's claim for defalcation under § 523(a)(4). Defalcation arises when the debtor breaches a fiduciary duty to the creditor. The concept of "fiduciary" under § 523(a)(4) is more narrow than the general common law and must involve express or technical trusts. This trust relationship must also exist prior to the indebtedness. The court likened LLCs in Texas to corporations, and said that Texas law long recognized that fiduciary duties owed by a corporate officer or director to the corporation meet the standards for a technical trust, and satisfy the narrow definition of "fiduciary" in § 523(a)(4). Therefore, when Hardee failed to pay taxes on the LLC's Zaxby's restaurants, Hardee failed to comply with his duty of care and loyalty required under Texas corporate law. Thus, Hardee was not permitted to discharge Tomlin and Scott's claim for the $248,027.12 they had to pay the IRS because of Hardee's defalcation.

The power of the Bankruptcy Code was apparent in *In re Center Field Properties, LLC*, No. 12-60854-11, 2013 Bankr. LEXIS 2694 (Bankr. D.

Mont. July 3, 2013). Franchisor Hawthorne Suites Franchising, Inc. filed a $85,736.08 post-petition administrative claim, seeking payment for the Montana hotel franchisee's use of Hawthorne's reservation system and advertising. The franchisee objected, stating that it received only $4,343.35 in actual benefit from these items.

The bankruptcy court agreed and granted Hawthorne a barely-higher amount of $4,489.26 as an administrative expense. The court found that for a claim to be recoverable as a post-petition administrative claim in the Ninth Circuit, the expense at issue must have directly and substantially benefitted the estate. Hawthorne had failed to establish any "direct and substantial benefit" to the estate. Therefore, the court made its own determination of the benefit to the estate and awarded Hawthorne $4,489.26 based upon what it described as "the Debtor's evidence."

II. RICO

In *Horowitz v. QFA Royalties*, No. 11-CV-6123, 2012 U.S. Dist. LEXIS 178456 (S.D. N.Y. Sept. 27, 2012), the court dismissed a Quiznos franchisee's complaint against the franchisor, Quiznos, under the Racketeer Influenced and Corrupt Organizations Act (RICO), 18 U.S.C. § 1961.

In order to successfully plead a RICO claim, a plaintiff must allege a "pattern of racketeering" activity. In order to satisfy a pattern of racketeering activity, a plaintiff must allege: (1) at least two predicate acts of racketeering activity that relate to one another and the enterprise, and (2) threaten continuous criminal activity. *U.S. v. Basciano*, 599 F.3d 184, 202 (2d Cir. 2010). A plaintiff may establish continuity through closed and open-ended conduct. Closed-ended conduct includes a series of related predicates extending over a substantial period of time, and open-ended continuity is established by showing the predicate acts are a regular way of conducting the defendant's ongoing business.

Here, the franchisee successfully alleged the first prong, two predicate acts of racketeering activity, but failed to allege sufficient facts to demonstrate a closed or open-ended threat of continuous racketeering activities. The court found the franchisor's false and misleading representations to the franchisee about Quiznos franchisees' profitability and previous failed Quiznos franchises in the same county to be two predicate acts of racketeering activity. However, the court found no closed-ended continuous pattern of racketeering because the fraudulent scheme did not exist over a "substantial" period of time. The court also found no open-ended threat of continuous racketeering going forward because the plaintiff alleged only that Quiznos fraudulent induced him as a single franchisee.

Because the plaintiff was unable to establish the elements of a RICO claim, the court dismissed the complaint.

In *Martin v. JTH Tax, Inc.*, No. 10-CV-03016, 2013 U.S. Dist. LEXIS 43035 (D. S.C. Mar. 27, 2013), Liberty Tax Service franchisees and former customers of Liberty Tax sued franchisor Liberty Tax and its founders, John and Danny Hewitt, for RICO claims and unjust enrichment, respectively. The court granted Danny Hewitt's motion for summary judgment on the franchisees' RICO claims, but denied summary judgment to John Hewitt. The court also granted the Hewitt brother's summary judgment motion on the former customers' unjust enrichment claim, but allowed the unjust enrichment claim to move forward against the franchisor Liberty Tax as an entity.

On the RICO claims asserted by the franchisees, the court found the plaintiff franchisees failed to allege sufficient facts to demonstrate that both Hewitt brothers engaged in "racketeering activity" to support a civil RICO complaint. The franchisees claimed that the franchisor founders, John and Danny Hewitt, individually caused fraudulent tax return forms to be sent from the Liberty Tax Newberry, South Carolina office to the IRS, violating 18 U.S.C. § 1343 (wire fraud), 18 U.S.C. § 2 (aiding and abetting wire fraud) and 18 U.S.C. § 1962(d) (RICO conspiracy) because the Hewitts encouraged the franchisees to fill out more forms than necessary in order to charge more fees from customers. The Court granted Denny Hewitt's motion because the evidence showed that Danny Hewitt was largely on the marketing side of the business and was not involved with franchisees. However, the court denied John Hewitt's motion because plaintiff alleged facts that showed John Hewitt was actively involved in training franchisees and instructing franchisees on how to maximize profits by filing multiple forms.

Next, the court dismissed the former customers' claims of unjust enrichment against John and Danny Hewitt as individuals, but allowed the customers' claims to move forward against the Liberty Tax franchisor as an entity. The court held that the consumers, merely by paying the Liberty Tax Service franchisees, who would then pay royalties to the franchisor entity, which would then distribute funds to John and Danny Hewitt as shareholders, did not confer the requisite direct benefit on the Hewitt brothers to survive their motion for summary judgment.

In a continuation of the long-running dispute involving The Coffee Beanery, in *WW, LLC v. Coffee Beanery, Ltd.*, No. 05-3360, 2012 U.S. Dist. LEXIS 121347 (D. Md. Aug. 27, 2012), the court considered The Coffee Beanery, Ltd.'s motion for partial dismissal of a former franchisee's RICO claim.

CHAPTER 7

WW, LLC was the corporate entity created by the franchisee plaintiffs to open a Coffee Beanery Café. The franchisee plaintiffs operated the café for approximately three years, but for a number of reasons, never made a profit. They claimed that the café had been represented as a "proven concept." After losing nearly $325,000, the franchisee plaintiffs filed suit. Following an arbitration award in favor of Coffee Beanery, the Sixth Circuit reversed and vacated the arbitration award. The underlying litigation was revived (after another trip to the 4th Circuit) and plaintiffs filed a Second Amended Complaint (SAC). The SAC contained four RICO counts and alleged that The Coffee Beanery and seven of its officers (the "individual defendants") (collectively, "franchisor defendants") had misrepresented and fraudulently omitted information in The Coffee Beanery's Uniform Franchise Offering Circulars (UFOC), which induced the franchisee plaintiffs to invest in a Coffee Beanery Café. The franchisor defendants' sought to dismiss the four RICO counts brought in the SAC.

The franchisor defendants first argued that the RICO claims were barred by the four year statute of limitations. Specifically, the franchisor defendants argued that the SAC did not relate back, pursuant to Federal Rule of Civil Procedure 15(c), to the Original or Amended Complaint because it "inject[ed] entirely new legal and evidentiary issues that drastically alter[ed] the scope and focus" of the litigation. Further, the franchisor defendants argued that the RICO counts did not "draw on the same nucleus" of operative facts as the Original Complaint. The court noted that when amendments to complaints seek to add RICO claims, courts typically find such amendments relate back so long as the Original Complaint included a claim of fraud. Thus, the court determined that the primary consideration was whether the factual allegations supporting the RICO claim were similar to allegations in the Original or Amended Complaint. The court found that the factual claims supporting the RICO counts were, in fact, similar to the factual allegations in the original Complaint because the Original Complaint alleged fraud using the same "nucleus of operative fact". Accordingly, the court held that the RICO claims were not barred by the statute of limitations.

Next, the franchisor defendants argued that the franchisee plaintiffs had failed to allege sufficient facts to support the RICO claims alleged pursuant to 18 U.S.C. § 1962(c) which requires that a plaintiff establish four elements: (1) conduct; (2) of an enterprise; (3) through a pattern; (4) of racketeering activity. The franchisor defendants argued that the franchisee plaintiffs had not proven the final three factors. The court disagreed and noted that the non-fraud elements of RICO claims do not have to be pled with particularity as required by Federal Rule of Civil Procedure 9(b). Rather, the court explained that the non-fraud elements of RICO claims may

154

be pled pursuant to the less stringent standard of Rule 8 and held that the franchisee plaintiffs had met this standard. The court found that the franchisee plaintiffs had demonstrated the existence of an enterprise by outlining the alleged scheme and the role of the individual defendants in The Coffee Beanery organization. By this, the court was able to infer that the individual defendants had played some role in directing the alleged fraud. The court found that the franchisee plaintiffs demonstrated a pattern of racketeering activity existed because the defendants provided the same fraudulent UFOCs and false representations to induce other potential franchisees. Finally, the court found that the franchisee plaintiffs had satisfied the "racketeering activity" factor. The franchisee plaintiffs alleged that The Coffee Beanery had participated in mail and wire fraud by sending copies of the fraudulent UFOCs to others through the mail. Further, the franchisee plaintiffs had outlined the purpose, time frame, and targets of the alleged scheme to defraud, as well as the contents of the allegedly fraudulent communications that were sent using the mails and wires.

Finally, the court addressed the defendants' argument that the RICO claims were barred by the intracorporate conspiracy doctrine. The intracorporate conspiracy doctrine holds that corporations lack the multiplicity of actors required to form conspiracies. There are two exceptions to the intracorporate conspiracy doctrine. One is when a corporate officer has an independent personal stake in achieving the illegal objectives of the corporation and the second is when the agent's acts are unauthorized. The court found that neither exception applied. Therefore, two of the four RICO claims were barred. Accordingly, the court granted in part and denied in part the defendants' partial motion to dismiss.

III.   The Telephone Consumer Protection Act

In *Freidman v. Massage Envy Franchising, LCC*, No. 12-CV-02962, 2013 U.S. Dist. LEXIS 84250 (S.D. Cal. June 13, 2013), defendants Massage Envy Franchising ("Massage Envy") and M6 Marketing, Inc. ("M6") each filed a motion to dismiss for failure to state a claim pursuant to Federal of Civil Procedure 12(b)(6). Massage Envy is the franchisor of personal health goods and massage services. M6 specialized in providing automated telephone calling and text messaging services ("ATDS") on behalf of its clients. Plaintiffs argued that each of the Defendant acted as an agent or employee of the other Defendants, and acted within the scope and knowledge of each of the other Defendants.

Plaintiffs alleged that using an automatic telephone dialing system, the Defendants sent spam text message advertisements and promotional offers in violation of the Telephone Consumer Protection Act ("TCPA")(47 U.S.C. § 227 et seq.). Plaintiffs argued that the text messages originated from M6 at the direction of Massage Envy. Further, the Plaintiffs asserted that they had not given consent to receive unsolicited text messages nor had they conducted business with the Defendants.

The court found that Plaintiffs had "not stated with a level of factual specificity a claim under the TCPA." Rather, Plaintiffs had simply offered a "formulaic recitation" of the elements for a cause of action under the TCPA. Thus, asserting that the text messages that they received were generic and impersonal was a mere speculation, not a plausible claim supported by factual details. The court noted that it was equally conceivable that the messages were sent by hand or not using ATDS.

The court also found that Plaintiffs did not have standing to pursue a TCPA claim against Massage Envy. Plaintiffs had not sufficiently plead an agency relationship, but instead "rel[ied] on legal conclusions as if they were facts." Plaintiffs argued that even if Massage Envy was not considered to be an agent of M6, Massage Envy would still be liable as a beneficiary of M6's actions. The court declined to follow Plaintiffs' reasoning, observing that the TCPA and case law do not suggest a broader standard of liability beyond any party who "makes" a call or text message. Accordingly, the court granted the Defendants' motions to dismiss, but with leave to amend.

IV.   The Americans With Disabilities Act

In *Vallabhapurapu v. Burger King Corp.*, Bus. Franchise Guide (CCH) ¶ 14,931(N.D. Cal. Oct. 26, 2012), the court considered a joint motion for final approval of a class settlement. The action was the second part of a class action asserted against Burger King in which Plaintiffs alleged that restaurants leased by Burger King Corporation to its franchisees in California violated the Americans with Disabilities Act (ADA), the Unruh Civil Rights Act, and the California Disabled Persons Act. Specifically, Plaintiffs alleged that Burger King Corporation pursued "discriminatory policies or practices that resulted in unlawful architectural or design barriers which denied customers who use[d] wheelchairs or scooters access to services" at the Burger King restaurants in California.

The proposed settlement provided significant injunctive relief and damages, even going beyond the settlement negotiated in the first part of the class action. The settlement required Burger King to eliminate all accessibility barriers and use mandatory checklists that included specific accessibility items for remodeling, alterations, repairs, and maintenance. The settlement also required Burger King to include a recommendation in its franchisee operations manual encouraging franchisees to "check the force required to open all public exterior and restroom doors twice per month to ensure that they do not require more than five pounds of pressure to open." Additionally, the settlement provided for a cash payment of $19,000,000 to satisfy and settle all claims for damages, attorney's fees, and costs, one of the largest ADA settlements involving a franchisor.

The court approved the settlement. The court considered several factors, including the terms of the agreement, proposed plan of distribution and adequacy of notice to class members. The court determined that the settlement was a product of good faith, arms-length negotiations and found that the settlement was fair, reasonable and adequate pursuant to Federal Rule of Civil Procedure 23(e).

In *Bunn v. Khoury Enterprises, Inc.*, No. 11-CV-1540, 2013 U.S. Dist. LEXIS 68267 (S.D. Ind. May 13, 2013), the court found that the defendant Dairy Queen franchisee did not violate the Americans with Disabilities Act (ADA) when it reduced a disabled employee's hours during a seasonal drop-off in business because the employer did not subject the employee to any discipline that other workers were not subject to, and the employee presented no evidence that he performed satisfactory work.

The court observed that a disabled employee establishes a prima facie case of indirect discrimination by showing: (1) he is disabled, (2) he met his employer's legitimate employment expectations, (3) he suffered adverse employment action, and (4) the employer treated similarly situated employees without disability more favorably. The court found that the employee, Bunn, was disabled due to his sight impairment, and also found that reduced hours are an adverse employment outcome, which satisfied the third prong. However, the court ruled that Bunn failed to allege facts sufficient to demonstrate that he met his employer's legitimate expectations. Specifically, the court found that Bunn failed to address Khoury's allegations that Bunn shoved a trash can at a manager and refused to follow managers' directions. Further, the court found that Khoury did not treat similarly situated employees more favorably than Bunn himself. Thus, because Bunn failed to allege facts sufficient to demonstrate all four elements of indirect discrimination under the ADA, the court dismissed Bunn's complaint on summary judgment.

In *Hile v. Jimmy John's Hwy. 55*, No. 12-CV-1672, 2012 U.S. Dist. LEXIS 151536 (D. Minn. Oct. 9, 2012), the court denied a Jimmy John's franchisee's motion to dismiss a discrimination complaint on grounds that the alleged victim waited beyond the statutory period to file his complaint under both the ADA and Minnesota Human Rights Act (MHRA). Title VII of the Civil Rights Act of 1964, which applies to ADA claims, provides that in order for a claimant to sue an employer for discrimination, the claimant must file a discrimination charge with the EEOC within three hundred days after the alleged unlawful employment practice occurred. Under the MHRA, the claimant must file within one year of the discriminatory act.

In this case, Hile, who is deaf, sought to work at Jimmy John's as a delivery driver in the summer or fall of 2009. Various Jimmy John's around the Twin Cities declined to hire Hile. Hile alleged Jimmy John's implemented an unlawful policy requiring delivery drivers to be able to verbally communicate with customers. Hile filed his EEOC charge against the defendant Jimmy John's franchisee in the winter of 2009. In January 2012, the EEOC invited Hile to amend his complaint to name the franchisor, which Hile did. Hile commenced his suit in July 2012, asserting the franchisee violated the ADA and MHRA by denying him employment because of his disability, and asserting that the franchisor implemented an unlawful policy that caused the franchisee to discriminate. In his complaint, Hile failed to plead that he had filed the charges with the EEOC within the three-hundred day statutory period. The franchisee and franchisor moved to dismiss for failure to file the EEOC charge within the statutory period. The court found the omission to be immaterial because once a person files an EEOC charge, it becomes a part of the public record and a plaintiff need not plead it in the complaint. The court also held that the appropriate time to challenge the statutory period for filing a charge with the EEOC is summary judgment and not a motion to dismiss.

The franchisor Jimmy John's also challenged the plaintiff's right to name the franchisor in the lawsuit when it was not a party to the EEOC charge. The court ruled that even when a claimant fails to name a specific defendant in an EEOC charge, the claimant may sue that party after administrative exhaustion when there is a "sufficient identity of interest" between the previously unnamed party and the named respondent. The court found that this permitted a claimant suing a franchisee to sue a franchisor even if the claimant failed to name the franchisor in the initial EEOC charge. In this case, Hile failed to name Jimmy John's, the franchisor, in the EEOC charge, but the court held there was a "sufficient identity of interest" between Jimmy John's, the franchisor, and Jimmy John's Highway 55, the franchisee, because Hile alleged that the franchisor originated the allegedly unlawful policy. Accordingly, the court denied the motion to dismiss.

In *Lema v. Comfort Inn, Merced*, No, 10-CV-00362, 2013 U.S. Dist. LEXIS 48408 (E.D. Cal. April 2, 2013), the court granted summary judgment to the plaintiff because the defendant, a Comfort Inn franchisee, denied the disabled plaintiff full and equal treatment during her hotel stay, in violation of Title III of the ADA.

The court observed that to succeed under an ADA, Title III, claim a plaintiff must prove that: (1) she is disabled under the ADA, (2) the defendant is the private entity that owns, leases, or operates a place of public accommodation, and (3) the defendant denied the plaintiff full and equal treatment due to her disability. *Molski v. M.J. Cable, Inc.*, 481 F.3d 724, 730 (9th Cir. 2007). Denying a disabled person the opportunity to benefit from the goods, services, privileges, advantages or accommodations of an entity, directly or indirectly is a violation of 42 U.S.C. § 12182(b)(1)(A)(iv). When a private entity has already constructed a building, the entity violates full and equal treatment of the disabled by failing to remove architectural barriers when such removal is readily achievable. *Id.* The ADA Accessibility Guidelines define whether a facility is "readily accessible" and meets ADA requirements.

Here, plaintiff was a wheelchair-bound woman who stayed at a Comfort Inn hotel, which operated a place of public accommodation. An expert witness examined the hotel and concluded: a wheelchair could not navigate the lobby; the pool and sauna were inaccessible by wheelchair; public restrooms lacked turning space and support bars, and; the main entrance was not accessible by wheelchair. As the nonmoving party, the court found the defendant franchisee failed its burden to provide evidence sufficient to create a genuine issue of material fact. Therefore, the court accepted the plaintiff's allegations as true. On the undisputed facts, the Comfort Inn franchisee failed to provide "full and equal treatment" to Lema. The Court awarded $8,000 in statutory damages under Title III of the ADA and invited a separate motion for attorney's fees and costs.

V.   Civil Rights/Employment Law

A.   CIVIL RIGHTS

In *Comeaux v. Trahan*, No. 12-0767, 2012 U.S. Dist. 158527 (W.D. La. Nov. 5, 2012), the court reviewed whether a Coldwell Banker franchisee racially discriminated against an African-American purchaser when the franchisee denied the purchaser the opportunity to buy a home when he was financially ready and able. Comeaux, the plaintiff, sued the franchisor, Coldwell Banker LLC; the franchisee, Coldwell Banker Pelican Real Estate; the franchisee owner, Angi Trahan and Freddie Mac. Coldwell Banker LLC moved to dismiss the complaint for failure to state a claim, arguing that it was not responsible for the acts of its franchisee's employees under the terms of the franchise agreement between the franchisor and Pelican. The plaintiff opposed the motion to dismiss on grounds that Coldwell Banker LLC exercised sufficient control over Pelican's business practice to be liable for its alleged discriminatory housing practices.

The Court denied Coldwell Banker LLC's motion to dismiss, finding Comeaux pled sufficient facts from which a court could infer that Coldwell Banker could be vicariously liable for the alleged misconduct. Specifically, the court pointed to the language in the franchise agreement that required that a "[f]ranchisee shall operate the Franchised Business in accordance with the Policy Manual…." Comeaux argued that at this point in the litigation, he had not had a chance to conduct discovery and view the Operations Manual. The court concluded that the Operations Manual could contain information that would indicate franchisor control over Pelican. On these grounds, the court denied the franchisor's motion to dismiss.

B.   FAIR LABOR STANDARDS ACT

In *Cano v. DPNY, Inc.*, No. 10-CV-7100, 2012 U.S. LEXIS 161284 (S.D. N.Y. Nov. 8, 2012) the court allowed the plaintiffs to amend their Fair Labor Standards Act complaint against a Dominos' franchisee to add as additional defendants Domino's Pizza LLC, Domino's Pizza Franchising LLC, and Domino's Pizza, Inc., all entities which grant franchises to operate Domino's Pizza stores in New York. The plaintiffs were employees who alleged that a Domino's franchisee paid them substandard wages, failed to reimburse them for necessary costs, and illegally deducted money from their paychecks. The plaintiffs sought to amend their complaint to add the franchisor under a theory that the franchisor also employed them, thus, making the franchisor liable for compliance with the Fair Labor Standards Act.

Domino's Pizza, Inc., which does business in New York through subsidiaries Domino's Pizza LLC and Domino's Pizza Franchising LLC, opposed the plaintiffs' motion to amend on grounds that joining the franchisor would be "futile." Domino's argued that because the franchisor did not employ the employees, they had no obligation to the employees under the Fair Labor Standards Act, and the plaintiffs' suit against them would be futile. Courts apply the same standard to a futility argument as they apply to a 12(b)(6) motion to dismiss. To overcome a defendant's futility objection, a plaintiff need only show it has "colorable grounds" for relief.

The court found "colorable" grounds for the plaintiffs' claim for relief against the franchisor without speaking to whether it thought the plaintiffs could ultimately prevail on its FLSA claim against the franchisor Domino's.

The court noted that no Second Circuit decision precluded the possibility of employees of an independently owned franchisee recovering against the franchisor. The fact that Domino's Pizza, Inc. promulgated compensation policies, implemented the policies through Domino's point of sale system and tracked hours, wages, payroll records and monitored employee performance all aggregated to demonstrate that the plaintiffs should be allowed to amend their complaint to join the franchisor as a potentially liable defendant.

In *Pares v. Kendall Lakes Automotive, LLC.*, No. 13-CV-20317, 2013 U.S. Dist. LEXIS 90499 (S.D. Fla. June 27, 2013) the court granted plaintiffs' motion for conditional certification of a collective action under the Fair Labor Standards Act ("FSLA"). Juan Pares, Emilio Alonzo, and Mario Gomez (collectively "Plaintiffs") brought a claim against their former employers Kendall Lakes Automotive, LCC and Miami Lakes AM, LCC, franchised car dealerships, (collectively "Defendants") for allegedly violating the FSLA by instituting a payment plan that failed to pay the minimum wage. Plaintiffs filed a motion seeking a conditional class certification for all the salespeople employed by Defendants subject to the payment plan.

When the plaintiff's began their employment, they received $600 on a biweekly basis plus all commissions earned from their sales during that period. The biweekly payment was not connected to the number of hours worked. In July 2012, the dealerships altered the payment plan at both locations by treating the $600 biweekly payment as a draw against the commissions earned. If the plaintiffs earned less than $600 in commissions on biweekly basis, the deficiency would then carry forward in perpetuity to subsequent months until the salesman could pay it back from future earnings. Other plaintiffs received in advance of $7.67 for every hour logged on a biweekly basis which was also treated as an advance against commissions earned. Because of the way the system worked, Plaintiffs began to underreport their hours worked because it had the effect of decreasing their compensation, even though they were working 60 to 70 hours per week. Plaintiffs alleged that the reduced commissions did not cover the minimum wage owed and cause the plaintiffs to receive less than the minimum wage because of the hours worked. Plaintiffs also submitted affidavits that approximately 100 other similarly situated employees were willing to opt-in to a class lawsuit.

The court found that there was a reasonable basis to certify a conditional class under the FLSA. The plaintiff demonstrated that there was a reasonable basis for his claim that there were other similarly situated employees who wanted to opt-in. The court emphasized that this was a decision based on a lenient standard at the beginning of the litigation. The court noted that the plaintiff would be subject to a more rigorous standard after the completion of discovery if and when the defendants moved to decertify the class..

Despite granting Plaintiffs request for conditional certification, the court limited discovery, the notice to other potential class plaintiffs, and refused to toll the statute of limitations. First, the court found that, because Plaintiffs requested expedited discovery within 15 days, the Defendants were only required to provide the last known address and telephone number of potential plaintiffs for a limited period of time. They were not required to dig through years of personnel records or conduct employee interviews within the timeframe requested by the plaintiffs. Finally, the court refused to toll the statute of limitations. Plaintiffs argued that it should be tolled for other potential plaintiffs for every day they are not given notice. The court disagreed, finding that the plaintiffs did not identify any extraordinary circumstances that would permit equitable tolling of the statute of limitations.

VI.   Taxation

One of the most interesting cases of the year is *Cavanaugh v. Commissioner*, No. 30825-09, 2012 T.C.M. LEXIS 325 (Nov. 26, 2012), which answers the question: "If our CEO takes his 27 year old girlfriend on vacation and she dies of a cocaine overdose, can we deduct the wrongful death settlement as a business expense?" The U.S. Tax Court said no, this is not a valid business expense, and denied the claimed $2.3 million deduction.

James Cavanaugh, then age 55, was the CEO of Jani-King International, Inc. For Thanksgiving 2002, he decided to take his 27 year old girlfriend, Anne (Claire) Robinson, with him to St. Martin in the Caribbean along with his bodyguard Ronald ("Rock") Walker and Erika Fortner (another Jani-King employee). The trip was, admittedly, a pleasure trip, and no Jani-King business was conducted.

Claire Robinson died on November 28, 2002 due to cardiac arrest caused by a cocaine overdose. Robinson's mother brought a wrongful death action against Cavanaugh, and Jani-King, alleging that he regularly (with Walker's help) supplied young women (including both of her daughters) with drugs and "forced them to participate in diverse debauchery." The Jani-King board of directors authorized a settlement up to $5,000,000. Unfortunately for Robinson, she accepted $2.3 million over two years, not even half of what Jani-King has set aside for settlement.

Jani-King deducted the $2.3 million over 2005 and 2006, plus its attorneys' fees incurred in defending the case. In 2009, the IRS advised Cavanaugh of various tax issues, all of which he settled . . . except for the deduction of $2.3 million plus attorneys' fees. (Jani-King was at the time an S corporation, its returns flowed through to Cavanaugh, its 100% owner).

The question for the tax court was whether the expenses were ordinary and necessary business expenses under IRS Code § 162. The court found they were not because the conduct in question did not "arise from Jani-King's profit-seeking activities." The activities creating the claim did not "arise from or further Jani-King's business, and were far from company property." Cavanaugh belatedly argued that he could deduct the expenses personally, but the court rejected that argument as waived. Even if the argument was not waived, it was also barred because Cavanaugh, at the time the claim arose, was also not engaged in any profit-seeking business activity.

The court also prohibited Cavanaugh or Jani-King from deducting the $250,000 Cavanaugh contributed to the settlement, but later was reimbursed by Jani-King.

As no superseding federal law was enacted preventing California from enforcing its Click-Through and Affiliate Nexus law, the provisions of the law became effective on September 15, 2012 according to a formal letter from the Department of Finance, Office of the Director, dated August 15, 2012.

In recent years, it has become very popular for individuals with poor credit and no substantial assets other than their retirement funds to start up their franchised businesses by using the retirement funds. This system of funding has been referred to as "ROBS" an acronym for "Rollovers for Business Startups." The benefit of this system of funding is that the franchisee does not need to withdraw the retirement funds and pay taxes and penalties, thus saving the franchisee 30-40% based upon today's typical tax rates.

These products have been sold aggressively by economic advisors (and sometimes by franchisors). The products have generally been ignored by the IRS. However, the validity of these ROBS products has been called into question as a result of the recent case of *Peek v. Commissioner,* No. 5951-11 6481-11, 2013 T.C. LEXIS 13 (May 9, 2013).

In *Peek*, the taxpayers sought to purchase a business in 2001, and, to do so, they established IRAs, transferred funds to the IRAs from existing IRAs, set up a new corporation, sold shares in the new corporation to the IRAs, and used the funds from the sale of shares to purchase the business. This is a typical ROBS transaction.

But, most importantly for the *Peek* case, the taxpayers also personally guaranteed a $200,000 promissory note to the seller. Later, in 2003 and 2004, the taxpayers rolled over the stock in the "traditional" IRAs they set up for the original ROBS transaction, to Roth IRAs and paid income tax on the appreciation. Then, in 2006, the taxpayers directed the Roth IRAs to sell the stock, which had significantly appreciated in value. Because the accounts were Roth IRAs and tax had already been paid on the conversion, the taxpayers believed that they were not subject to tax on the gains.

The Tax Court disagreed and said the 2001 transaction destroyed the tax exempt status of the ROBS IRA on the date that the loan guaranties were signed. The guaranties created a "prohibited transaction" under IRC Section 4975, which disqualified the IRA *ab initito*. The court wrote, "The loan guaranties were not a once-and-done transaction with effects only in 2001 but instead remained in place and constituted a continuing prohibited transaction, thus preventing [the taxpayers'] accounts that held the FP Company stock from being IRAs in subsequent years." The tax deficiencies asserted by the IRS were upheld at approximately a quarter of a million dollars each.

Additionally, there was a 20% undervaluation penalty which was upheld in the face of the taxpayers' argument, because the certified public accountant on whose advice the taxpayers claimed to have reasonably relied was, as noted by the court, not a disinterested professional but a promoter of the plan employed by the taxpayers, so they could not claim a "reasonable cause" defense under Code Sec. 6664(c)

Peek raises a huge red flag for franchisees using ROBS financing. Based upon the result in *Peek*, a good argument could be made that if a franchisee funds its franchise purchase with funds from a Rollover IRA and the franchisee guarantees the business' loans or lends money to the business, the franchisee could have been found to have destroyed the tax exempt nature of the IRA and could have substantial liability for taxes, interest and penalties.

VII. Privacy

In *Ignat v. YUM! Brands, Inc.*, No. 046343, 2013 Cal. App. LEXIS 210 (Cal. Ct. App. Mar. 13, 2013), the California state appellate court reaffirmed a common-law right to privacy in California and held that an employer may violate a current or former employee's common-law right to privacy by disclosing "private facts" to coworkers in writing *or orally*. The court further held that the common-law right to privacy and a constitutional right to privacy are different, albeit related. The court may find a person violates another's common-law privacy right if that person publicizes a private fact that is offensive or objectionable to a reasonable person. The court may find a person violates a constitutional right to privacy if he discloses any private record that is supposed to be kept confidential.

In this case, the plaintiff, Ignat, was an assistant in the YUM! corporate office and suffered from bipolar disorder. Ignat took medicine for her condition, and side effects occasionally caused her to miss work. After one such medical absence, Ignat returned to work and learned that during her absence her supervisor informed her coworkers that Ignat was bipolar. The court found that the supervisor's oral disclosure of Ignat's disorder would be objectionable and offensive to reasonable person and violated Ignat's common-law right to privacy. Previously, California courts held that a person could only violate another person's common-law right to privacy by disclosing an objectionable private fact in writing. Based on this ruling, employers may now violate their employee's right to common-law privacy by orally disclosing a private fact that would be considered offensive or objectionable to a reasonable person.

VIII. Consolidated Appropriations Act

In *Colonial Chevrolet Co., Inc. v. U.S.*, No. 10-647, 2012 U.S. Claims LEXIS 997 (Fed. Cl. Aug. 20, 2012) and *Alley's of Kingsport, Inc. v. U.S.*, No. 10-100, 2012 U.S. Claims LEXIS 1006 (Fed. Cl. Aug. 20, 2012), the court reviewed former car dealers' public takings claim against the United States for causing GM and Chrysler to rescind their dealership contracts while the U.S. restructured the auto giants. The United States sought an interlocutory appeal of the denial of its motion to dismiss the "unique" former dealers' takings claims. The court noted that the interlocutory appeal could materially advance the ultimate termination of the litigation, which was important because the case had the possibility of expanding to numerous additional plaintiffs.

The plaintiff's complaint alleged that the government's conduct in the manner at which it controlled GM and Chrysler's bankruptcy proceeding facilitated the repudiation of the plaintiff's franchise agreements with the auto makers. In order for the bankruptcy court to approve the rescission of the franchise agreements, it had to make a finding that the government did not "control" GM and Chrysler. The government sought a ruling that the bankruptcy court's finding had a preclusive effect on the district court and the plaintiff's taking's claim. In essence, the government argued that since the bankruptcy court made a preliminary ruling that the government did not control GM and Chrysler, the plaintiff could not hope to prevail on a government taking's claim. The court rejected the government's argument reasoning that even if the bankruptcy court found the government did not control the automakers' bankruptcy proceedings, the plaintiffs could still show their business losses were a "direct, natural, and probable result" of the government's restructuring of Chrysler and GM. This could be an alternate method to show the government took the dealer's property without just compensation.

The U.S. Court of Appeals consolidated the *Colonial Chevrolet* and *Alley's of Kingsport* cases and granted the United States' motion to certify the district court's ruling denying its motion to dismiss on appeal. *Alley's of Kingsport v. U.S.*, 494 Fed. Appx. 89, 91 (Fed. Cir. 2012).

In *Los Feliz Ford v. Chrysler Group LLC*, No. 10-CV-6077, 2012 U.S. Dist. LEXIS 147370 (C.D. Cal. April 9, 2012), the court reviewed Section 747 of the Consolidated Appropriations Act of 2010 and its application to dealership contracts that Chrysler rescinded in bankruptcy.

Congress passed the Consolidated Appropriations Act of 2010 after terminated Chrysler dealers lobbied Congress for a legislative remedy. Section 747 of the Act established an arbitration process for dealers who sought continuation, reinstatement of a franchise agreement, or to be added as a franchisee to the reorganized auto manufacturers' new dealer networks. Section 747 entitled dealers who petitioned for arbitration and met Section the 747(b) standards to receive a "customary and usual letter of intent" to enter into a sale and service agreement with the newly organized Chrysler (the "New Chrysler").

In this case, plaintiff Los Feliz pursued arbitration, and the arbitrator directed New Chrysler to provide Los Feliz Ford with a customary and usual letter of intent to add Los Feliz as a dealer. Los Feliz claimed the letter New Chrysler provided them was not customary and usual, and filed a lawsuit contending that Section 747 entitled Los Feliz to a reinstatement of its previous Old Chrysler contract with the New Chrysler post-bankruptcy entity. The court disagreed, and granted defendant New Chrysler's motion for summary judgment, finding that a "customary and usual" letter of intent refers to "customary and usual" at the present time, not what would have been "customary and usual" for the dealer under its previous contract. Because Los Feliz's previous dealership contract with Old Chrysler terminated and Old Chrysler ceased to exist, Los Feliz could not be "reinstated" or "continue" as a dealer under Section 747. Therefore, the only remedy available to Los Feliz under the Act was to be added as a franchisee under terms consistent with similarly recently added dealers.

In *Quality Jeep Chrysler, Inc. v. Chrysler Group LLC*, No. 10-CV-00900, 2011 U.S. Dist. LEXIS 156450 (D.N.M. Mar. 22, 2011) the court reviewed the scope of discoverable materials in Section 747 arbitration proceedings. Quality Jeep was a former Chrysler dealer that Chrysler terminated during its bankruptcy. Quality Jeep initiated arbitration against New Chrysler under section 747 of the Consolidated Appropriations Act of 2010 and sought discovery relating to the contents on letters of intent issued by New Chrysler to other former dealers. New Chrysler resisted the discovery and Quality Jeep brought a motion to compel.

The court found that sales and service agreements between New Chrysler and continued dealers were not subject to discovery because they were not instructive concerning what constituted a "customary and usual" letter of intent for dealers seeking a new dealer agreement from New Chrysler pursuant to Section 747. However, sales and service agreements between New Chrysler since its inception and dealers added after emerging from bankruptcy were relevant and open for discovery, along with any communication and other documents related to this narrow band of sales and service agreements. The court found that only letters of intent to dealers it added after its bankruptcy were relevant and discoverable. The court also decided that Quality Jeep could not access information about Chrysler's lobbying efforts during the Consolidated Appropriations Act of 2010.

In *Eagle Auto Mall Corp. v. Chrysler Group LLC*, No. 10-CV-3876, 2012 U.S. Dist. LEXIS 146562 (E.D. N.Y Sept. 28, 2012), the court reviewed the terms of a "customary letter of intent" between two terminated Chrysler auto dealers and New Chrysler that resulted from Section 747 arbitration. The issue before the court on defendant New Chrysler's motion for summary judgment was whether the terms of the letter New Chrysler offered to the dealerships was "substantially the same" as those New Chrysler offered to new franchisees in the dealer network during the same time period. New Chrysler moved for summary judgment on the dealer's claims.

The plaintiff dealerships prevailed in arbitration under Section 747 of the Consolidated Appropriations Act of 2010. However, the same court held a year prior that prevailing in arbitration did not entitle the dealers to reinstatement on the same terms of their prior dealer agreement before Old Chrysler rescinded the dealership contract in bankruptcy. Instead, the plaintiffs were only entitled to an offer under terms that were usual and customary at the time of the offer. The dealers believed that New Chrysler subjected them to onerous terms in the new letters of intent. The court determined that whether the offer was "usual and customary" or onerous was a question of fact, and denied New Chrysler's motion for summary judgment. Subsequently, in *Eagle Auto Mall Corp. v. Chrysler Group LLC*, No.10-CV-3876, 2013 U.S. Dist. 27943 (E.D.N.Y. June 24, 2013) the court ruled as a matter of law that New Chrysler's letter of intent to plaintiffs was customary and usual.

The plaintiff auto dealers alleged that four terms in the letter of intent violated Section 747 of the Act. The four terms at issue were: (1) a dealership site approval provision, (2) the time in which to resolve protests raised by opposing dealers, (3) architectural requirements, and (4) a site option to purchase the facility. In its fact finding, the court considered terms from 135 different letters of intent offered by New Chrysler from June 2009 through April 2011. Fifty of the letters were between New Chrysler and dealers from pre-arbitration settlement, 32 letters were to terminated dealers that prevailed in Section 747 arbitration, and 53 letters were from New Chrysler to new dealers not previously affiliated with Old Chrysler. Using the 135 letters of intent from the relevant time period, the court found the four terms to be usual and customary; 97% of the 135 letters had site approval requirements; the dispute resolution term appeared in 55% of letters of intent; the architectural requirements appeared in 90% of the 135 letters, and; the site option requirement appeared in 83% of the 135 letters. Thus, the court found as a matter of law that the terms of the letters of intent offered by New Chrysler to Plaintiff Eagle Auto Mall were customary and usual and, thus, legal under the Consolidated Appropriations Act.

IX.   Sailors And Servicemembers' Civil Relief Act

In *In re: Oil Spill by the Oil Rig "Deepwater Horizon"*, No. 2179, 2012 U.S. Dist. LEXIS 141546 (E.D. La. Oct. 1, 2012), the court reviewed the collective BP dealers' claim against BP corporate for lost profits and brand damage due to consumer animosity after BP corporate's negligence in causing the Deepwater Horizon oil spill and subsequent failure to quickly stop the spill. The plaintiffs were BP gas station franchisees around the country that based their claims solely on consumer animosity and not actual property damage due to the spill.

The court first applied the Oil Pollution Act, 33 U.S.C. § 2702 (1991), to plaintiffs' claims. The Oil Pollution Act (OPA) allows a party to recover economic losses resulting from destruction of real or personal property due to an oil spill caused by another party. The court held that the BP franchisees could not recover from BP corporate for "brand damage" under subsection B because subsection B applies only to injury to tangible physical property.

The court further held that admiralty law applied and precluded the court from applying any other tort law, including the OPA. The court determined that the case met the locus and nexus requirements of admiralty tort jurisdiction, because the tort occurred on navigable water (locus) and the tort disrupted maritime commerce (nexus). The court rejected plaintiffs' argument that because BP corporate made decisions regarding how to respond to the spill on dry land, it should defeat the "locus" requirement.

Using admiralty law, the court then applied the *Robins Dry Dock Rule* to the dealers' claim, which bars tort claims for purely economic losses when they are unaccompanied by physical injury to the plaintiff's property interest. Because the Rule does not bar suits on intentional torts, insofar as the actor intends both the act itself and the consequences of the act, the plaintiffs attempted to come within the exception by alleging that BP corporate intentionally decided to attempt to save the leaking well rather than block it, which increased the oil spilled into the ocean and caused Plaintiff's lost profits and brand damages. The court applied the *Iqbal* plausibility standard to the plaintiffs' claim that BP intentionally failed to stop the flow of oil and found the plaintiffs did not allege sufficient facts to meet the standard. Accordingly, the franchisees' claims were dismissed.

CHAPTER ❖ 8

Other State Law Issues

I.   Unfair And Deceptive Trade Practices

Case law was skimpy this year on claims based upon state unfair and deceptive trade practices acts. However, a few franchisees and distributors were able to survive dispositive motions on such claims.

Oliver Stores v. JCB, Inc., No.11-CV-353, 2012 U.S. Dist. LEXIS 144348 (D. Me. Oct. 5, 2012) involved a claim by a dealer under the Maine Franchise Act, 10 M.R.S.A. §§ 1361, *et seq.* and under the Maine Unfair Trade Practices Act, 5 M.R.S.A. §§ 201, *et seq.* The manufacturer moved for judgment on the pleadings, arguing that a dealer could not bring a claim under the MUTPA because the dealer did not purchase or lease goods, services or property primarily for personal, family or household purposes, as was required to bring a private civil action under 5 M.R.S.A. § 213.

The dealer countered that the MFA had been revised in 1993 to state that a violation of the MFA "constitutes an unfair trade practice" under the MUTPA. 10 M.R.S.A. § 1370. There was no reason for the legislature to make this amendment if it did not want to provide a dealer with a private right of action under the MUTPA.

The court ruled for the manufacturer. The court found that the specific "primarily for personal, family or household purposes" language of the MUTPA overrode the legislature's incorporation of the MFA into the MUTPA. Therefore, the Maine Attorney General could sue to enjoin violations of the MFA (under the AG's MUTPA authority) but the dealer had no private right of action under the MUTPA.

G.L.M. Security & Sound, Inc. v. Lojack Corp., No. 10-CV-4701, 2012 U.S. Dist. LEXIS 142549 (E.D. N.Y. Sept. 28, 2012) involved a distributor of Lojack car security systems and tracking devices suing Lojack, stating that Lojack had promised G.L.M. the best price for its systems but, subsequently, Lojack gave other dealers a far better price.

While dismissing a number of claims, the court refused to dismiss G.L.M.'s claim under Massachusetts' General Law Chapter 93A, which prohibits unfair, immoral and unscrupulous conduct. The court found that Massachusetts would recognize a Chapter 93A for the "best price" claim, which it described as, "Lojack's lie and the effect of that lie on G.L.M's business."

In *Beaver v. Inkmart, LLC* (summarized in Chapter 5.X.C.), while dismissing Beaver's Florida Franchise Act claim, the Court refused to dismiss a Florida Unfair and Deceptive Trade Practices Act claim against the franchisor, finding that Beaver had adequately pled a deceptive or unfair practice, causation, and damages. In addition, the FDD omissions alleged by Beaver were *per se* violations of the FDUPTA.

In *Chicago Male Medical Clinic, LLC v. Ultimate Management, Inc.*, summarized at Chapter 1.I., the court found that Chicago Male had failed to plead common law or statutory fraud with particularity and had failed to establish a right to sue under the Illinois Consumer Fraud Act.

In *AdvoCare International, L.P. v. Ford*, Bus. Franchise Guide (CCH) ¶ 14,999 (Tex. App. Feb. 5, 2013), the Texas Court of Appeals, reversing the trial court, found that 29 distributors who were terminated without good cause by AdvoCare were not "consumers" protected by the Texas Deceptive Trade Practice Act because their claims related to the distributorships themselves and <u>not</u> to any defects related to the goods and services purchased from AdvoCare.

The court indicated that the result may have been different had a distributor been an actual "franchisee" (citing *Texas Cookie Co. v. Hendricks & Peralta, Inc.*, 747 S.W.2d 873 (Tex. App. 1988)), however, the distributors had made no such claim, so their claims were invalid as a matter of law. The court reversed the judgment of the trial court and rendered judgment that the distributors "take nothing on their claims."

In *Center City Periodontists, P.C. v. Dentsply International, Inc.*, No. 10-774, 2013 U.S. Dist. LEXIS 109545 (E.D. Pa. June 28, 2013), a periodontist made a New Jersey Consumer Fraud Act ("NJCFA") claim against a supplier for selling a defective Cavitron – a prescription medical devise.

The court found that since the device was <u>not</u> available for purchase to anyone other than a licensed physician, it was not "merchandise" under the NJCFA. The court distinguished a case involving a hair removal franchisee who purchased an expensive laser for its practice, stating that no license was required to purchase said laser.

In *Camasta v. Jos. A. Bank Clothiers, Inc.*, No. 12-CV-7782, 2013 U.S. Dist. LEXIS 103905 (N.D. Ill. July 25, 2013) a suit for fraud failed because of the plaintiff's failure to prove actual damages. Camasta filed a class action under the Illinois Consumer Fraud and Deceptive Business Practices Act ("ICFA") against the clothier, Jos. A. Bank, for its sales practices. Specifically, the plaintiff alleged that the defendant had a sale practice of advertising certain items as "on sale" when, in fact, the items were merely being sold at their normal retail price.

The plaintiff had seen an advertisement stating "sale prices" and proceeded to the defendant's store, where he purchased six shirts for $167.00. The plaintiff alleged, but for the "sale" price, he would not have purchased the shirts or may have purchased them for less elsewhere. In order for a private party to bring an action to rectify an "unfair or deceptive ac[t] or practice" under the ICFA, the plaintiff must prove "actual damage." First, the court found Camasta had failed to allege fraud with particularity, and then the court concluded the plaintiff had failed, as he must, to allege "that he was deprived the benefit of the bargain because he paid more than the actual value of the shirts." For these reasons, the court granted the defendant's motion to dismiss.

II. Taxation

In 2012, Virginia enacted legislation requiring certain remote sellers to collect Virginia sales tax if they utilize in-state facilities. The law establishes a presumption that a dealer has nexus with the state if the seller or any commonly-controlled person maintains a distribution center, warehouse, fulfillment center, office, or similar location in Virginia that facilitates the delivery of tangible personal property sold by the seller to its customers. *See* Ch. 590 (S.B. 597), Laws 2012, effective September 1, 2013.

In late August of 2012, the Alabama Department of Revenue adopted a new rule which requires certain out-of-state sellers to register with the department for a sales tax license and collect and remit sales tax on all sales of tangible personal property made within the state. The rule also provides that a seller may have substantial nexus with the state due to the business activities conducted in the state by the seller's affiliates as set forth in Ala. Code §40-23-190. A seller has substantial nexus with the state for the collection of use tax if, among other things:

> the seller and the in-state business use an identical or substantially similar name, trade name, trademark, or goodwill, to develop, promote, or maintain sales, or the in-state business and the seller pay for each other's services in whole or in part contingent upon the volume or value of sales, or the in-state business and the seller share a common business plan or substantially coordinate their business plans, or the in-state business provides services to, or that inure to the benefit of, the business related to developing, promoting, or maintaining the in-state market.

Rule 810-6-2-.90.01, Alabama Department of Revenue, effective August 24, 2012.

The Kansas Department of Revenue has issued guidance on recent changes to state law that impose a duty on certain remote retailers to register with the department as retailers and to collect and remit Kansas retailers' sales tax or use tax on taxable sales of tangible personal property for use, consumption, or storage in Kansas. The click-through nexus provisions take effect on October 1, 2013, and the affiliate nexus provisions and various amendments to the definition of "retailer doing business in this state" take effect on July 1, 2013. The department also emphasizes that under Kansas law, each retailer doing business in Kansas who makes taxable sales of tangible personal property for use, storage, or consumption in Kansas has a duty to collect from customers the Kansas state and local use tax due, and to timely report and remit the taxes. Notice 13-05, Kansas Department of Revenue, May 10, 2013.

In *Avis Budget Group, Inc. v. City of Newark*, 48 A.3d 1113 (N.J. Super. Ct. App. Div. 2012), the New Jersey Superior Court, Appellate Division, affirmed a district court ruling that an ordinance enacted by the City of Newark which levied a rental tax on all car rental transactions within specified industrial zones of the city, including the Newark Airport, was not a discriminatory tax or otherwise in violation of the federal Anti-Head Tax Act (AHTA) or the dormant Commerce Clause. The Appellate Division ruled that the car rental tax was a valid exercise of municipal authority.

Cavanaugh v. Commissioner, No. 30825-09, 2012 T.C.M. LEXIS 325 (Nov. 26, 2012), summarized at Chapter 7.V., would appear to raise issue relevant to state income tax deductions if they have been taken for similar acts.

III. Employment/Civil Rights

In *Hayes v. Jani-King Franchising, Inc.*, No.10-CV-382, 2012 U.S. Dist. LEXIS 182690 (S.D. Miss. Dec. 28, 2012), the court denied Jani-King's motion for reconsideration, finding that the issue of whether an "employee/employer" relationship existed was to be determined not by the franchise agreement's terms, but by facts surrounding the actual relationship of the parties, which facts were in dispute.

Was an area developer for franchisor Mossy Oak Properties a "sales representative" under Alabama's State Sales Representatives Commissions Contracts Act, Ala. Code § 8-24-1 (1975)? The court in *Johnson v. Mossy Oak Properties, Inc.*, No. 11-CV-4205, 2012 U.S. Dist. LEXIS 167605 (N.D. Ala. Nov. 27, 2012) said no. While the area developer (called a "Development Agent" by Mossy Oak) did, in fact, solicit sales of franchises, he was not protected by the anti-termination provisions Alabama Act applicable to sales representatives because franchises were an intangible item and, therefore, not a "product" under the Alabama Act. In addition, the franchises were not sold "at wholesale," but instead were sold at retail to an end user. Therefore, Mossy Oak was granted partial summary judgment on this issue.

IV. Breach of Warranty

In *Manley v. Doe*, 849 F. Supp. 2d 594 (E.D. N.C. 2012), the court considered Defendants Wendy's International, Inc. ("Wendy's") and its franchisee First Sun Management's ("First Sun") (collectively "Defendants") motion for summary judgment dismissing plaintiff's complaint. Plaintiff John Manley sought to recover damages as a result of Defendants' alleged breach of an implied warranty of merchantability and negligence, and Plaintiff Karen Manley's derivative claim for loss of consortium. The dispute arose out of a 2 inch plastic fragment, embossed with a portion of Wendy's logo that was removed from Mr. Manley's lung. According to Mr. Manley, he unknowingly ingested the fragment two years earlier while eating a hamburger from Wendy's.

The court first considered Mr. Manley's breach of implied warranty of merchantability claim. The court addressed an issue of first impression in North Carolina: whether a plaintiff must prove the existence of a specific good when claiming a breach of implied warranty of merchantability. The court conducted case law research and found that no North Carolina appellate decisions had permitted "a breach of warranty claim to go to a jury where a plaintiff failed to identify with particularity a specific good when claiming breach of an implied warranty of merchantability." The court concluded that the appellate case law stated that a plaintiff alleging breach of an implied warranty of merchantability must establish that the goods were defective at the time of sale. Mr. Manley failed in this regard. Further, the court noted that even if Mr. Manley was not required to prove a specific defective good, his claim would still fail because he was not able to prove that a hamburger sold to him by Wendy's caused his injuries. He could not support his claims by inference.

The court next addressed Mr. Manley's claim that Defendants were negligent in preparing his food. Once again, the court found that Mr. Manley was seeking to establish negligence through circumstantial evidence, and lacked the direct evidence necessary to support such a claim. The court found that Mr. Manley essentially made a *res ipsa loquitor* claim, which was not available under North Carolina law because the injury was allegedly from the "ingestion of an adulterated food product."

Finally, the court dismissed Mrs. Manley's derivative claim of loss of consortium because Mr. Manley's claims, from which it was derived, were dismissed, and granted the Defendants' Motion for Summary Judgment.

CHAPTER ❖ 9

Litigation

It has been another busy year for franchise litigants. As in the past, a large number of cases involve the determination of where the parties are going to ultimately litigate their dispute. Federal courts continue to be careful about asserting jurisdiction over parties that have insufficient contact with the forum state. However, franchisors continue to be successful enforcing forum selection clauses in contracts with their franchisees. Arbitration continues to be a prolific source of litigation. Significantly, the United States Supreme Court weighed in on the class waiver issue and continued the trend of rigorously enforcing arbitration provisions, including class action waivers. Outside of the arbitration context, wage and hour class action litigation against franchisors continues to be very popular, especially on the West Coast. Add to this a panoply of procedural and contractual issues and you have this year's litigation summary of cases.

I. Jurisdiction

A. STATE OR FEDERAL COURT?

In *Ranjer Foods, LLC v. Quiznos Franchising II, LLC*, No. 13-CV-00256, 2013 U.S. Dist. LEXIS 18132 (D. Colo. Feb. 8, 2013), the court reviewed its own jurisdiction, sua sponte, after the defendant franchisor removed the case to federal court from county court in Denver, Colorado. The plaintiff's complaint alleged 28 causes of action against Quiznos, including violations of the Colorado Organized Crime Control Act ("COCCA"), violation of the Colorado Consumer Protection Act and the Civil Theft Act, as well as breach of contract, unjust enrichment, fraud and other related claims. Quiznos removed the case to the District of Colorado arguing that the district court had subject matter jurisdiction because plaintiff's state law claims raised "substantial federal questions." Although the plaintiffs did not file a motion to remand, the court took it upon itself to address the issue. The court acknowledged that a plaintiff may not avoid federal jurisdiction by artfully invoking only state law when federal questions are "essential" to the asserted claims. However, a federal court must satisfy itself that it has jurisdiction before proceeding in a case.

Quiznos alleged that the complaint raised two federal questions: (1) whether Quiznos complied with the Franchise Rule promulgated by the Federal Trade Commission ("FTC") and (2) whether Quiznos violated federal laws prohibiting fraud and racketeering. With respect to the first claim, Quiznos alleged that resolving the plaintiff's claims would require an analysis of the FTC Franchise Rule, which describes what a franchisor can, and cannot, say to prospective franchisees. The court dispatched this argument quickly by noting that there is no private right of action to enforce the FTC Act. The absence of a private right of action is evidence that Congress did not intent for the Franchise Rule to serve as a basis for federal jurisdiction in a private lawsuit. Quiznos also argued that plaintiff's COCCA claims raised federal questions because plaintiff alleged violation of federal law as the requisite predicate acts. Again, the court rejected Quiznos' argument by noting that violations of federal law as an element of a COCCA claim does not support federal question jurisdiction. Additionally, none of the plaintiff's COCCA claims relied exclusively on federal law for the alleged predicate acts. Therefore, the court could resolve those claims without addressing federal law. Based on the court's holding, the court remanded the case to county court.

In *MMXII, Inc. v. QFA Royalties*, LLC, No. 13-CV-00253, 2013 U.S. Dist. LEXIS 20869 (D. Colo. Feb. 15, 2013), plaintiff franchisees brought a claim against Quiznos for allegedly stealing millions of dollars from the franchisees. Plaintiff's complaint asserted 28 claims for relief, including Colorado state law causes of action. Quiznos removed to federal court, arguing that plaintiff's state law claims actually raised substantial federal questions.

The court remanded the matter to state court finding that there is a general presumption against federal jurisdiction and that federal courts should strictly construe the federal removal statute. The court observed that to create subject-matter jurisdiction, the "well-plead complaint [must] establish[] either that federal law creates the cause of action or that the plaintiffs' right to relief necessarily depends on resolution of a substantial question of federal" law.

Attempting to satisfy this standard, Quiznos first argued that plaintiff's claims implicated the Federal Trade Commission's ("FTC") Franchise Rule. The Franchise Rule sets forth disclosure requirements for the sale of franchises. Quiznos argued that any analysis of a failure to disclose claim requires an analysis of whether it also complied with the Franchise Rule. The court rejected Quiznos' argument. Instead, the court found that plaintiff's claim did not raise a substantial federal issue under the FTC Franchise Rule. Although Quiznos intended to rely on the Franchise Rule in defense of the plaintiff's claims, the court held that was not a proper basis for removal.

Quiznos also argued that plaintiff's claims under the Colorado Organized Crime Control Act involved a federal question because proving a claim under the statute required proof of federal crimes. The court emphasized that the mere presence of a federal issue in a state cause of action does not automatically create federal-question jurisdiction. Instead, a "state-law claim [must] necessarily raise a stated federal issue." The court found that the determination of a federal issue usually depends on the whether Congress intended to provide a federal forum by including a private right of action. Because the federal criminal code does not confer a private cause of action, there was no substantial question of federal law. The court remanded the case to state court.

In *Light House, Inc. v. QFA Royalties LLC*, No. 13-CV-00263, 2013 U.S. Dist. LEXIS 95388 (D. Colo. July 9, 2013), the court denied the plaintiffs' motion for attorneys' fees under 28 U.S.C. § 1447(c), which concerns remand of a case improperly removed to federal court. The plaintiffs brought 28 state and common law claims against Quiznos Franchising II LLC and related defendants. Citing federal subject matter jurisdiction, the defendants removed the case, and nine similar cases, to federal court. Judges reviewing two of the similar cases remanded them to state court *sua sponte*.

Notwithstanding the orders entered by judges in the same district granting remand, the defendants refused consent to remand in *Light House*. Accordingly, the plaintiffs filed a motion to remand, which the court granted. The plaintiffs then sought attorneys' fees under 28 U.S.C. § 1447(c), which allows the court to award attorneys' fees if it remands a removed case. The court observed that the Supreme Court has explained that the purpose of § 1447(c) is to discourage parties from needlessly prolonging litigation and imposing costs on the other party. The court further observed that a party should only receive attorneys' fees if the removing party lacked an objectively reasonable basis for seeking removal.

When determining reasonableness, the court looks to the time the party filed the petition for removal. In *Light House*, the defendants sought removal before the other courts remanded the sister cases. The court held that at the time the defendants sought to remove, their motion was reasonable. Accordingly, the court denied the plaintiffs' motion for attorneys' fees.

In *Ridgestone Bank v. Dunkin' Donuts Franchising LLC*, No 13-CV-3126, 2013 U.S. Dist. LEXIS 60859 (N.D. Ill. April 29, 2013), the court found that removal was flawed because Dunkin' Donuts ("Dunkin'") failed to join all defendants in the removal petition. Dunkin' removed the action from Cook County Circuit Court to Federal District Court. An individually named defendant, Shree, did not join in removal. Dunkin' claimed that the plaintiff franchisee had fraudulently joined Shree and therefore it was not necessary for Shree to join the removal. Dunkin' claimed that Shree was not a proper defendant because plaintiff Ridgestone's claim against Shree was for injunctive relief, which Dunkin' asserted was not a separate cause of action. The court rejected Dunkin's assertion that Ridgestone did have a substantive claim against Shree because of Ridgestone's security interest in the company that Shree purchased, including the equipment, fixtures, and inventory. Based on Ridgestone's allegations regarding its right to the equipment being used by Shree, removal was flawed without all defendants. The court gave Ridgestone one week to decide whether to remand or waive the procedural defect and stay in federal court.

In *Major Brands, Inc. v. Bacardi, USA, Inc.*, No. 13-CV-00706, 2013 U.S. Dist. LEXIS 61126 (D. Mo. April 30, 2013), the court granted Major Brands' motion to remand the case to Missouri state court. Major Brands had a distribution agreement with Bacardi. On March 5, 2013, Bacardi sent notice of termination of the agreement "for cause" citing Major Brands' failure to grow net sales, adhere to its sales strategies, and comply with inventory requirements. Major Brands then filed an eight-count action in the state Circuit Court of St. Louis City, Missouri, against Bacardi and Glazer's, another wholesale dealer. While the first seven counts were against Bacardi, count eight was for tortious interference against Glazer's. After the case was removed to federal court, Bacardi claimed that Glazer's was fraudulently joined merely for the purpose of defeating diversity jurisdiction. Major Brands argued that its claim against Glazer's was not fraudulent and asked the court to remand the case back to state court with an award for attorneys' fees and costs.

After reviewing the record and the parties' arguments, the court concluded that it could not "say that Plaintiff does not have a colorable claim for tortious interference against Glazer's." Therefore, the court remanded the case to state court. However, because the court also found that Major Brands' complaint, by itself, lacked a clear factual basis to support its claim against Glazer's, the court denied Major Brands' request for attorneys' fees incurred in pursuing the remand motion.

In *AKC, Inc. v. ServiceMaster Clean*, No. 13-CV-388, 2013 U.S. Dist. LEXIS 64361 (N.D. Ohio May 6, 2014), the court granted plaintiff franchisee's motion to remand to state court. Plaintiff brought a lawsuit alleging that ServiceMaster breached its contracts with plaintiff and ServiceMaster's action demonstrated bad faith and unclean hands." Plaintiff had five franchise agreements with defendant. Defendant removed the case and filed a motion to transfer venue to United States District Court in Tennessee based on the franchise agreements' forum selection clauses. In response, plaintiff filed a motion to remand the case to state court because the amount of controversy alleged in the complaint was less than $75,000 and, therefore, diversity jurisdiction did not exist.

The court observed that plaintiff stipulated that the amount in controversy was less than $75,000. Defendant claimed that this calculation was speculative and that the actual amount in controversy exceeded one million dollars. The court found that ServiceMaster failed to meet its burden of proof showing that the claim would meet the jurisdictional requirement. The court granted the motion to remand to state court and held that the plaintiff was barred from seeking damages in excess of $75,000.

In *Lou Bachrodt Chevrolet Co. v. General Motors, LLC*, No. 12-CV-7998, 2013 U.S. Dist. LEXIS 98870 (N.D. Ill. July 15, 2013) the court remanded the case to the Illinois Motor Vehicle Board ("MVRB"). Plaintiffs (collectively "Bachrodt") were two affiliated car dealerships operating in Illinois. Defendant was franchisor General Motors, LLC ("GM"). Despite an agreement to the contrary, GM did not permit Bachrodt to relocate one of its dealerships. Bachrodt filed two notices of protest with the MVRB to compel GM to allow relocation. GM then filed a notice of removal pursuant to 28 U.S.C. § 1441, claiming federal question, diversity, and bankruptcy jurisdiction. Bachrodt argued that removal was improper because MVRB was not a state "court" from which a case could be removed pursuant to § 1441.

First, the court considered if it all had subject matter jurisdiction. The court found that the dispute did not arise under the Constitution, was not related to a federal question, or related to the bankruptcy proceedings. Instead, the court found that the agreement was a private contract and that disputes involving the terms of settlement agreements are under state contract law, not federal law. Therefore, the court found it did not have subject matter jurisdiction.

Next, the court considered whether it had diversity jurisdiction over the parties. The court found that because Bachrodt's claims were worth more than $75,000 and there was no dispute that complete diversity existed, the court had diversity jurisdiction.

Although the court found it had jurisdiction to hear the case, it considered whether the dispute was subject to removal from the MVRB. The court applied the "functional test" to determine if the MVRB qualified as a "state court" from which a case could be removed. To apply this test, the court examined the "courtness" of the MVRB and the federal and state interests involved. The court found that even though the MVRB had some power beyond the scope of a traditional court, it still functioned like a "court" within the meaning of the removal statute. The court noted that administrative agencies also have extra-judicial power, but they are still subject to removal statutes.

Despite finding that MVRB was similar enough to a court to be subject to removal, the court found that the issue was not a matter of substantial federal concern. The court observed that "[n]o aspect of federal law will be implicated in any way by the parties' resolution of their private dispute." In addition, because the Illinois legislature has declared the importance of dealerships to the state's economy, the court found that state's interest substantially outweighed any federal interest and remanded the case to the MVRB.

B.   SUBJECT MATTER JURISDICTION

In *Racetime Investments, LLC v. Robert Moser*, No. 12-CV-860, 2013 U.S. Dist. LEXIS 36263 (D.Va. Feb. 5, 2013), the magistrate judge recommended that the District Court grant plaintiff's motion to remand but deny the request for costs and attorney's fees. Racetime Investments, LLC ("RI") filed an action against Robert Moser, Robert Morgan, Morgan RV Reports, LLC, and Racetime RV Reports, LLC (collectively, "defendants"). At issue was the manner in which the court should consider the citizenship of a joint venture in a derivative action.

RI along with Moser and Morgan (through Morgan RV Resorts, LCC) ("Morgan RV") created Racetime RV Resorts, LLC (the "JV"), a joint venture to franchise NASCAR themed RV parks. The JV entered into agreements with NASCAR. RI claimed it contributed millions of dollars to the JV but that defendants intentionally used the money for other entities, making fraudulent entries in the JV's books and records. Because of the corporate structure, both Morgan RV and RI were participants in the JV. RI was a plaintiff but it was also one of the members of the JV which was a defendant. Thus, if the court took into consideration the JV's citizenship, diversity jurisdiction would be destroyed because the same entity, RI, was on both sides of the dispute.

Defendants argued that diversity existed because the JV was a nominal defendant whose citizenship should be disregarded for diversity purposes. The court found that even if the parties were realigned to other side of the dispute, diversity jurisdiction would still be defeated because then another state would appear on both sides. The court also refused to disregard the citizenship of the JV. Instead of being a nominal party, the court found that the JV was a real party in interest because the JV had entered into a franchise agreement with NASCAR which was directly affected. In addition, it emphasized that it is a well-established principle that in derivative actions, the corporation is taken into consideration when assessing diversity jurisdiction.

Despite finding that diversity jurisdiction did not exist, the court rejected RI's motion for costs and attorney's fees. It found that defendants had a reasonable basis for seeking removal. Although the court initially did not find the authority cited by defendants persuasive, it did find that it was reasonable for the defendants to have relied on it and, therefore, denied the motion for attorneys' fees and costs.

In *Just Tacos, Inc. v. Michael Zezulak*, No. 11-00663, 2013 U.S. Dist. LEXIS 97438 (D. Haw. July 12, 2013) the court denied the defendants' motion to dismiss for lack of subject matter jurisdiction. Franchisor Just Tacos, Inc. ("franchisor") brought a claim under the Lanham Act against defendant Michael Zezulak and his two corporate franchises (collectively "franchisee") after Franchisee repudiated the franchise agreements, but continued to improperly use its trade name/mark, trade dress, menus, and trade secret recipes after termination. Franchisee filed a motion to dismiss for lack of subject matter jurisdiction claiming that the franchisor could not prove that the franchisee was using the trademark in interstate commerce.

The key jurisdictional issue was whether the phrase "uses in interstate commerce" in the Lanham Act was a jurisdictional prerequisite or substantive requirement to prove infringement. The court followed the test set forth in *Arbaugh v. Y&H Corp.*, 546 U.S. 500 (2006) and as applied by the Ninth Circuit. Under this test, to determine something is a jurisdictional element, the court considers if the "1) provision is clearly labeled jurisdictional; 2) the provision is located in a jurisdiction-granting provision;

and 3) other reasons necessitate that the provision be construed as jurisdictional."

The court found that 11 U.S.C. § 1125 did not address jurisdictional terms or refer in any way to the jurisdiction of the district courts. Nor was the operative language contained in a jurisdiction granting provision in the statute. Finally, the court could not discern any other reason that would make it necessary to interpret the phrase as a jurisdictional prerequisite. Thus, because Congress did not clearly state that "uses in commerce" is a jurisdictional limitation, the court found that such a limitation is a substantive element of a Lanham act claim. Because the franchisee's motion was based on the incorrect premise that the "uses in commerce" requirement was jurisdictional, the franchisee's motion to dismiss for lack of subject matter jurisdiction was denied.

In *Duncan Oil Co., v. Edward Johnson*, No. 12-27, 2012 U.S. Dist. LEXIS 127300 (D. Ky. Sept. 7, 2012), the court denied defendant Edward Johnson's ("Johnson") motion to dismiss for lack of subject-matter jurisdiction. Johnson argued that plaintiff Duncan Oil Company's ("Duncan Oil") claim was less than the $75,000 required to establish subject-matter jurisdiction because Duncan Oil was limited in the amount it could recover under its contract.

Duncan Oil brought a claim for breach of contract seeking $99,338 in damages, in addition to interest and attorney's fees. Because there were no federal claims alleged, Duncan Oil had the burden to show that it could recover more than $75,000 in order to satisfy the jurisdictional threshold. The dispute centered on how the agreement defined "image money." Image money is the money used to propose new signs and otherwise show the products. Duncan Oil claimed that Johnson would be required to pay back about $40,000 in image money because it breached its contract. Johnson, however, claimed that it did not owe any image money because the marks and images had already been paid and provided for. The court found that in the event of breach the contract required supplier reimbursement, which included image money. The same provision also provided for the recovery of legal fees. The court held that it could not conclude that the total amount of the controversy would be under $75,000 once legal fees were included. Therefore, the court denied Johnson's motion to dismiss.

In *ERA Franchise Systems, LLC v. Hoppens Realty, Inc.*, No. 12-CV-594, 2013 U.S. Dist. LEXIS 107078 (W.D. Wis. July 31, 2013), the Court was faced with the interesting procedural dilemma of whether to deny a prematurely filed Rule 12(c) motion for judgment on the pleadings or convert it to a motion to dismiss under Rule 12(b)(6). The franchisor ERA

Realty initiated litigation against a terminated franchisee in Wisconsin after the franchisee continued to use ERA's marks. The franchisee filed an answer and counterclaim asserting causes of action for breach of contract, conversion, unjust enrichment, misrepresentation and violation of the Wisconsin Fair Dealership Act. ERA responded to the counterclaim by filing a motion for judgment on the pleadings pursuant to Fed. R. Civ. P. 12(c). Unfortunately, ERA filed its Rule 12(c) motion too quickly. Under Rule 12(c), a party is permitted to move for judgment on the pleadings after the pleadings are closed, but early enough not to delay trial. Unless the court orders a reply to the answer or third-party answer, pleadings close after the last of the following pleadings in the case have been filed: Answer, Reply to Counterclaim, Answer to Cross claim and Third-Party Answer. In this case, ERA filed its Rule 12(c) motion on the pleadings in lieu of an answer to the counterclaim. Because the pleadings were not closed, ERA's motion was premature.

The Court was then faced with the prospect of denying ERA's motion outright or treating it as a motion to dismiss under Rule 12(b)(6). Because the Court employs the same standard for a motion to dismiss under Rule 12(b)(6) or 12(c), the Court decided to treat ERA's motion as if it was filed pursuant to Rule 12(b)(6).

Given the initial confusion regarding which Rule applied to ERA's motion, the Court found it necessary to identify the materials properly within the scope of the Court's review. Because ERA's motion was to dismiss the franchisee's counterclaim, the Court determined that it was free to consider any facts set forth in the counterclaim, as well as exhibits attached to the counterclaim or documents referenced in those pleadings that are central to the claim. Using this guideline, the Court determined that it could consider the franchise agreement and ERA's termination letter, both of which were referenced in the counterclaim. The Court would not consider however, documents not referenced in the counterclaim that were attached to ERA's complaint or documents attached to ERA's motion to dismiss. Having established the framework for ERA's motion, the Court proceeded to consider the merits of ERA's motion to dismiss, which is discussed in Chapter 5 above at Pages 89-90.

C.   PERSONAL JURISDICTION

Reflecting reluctance to exercise jurisdiction over those without sufficient contact with the jurisdiction, all but one court in the eight cases discussed either dismissed or transferred cases in response to a personal jurisdiction challenge.

In *Daimler AG v. Shuanghuan Automobile Company, LTD.*, No. 11-CV-13588, 2013 U.S. Dist. LEXIS 72166 (D. Mich. May 22, 2013), the court granted defendant Des Moines Motors' motion to dismiss for lack of personal jurisdiction. Plaintiff Daimler AG filed claims against defendants alleging trademark and trade dress infringement, trademark counterfeiting, patent infringement, unfair competition, and trademark dilution arising out of defendants' manufacture and sale of "smart vehicles."

Daimler is a company based in Germany which holds several trademarks on "smart" vehicles including its "smart fortwo." Shuanghuan Automobile Company ("SAC") is a Chinese car manufacturer. Des Moines Motors, Inc. is a car dealership and an Iowa Corporation. Although Des Moines Motors does not sell cars online, they advertise Daimler's and SAC's cars on its website. Des Moines Motors also operates a franchise for defendant Wheego, a manufacturer that sells "smart" cars.

The court found that Daimler had the burden of establishing that personal jurisdiction exists. It also found that Des Moines Motors has no contacts with Michigan. The court dismissed Daimler's arguments that it should exercise jurisdiction over Des Moines Motors because of its website and because Des Moines Motors intended to sell cars in Michigan.

Under the Michigan Long-Arm Statute, to satisfy due process requirements there are three conditions. They are:

First, the Defendant must purposely avail himself of the privilege of acting in the forum state or causing a consequence in the forum state. Second, the cause of action must arise from the defendant's activities there. Finally, the acts of the defendant or consequences caused by the defendant must have a substantial enough connection with the forum state to make the exercise of jurisdiction over the defendant reasonable.

Considering these factors, the court first found that Des Moines Motors' only contact with Michigan was through its website. However, the nature of the website was not "highly interactive" because it did not actually sell the cars from its website. Because of this factor and because Des Moines Motors had never sold any products or engaged in any business with a Michigan resident or company, the court found Des Moines Motors did not purposely avail itself of the privilege of Michigan's laws. In addition, because there were no activities there, the court also found that the "cause of action [did not] arise from the defendant's activities" in Michigan.

Finally, the court used the effects test to determine if "the acts of the defendant or consequences caused by the defendant [had] a substantial enough connection with the forum state to make the exercise of jurisdiction over the defendant reasonable." The court observed that effects test applies if the defendant "(i) commits intentionally tortious actions; (ii) which are expressly aimed at the forum state; (iii) which cause harm to the plaintiff in the forum state which the defendant knows is likely to be suffered." The court held that the test did not apply in this case because Daimler did not establish that the brunt of its injuries were aimed at or felt in Michigan because Daimler is not a Michigan corporation. Therefore, the court found that overall it would be unreasonable to exercise personal jurisdiction due to the extreme scarcity of Des Moines Motors' contacts with the forum state.

Zuchowski v. Doctor's Associates, Inc. dba Subway Restaurants and Ghazi Faddoul, UWYCV126014020S, 2012 Conn. Super. LEXIS 3102 (D. Conn. Dec. 21, 2012), involved the establishment of kosher Subway stores. Plaintiff Zuchowski brought an action against defendants Subway Restaurants and Ghazi Faddoul for violation of Connecticut's Unfair Trade Practices Act, breach of fiduciary duty, and common law fraud. Faddoul filed a motion to dismiss the complaint for lack of personal jurisdiction under Connecticut's long-arm statute.

Faddoul asserted that he was an Ohio resident and had never lived in Connecticut. Faddoul alleged that he was the development agent for the franchisor of Subway, Doctor's Associates, Inc. Doctor's Associates' principal place of business is in Connecticut. Faddoul stated that he was called upon to travel to Connecticut less than once a year. Zuchowski approached Faddoul about establishing kosher Subway restaurants. Doctor's Associates, Inc. approved this idea. Zuchowski then invested in the first kosher Subway. Zuchowski claimed that Faddoul sold a percentage of the ownership of the first kosher Subway to a third party, non-party. Later Faddoul started several additional kosher Subways without the involvement or knowledge of Zuchowski. Zuchowski claimed that this violated an agreement he had with Doctor's Associates that permitted him the exclusive right to develop all kosher Subway restaurants.

The court found that Faddoul lacked contacts with Connecticut necessary to satisfy the state's long-arm statute and that the exercise of the court's jurisdiction over Faddoul would violate due process. Zuchowski contended that Faddoul did have contacts with Connecticut through his business transactions and specifically through his receipt of royalties as a development agent. However, the court found that the royalties collected were only from Faddoul's franchise territory, none of which was in Connecticut. The court also found that an arbitration clause between Faddoul and the franchisor naming Connecticut as the forum was also irrelevant because that involved Faddoul's role as a franchisee and was not included in the governing documents relating to his role as a development agent.

In addition, the court found that it would be unreasonable to exercise jurisdiction because of the burden on Faddoul if the case was litigated in Connecticut. None of his franchises were located there, he did not have any property there, and he only traveled here about once a year. The court also found that Connecticut had a sufficient interest in the case. Therefore, the court granted Faddoul's motion to dismiss.

In *Myers v. Holiday Inns, Inc.*, No. 11-CV-1948, 2013 U.S. Dist. Lexis 6250 (D. D.C. Jan. 16, 2013), the franchisor Holiday Inn moved to dismiss the case for lack of personal jurisdiction and improper venue. Plaintiff Myers, a District of Columbia ("D.C.") resident, was injured in a Holiday Inn in Georgia. She brought a claim in D.C. against Holiday Inn, Island Group, and Holiday Hospitality Franchising, Inc., a licensing company. Holiday Inn is a Georgia corporation. Island Group is a Georgia franchisee that owns the Holiday Inn where Myers was injured. Defendants argued that Island Group was the only proper defendant and that the appropriate venue was Georgia.

To determine whether jurisdiction existed, the court examined whether Holiday Inn's contacts in the forum were of such quality that they manifested a "deliberate and voluntary association with the forum." Myers claimed that, because Island Group advertised in D.C., it conducted business in the forum state. However, the court found that advertisements alone are not generally sufficient to establish personal jurisdiction. This was true in this case because the advertisements never directly encouraged D.C. residents to stay at Island Group Holiday Inns. According to the court, even if Island Group was transacting business, Myers failed to show that the duty of care by the hotel arose from the advertisements. The court found that absent a claim arising out of the transacted business, there was no personal jurisdiction. In addition, the court found that the other defendants also had not transacted business in D.C. and, therefore, did not have sufficient minimum contacts to properly exercise of personal jurisdiction over them.

The court also found that while D.C. was an improper venue because of the lack of personal jurisdiction, Georgia would be able to exercise jurisdiction over the defendants. Therefore, in the "interest of justice" the court transferred the case to Georgia.

In *KFC Corporation v. Texas Petroplex, Inc.,* No. 11-CV-00479, 2012 U.S. Dist. LEXIS 144342 (D. Ky. Oct. 4, 2012), the court was faced with a situation where the individual personal guarantors of a corporate Texas franchisee moved to dismiss a complaint against them for lack of personal jurisdiction in Kentucky, the franchisor's home state. The court granted the motion to dismiss, finding that it could not exercise personal jurisdiction over individual defendants Mohammad Tatari, Naim Tatari, and Lama Tatari ("the Tataris"). It transferred the action to the United States District Court of the Northern District of Texas.

Franchisor KFC Corporation ("KFC") is a Delaware Corporation with a principal place of business in Kentucky. It brought claims in Kentucky against Texas Petroplex and the Tataris for breach of two franchise agreements, trademark infringement and false representation. The Tataris, Texas residents, signed personal guaranties of the obligations of the franchise agreements. KFC sought a declaratory judgment that the franchise agreements were terminated and that defendants were obligated to comply with franchise agreement's post-termination obligations.

The franchise agreements between KFC and Texas Petroplex contained Kentucky forum selection clauses. The court observed that Texas Petroplex transacted business in Kentucky by entering into these contracts which created obligations in Kentucky, and the breach arose from the contracts, creating a "reasonable and direct nexus." Accordingly, the court found that the exercise of personal jurisdiction over the corporate franchisee, Texas Petroplex, was proper.

The court next examined whether it had personal jurisdiction over the Tataris as guarantors who operated the Texas franchises. The court found that standing alone, signing the guaranty agreements did not confer power on the court to exercise personal jurisdiction over the Tataris. The court concluded that because the Tataris had not traveled to Kentucky, did not have any real connections to Kentucky, and had not done anything to personally avail themselves of Kentucky's laws, exercising personal jurisdiction over these defendants would violate due process. Therefore, the court transferred the case to Texas because the Texas court would have jurisdiction over all defendants and it would be more convenient for the witnesses.

In *KFC Corporation v. Wagstaff,* No. 11-CV-00674, 2013 U.S. Dist. LEXIS 86758 (D. Ky. June 19, 2013), plaintiff franchisor KFC brought a claim in Kentucky against six California corporations operating KFC franchises in six states. KFC alleged that the franchisees had defaulted on the original franchise agreements governing their collective seventy-seven KFC restaurants by failing to pay royalties and advertising costs. All six of the franchisee corporations filed Chapter 11 bankruptcy in Minnesota and KFC was a creditor in those proceedings.

KFC argued that jurisdiction was proper in Kentucky because the franchisees consented to the jurisdiction in a number of documents and contracts. The franchisees argued that they did not consent to personal jurisdiction in Kentucky and that it was not proper because they were not transacting business in Kentucky and, thus, under Kentucky's long-arm statute.

To determine if the franchisees consented to personal jurisdiction in Kentucky, the court examined the guaranty along with the underlying agreements. KFC argued that the franchisees consented to jurisdiction when they signed the pre-negotiation agreement. The agreement contained language indicating that defendants had consented to personal jurisdiction in Kentucky. However, the court found that the pre-negotiation agreement was not evidence of franchisee consent because KFC's claims did not arise from the agreement. The pre-negotiation agreement was a separate instrument from the promissory notes and guaranties and it did not provide for repayment or bind either party to accept or pay any debts. Therefore, the court found that the franchisees' consent to jurisdiction in Kentucky in the pre-negotiation agreement was not relevant to the issue of whether defendants consented to Kentucky jurisdiction with respect to claims under the guaranties.

Next the court considered whether the franchisee defendants were bound by the forum selection clause in the promissory notes in their personal capacity when the notes only obligated the corporation, not the individuals. The guaranty in question only stated that individual defendants were liable for the payment of the notes, not for "all obligations." The court found that this suggested that the guarantor was not bound by the entire agreement, including the forum selection clause. In addition, while the notes contained both a choice of law and forum selection clause, the guaranty only contained a choice of law clause. Therefore, the court found it was "not clear that the guarantor undertook to honor the forum selection clause in the [p]romissory [n]otes." Finally, the court found that the individual defendant representatives were not parties to the notes in their individual capacity and, therefore, did not consent to personal jurisdiction simply by guarantying the notes.

Next the court considered jurisdiction under Kentucky's long-arm statute. The court found that the franchisees did not transact business in Kentucky and lacked the requisite minimum contacts with the state. Signing guaranties that created obligations to a Kentucky corporation was not enough to constitute transacting business. Therefore, the court found that it did not have personal jurisdiction over the guarantor defendants.

The court then determined whether to dismiss the claims or transfer them to a more suitable venue. The court transferred the case to the U.S. District Court for the District of Minnesota. The court found that the claims were related to, and affected by the bankruptcy proceedings in Minnesota. For example, indemnification claims could also affect the size of the debtors' estates, and the length of the bankruptcy proceedings. The court also found that a transfer served the interest of justice because, it created judicial efficiency with the same parties and witnesses in both of the actions. Therefore, the court granted the motion to transfer.

In *C&K Auto Imports v. Daimler AG.*, No. A-2982-12T1, 2013 N.J. Super. Unpub. LEXIS 1568 (App.Div. June 21, 2013), the court considered defendant Garff Enterprises' ("Garff") motion to dismiss on jurisdictional grounds. Garff was a franchise dealer of Mercedes Benz automobiles. Garff was incorporated in Utah and had its principal place of business in Salt Lake City. The case concerned a Mercedes Benz coupe that Mercedes Benz USA, LLC ("MBUSA") sold to Garff. Garff leased the vehicle to between one to ten people ("John Does"). John Does also leased the vehicle from Daimler Trust ("Daimler"), who held the title. When the lease expired, Daimler took possession of the vehicle and sent it to be auctioned in Las Vegas. The vehicle was purchased online by Crossroads of Lynchburg ("Crossroads"). Crossroads sold the vehicle to plaintiffs and shipped the vehicle directly to plaintiffs in Florida. Plaintiffs shipped the vehicle to their warehouse in New Jersey. Plaintiffs then sold the vehicle to an overseas buyer, and prior to shipping it had an inspection conducted to address the cause of a noise that plaintiffs had noticed. The inspector, an authorized MBUSA and Daimler dealer, determined that the vehicle's engine had been damaged by water. Plaintiffs repaired the vehicle for $20,000. Plaintiffs then sued, asserting claims against Daimler and MBUSA for, among other things, breach of implied warranty of merchantability.

Defendant Garff filed a motion to dismiss the complaint on jurisdictional grounds. Garff argued that the court did not have personal jurisdiction over Garff because Garff had no place of business in New Jersey, Garff was not registered to do business in New Jersey, and Garff had no salespeople in New Jersey. Further, Garff argued that because it only sold Mercedes Benz vehicles in Utah and did not have control over the vehicle once leased to a customer, the court did not have personal jurisdiction over Garff. Plaintiffs argued that personal jurisdiction could be properly exercised over Garff pursuant to the "stream of commerce" theory. The stream of commerce theory "refers to the movement of goods from manufacturers through distributors to consumers." The trial court denied Garff's motion.

Garff appealed. The appellate court referred to its prior decision in *Mische v. Bracey's Supermarket*, 420 N.J. Super. 487 (App. Div. 2011), which reviewed the "principles applicable to a determination of whether a defendant has sufficient contacts with a state to warrant the exercise of jurisdiction." The threshold for having sufficient contact is high and difficult to meet, as it requires "extensive contacts between a defendant and a forum." The court determined that the plaintiff failed to meet the threshold because Garff had simply leased the vehicle two years before it made its way to New Jersey and had had no control over the vehicle thereafter. Further, relying on the New Jersey Supreme Court's decision in *Nicastro v. McIntre Mach. Am. Ltd.*, 201 N.J. 48 (2010), the court rejected plaintiffs' stream of commerce theory of jurisdiction. The court explained that *McIntre* made clear that in order to prevail on a stream of commerce theory, the defendant had to engage in activities that purposefully targeted the forum state. Because Garff took no targeted action to send the vehicle to New Jersey, or participate in any commercial transactions in New Jersey, the stream of commerce theory failed. Accordingly, the court reversed the trial court's denial of the motion to dismiss.

Following the appellate court's reversal, the court considered the exact same motion to dismiss based on lack of jurisdiction from defendant Crossroads in *C&K Auto Imports v. Daimler AG.*, No. A-2982-12T1, 2013 N.J. Super. Unpub. LEXIS 1568 (App.Div. June 21, 2013). Like Garff's motion to dismiss, Crossroads motion to dismiss was denied by the trial court. Crossroads then appealed and made the same arguments as Garff, mainly that: it had no place of business or physical presence in New Jersey; its only place of business was in Virginia; and it had no office, employees, or agents in New Jersey. Plaintiffs made an argument identical to the one used to oppose Garff's motion, however, the court was not persuaded and, as for Garff, reversed the trial court's denial of the motion to dismiss.

In *MIO, LLC v. Valentino's of America, Inc.*, No. 13-CV-191, 2013 U.S. Dist. LEXIS 93660 (M.D. Fla. July 3, 2013), plaintiff MIO, LLC ("MIO") brought action against defendant franchisor Valentino's of America, Inc. ("Valentino's"), alleging trademark infringement in Florida. MIO operated a restaurant in Tampa called "Valentino Pizzeria Trattoria" MIO's amended complaint alleged personal jurisdiction over Valentino's based on specific jurisdiction "related to defendant's engaging in a business venture in Florida," and general jurisdiction "related to defendant's substantial and not isolated activities in Florida." Finding that Valentino's desire to start franchising in Florida did not subject it to personal jurisdiction in the State, the court granted Valentino's motion to dismiss for lack of personal jurisdiction.

The court engaged in a two-part inquiry to determine whether it had personal jurisdiction over Valentino's, a Nebraska corporation. First, the court inquired whether there were grounds for application of the Florida long-arm statute, and second, the court applied a due process analysis to see whether constitutional minimum contacts between Valentino's and Florida were sufficient to satisfy "traditional notions of fair play and substantial justice."

Valentino's argued that Florida's long-arm statute did not confer general or specific jurisdiction over it. Agreeing with Valentino's, the court explained that general jurisdiction could not exist, because Valentino's had not "engaged in substantial and not isolated activity" in Florida. In support of its finding, the court found that: Valentino's never consummated a sale of its franchise in Florida; Valentino's did not market its restaurant franchise in Florida; a Nebraska resident initially expressed interest in the possibility of such a franchise in Florida; Valentino's operated restaurants in the Midwest since 1957, but it never held any office or any other real estate in Florida; Valentino's never sent a representative to Florida; the legal work for all Florida negotiations was done by individuals other than the defendant and no franchise agreement was ever executed with any Florida individuals or entities.

Although Valentino's had filed a Franchise Exemption Application in Florida, the court found that act would not satisfy the "substantial and not isolated" requirement. The court explained that to "even entertain the inquiry regarding a franchise in Florida, [Valentino's] was required to seek an exemption pursuant to Florida law." Further, though Valentino's had designated a state agent to accept service in the Franchise Disclosure Document, the designation did not establish the continuous general business contacts in Florida necessary to support general jurisdiction.

Similarly, specific jurisdiction did not exist. MIO argued that Valentino's activities showed a "general course of business activity in the State for pecuniary benefit.'" Disagreeing with MIO, the court explained that the infringement was directed at MIO, who was not part of the plans to start a franchise. Further, the four individuals who initially brought the idea to Valentino's and searched for a franchise location in Florida were not charged with infringement. Finally, the absence of any franchise relationship in Florida confirms that Valentino's was not involved in a general course of activity in the State. Accordingly, the case was dismissed for lack of personal jurisdiction over Valentino's.

In *Knauf Insulation, GMBH v. Southern Brands, Inc.*, No. 12-CV-00273, 2013 U.S. Dist. LEXIS 38435 (D. Ind. Mar. 19, 2013), the court denied defendants' motion to dismiss for lack of personal jurisdiction and failure to state a claim. Plaintiff Knauf Insulation ("Knauf") is an international company that produces fiberglass insulation products. Its United States' headquarters is in Indiana. Defendant Southern Brands ("SBI") is a Georgia corporation owned by Albert and Rosemary Dowd. Knauf and SBI entered into a distributor agreement whereby SBI sold Knauf fiberglass insulation to its Florida customers.

By December 2007, SBI owed Knauf about $1.8 million dollars. SBI entered into a series of promissory notes with Knauf. Mr. Dowd also signed a personal guaranty for the obligations. The notes, including the last one signed, included an Indiana forum selection and choice of law clause. When SBI failed to pay the debt, Knauf filed suit in Indiana. SBI moved to dismiss.

First, the court determined whether the Indiana forum selection clause was enforceable. The Dowds acknowledged that they signed the agreement but claimed that the agreement was not 'freely negotiated' nor 'just and reasonable' and, thus, should not be enforced. *Id.* at 14. Indiana law presumes that contracts are the result of freely bargained agreements. The court found that although Knauf was the stronger party, defendants went too far in their claims that Knauf was an "overreaching...corporate Goliath." It found defendants' assertions unconvincing because there was no evidence that the Dowds ever raised objections to any of the terms of the agreement or were forced to sign the agreement. The Dowds also did not present other evidence of undue influence or unfair bargaining. Therefore, the court found that the Indiana forum selection clause was binding and enforceable.

After finding the forum selection clauses enforceable, the court also examined whether it had personal jurisdiction over the Dowds. Defendants claimed that plaintiff failed to allege sufficient facts to establish jurisdiction. The court compared the case to *Burger King v. Rudzewicz*, 471, U.S. 462 (1985). The court emphasized that in *Burger King*, although the defendant was never physically in the forum state, the court found that defendant's "continuous course of direct communications" with Knauf was proof of purposeful availment of the law and protection of the forum state. As in *Burger King*, Mr. Dowd's extensive, long-term association with Knauf supported a finding that personal jurisdiction over the defendants existed. The court found that the "record [was] replete with indications that defendants created 'continuous obligations' between themselves and residents of Indiana." In addition, the court found that there were multiple acts connecting the Dowds to Indiana which created the type of relationship contemplated by *Burger King*. Therefore, the court denied the Dowd's motion to dismiss for lack of personal jurisdiction.

II.   Choice of Forum

A.   CASES ENFORCING FORUM SELECTION CLAUSES

In *Goddard Systems, Inc. v. Overman*, No. 12-5368, 2013 U.S. Dist. LEXIS 5468 (D. Pa. Jan. 14, 2013), plaintiff Goddard Systems ("Goddard") alleged that Overman misappropriated the plaintiff's business opportunity, trade secrets, and proprietary information after Overman opened a competing preschool in a former Goddard location in Florida. Goddard is a Pennsylvania franchisor with a principal place of business in Pennsylvania. Overman is a citizen of Florida. In 2010, Overman, with her parents and brother and sister-in-law, entered into a franchise agreement to open a Goddard preschool early education center in Florida. Under the terms of the agreement Overman agreed to not divulge any of Goddard's material that had copyright protection, trade secrets, or confidential information. Later Overman became the Educational Director for the Florida franchise. Under the Goddard System, the Educational Director cannot be a franchisee. Therefore, Overman was removed from the agreement through an Addendum and Release. In 2012, she left her post as Educational Director to open a new school where a Goddard school had just closed.

Goddard sued in its home state of Pennsylvania and claimed that Overman engaged in a scheme to usurp a business opportunity and was using confidential and proprietary information from the Goddard System. Overman moved to dismiss for improper venue.

The court found that venue can be waived when parties contractually agree to a forum. The forum selection clause in the Addendum and Release signed by Overman identified Pennsylvania as the agreed forum for any actions "arising out of or relating to [the Addendum]" and applied to "any disputes" between them. In addition, the court found that Overman had not shown any evidence of fraud, violation of public policy, or unreasonable inconvenience. Therefore, the court held that Overman waived any objection to venue in Pennsylvania in the Addendum and Release. Additionally, the court found that even if the forum selection clause didn't apply, the underlying facts and development of materials and trade secrets occurred in Pennsylvania, making it the proper venue. The court denied Overman's motion to dismiss.

In *Days Inn Worldwide, Inc. v. Royal Hospitality Groups,* No. 12-CV-05028 (D. N.J. February 13, 2013), the court denied the franchisee defendants' motion to dismiss based on lack of personal jurisdiction and improper venue. The dispute involved a breach of franchise agreement between Days Inn Worldwide, Inc. ("Days Inn") and Royalty Hospitality and Mike B. Barry (together "Franchisees"). Days Inn is a Delaware corporation with its primary location of business in New Jersey. Franchisee Royal Hospitality is also a Delaware company with its primary location of business in California. Days Inn claimed that Franchisees breached their financial obligations under the franchise agreement. The forum selection clause in the agreement provided that Franchisees consented and waived any objection to personal jurisdiction in the state and federal courts of New Jersey. Despite the forum selection clause, Franchisees claimed lack of personal jurisdiction and venue because that they did not have sufficient contacts with New Jersey to support jurisdiction under New Jersey's long-arm statute. Franchisees claimed that enforcing the venue clause would violate their due process rights.

The court rejected these claims and found the venue clause valid. The court found that "forum selection clauses are routinely upheld as prima facie evidence that a court has personal jurisdiction over all defendants that are party to a franchise agreement." To determine if the clause is valid the court considered whether the clause "(i) contained an express provision that conferred personal jurisdiction; (ii) selected the District Court of New Jersey as its forum; and (iii) selected New Jersey law as the governing authority." Because the clause in this case expressly provided consent and clearly named New Jersey as the forum and governing authority, the court found that it had personal jurisdiction over the defendants. The court also denied the claims of improper venue because the clause specifically named New Jersey.

Huntington Learning Center, Inc. v. Read It, N.C., Inc., No. 12-CV-03598, 2013 U.S. Dist. LEXIS 77258 (D. N.J. May 30, 2013), involved a motion to dismiss for improper venue and lack of personal jurisdiction. Plaintiff Huntington Learning Centers, Inc. ("Huntington") brought a claim against Read It, N.C., Wallace Educational Holdings, and individual defendants (collectively "defendants"). The parties had a franchise agreement to establish Huntington franchises in North Carolina. The agreement had a New Jersey forum selection clause. Huntington's principal place of business is New Jersey. The individual defendants personally guaranteed the franchise agreements. Huntington filed a complaint in New Jersey against defendants alleging trademark infringement and breach of contract.

Defendants then filed a motion to dismiss for lack of personal jurisdiction and improper venue, and requested a transfer to North Carolina. The court denied the motion.

The court first considered the forum selection clause and found that it was valid. The court found that defendants expressly consented to the jurisdiction in three separate provisions. Defendants argued that the clauses were invalid under the New Jersey Franchise Practices Act, which contains exceptions to the presumed enforceability of forum selection clauses. The court rejected this argument and found that the Act applies only to franchises in New Jersey. Because the franchises in this case were in North Carolina, the act did not apply. The court rejected all other arguments of unconscionability and inconvenience and found the clause enforceable.

The court then considered public and private interests in deciding whether to transfer the case. The court found that transferring the case would not necessarily serve judicial economy and there was no evidence that defendants would not be able to litigate in New Jersey. Considering the circumstances as a whole, it denied the motion for transfer.

In *Duggan O'Rourke Inc. v. The Intelligent Office System*, No.12-CV-550, 2012 U.S. Dist. LEXIS 131482 (D. Ind. Sept. 14, 2012), the court enforced a forum selection clause between the parties and granted the defendant franchisor's motion to dismiss for lack of jurisdiction. Franchisor, The Intelligent Office System ("IOS"), entered into an agreement with franchisee Duggan O'Rourke, Inc. ("Duggan") in 2000. Under the agreement there was a "governing law/consent to venue and jurisdiction" clause specifying Colorado as the governing law and venue for any dispute between the parties. In 2009, the two parties and MMA Business Solutions, Inc. ("MMA") entered into a transfer agreement, whereby Duggan assigned its rights, title, and interest under the franchise agreement to MMA. However, it also provided that 'nothing herein shall be deemed to release [Duggan] from liability under the Franchise Agreement…'. The transfer agreement also selected Colorado as the dispute resolution forum and applicable law. Duggan claimed that IOS and MMA subsequently issued a new franchise agreement thereby terminating Duggan's ongoing liability. Duggan filed a declaratory judgment action in Indiana to confirm its lack of ongoing liability. IOS moved to dismiss for improper venue.

First, the court considered the applicable law. The court observed that the validity of a forum selection clause "depends on the law of the jurisdiction whose rules will govern the rest of the dispute." Applying this rule, the court applied Colorado law to determine the validity of the clause. The court found that Duggan failed to establish that the forum selection clause in the franchise agreement was unfair or unreasonable under Colorado law. Duggan argued that the forum selection clause was unenforceable because it terminated when IOS signed the new agreement with MMA. The court rejected this argument because the transfer agreement stated that Duggan was not released from liability under the initial franchise agreement. The court found that there was nothing in the record to show that the parties intended to terminate the forum selection clause. Therefore, the court granted IOS's motion to dismiss. It ordered Duggan to report on whether it preferred the action be dismissed or transferred to Colorado.

In *Alloy Wheels, Inc. v. Wheel Repair Solutions Int'l, Inc.* No. 12-80716, 2012 U.S. Dist. LEXIS 118600 (S.D. Fla. Aug. 21, 2012), the court granted defendant franchisor's motion to dismiss based on the language in the franchise agreement. Plaintiff Alloy Wheels brought an action against defendant Wheel Repair for failing to provide an exclusive franchise territory. In 2008, the plaintiff and defendant began negotiating for the sale of a franchise to plaintiff. Plaintiff was shown an agreement with exclusive territory. However, there was dispute over the agreement because neither party produced a signed agreement for the court. Defendant moved to dismiss for improper venue because it claimed that the agreement required that all litigation be brought in Georgia. It submitted a copy of a complaint it filed in Georgia against plaintiff and a copy of the unsigned franchise agreement.

While the court found that the forum selection clause was enforceable, it also conducted a fact-specific inquiry to determine if it applied. The court found that the franchisee asserted that no franchise agreement existed, but also referred to the agreement as a basis for its claims. On the other hand, the franchisor submitted evidence that it mailed the agreement to the franchisee and included an affidavit claiming that the parties signed the franchise agreement with the forum selection clause. Franchisee did not counter the franchisor's evidence. Therefore, the court found that franchisee failed to meet its burden to show that the agreement was not executed. It found that the clause applied and dismissed the Florida case.

In *TGA Premier Junior Golf Franchise v. B P Bevins Golf, LLC,* No. 12-4321, 2012 U.S. Dist. LEXIS 147785 (D. N.J. Oct. 12, 2012), the court granted the pro se defendant's motion to dismiss. The case involved plaintiff franchisor TGA Premier Junior Golf Franchise ("TGA") seeking an injunction preventing franchisee B P Bevins Golf LLC ("BP") from operating a competitive golf instruction business after expiration of the franchise agreement. TGA initiated litigation in New Jersey and moved for an injunction to enforce the noncompetition covenant in the franchise agreement between the two parties. Despite being a New Jersey resident, the individual defendant, Bevins, appearing pro se, moved to dismiss the case claiming that the forum selection clause required the action be filed in California.

The court examined the franchise agreement as well as the personal guaranty signed by Bevins. The franchise agreement included a noncompetition provision and a forum selection clause. The clause named the State of California as the location for any action "and the parties hereby waive all question of personal jurisdiction or venue for the purpose of carrying out this provision." Therefore, it found California to be the proper forum.

The court then considered whether a motion to dismiss was a proper mechanism for enforcing a forum selection clause or if it must be transferred. The court found that in the Third Circuit a forum selection clause may be enforced through dismissal. Because the forum selection clause in the franchise agreement was clear and unambiguous, and plaintiff failed to provide evidence of why it was unenforceable or gravely inconvenient, the court found that the appropriate forum was California and granted the motion to dismiss. In an interesting footnote, the court commented that because New Jersey resident Bevins exercised this right to enforce, rather than waive, the forum selection clause, he should not be heard to complain that he will be required to litigate in California if TCA re-files there.

In *Spencer Franchise Services of Georgia, Inc. v. Wow Café and Wingery Franchising Account, LLC*, No. 12-CV-470, 2013 U.S. Dist. LEXIS 42067 (D. Ga. Mar. 26, 2013), the court granted the defendant franchisor's motion to dismiss based on a valid forum-selection clause. Plaintiff Spencer Franchise Services of Georgia, Inc. ("Spencer") and defendant WOW Café & Wingery Franchising Account, LLC ("WOW") entered into an Area Developer Agreement and Addendum in 2007. The agreement contained a forum selection clause providing for the franchisor's home state of Louisiana as the venue for any action brought by either party to the agreement.

Although neither party contested the validity of the clause, Spencer argued that WOW waived its right to challenge venue because it filed a motion to appear, a stipulation extending time, an answer and counterclaim, and a supplemental/amended answer and counterclaim. WOW argued that it did not waive its objection to venue because it filed a motion to dismiss for improper venue before its answer and counterclaim. The court agreed with

WOW. The court found that because WOW moved to dismiss for improper venue in a separate filing before its answer and counterclaim, it did not waive its defense.

Next, the court considered whether a transfer or dismissal was appropriate. The court examined Eleventh Circuit precedent from *Slater v. Energy Services Group International*, 634 F.3d 1326 (11th Cir. 2011), which requires the court to enforce a valid forum-selection clause by dismissing the cause. Even though transfer was appropriate before *Slater*, the court found that *Slater* made dismissal the appropriate mechanism. Therefore, the court granted the motion to dismiss.

In *Maaco Franchising, Inc. vs. Tainter*, No. 12-5500, 2013 U.S. Dist. Lexis 80790 (E.D. Pa. June 6, 2013), the franchisor brought an action in Federal Court in Pennsylvania against an existing California based franchisee for failure to pay franchise and advertising fee and to comply with an audit. The franchise agreement included a choice of law provision and a forum selection clause requiring all litigation in Pennsylvania and the application of Pennsylvania law. The franchisee challenged the enforceability of the forum selection clause and moved to transfer the case to the Northern District of California, where they resided. The franchisee argued that the forum selection clause was invalid because the parties did not "reach a meeting of the minds" and therefore never agreed to a forum outside California. Franchisee also argued that the venue provision contravened California's public policy disfavoring the enforcement of out of state forum selection clauses pursuant to the California Franchise Act. Finally, the franchisee argued that other factors weighed in favor of transferring the action to the Northern District of California.

The court rejected all of the franchisee's claims and enforced the venue provision in the franchise agreement. First, the court confirmed the general rule that forum selection clauses are presumptively valid and enforceable, unless enforcement is shown by the resisting party to be unreasonable under the circumstances. The court noted that the franchisee did not allege any fraud or overreaching on the part of Maaco that would render the forum selection clause unenforceable. Nor did the franchisee argue that the expense or inconvenience of litigating in Pennsylvania would deprive him of his day in court. Instead, the franchisee argued that because the Franchise Disclosure Document he received before signing the franchise agreement stated that some states, including California, "might have statutes that supersede the franchise agreement," the Franchisee believed that regardless of the language in the franchise agreement, Maaco would be required to comply with the California Franchise Act, which voided out of state forum selection clauses. The franchisee cited *Laxmi Investments, LLC vs. Golf USA*, 193 F 3d 1093, 1097 (9th Cir. 1999) for support. The court found that the reasoning in *Laxmi* was not persuasive in this case. The court found that the Pennsylvania venue and choice of law provisions were "perfectly clear and unambiguous." Furthermore, the court found that the integration clause in the franchise agreement confirmed that the franchisee was not relying on any representations, promises or agreements outside of the franchise agreement. A separate franchise disclosure document stating that some of the terms of the franchise agreement might be superseded by certain California law was insufficient to negate the franchisee's express agreement to litigate in a Pennsylvania forum.

Secondly, with respect to the franchisee's argument that the forum selection clause contravened the anti-waiver provision in the California Franchise Act, the court held that the proper inquiry is not whether enforcement of a forum selection clause would contravene *any* strong public policy, but whether it would contravene a strong public policy of the forum in which the suit is brought. Because the forum selection clause did not violate any public policy in Pennsylvania, it was enforceable.

Finally, the court review the convenience factors set forth in 18 U.S.C. §1404(a), and concluded that they either weighed against transfer or were neutral. As a result, the court enforced the venue provision and denied the franchisee's motion to transfer the case to Northern District of California.

In *BK Tax Service, Inc. v. Jackson Hewitt, Inc.*, No. 12-CV-676, 2013 U.S. Dist. LEXIS 102761 (S.D. Miss. July 23, 2013), the court held that "a forum selection clause is prima facie valid and should be enforced unless the resisting party shows that enforcement would be unreasonable." A Mississippi franchisee, BK Tax Service, Inc., ("Franchisee") alleged that franchisor Jackson Hewitt violated the exclusivity provision in the parties' Franchise Agreement when it awarded Franchisee's competitor, defendant Central Mississippi Tax Consultants, Inc. ("CMTC") another franchise in the same county.

The franchisee previously entered negotiations to sell its franchise to CMTC but negotiations failed. A few months later, CMTC negotiated a deal with the Jackson Hewitt to open a "highly lucrative Wal-Mart location, only a few miles from the [franchisee's location]." The franchisee filed suit in state court against Jackson Hewitt and CMTC, claiming a loss of the prospective sale of its franchise, as well as the opportunity to open a highly lucrative Wal-Mart location.

Jackson Hewitt removed the action, alleging that CMTC was fraudulently joined for the purpose of defeating diversity jurisdiction. It then filed a motion to transfer venue to the United States District Court for the District of New Jersey pursuant to the venue provision in the parties' franchise agreement. CMTC filed a motion to dismiss. Finally, the franchisee denied that CMTC was fraudulently joined and moved to remand to state court.

As the removing party, Jackson Hewitt had the burden of demonstrating the existence of federal jurisdiction. In order to meet this burden, Jackson Hewitt had to show, by clear and convincing evidence, all either: (1) actual fraud in the pleading of jurisdictional facts or the citizenship status of CMTC, or (2) inability to establish a cause of action against CMTC in state court. The court focused on the second prong, applying a Rule 12(b)(6)-type analysis—whether the allegations presented in the complaint made out a claim against CMTC.

The court found that the franchisee failed allege facts sufficient to state a claim for tortious interference against CMTC under Mississippi law, the law of the forum state. The franchisee's allegations suggested only that CMTC pursued a contract with Jackson Hewitt after CMTC's negotiations with the franchisee failed. There was no allegation that CMTC knew of the nature of the franchisee's agreement with Jackson Hewitt or of the franchisee's plan to expand to Wal-Mart. Because the franchisee could not state a cause of action, and the court granted CMTC's motion to dismiss and denied the franchisee's motion to remand.

As for Jackson Hewitt's motion to transfer venue, the parties' franchise agreement plainly provided that all litigation must be venued in the United State District Court in New Jersey, and the franchisee presented no arguments as to why that clause should not be binding. Accordingly, the court granted Jackson Hewitt's motion to transfer to the United State District Court for the District of New Jersey.

In *Great Clips, Inc. v. Ross*, No. 12-1886, 2013 U.S. Dist. LEXIS 12530 (D. Minn. Jan. 30, 2013), the court considered the franchisee Defendants' motion to transfer venue of Great Clips' Declaratory Judgment claim that it did not breach the franchise agreements between the parties. The Defendants, Ross and Cool Otter, LLC, were franchisees of eleven Great Clips salons in Texas. Great Clips terminated the Defendants' Franchise Agreements (Agreements) based on "numerous problems with the Defendants' performance as a franchisee." After Ross refused to acknowledge that he would not oppose the termination, Greats Clips, a Minnesota corporation, filed an action in federal district court in Minnesota seeking a declaratory judgment that it did not breach the Agreements. The Agreements contained forum selection clauses mandating that disputes "be venued exclusively and solely in federal or state court in Hennepin County, Minnesota." The Defendants also agreed to submit to personal jurisdiction in Minnesota and waived any rights they may have to contest venue and jurisdiction in Minnesota.

Great Clips and the Defendants entered into a Settlement Agreement that released the federal lawsuit against the Defendants and contained a confidentiality/non-slander clause. The Defendants requested that Great Clips draft the Settlement Agreement, and after receiving a draft, contacted Great Clips' Chief Legal Officer, in Minnesota, to request changes and modifications. The Chief Legal Officer made the revisions and sent the revised draft to the Defendants in Texas. The Defendants contacted the Chief Legal Officer again to request additional changes, most notably, a forum selection clause designating Texas as the appropriate forum for future disputes. The Chief Legal Officer emailed the Defendants a rejection of their changes and sent a revised draft. Ross signed the Settlement Agreement and mailed it to the Chief Legal Officer in Minnesota, where Great Clips then signed it.

After both parties had signed the Settlement Agreement, Great Clips learned that a Dallas newspaper had obtained a copy of the original termination complaint filed by Great Clips and had written an article about Ross and Great Clips. The Defendants were concerned about the article and through their attorney, sent a letter to Great Clips, asserting that Great Clips had breached the confidentiality/non-slander clause of the Settlement Agreement. Great Clips then filed suit in federal court in Minnesota, seeking a declaratory judgment that it did not breach the Settlement Agreement.

The court noted that because the allegedly wrongful conduct occurred after the Franchise Agreements were terminated, that it was unclear how the forum selection clauses in the Franchise Agreements would apply to the breach of Settlement Agreement claim. Ultimately, the court held that venue was proper in Minnesota because "a substantial part of the events or omissions" that gave rise to the breach of contract claim arose in Minnesota. Further, the court found that there was no evidence that the conduct at issue—whether Great Clips disclosed confidential information—occurred anywhere other than in Minnesota.

In the alternative, the Defendants' moved to transfer the action to the Northern District of Texas. The court agreed with Great Clips' argument that transferring the case would merely shift the burden from one party to another. Accordingly, the court denied the Defendant's motion to transfer.

In *Crazy Willy's Inc., v. Halloween Express, LLC.*, No. 12-CV-01496, 2013 U.S. Dist. LEXIS 36896 (D. Colo. Mar. 18, 2013) the court enforced a choice of venue provision in a franchise agreement requiring arbitration in Summit County, Ohio. Two Colorado Halloween shop franchisees, Crazy Willy's and Jack's Halloween sued the franchisor, Halloween Express, in the U.S. District Court for the District of Colorado. The District of Colorado ruled that where the dispute involved the franchise relationship, was between the franchisor and franchisees, and the parties conducted business under the franchise agreement containing the venue provision, the plaintiff's claims are subject to dismissal without prejudice because they were filed in an improper venue.

B.   CASES REFUSING TO ENFORCE FORUM SELECTION CLAUSES

In *Valvoline Instant Oil Change Franchising, Inc. v. RFG Oil, Inc.*, No. 12-CV-39, 2012 U.S. Dist. LEXIS 118571 (E.D. Ky. Aug. 22, 2012), the court transferred a case from the Eastern District of Kentucky to the Southern District of California, even though the franchise agreement contained a Kentucky forum selection clause. The plaintiff, franchisor Valvoline, argued venue was proper under 18 U.S.C. § 1391(b)(1) because of the franchisee RFG's long-standing business connection with Valvoline based in Kentucky. The franchisor also argued that the Kentucky venue was proper because a substantial part of the events which gave rise to Valvoline's claim against RFG occurred in Kentucky.

The court disagreed that Kentucky was the proper forum and disregarded the forum selection clause. 28 U.S.C. § 1404 allows a district court to exercise its discretion in transferring cases by weighing the private interests of the parties against public interest concerns. The court focused on the location of a key witness, RFG founder David Gong, who lived in San Diego and who was a quadriplegic. Under § 1404(a), witnesses' convenience is one of the most important factors the court will consider to determine whether to grant a motion to change venue. *Thomas v. Home Depot*, 131 F. Supp.2d 934, 937 (E.D. Mich. 2001). Gong could only travel at great expense and inconvenience. Gong's condition substantially undermined the court's predisposition to the plaintiff's forum choice.

The court also focused on the location of the cause of action. Valvoline alleged RFG infringed its trademark by representing competitor's oil as Valvoline oil for sale to consumers. RFG operated 35 stores in California and none in Kentucky. Because the events giving rise to Valvoline's claims occurred in California, the court found Kentucky had "little connection" to the claims at issue, except for Valvoline alleging that it suffered economic harm in Kentucky, which was insufficient to establish minimum contacts with a forum state. For a trademark infringement case, the appropriate forum is where the alleged infringer wrongfully passes off a good under another's trademark. Because of the unique circumstances of the primary witness and location of the alleged trademark infringement, the court disregarded the forum selection clause and transferred the case to the Southern District of California.

In *Myers v. Jani-King of Phila., Inc.*, No. 09-1738, 2012 U.S. Dist. LEXIS 172782 (E.D. Pa. Dec. 5, 2012), the court denied Defendant Jani-King's motion to transfer venue in spite of a Texas choice of venue clause. Plaintiffs Pamela Myers, et al ("Myers") filed a class action against Jani-King and its subsidiaries ("Jani-King"), alleging that the Jani-King franchise agreements were illegal employment agreements. The complaint alleged the following claims: Violation of the Pennsylvania Minimum Wage Act ("MWA"), Violation of the Pennsylvania Wage Payment and Collection Law, breach of contract, breach of the duty of good faith and fair dealing, and unjust enrichment. Jani-King filed a motion to dismiss or transfer venue, arguing that the forum selection clause in the franchise agreements mandated that the case be dismissed in its entirety, or in the alternative, transferred to the Northern District of Texas. The forum selection clause provided that "[j]urisdiction and venue is declared to be exclusively in Dallas County, in the State of Texas."

Pursuant to 28 U.S.C. § 1404(a), a district court may transfer any civil action to any other district or division where it could have been brought "for the convenience of the parties and witnesses, in the interest of justice." The district court has discretion in adjudicating motions to transfer based on the weighing of public and private interests. *Jumara v. State Farm Ins. Co.*, 55 F.3d 873, 878 (3d Cir. 1995). Before balancing the public and private interests, the court determined that the forum selection clause was valid. Myers argued that the forum selection clause was the product of undue influence and overweening bargaining power and was both procedurally and substantively unconscionable. However, Myers had notice of the forum selection clause and had the opportunity to reject the franchise agreement. The fact that the agreement was a form contract and Myers did not engage in negotiations did not render the forum selection clause procedurally unconscionable. Substantive unconscionability exists when the terms of an agreement so unreasonably favor one party that they "shock the conscience." This was not the case. The court found that it was not unreasonable for a national company with franchisees throughout the country to focus litigation in a particular forum. Therefore, the court found that the forum selection clause in the franchise agreement was valid.

However, in addressing the *Jumara* factors, the court found that both private and public factors weighed in favor of Myers. With regard to private factors, although plaintiff's choice of forum is ordinarily given deference, where the plaintiff has contractually agreed to a proper venue, such deference is inappropriate. The court found this factor neutral. Further, the convenience of the parties and witnesses weighed in favor of Myers and the location of the books and records weighed in favor of Myers. The court noted that Jani-King had a regional office in Pennsylvania and it would be unreasonable to require anyone who wishes to participate in the litigation to appear in Texas when Jani-King had an office in Pennsylvania and the work was performed in Pennsylvania by Pennsylvania residents. With regard to public factors, enforceability of a Texas judgment would be problematic because putative class members all live and work in the Pennsylvania area. The court also found that practical considerations make litigation easier and more efficient in Pennsylvania because the location of parties, the location of witnesses, in the place where the claim arose all make Pennsylvania and easier and more efficient location to conduct litigation. Finally, Pennsylvania has a local interest in interpreting and enforcing Pennsylvania law. Based on these reasons, the court denied Jani-King's motion to transfer the case to the Northern District of Texas.

See also, *KFC Corporation v. Texas Petroplex, Inc.*, No. 11-CV-00479, 2012 U.S. Dist. LEXIS 144342 (D. Ky. Oct. 4, 2012)(court enforced forum selection clause against Corporate Franchisee, but not against individual personal guarantors, thus requiring transfer to franchisee's forum state).

C.   CASES WITH NO FORUM CLAUSE

In *JTH Tax, Inc., v. Callahan*, No. 12-CV-691, 2013 U.S. Dist. LEXIS 84684 (E.D. Va. June 6, 2013) the court denied the defendant franchisee's motion to transfer venue and conditioned its ruling upon defendant's payment of plaintiff's attorney's fees and costs associated with pursuing competing default motions. The franchisor brought a claim in the Eastern District of Virginia against franchisee relating to the franchisee's post-termination obligations.

First the court considered the franchisee's motion to transfer venue from the Eastern District of Virginia to the Western District of Virginia. The court denied the motion because, although the claim could have been brought in Western District, the "interest of justice and convenience of the parties and witnesses [did not] justify a transfer to that forum." Here, the court found that the Eastern District of Virginia was the most appropriate forum. Plaintiff's headquarters is located there and both parties agreed in the franchise agreement that Eastern District of Virginia would be "an appropriate federal forum for contract disputes."

Witness and party convenience also supported a denial of a transfer. While the franchisee named a few potential witnesses that he claimed were not subject to service of process in the Eastern District, he provided no affidavits to support his claim. Instead, defendant's motion and memorandum focused almost entirely on inconvenience to the defendant himself, as opposed to the inconvenience of any witnesses who would testify on his behalf. In addition, although the franchisee argued that his health prevented him from traveling, the court found that he had recently made similar trips and had failed to show why accommodations could not be arranged to make the travel easier. In contrast, the franchisor named five specific witnesses, all of whom reside in the Eastern District of Virginia. The plaintiff provided timely affidavits explaining the topic on which each witness is expected to testify and the asserted inconvenience each would face should transfer occur. The court also found that the interests of justice would be equally served in the existing forum because both forums were in the same state and had similar case loads and laws. All these factors together weighed against a transfer.

In *Easton-Bell Sports v. E.I. DuPont de Nemours & Co.,* No. 13-CV-00283, 2013 U.S. Dist. LEXIS 43832 (N.D. Cal. Mar. 26, 2013) the court denied defendant's motion to dismiss or transfer the case. Defendant DuPont argued that Plaintiff Easton-Bell's complaint for declaratory relief was anticipatory and made with the purpose of improper forum shopping. DuPont asked the Court to depart from the first-to-file rule, which dictates that a later filed action usually defers to an earlier filed action with the same parties and issues. The court found that the suit was not anticipatory, brought in bad faith, or the product of improper forum shopping and that convenience and interest of justice did not weigh in favor of transferring the action.

DuPont is a manufacturer, seller, and distributor of Kevlar, a synthetic fiber that is ballistic, stab-resistant, and used to finish products. DuPont owns multiple federal trademark registrations for the Kevlar trademark. DuPont contacted Easton-Bell regarding its use of the Kevlar mark on its bike tires and locks. The two parties entered into an agreement to explore the possibility of a licensing agreement. However, Easton-Bell claimed that the licensing agreement fees were too high given its limited and fair use of the mark. Later DuPont asked Easton-Bell to provide accounting for a proposed settlement agreement relating Easton-Bell's use of the Kevlar mark. When Easton-Bell failed to respond, DuPont emailed Easton-Bell on January 18, 2013, asking them to respond by January 23, 2013. Easton-Bell filed suit in California on January 18, 2013. Ten days later, DuPont filed an infringement action in Delaware.

In Easton-Bell's complaint, it sought declaratory judgment that it did not infringe DuPont's trademark under the Lanham Act. It argued that its use of the Kevlar mark was limited and constituted fair use, was not likely to cause confusion or mistake, and was not likely to deceive consumers regarding its origins. DuPont countered that the use of the mark was likely to confuse consumers and lead them to believe that the products were endorsed by DuPont.

The court found that the complaint was not anticipatory or brought in bad faith. Even though DuPont emailed Easton-Bell threatening litigation on January 18, 2013, Easton-Bell had already filed its complaint that morning. Therefore, the court found that Easton-Bell did not file as a reaction to DuPont's email. There were no facts to show that there was a specific and concrete indication of an imminent suit by DuPont. In fact, DuPont's counsel offered no less than three extensions to respond to its offer of settlement. As the court put it: "These never-ending extensions do not give specific, concrete indications that suit was imminent." In addition, DuPont failed to allege any facts that indicated bad faith in the negotiations.

The court then considered if Easton-Bell was forum shopping. When Easton-Bell filed suit in California rather than Delaware, there was nothing to show that it did so to forum shop. The substantive law was federal and would not motivate forum shopping. In addition, DuPont failed to show any specific or concrete indications that there were other motivations behind where Easton-Bell filed. For these reasons, in addition to the location of potential witnesses weighing in favor of Easton-Bell, the court denied DuPont's motion to transfer venue.

In *Long John Silver's Inc. v. Nickleson*, No. 11-CV-93, 2013 U.S. Dist. LEXIS 2010 (W.D. Ky. Jan. 7, 2013), the court denied Defendant Nickleson's motion to transfer venue, or in the alternative, to abstain, finding all factors other than the home-court presumption were either neutral or weighed in favor of Plaintiff Long John Silver's choice of forum.

Long John Silver's filed breach of contract, trademark infringement and unfair competition claims in the United States District Court for the Western District of Kentucky on the basis of diversity jurisdiction. Nickleson counterclaimed, alleging breach of contract, violations of the Minnesota Franchise Act and common law fraud. Nickleson filed for bankruptcy in Minnesota while this action was pending in Kentucky. On behalf of

Nickleson, the trustee of his bankruptcy estate moved to transfer the case to the United States District Court of Minnesota pursuant to 28 U.S.C. § 1412, or in the alternative, to abstain from deciding the action.

The court had previously denied Nickleson's motion to transfer venue pursuant to 28 U.S.C. § 1404(a) before he filed bankruptcy. Both §1404 and § 1412 permit a district court to transfer a case or proceeding in the interests of justice or for the convenience of the parties. The standards applied under § 1404 and § 1412 are similar, other than that § 1412 applies to bankruptcy-related matters. There are two requirements under § 1412: (1) there must be a case or proceeding under title 11, and (2) the transfer must either be in the interests of justice or for the convenience of the parties. Transfer is granted at the discretion of the district court; however, the moving party must establish that transfer is appropriate by a preponderance of the evidence. Although proper venue is presumed in the district in which the bankruptcy case is pending, there is also a strong presumption favoring the Plaintiff's choice of forum.

Courts consider the following factors to determine whether a transfer of venue under § 1412 will serve the interests of justice: (1) whether the transfer would promote the economic and efficient administration of the bankruptcy estate; (2) whether the interests of judicial economy would be served by the transfer; (3) whether the parties would be able to receive a fair trial in each of the possible venues; (4) whether either forum has an interest in having the controversy decided within its borders; (5) whether the enforceability of any judgment obtained would be affected by the transfer; and (6) whether the plaintiff's original choice of forum should be disturbed. The most significant factor is whether the transfer would promote economic and efficient administration of the estate. The Court found that all factors were either neutral or weighed in favor of Long John Silver's choice of forum, other than the home-court presumption. Significantly, the court found that transferring the action to Minnesota would be unlikely to have any material impact on the administration of Nickleson's bankruptcy case because he already assigned his equitable and legal interest in the litigation to his primary secured creditor. The court also found that a transfer would likely result in delay and needless waste of judicial and party resources. Nickleson's motion to transfer venue was denied.

In a lengthy and complex case involving many issues surrounding choice of forum, the plaintiff in *Difederico vs. Marriott International, Inc.,* 714 F 3d 796 (4th Cir. 2013) initiated a wrongful death action against the franchisor Marriott when her husband was killed at the Marriott Islamabad Hotel in September 2008. A truck containing over 1,000 pounds of explosives, artillery shells, mortar bombs and shrapnel detonated killing 56 people and injuring at least 266 more. The plaintiff was the widow of a formal Navy commander serving as a civilian contractor for the State Department. The plaintiff made a decision to only sue the franchisor Marriott in Maryland, even though the hotel was owned by a franchisee and located in Pakistan. The plaintiff alleged that Marriott controlled all aspects of hotel security and was vicariously libel based on a negligent security theory. Marriott moved to dismiss based on the doctrine of forum non-conveniens claiming that the case should have been brought in Pakistan. The district court granted Marriott's motion finding that, although the statute of limitations might bar the plaintiff's claim in Pakistan, it posed no bar to dismissal because the plaintiff was responsible for the tactical decision not to litigate within the statute of limitations in Pakistan. The district court also found that Pakistan provided an adequate forum for adjudication, relying on the affidavit of Marriott's expert witness, an experienced Pakistani attorney. The district court also found that applicable public and private interests factors weighed heavily in favor of dismissal. The plaintiff appealed to the Fourth Circuit.

Plaintiff argued that the district court erred when it decided that the Pakistani forum was available even though the 1-year statute of limitations had run on her claims in Pakistan. Marriott argued that a "reasonable interpretation" of the Pakistani Limitations Act was that the limitation period did not begin to run until Marriott submitted itself to the jurisdiction of Pakistan. The Fourth Circuit found this argument unpersuasive because Marriott did not provide any evidence of the viability of its interpretation. Normally, if the plaintiff can demonstrate that the statute of limitations would bar its claim in another jurisdiction, that fact is dispositive in a forum non-conveniens analysis. However, the Fourth Circuit has recognized an exception where it can be shown that the plaintiff made a deliberate and tactical decision to run the statute of limitations for the purpose of avoiding dismissal in the preferred forum. In this case, after acknowledging that the plaintiff may not be able to pursue her claim in Pakistan, the district court determined that she made a strategic decision to avoid trying the case in Pakistan and concluded that the exception applied in this case. The Fourth Circuit disagreed, finding that courts cannot invoke the exception without specific evidence establishing a plan of deliberate maneuvering to avoid trying the case in the alternative form. The Fourth Circuit scoured the briefs, the record, and the transcript of the hearing and found no evidence of the plaintiff's motives, much less evidence of a deliberate and tactical decision to let the statute of limitations run in Pakistan to avoid dismissal. As a result, the Fourth Circuit held that the district court abused its discretion in applying the exception and that Marriott failed to carry its burden of establishing Pakistan as an available forum.

With respect to the district court's analysis of the public and private factors relative to the forum non-conveniens analysis, the court reiterated that a citizen plaintiff's choice of forum is entitled to great deference when the plaintiff chooses her "home forum" and can only be overridden when the defendant "establishes such oppressiveness and vexation to a defendant as to be out of all proportion to plaintiff's convenience, which may be shown to be slight or non-existent." The Fourth Circuit found that the District Court abused its discretion because it failed to clearly acknowledge the greater deference given to a citizen plaintiff or to analyze the case accordingly. With respect to the so-called "private factors," the Fourth Circuit found that the fear and emotional trauma involved in traveling to Pakistan for a trial concerning such a politically charged event, would give rise to a bevy of logistical concerns and expenses for the plaintiff, including: 1) avoiding hotels, restaurants, shops and stores identified by the State Department as targets for potential attack; 2) hiring local assistance to help plaintiff access basic amenities; and 3) hiring body guards for protection. Although Marriott argued that the plaintiff may not need to travel to Pakistan for the trial, the court rejected this assertion finding that the plaintiff had a right to attend trial proceedings and may be necessary as a witness on the issue of damages. Ultimately, the Fourth Circuit concluded that it would be a perversion of justice to force a widow and her children to place themselves in the same risk-laden situation that led to the death of a family member, and they would be inconvenienced by the fear, emotion trauma and associated logistical complexity that would afflict them if the case were dismissed and decided in Pakistan.

The court also found that review of private factors provided additional support for the conclusion that the district court abused its discretion in dismissing the case. For example, the plaintiff's theory centered on Marriott's failure to properly control security at its franchised hotel. As such, the essential sources of proof shifted to policies and procedures developed by Marriott at its corporate offices in the United States. The Fourth Circuit also criticized the district court's finding that the availability of compulsory process for attendance of unwilling witnesses and the cost of bringing witnesses to court weighed in favor of Marriott. The court found that although Marriott made a generalized assertion that the court cannot compel Pakistani witnesses to give testimony, it failed to allege or offer proof that any witnesses would be unwilling to cooperate with a trial in the United States. The Fourth Circuit also found that the district court erred in finding there was no compelling local interest in having localized controversies decided at home. However, because the plaintiff's central theory revolved around Marriott's coordination of security from its principal place of business in the United States, there is inherent convenience to bringing the case in Marriott's own legal backyard. The Fourth Circuit also found that the district court erred in finding that the difficulty in applying foreign law weighed in favor of dismissal. Without deciding whether Pakistani law would apply, the district court provided no reason why Pakistani law would create any particularly difficulty in application or interpretation.

Finally, the Fourth Circuit held that the district court erred in concluding that it would be burdensome to have members of a jury hear evidence regarding a terrorist attack that has little to do with the forum, other than the fact that Marriott's headquarters is in Maryland. The Fourth Circuit noted that the case involved an American citizen suing an American corporation within the community where the case would be tried. As such, a Maryland jury has a strong interest in deciding the case. The Fourth Circuit reversed and remanded.

In *Motorscope, Inc. v. Precision Tune, Inc.*, No. 12-1296, 2012 U.S. Dist. LEXIS 143735 (D. Minn. Oct. 4, 2012), the court ruled that franchisor, Precision Tune, could not meet its heavy burden to transfer the case by its former franchisee from the franchisee's home state in the District of Minnesota to Precision Tune's home turf in the Eastern District of Virginia. The district court recognized a presumption for the plaintiff's "home" forum and that a court should deny a motion to transfer unless a balance of factors strongly favors the moving party.

The court found that Precision Franchising failed to satisfy its burden to demonstrate that the scale of factors weighed in its favor because Motorscope, the franchisee, met all of Precision's arguments with equal force. All of the witnesses for Motorscope were located in Minnesota, but Precision's witnesses were located in Virginia. An unfavorable outcome for Motorscope would cause more injuries in Minnesota, but an unfavorable outcome for Precision would cause more injuries in Virginia. Both parties have an equal connection to the case. Accordingly, the court determined that Precision Tune had not met its burden to transfer the case under 28 U.S.C. §1404(a).

In *Capriotti's Sandwich Shop, Inc. v. Taylor Family Holdings, Inc.*, 857 F. Supp. 2d 489 (D. Del. 2012), Plaintiff Capriotti's Sandwich Shop, Inc., a Nevada corporation with its principal place of business in Las Vegas, filed suit in Delaware against its franchisee Taylor Family Holdings, Inc. ("Defendant") and Natalie Delucia Taylor, the president and partial owner of

TFH for breach of a franchise agreement. Capriotti's filed in Delaware because it's prior owners were based in Delaware. Capriotti's learned that a Las Vegas-based gentlemen's club was offering a happy hour promotion in which customers could receive a 6 inch Capriotti's sandwich and a beer for five dollars. A promotional flyer prepared by the gentlemen's club advertised the promotion and featured an exotic dancer along with one of Capriotti's trademarks. The club also advertising the deal on its Facebook page and the local ESPN radio affiliate. Capriotti's alleged that the publicity falsely suggested that the promotion was sponsored or authorized by Capriotti's and sought a preliminary injunction. In response, Defendant filed a separate action in Delaware state court against Capriotti's seeking to prevent Capriotti's from terminating the franchise agreement. Defendants then moved to dismiss the action filed by Capriotti's, as well as a motion to transfer.

The court found that by filing suit in the Delaware state court, Defendants waived jurisdictional defenses and consented to the jurisdiction of the federal court in the same state. The court explained that Defendant could not claim unfairness based upon the court's exercise of jurisdiction over them, because one who enjoys the full benefits of access to the forum's courts as a Plaintiff cannot also claim immunity from the forum's authority as a Defendant. Accordingly, venue was proper in Delaware. However, that was not the end of the issue.

With respect to the defendant's motion to transfer the action to Nevada, the court determined that the reasons to transfer strongly favored the defendant. Although Delaware was a legitimate venue, with both parties choosing it as a forum in the first instance, the dispute between the parties could not be properly resolved in Delaware. The dispute arose in Nevada between two Nevada-based businesses and only a Nevada court could exercise personal jurisdiction over a critical fact witness, the owner of the gentlemen's club who worked with the local Nevada franchisee on the sandwich and beer promotion. Thus, both public and private factors weighed in favor transfer to the district of Nevada for ultimate disposition of Capriotti's motion for preliminary junction.

In *Tittl v. Hilton Worldwide, Inc.*, No.: 12-CV-02040, 2013 U.S. Dist. LEXIS 35680 (E.D. Cal. Mar. 13, 2013), the court granted Defendant Hilton Worldwide, Inc.'s ("Hilton") motion to transfer in the interest of justice. Plaintiff Pete Tittl initiated a class action in Kern County Superior Court alleging that Hilton illegally recorded his phone conversations and was liable for violations of Ca. Penal Code § 630 and Cal. Bus. & Prof. Code § 17200. Hilton removed the case to the Eastern District of California and filed motions to dismiss the complaint for failure to state a claim and to change venue to the Central District of California pursuant to 28 U.S.C. § 1404(a), or in the alternative, to stay the action. The court found that Hilton sufficiently demonstrated that transfer was appropriate in the interest of justice, based on the pendency of a related action in the Central District of California, the familiarity of the forum with applicable law, and comparative levels of court congestion in each forum.

Additionally, the Central District had previously sustained a motion to dismiss in a substantially similar case: *Young v. Hilton*, No. 12-CV-1788, 2012 U.S. Dist. LEXIS 84163 (C.D. Cal. June 18, 2012). At the time of Hilton's motion to transfer, the decision to dismiss in *Young* was pending before the Ninth Circuit Court of Appeals. Though Tittl was not a party in *Young*, the putative classes, defendants, legal claims and allegations were virtually the same. Further, the Central District Court was more familiar with applicable law and a local rule in the Central District assured the *Tittl* action would be assigned to the same District Judge that dealt with identical legal issues in *Young*. The local rule applied regardless of whether there was an existing case pending before the newly-filed case was assigned to the judge who handled the earlier case. Finally, based on the *Statistic Tables for the Federal Judiciary*, the median time interval from a civil filing to disposition was approximately three months shorter in the Central District of California than in the Eastern District of California. Although the court found the convenience of parties and witnesses did not weigh in favor of a change in venue, the interests of justice and the need to conserve judicial resources weighed in favor of transferring the matter to the Central District of California.

In *Brugger v. Jani-King of Minnesota, Inc.*, No. 13-CV-05, 2013 U.S. Dist. Lexis 74548 (D. Minn. May 28, 2013), the plaintiff, Brugger, initiated a purported class action against Jani-King under the Fair Labor Standards Act. Brugger worked for Jani-King as an assistant Operations Manager or Operations Manager and alleged that Jani-King misclassified him as an exempt employee and failed to pay him overtime compensation. Brugger claimed that he intended to seek certification of a nationwide collective action of approximately 133 individuals throughout the United States who worked as Operations Managers or Assistant Operations Managers for Jani-King or its affiliate corporations. Jani-King moved to transfer venue to the Northern District of Texas under 28 U.S.C. §1404(a) "for the convenience of the parties and witnesses and the interests of justice." Noting that Brugger only named one of Jani-King's affiliate corporations as a defendant, the court observed that the remaining corporate affiliates would likely be required in order to seek certification of a nation-wide collective action. Jani-King alleged that the remaining Jani-King corporate affiliates were not subject to personal jurisdiction in Minnesota, but they would be subject to personal jurisdiction in the Northern District of Texas, where Jani-King is located. Under these circumstances, the Northern District of Texas seemed to be the only appropriate venue where the case could proceed as a collective action. Furthermore, of the 133 potential class members, only 5 worked for Jani-King in Minnesota while the rest were distributed throughout the United States. This fact tempered the deference that would normally be associated with Brugger's choice of forum. With respect to potential witnesses, Jani-King identified several individuals who resided in Texas that were expected to testify about the policies and guidelines that affected all corporate affiliates while the plaintiff identified only a few witnesses in Minnesota. The court also found that a majority of the documents relating to Assistant Operations Managers and Operations Managers were located in Texas, not Minnesota. Finally, although the court acknowledged Brugger's claim that he could not afford to bring a case in Texas, he failed to substantiate that claim with any proof of his inability to pursue litigation in Texas. As a result, the court granted Jani-King's motion and transferred the case to the Northern District of Texas.

In *FTC v. Wyndham Worldwide Corp.*, No. 12-CV-1365, 2013 U.S. Dist. LEXIS 41494 (D. Ariz. Mar. 25, 2013), the court reviewed franchisor Wyndham's motion to transfer the case from the United States District Court for the District of Arizona to New Jersey or the District of Columbia.

The FTC sued Wyndham and its franchisees in the U.S. District Court for the District of Arizona for allegedly violating the FTC Act, 15 U.S.C. § 45(a), for "unfair or deceptive acts or practices in or affecting commerce." The FTC alleged Wyndham deceived consumers by advertising that the company used industry-standard security measures to protect guests' personal information. The FTC alleged Wyndham acted improperly by failing to implement "reasonable and appropriate measures to protect personal information against unauthorized access." Intruders obtained unauthorized access to Wyndham's Arizona-based computer network three times in two years.

Wyndham and its franchisees moved to transfer the case to the U.S District Court for the District of New Jersey or the District of Columbia under 28 U.S.C. § 1404. The FTC opposed the motion, claiming the "operative facts" occurred in Arizona, the key witnesses resided in Arizona and the court should give deference to the FTC's forum choice. The court disagreed. The court found that New Jersey would be the appropriate forum because it is Wyndham's principle place of business and it developed the advertising at issue in New Jersey. Further, the employees that developed the advertising were in New Jersey and it would be most convenient for them as witnesses if the case were in New Jersey. Further, the plaintiff FTC had no significant connection to Arizona. On these facts, the court transferred the case to the District of New Jersey.

III.   Choice of Law

In *Lynch v. Math-U-See, Inc.*, No. 11-CV-233, 2013 U.S. Dist. LEXIS 29460 (N.D. Ind. Mar. 4, 2013), the court reviewed which state's law would govern a case between Math-U-See distributors in Idaho, Indiana and Pennsylvania that sued Math-U-See for violating its Distributor Agreements which contained a Pennsylvania choice of law provision. The plaintiff alleged various torts, including breach of fiduciary duty, tortious interference with contract, violation of the Idaho Consumer Protection Act, violation of Indiana Franchise Act and violation of the Tennessee Consumer Protection Act. Math-U-See argued that the state causes of action should be dismissed under 12(b)(6) and the tortious interference and breach of fiduciary duty claims were merely attempts by the distributors to recast breach of contract claims as tort claims.

The court denied Math-U-See's motion to dismiss. The court held that Pennsylvania law applied to all contract claims because the Distributor Agreement applied to contract-based claims. Additionally, the court applied Pennsylvania law to the tort claims because under Indiana choice of law rules, the law of the place where the injury occurred would apply. Because the court could not apply different jurisdictions' laws to the same claim, the court determined that Pennsylvania law would apply because it had the most significant contacts to the action as a whole. Further, the "gist of the action" applied in Pennsylvania, even if the injuries were spread among three states.

In *Wingate Inns International v. Swindall*, No. 12-248, 2012 U.S. Dist. LEXIS 152608 (D.N.J. Oct. 22, 2012), the court reviewed which state's law would govern Wingate's action against a former franchisee who allegedly transferred a Florida-based hotel property in violation of the franchise agreement. Wingate filed suit in New Jersey for an accounting of the revenues the franchisee earned while it operated as Wingate in order to recover outstanding royalties and fees. The franchisee counterclaimed for fraud, violation of New Jersey Consumer Fraud Act, breach of contract, breach of implied duty of good faith, lost income, violation of the Georgia Fair Business Practices Act and violation of the Florida Franchise and

Distributorship Law. Wingate moved to dismiss all the counterclaims except breach of contract and breach of implied duty of good faith.

Even though the hotel property was in Florida, the court dismissed the franchisee's Florida Franchise and Distributorship Law claim because the franchise agreement stated that New Jersey law would govern all disputes arising from the franchise agreement. The court cited prior precedent that choice of law clauses should apply, unless the chosen state: (a) has no substantial relationship to either party or the transaction and no reasonably basis exists for the parties' choice, or (b) applying the chosen state's law would be contrary to another states' public policy with a materially greater interest than the chosen state in determining the particular issue. The court found that Wingate had substantial contact with New Jersey because its principle place of business is in Parsippany, New Jersey. It also found that Florida likely did not have a materially greater interest in applying its laws to the case. The court found support in other Florida district court cases where the courts have allowed choice of law agreements to bar application of the Florida Franchise Act. The court also reasoned that defendant waived its right to protection under Florida law by agreeing that New Jersey law would govern the agreement.

IV.   Arbitration

A.   ENFORCEABILITY

1.   Arbitration in Class Actions

There were a number of decisions issued in the last twelve months regarding the enforcement of class waivers in arbitration provisions. Most significantly, the United States Supreme Court in *American Express Co. vs. Italian Colors Restaurant* confirmed the absolute enforceability of class action waivers in the face of virtually any challenge. The decision forced the Massachusetts Supreme Court to rescript two recently issued opinions, reversing itself in one of them. Several other decisions confirmed what the Massachusetts Supreme Court apparently didn't grasp-- class action waivers in arbitration agreements are enforceable.

In a case with significant implications for franchise litigation, the United States Supreme Court in *American Express Co. vs. Italian Colors Restaurant,* 133 S. Ct. 2304 (2013) held that the Federal Arbitration Act does not permit courts to invalidate a contractual waiver of a class arbitration on the ground that the plaintiff's costs of individually arbitrating a federal statutory claim exceeds the potential recovery.

This case involved an agreement between American Express and merchants who accept American Express cards. The parties' agreement required that all disputes be resolved by arbitration, and stated that there "shall be no right or authority for any claims to be arbitrated on a class-action basis." Regardless, a group of merchants initiated a class-action claiming violation of the Sherman Act and seeking treble damages for the class under the Clayton Act. American Express moved to compel individual arbitration under the FAA. The merchants countered that the cost of expert analysis to prove the anti-trust claims would greatly exceed the maximum recovery for any individual plaintiff. The district court rebuffed the merchant's argument and granted American Express's motion to dismiss the lawsuit.

On appeal, the Second Circuit reversed and remanded, holding that the class-action waiver was unenforceable because of the prohibitive costs the merchants would face if they had to individually arbitrate. The Supreme Court granted *certiorari*, vacated the judgment and remanded for further consideration in light of *Stolt-Nielsen S.A. v. AnimalFeeds Int'l Corp.*, 559 US 662 (2010), which held that a party may not be compelled to submit to class arbitration absent an agreement to do so. *American Express Co. vs. Italian Colors Restaurant*, 559 U.S. 1103 (2010).

On remand, the Second Circuit stood by its original ruling. Shortly thereafter, the Second Circuit reconsidered its ruling *sua sponte*, in light of *AT&T Mobility LLC v. Concepcion*, 131 S. Ct. 1740 (2011), which held that the FAA preempts any state law barring enforcement of a class arbitration waiver. However, the Second Circuit found that the *AT&T* case was inapplicable because it addressed preemption, not class waiver. Therefore the Second Circuit reversed for the third time. *In re American Express Merchants Litigation*, 667 F. 3d 204, 213 (2nd Cir. 2011). The Second Circuit also denied rehearing *en banc* with five judges dissenting.

The Supreme Court granted *certiorari* and again reversed the Second Circuit. The Supreme Court reinforced the notion that courts must "rigorously enforce" arbitration agreements according to their terms, even for claims alleging a violation of a Federal Statute, unless the FAA's mandate has been "overridden by a contrary congressional command." In this case, the Supreme Court found no contrary congressional command requiring rejection of the class arbitration waiver. With respect to the argument that the cost of expert analysis of antitrust claims would greatly exceed the maximum recovery for any individual plaintiff, the Supreme Court stated that the antitrust laws "do not guarantee an affordable procedural path" to the vindication of every claim. By analogy, the Court noted that it has rejected the assertion that the class notice requirement may be waived because the "prohibitively high cost" of compliance would frustrate the Plaintiff's attempt to vindicate the policies underlying antitrust laws.

The merchants also cited a common law exception to the FAA which serves to harmonize the competing federal policies by allowing courts to invalidate agreements that prevent the "effective vindication" of a federal statutory right. The merchants argued that enforcing the class waiver effectively bars vindication of their rights because they have no economic incentive to pursue their antitrust claims individually in arbitration. The Supreme Court noted that the "effective vindication" exception originated in dictum in *Mitsubishi Motors Corp. vs. Soler Chrysler-Plymouth, Inc.* 473 U.S. 614, 637, n.19 (1985). The exception finds its origin in the desire to prevent prospective waiver of a party's right to pursue statutory remedies. However, "the fact that it is not worth the expense involved in *proving* a statutory remedy does not constitute the elimination of the *right to pursue* that remedy." *American Express Co. vs. Italian Colors Restaurant*, 133 S. Ct. 2304, 2311 (2013). Put differently, the Court stated that individual claims that were considered adequate to assure effective vindication of a federal right before adoption of class action procedures in Rule 23 did not suddenly become ineffective vindication after Rule 23 went into effect.

Given this most recent ruling by the United States Supreme Court, franchisors with class action waivers in their arbitration agreements should rest assured that franchisees will not be able to arbitration class-wide claims against the franchisor.

Had the Massachusetts Supreme Court waited eight days, they could have avoided issuing their decision in *Feeney v. Dell, Inc.*, No. SJC-11133, 2013 Mass LEXIS 462 (Mass. June 12, 2013), which conflicted with the *American Express* Case. Feeney and other plaintiffs filed a class action lawsuit against Dell for allegedly collecting money falsely characterized as a sales tax. Dell moved to compel individual arbitration under the agreement between the parties. The arbitration clause mandated all claims to be arbitrated "on an individual basis." The court initially found that the arbitration clause was invalid because it violated Massachusetts public policy. Specifically, the court found that Massachusetts favored consumer class actions, and enforcing the clause would insulate Dell from class action claims.

After the court's initial finding in Feeney ("Feeney I"), the Supreme Court decided *AT&T Mobility LLC v. Concepcion*, 131 S. Ct. 1740 (2011). In *Concepcion*, the Supreme Court found that the Federal Arbitration Act ("FAA") "prohibits States from conditioning the enforceability of certain arbitration agreements on the availability of class-wide arbitration procedures."

After *Concepcion*, the court in *Feeney* ("Feeney II") considered whether the Supreme Court's decision abrogated Feeney I. In Feeney II, the court considered "whether a class action waiver provision in an arbitration clause in a consumer contract is enforceable where the plaintiff can demonstrate, as a factual matter, that the class action waiver effectively denies him or her a remedy and insulates the defendant from private civil liability for violations of State law." Despite *Concepcion*, the court held that when the clause denies a plaintiff remedy, it is invalid.

In its reasoning, the court found its initial holding in Feeney I invalid after *Concepcion* because it was based solely on a violation of Massachusetts policy. However, the court also found that the Supreme Court did not foreclose invalidating arbitration agreements with a class action wavier when the alternative would leave the plaintiff unable to pursue a claim. The court found that the plaintiffs in Feeney II were able to demonstrate that in light of the complex nature of their claims and the modest amount of their individual damages, they could not pursue their individual statutory claim under the individual claim arbitration process. Therefore, the class waiver provision in the arbitration agreement was invalid.

Eight days after the Massachusetts Supreme Court issued its opinion in *Feeney II*, the United States Supreme Court issued its opinion in *American Express Co. vs. Italian Colors Restaurant,* 133 S. Ct. 2304 (2013). This prompted the defendants in *Feeney II* to file a petition for rehearing on the grounds that *American Express* abrogated *Feeney II*. On August 1, 2013 the Massachusetts Supreme Court issued a rescript of *Feeney II* and concluded that its analysis in *Feeney II* no longer comported with the Supreme Court's interpretation of the FAA. Although it found "untenable the Supreme Court's view that the FAA's command to enforce arbitration agreements trumps any interest in ensuring the prosecution of low value claims," it was bound to accept that view as the controlling statement of federal law. As a result, it reversed its prior decision affirming the Superior Court's decision in *Feeney II* invalidating the class waiver provision. *Feeney v. Dell, Inc.,* No. SJC-11133, 2013 Mass LEXIS 635, (Mass. Aug. 1, 2013)

In a case decided on the same day as *Feeney v. Dell*, but with a different result, in *Edson Teles. Machado v. System4, LLC*, No. SJC-11175, 2013 Mass. LEXIS 461 (Mass. June 12, 2013), the court found that because plaintiffs were unable to demonstrate that they lacked a means to pursue their claims on an individual basis, the arbitration clause with a class waiver was valid. In the *Machado* case, the plaintiffs entered into "local franchise agreements" with defendants Systems 4 LLC ("Systems 4") and NECCS, Inc. ("NECCS") for commercial janitorial services. Plaintiff claimed that Systems 4 and NECCS misclassified the plaintiffs and other similarly situated individuals as independent contractors in violation of Massachusetts wage law. The plaintiffs sought return of their franchise fees, which ranged from approximately $9,500 to $21,800 per plaintiff. The local franchise agreements contained an arbitration clause that barred class proceedings and prohibited an award of multiple damages.

The court applied its interpretation of *AT&T Mobility LLC v. Concepcion*, 131 S. Ct. 1740 (2011) from *Feeney v. Dell, Inc.*, No. SJC-11133, 2013 Mass LEXIS 462 (Mass. June 12, 2013) to this case. The court in Feeney II found that *Concepcion* preempted state law and eliminated the public policy rationale favoring consumer class actions and invaliding class action waivers. However, a class waiver clause may still be invalid if it would mean that plaintiffs are unable to pursue their claims individually. The court found that the claims in the *Machado* case were large enough to pursue on an individual basis, although damages were not the only criteria for considering if a claim is remediable in individual arbitration. Because the court found that the class waiver clause did not prevent recovery in any other way under the Massachusetts Wage Law, it declined to invalidate the class waiver provision. However, it did declare the waiver of multiple damages unenforceable because it did not impinge on the fundamental characteristic of arbitration or frustrate the purpose of the arbitral forum. Calculating multiple damages is a purely clerical task easily accomplished by the arbitrator. Therefore, the court ruled that enforcement of the mandatory multiple damages provision of the Massachusetts Wage Act did not frustrate the FAA's objectives and could not be waived.

On August 1, 2013, the Massachusetts Supreme Court issued a rescript in the *Machado* case addressing whether the decision in *American Express Co. vs. Italian Colors Restaurant*, 133 S. Ct. 2304 (2013) had any effect on its holding in *Machado*. Although it agreed that the *American Express* case abrogated so much of its analysis in *Machado* as relied on its decision in *Feeney II*, it's analysis on the issue of the waiver of multiple damages, as well as its ultimate holding, remained sound. *Edson Teles. Machado v. System4, LLC*, No. SJC-11175, 2013 Mass. LEXIS 634, (Mass. Aug. 1, 2013).

In *Ace Hardware Corp. v. Advanced Caregivers, LLC*, No. 12-CV-01479, 2012 U.S. Dist. LEXIS 150877 (N.D. Ill. Oct. 18, 2012), the court ruled that the franchisee must arbitrate a putative nationwide class action against Ace

Hardware alleging fraud in connection with franchise sales. While no arbitration clause was included in the first franchise agreement signed in January 2009, Ace Hardware notified the franchisee in May 2009 that it needed to sign a new franchise agreement in order to correct an error in the street address of the franchisee's store. The "corrected" agreement included the arbitration clause. The addition of the arbitration clause was never mentioned by Ace.

The franchisee sought to defeat the arbitration clause by arguing that the clause was unenforceable on grounds of mutual mistake, failure to give notice, procedural unconscionability and fraud. Ace replied that it began inserting the arbitration clause in its agreements in March 2009, and the franchisee had sufficient time to read the agreement in the three weeks that it had the document before signing and returning it to Ace.

The court found that Illinois law presumes a party who signs a contract knows its terms and consents to be bound by them. The court also held that Ace had no duty to give the franchisee notice of the new arbitration clause. The court rejected the procedural unconscionability claim, stating that the arbitration clause appeared directly above the signature lines of the franchise agreement and was not hard to locate, read, or understand. For the same reasons, the court held that the franchisee's fraud claim failed as a matter of law. The court granted Ace's motion to compel arbitration.

In *Kairy v. Supershuttle International, Inc.*, No. 08-02993, 2012 U.S. Dist. LEXIS 134945 (N.D. Cal. Sept. 20, 2012), Kairy and a group of airport shuttle franchisees sued Supershuttle International, Inc., asserting that Supershuttle violated the federal Fair Labor Standards Act (FLSA), 9 U.S.C. § 1 et seq., and California law by classifying them as franchisees and independent contractors when they were, in fact and in law, employees eligible for overtime and other wages. Supershuttle moved to stay the litigation and compel individual arbitration pursuant to the arbitration provision in the franchise agreements.

Since the franchise agreements specifically prohibited class-wide arbitration, the franchisees opposed the motion to compel arbitration, arguing that: (1) Supershuttle waived any right to require arbitration by first litigating; (2) statutory claims such as those under the FLSA are properly resolved through legal proceedings, not arbitration; (3) the arbitration provision was unconscionable; and (4) some of the plaintiffs, who were "secondary drivers," were not signatories to the franchise agreement and thus could not be required to arbitrate.

The court rejected Kairy's arguments, relying in part on the U.S. Supreme Court's decision in *AT&T v. Concepcion*, 131 S. Ct. 1740 (2011), in which the court held that an arbitration provision excluding class-wide arbitration is not unconscionable.

The court held that Supershuttle did not waive its right to arbitrate because it acted promptly to compel arbitration once it became clear that class-wide arbitration prohibitions were enforceable. The court also held that the FLSA claims fell within the scope of the arbitration provision. The court rejected all other arguments regarding procedural unconscionability, including unequal bargaining power and surprise. Finally, the court held that the non-signatory secondary drivers were bound by the arbitration provision in the franchise agreements because they were third-party beneficiaries of the agreements who "knowingly exploited the rights and privileges under the agreements." Therefore, they could not accept the benefits of the agreement and then reject the portions of the agreement they did not like.

In a small victory for plaintiffs, the court held that the arbitration fee-splitting provision in the franchise agreement was unconscionable because the plaintiffs demonstrated a strong likelihood that they would not be able to afford arbitration on an individual basis. Accordingly, the court severed that provision from the rest of the agreement to arbitrate.

In *Muriithi v. Shuttle Express, Inc.*, 712 F.3d 173 (4th Cir. 2013), the Fourth Circuit considered the implications of the Supreme Court's holding in *AT&T Mobility LLC v. Concepcion*, 131 S. Ct. 1740 (2011) on the lower court's refusal to compel arbitration based on three provisions it held were unconscionable. At issue was the enforceability of an arbitration clause between Muriithi, a Shuttle Express franchisee, and Shuttle Express. The franchise agreement between the parties contained a broad arbitration clause that required arbitration of any controversy that arose from the agreement. Further, the arbitration clause contained a class action waiver that required disputes to be prosecuted on an individual basis.

Muriithi filed a claim under the Fair Labor Standards Act, 29 U.S.C. §§ 201-209, alleging that Shuttle Express induced him to sign the franchise agreement by misleading him about the compensation that he would receive. Muriithi also claimed that Shuttle Express improperly classified him as a "franchisee" or "independent contractor," thereby denying him overtime pay and minimum wage compensation. Shuttle Express moved to compel arbitration, and the district court denied the motion based on three provisions that it found unconscionable; a class action waiver, a fee splitting requirement and a one year contractual statute of limitations.

Shuttle Express challenged the district court's ruling, arguing that under *Concepcion*, the class action waiver was not unconscionable. The Fourth

Circuit agreed. The court explained that the *Concepcion* holding "prohibited courts from altering otherwise valid arbitration agreements by applying the doctrine of unconscionability to eliminate a term barring class wide procedures," and that therefore, the district court had erred in holding that the class action waiver was unconscionable.

With respect to the fee splitting provision, the court concluded that the holding in *Concepcion* did not alter the long-standing principle that a fee splitting provision can render an arbitration agreement unenforceable if an aggrieved party must pay arbitration fees and costs that are so prohibitive as to effectively deny the party access to the arbitral forum. The Fourth Circuit noted, however, that a party seeking to invalidate an arbitration agreement on this basis bears a substantial burden which must be established with firm proof. Because Muriithi failed to establish even the most basic elements of the challenge, including the value of his claim or the anticipated costs of the arbitration, he failed to carry his burden.

Finally, with respect to the one year contractual statute of limitations, the Fourth Circuit held that the district court erred in holding the one-year limitations period unconscionable as part of the court's resolution of the motion to compel because the one-year limitation provision was not part of the arbitration clause in the franchise agreement. A party challenging the enforceability of an arbitration clause must rely on grounds that relate specifically to the arbitration clause and not the contract as a whole. Thus, it was for the arbitrator to determine whether the one-year limitation provision was enforceable as part of the case on the merits. The Fourth Circuit vacated the district court's order and remanded the case with instructions that the district court enter an order compelling arbitration.

In *Chatman v. Pizza Hut, Inc.*, No. 12-CV-10209, 2013 U.S. Dist. LEXIS 73426 (N.D. Ill. May 23, 2013), Chatman filed a class action against Pizza Hut, the franchise owners, and JGJ Management under the Illinois Wage Payment and Collection Act (IWPCA), 820 ILCS § 115/1, *et seq.*, and the Illinois Minimum Wage Law (IMWL), 820 ILCS § 105/1, *et seq.* Chatman filed the complaint on behalf of all other similarly situated employees, and alleged that the defendants violated the IWPCA and IMWL by insufficiently reimbursing delivery drivers for automobile expenses incurred in the performance of their duties and failing to compensate delivery drivers for the actual time they worked each week. Pizza Hut filed a motion to compel arbitration on an individual basis based on the arbitration provision contained in the online job application submitted by Chatman.

The arbitration provision provided that any disputes between an employee and Pizza Hut would be resolved through confidential binding arbitration. Under the Federal Arbitration Act, 9 U.S.C § 4, a court must grant a motion to compel arbitration where there is (1) a written agreement to arbitrate, (2) a dispute within the scope of the arbitration agreement, and (3) one party refuses to arbitrate. Pizza Hut contended that the arbitration provision found within the employment application constituted a valid written agreement to arbitrate. Chatman argued that there was no valid agreement because the employment application lacked consideration, and that even if arbitration was compelled, that it should be done on a class basis.

The court first addressed whether the employment application was supported by consideration. Pizza Hut argued that the employment application was supported by three forms of consideration: (1) Pizza Hut's promise to consider Chatman for employment; (2) Pizza Hut's obligation to submit to binding arbitration; and 3) Pizza Hut's continued employment of Chatman. The court agreed with Pizza Hut and held that under Illinois law, each of the three acts was sufficient consideration.

The court then addressed Chatman's contention that there was no mutual promise to arbitrate because the employment application allowed Pizza Hut to change its rules and policies without notice via an "escape clause". Pizza Hut argued that the escape clause was unrelated to the arbitration provision. The court held that even if the escape clause were read to support Chatman's argument, there was still ample consideration. Further, the court referenced a recent case, *Collier v. Real Time Staffing Services, Inc.*, No. 11-CV-6209, 2012 U.S. Dist. LEXIS 50548 that rejected a similar argument. The *Collier* court declined to hold "that employment at-will language, which is standard in most employment contracts, renders an otherwise enforceable promise to arbitrate illusory."

Finally, the court addressed whether or not the arbitration provision prohibited class arbitration. Pizza Hut argued that because the arbitration provision did not mention class arbitration, that only individual arbitration should be allowed. Chatman argued that because the arbitration provision was drafted broadly enough to encompass "any claims", that class actions were included. The court found that it was the arbitrator's duty to decide whether or not the arbitration provision prohibited class arbitration. The court relied on *Price v. NCR Corp.*, No. 12-CV-3413, 2012 U.S. Dist. LEXIS 176166 (N.D. Ill. Dec. 10, 2012), in which the court faced a similar question. The *Price* court was guided by cases relating to the analogous question of whether an arbitrator should decide whether an arbitration agreement forbids consolidated arbitration. Based on Seventh Circuit cases that held that arbitrators have the discretion to analyze whether an arbitration provision permitted consolidated arbitration, the *Price* court reasoned that whether or not an arbitration provision prohibited or compelled class arbitration was for the arbitrator to decide.

Accordingly, the court granted Pizza Hut's motion to compel arbitration and left to the arbitrator the question of whether to arbitrate individually or on a class wide basis.

2.   *Enforcement of Arbitration Clause*

Even before *American Express Co. vs. Italian Colors Restaurant,* 133 S. Ct. 2304 (2013), arbitration provisions are almost universally enforced absent unusual circumstances. Below is a collection of cases in which the courts enforced arbitration provisions notwithstanding various challenges.

In *Woodbridge Center Property, LLC v. AMP Food Holdings, LLC*, No. A-6277-11T2, 2013 N.J. Super. Unpub. LEXIS 1521 (N.J. Super. Ct. App. Div., Jan. 20, 2013), the court reversed an order denying third-party defendants' motion to compel arbitration.   AMP Food Holdings, LLC ("AMP") entered into a franchise agreement with Panchero's Franchise Corporation to establish a Panchero's Mexican Grill. The individual owners of AMP all signed guaranty agreements. The franchise agreement stated that the contract was subject to arbitration.

AMP entered into a lease with plaintiff Woodridge Center Property, LLC ("Woodbridge") but AMP failed to take possession of the property. Woodridge filed an action against AMP as well as the guarantors. AMP then filed a third-party complaint against Panchero's, alleging that Panchero's was liable for all it owed Woodbridge. Panchero's then filed a motion to compel arbitration. It argued that "based on the language in the arbitration [clause], all claims and disputes have to be moved to arbitration." (internal citation omitted). The trial court denied the motion because it would create multiplicity of litigation. Panchero appealed. The Court of Appeals found that the terms of the franchise agreement were unambiguous and compelled arbitration of AMP's claims against Panchero's, notwithstanding the fact that it may be forced to continue litigation with Woodbridge in a separate proceeding. The clause required arbitration for "all controversies, disputes, or claims" and therefore, covered any claims by AMP against Panchero's. Thus, all the claims were within the scope of the arbitration clause.

In *Awuah v. Coverall North America, Inc.*, No. 12-1301, 2012 U.S. App. LEXIS 26461 (1st Cir. Dec. 27, 2012), the First Circuit held that a sub-group of purported class members who became Coverall franchisees by signing Consent to Transfer Agreements or personal guaranties to Coverall's franchise agreements must arbitrate their claims against Coverall. The district court ruled that this sub-group did not have to arbitrate their claims because its members did not have adequate notice of the arbitration clauses contained in the franchise agreements. Coverall appealed this determination, and the First Circuit reversed.

The franchisees become franchisees by entering into Consent to Transfer Agreements or by personal guaranties, but they did not sign the franchise agreements which contained or incorporated by reference a mandatory arbitration provision. They argued that the language of these consents and guaranties did not sufficiently incorporate the franchise agreements' arbitration clause. The consents and guaranties did explicitly state that the franchisees agreed to perform all responsibilities, duties, and obligations under the franchise agreements. The First Circuit held that no "magic terms" such as "incorporated by reference" are required in order to bind a party to a contractual provision. Rather, if the agreement at issue clearly communicates the obligation to arbitrate, as it did in this case, then it is enforceable.

The franchisees also argued that they could be not be bound by the arbitration provision because they did not receive appropriate notice of the arbitration requirement. They relied primarily on cases involving federal employment statutes, including the Americans With Disabilities Act, the Civil Rights Act of 1991, and the Age Discrimination in Employment Act, all of which held that a special heightened notice standard applied to agreements to arbitrate disputes involving federal employment statutes. The First Circuit held that the district court erred by relying on cases interpreting these statutes. Instead, the district court should have looked to Massachusetts state commercial contract law, which does not impose a special notice requirement upon agreements containing arbitration clauses. Even if Massachusetts law did impose a special notice requirement, any such requirement would have been preempted by the Federal Arbitration Act.

In *CPR - Cell Phone Repair Franchise Systems, Inc. v. Nayrami*, 896 F. Supp. 2d 1233 (N.D. Ga. 2012), Cell Phone Repair Franchise Systems, Inc. (CPR) moved to compel arbitration with a franchisee, Nayrami. The Franchise Agreement contained a mandatory arbitration provision delegating "all disputes relating to arbitrability," including unconscionability, to be exclusively decided by the arbitrator. Nayrami filed a lawsuit against CPR, alleging that CPR failed to register as a franchisor in violation of California Franchise Investment Law and that CPR misrepresented the profitability of the franchise in the negotiations leading up to the execution of the Agreement. In response to the filing, CPR filed a demand for arbitration and a motion to compel. Nayrami argued that the motion should be denied because: (1) the Agreement was not a result of a meeting of the minds; (2) the Agreement mandated California law, which declared the dispute resolution provision void; and (3) the dispute resolution provision was unconscionable.

The court agreed with CPR's position and granted the motion to compel arbitration based on the Eleventh Circuit's decision in *Given v. M & T Bank Corp.* (*In re* Checking Account Overdraft Litig.), 674 F.3d 1252 (11th Cir. 2012). *Given* involved a delegation provision that required the arbitrability of any issue, which the court named a "gateway question," to be decided by the arbitrator. The *Given* court stated that delegation provisions should be enforced if there is "clear and unmistakable evidence" that the parties intended to arbitrate a gateway question. Relying on this standard, the court found that the specific language in the Agreement "evidence[d] a clear and unmistakable intent by both parties to arbitrate the questions of arbitrability and unconscionability." The court granted the motion to compel arbitration.

STS Refills, LLC v. Rivers Printing Solutions, Inc., 896 F. Supp. 2d 364 (W.D. Pa. 2012) addressed whether the franchisor STS Refills, (STS) as assignee of an existing franchise agreement with Cartridge World, could enforce the included mandatory arbitration provision. The franchise agreement permitted assignment by Cartridge World with the one restriction; that the transferee have sufficient resources to fulfill its obligations.

The franchisee Rivers Printing challenged the validity of the assignment and argued that STS did not have sufficient resources to fulfill its obligations. STS filed a summary judgment motion to compel Rivers Printing to arbitrate disputes arising from the assigned franchise agreement. STS argued that because the disputed issues were within the scope of the agreement's arbitration provision, that the disputes should be arbitrated. STS also argued that Rivers Printing should be estopped from challenging the validity of the agreement because Rivers Printing continued to operate and conduct business with STS pursuant to the agreement after the assignment.

Under North Carolina law, contract rights are assignable unless prohibited by statute, public policy, the terms of the contract, or if the contract is one for personal services or is entered into out of personal confidence in the other party. The court concluded that the arbitration provision could be enforced only if the assignment was valid. Thus, because the validity of the assignment was a disputed issue of material fact, the court denied STS's motion for summary judgment.

EA Independent Franchisee Association v. Edible Arrangements International, Inc., No.10-CV-1489, 2012 U.S. Dist. LEXIS 166082 (D. Conn. Nov. 21, 2012), involved EA Independent Franchisee Association's suit against its franchisor, Edible Arrangements International, Inc. and its associates. The association claimed that the franchisor breached their franchise agreements, violated the implied covenant of good faith and fair dealing, and violated the Connecticut Unfair Trade Practices Act, Conn. Gen. Stat. § 42-110a et seq., by "unfairly imposing a series of system-wide changes on its franchisees." The alleged changes included imposing certain mandates concerning extended hours and purchase of produce from certain vendors, as well as instituting certain practices that unfairly drained profits away from the franchisees. In response, Edible Arrangements sought to compel arbitration pursuant to the arbitration provision in the agreements.

The court swiftly dismissed the association's arguments regarding associational standing and ripeness. The court stated that its prior ruling regarding the association's standing to pursue claims did not bear on the franchisor's right to compel arbitration of those claims. Further, the court found that the dispute was ripe, as the franchisor asserted rights that were challenged by the members of the association, all of which had arbitration clauses in their franchise agreements. The court granted the franchisor's motion, as the arbitration provision was broad in scope and expressly included disputes concerning any system standards.

In *Oneonta Motor Sports v. Arctic Cat Sales, Inc.*, No. 12-1100, 2012 U.S. Dist. LEXIS 137534 (D. Minn. Sept. 26, 2012), Arctic Cat moved to compel arbitration of disputes arising from a dealer agreement with one of its dealers, Oneonta Motor Sports (OMS). OMS, a snowmobile and ATV dealer, alleged that Arctic Cat's dealer incentive programs violated New York's Franchised Motor Vehicle Dealer Act (Act), and that the violation constituted fraud and misrepresentation. OMS did not challenge the enforceability of the agreement or dispute that the agreement's arbitration provision was very broad. Rather, OMS argued that the agreement's arbitration provision conflicted with the Act and that as a result, Arctic Cat could not force OMS to arbitrate.

OMS relied on the choice-of-law provision in the agreement which provided for Minnesota law unless any provisions of the agreement were inconsistent with any applicable laws relating to OMS. The Act provides that arbitration may be required only if after a controversy arises all parties to the controversy consent in writing to arbitrate the dispute. Further, the Act prohibits franchisors from requiring dealers:

228

to agree to a term or condition in a franchise, or as a condition to the offer, grant or renewal of the franchise, lease, or agreement which

> (1) unless preempted by federal law, requires the [dealer] to waive trial by jury in actions involving the franchisor; or

> (2) unless preempted by federal law, specifies the jurisdiction, venues or tribunals in which disputes arising with respect to the franchise, lease or agreement shall or shall not be submitted for resolution or otherwise prohibits a [dealer] from bringing an action in a particular forum otherwise available.

N.Y. Veh. & Traf. Law § 463(2)(x). According to OMS, its agreement with Arctic Cat is inconsistent with the Act, which provides that OMS cannot be required to waive its rights under the Act. As such, OMS argued that the dealer agreement did not preempt the Act and OMS could not be compelled to arbitrate its claims against Artic Cat.

The court found little merit with OMS's argument and granted Arctic Cat's motion to compel arbitration. Most importantly however, relying on nearly 30 years of undisputed case law, the court ruled that the provisions of the Act were contrary to the Federal Arbitration Act (FAA) and were thus preempted. The FAA provides that a written agreement to arbitrate "shall be valid, irrevocable, and enforceable, save upon such grounds as exist at law or in equity for the revocation of any such contract." Because the provisions of the Act that prohibit arbitration absent a post-dispute agreement are contrary to the FAA, they are preempted. The court granted Arctic Cat's motion to stay and compel arbitration.

In *Cold Stone Creamery, Inc. v. Nutty Buddies, Inc.*, No. 12-CV-0420, 2012 U.S. Dist. LEXIS 142955 (D. Ariz. Oct. 3, 2012), Cold Stone filed a petition in Arizona to compel arbitration with Nutty Buddies, a Cold Stone franchisee and a member of the National Independent Association of Cold Stone Creamery Franchisees, Inc. (NIACCF). The NIACFF filed suit in Florida against Cold Stone, alleging that Cold Stone failed to provide information pertaining to, nor did it properly account for, certain monies it received from third parties designated for the benefit of franchisees. In response to the Florida lawsuit, Cold Stone filed its petition to compel arbitration in its home state of Arizona. In a strange procedural twist, Nutty Buddies moved to dismiss Cold Stone's petition to compel arbitration, but did not identify the rule of civil procedure under which it sought relief. The court assumed that the motion was brought under Rule 12(b)(6).

The court held that the allegations in Cold Stone's petition to compel stated a claim upon which relief could be granted, thereby satisfying the requirements to resist a 12(b)(6) motion. Specifically, the court relied on Cold Stone's allegations that: (1) Nutty Buddies entered into a franchise agreement with Cold Stone; (2) the agreement contained a broad arbitration clause requiring arbitration of all disputes that in any way related to the agreement or the relationship between the parties; (3) the disputed claims arose out of the agreement and were related to the relationship between the parties; and (4) therefore, the disputed claims were subject to arbitration. Taken as true, these allegations stated a claim to compel arbitration. Accordingly, the court denied Nutty Buddies' motion to dismiss.

In *Mariposa Express, Inc. v. United Shipping Solutions, LLC*, 2013 UT App 28 (Utah Ct. App. 2013), the plaintiff Mariposa franchisees appealed from a district court order compelling them to arbitrate their dispute with United Shipping Solutions (USS). USS operates a franchise system in which franchisees resell small parcel shipping services under a reseller agreement with DHL Express USA, Inc. (DHL). In breach of the reseller agreement, DHL announced that it was discontinuing its express domestic shipping service. Under the non-compete provision of the franchise agreements, the Mariposa franchisees could not contract with other providers to provide replacement services or products. Following DHL's breach, the Mariposa franchisees brought suit against USS seeking to void all obligations under their franchise agreements.

The Mariposa franchisees eventually entered into a settlement agreement with USS, which included a provision stating that the Mariposa franchisees would be given access to certain data to help determine how much they owed to USS for freight services. The provision provided that if the Mariposa franchisees did not agree with USS's assessment of how much was owed for the freight, that the dispute, like all others arising from the settlement agreement, would be resolved "exclusively by binding arbitration." The Mariposa franchisees disputed the amounts owed, and after filing a lawsuit, sent a letter to USS stating that they would not participate in arbitration. The district court ordered the parties to arbitrate their disputes pursuant to the arbitration provision in the settlement agreement.

The appellate court affirmed the trial court's decision, reasoning that when reading the settlement agreement in its entirety in an attempt to "harmonize all provisions," the parties clearly indicated their intent to arbitrate any further disputes between them. At the time of the settlement agreement, the parties had resolved all but two issues, and the court reasoned that it was logical to leave the two unresolved issues to be decided at a later time, with the ultimate resolution through arbitration.

In *Cahill v. Alternative Wines, Inc.*, No. 12-CV-110, 2013 U.S. Dist. LEXIS 14588 (N.D. Iowa Feb. 4, 2013), the franchisor Alternative Wines moved to dismiss the franchisee's complaint and compel arbitration in North Carolina. The franchisee resisted the motion based on Iowa Code Section 537A.10(3)(a) which makes void any provision in a franchise agreement restricting jurisdiction to a forum outside the State of Iowa. The franchisee further argued that because Section 537A.10(3)(a) applied to all franchise agreements, including but not limited to arbitration agreements, the Federal Arbitration Act did not pre-empt it. The franchisee also argued that generally applicable contract defenses, such as fraud, duress or unconscionability may be applied to invalidate arbitration agreements without contravening the Federal Arbitration Act.

The court disagreed and found that the Iowa Code provision was not a "generally applicable" contract defense, but only applied to franchise agreements and therefore violated the supremacy clause of the United States Constitution because it directly conflicted with the Federal Arbitration Act. Because the court found that all of the franchisee's claims fell within the broad arbitration provision, it was appropriate to dismiss the case instead of staying it pending arbitration.

In *Ironson v. Ameriprise Financial Services, Inc.*, No. 11-CV- 899, 2012 U.S. Dist. LEXIS 128393 (D. Conn. Sept. 10, 2012), the court considered Ameriprise's motion to compel arbitration after being sued by Ironson for alleged violations of the Connecticut Franchise Act and the Connecticut Unfair Trade Practices Act.

Ironson worked as a financial advisor affiliated with Ameriprise. In 2000, Ameriprise instituted a policy requiring all of its affiliated financial advisors to choose whether to become Ameriprise employees or independent Ameriprise franchisees. Ironson chose to become a franchisee and signed a franchise agreement (agreement). The agreement contained an arbitration clause that subjected any disputes, claims, or controversies to arbitration. Further, the agreement stated that either the franchisee or Ameriprise could compel arbitration of any claims filed in a court of law. A month before signing the agreement, Ameriprise sent Ironson a copy of the agreement, which contained an acknowledgment clause stating that Ameriprise had accorded him ample time and opportunity to consult with advisors of the franchisee's choosing. In 2010 Ameriprise gave Ironson notice of termination for repeated failure to complete an annual written portfolio report for his clients. Ironson responded by filing suit against Ameriprise, who moved to dismiss and compel arbitration.

Ironson's first argument was that the arbitration clause was unenforceable based on economic duress. The agreement contained a choice-of-law provision stating that Minnesota law would govern, but both of the parties briefed the issue under Connecticut law, so the court addressed both jurisdictions. Ironson claimed that he was told that the terms of the agreement were being offered on a "take it, or leave it" basis, and that if he did not sign the agreement "his clients would be transferred and he would be assigned to another Ameriprise office." Further, he claimed that if he did not immediately sign the agreement, he would lose everything that he had worked for over his career and would have no way to support his family. However, Minnesota law does not recognize the defense of economic duress and under Connecticut law, economic necessity cannot be the sole reason for a claim of economic duress. Connecticut law requires that a plaintiff must prove that there was "(1) a wrongful act or threat, (2) that left the victim no reasonable alternative, and (3) to which the victim in fact acceded, and that (4) the resulting transaction was unfair to the victim." The court found that the arbitration clause was valid because: (1) Ironson was an "educated businessperson capable of understanding a contract" and had ample time to consult with an attorney; and (2) Ironson would have been given the opportunity to continue working as an Ameriprise employee if he had rejected the agreement.

Ironson's second argument was that his claims were expressly excluded from the scope of the arbitration provision in the agreement. The court swiftly rejected this argument based on the broad language in the arbitration provision that applied to "any dispute, claim or controversy that may arise between" Ironson and Ameriprise. Accordingly, the court dismissed Ironson's argument and granted Ameriprise's motion to compel arbitration.

In *Champion Auto Sales, LLC v. Polaris Sales Inc.*, No. 12-CV-1842, 2013 U.S. Dist. LEXIS 65219 (E.D. N.Y. Mar. 27, 2013), the court considered Polaris' motion to compel arbitration and/or stay Champion's breach of contract claim. Champion and Polaris entered into a Dealer Agreement that authorized Champion to sell and service Polaris-brand snowmobiles, all-terrain vehicles (ATVs), Ranger vehicles, low-speed vehicles (LSVs), and Victory Motorcycles. The agreement contained an arbitration provision that provided that all disputes, including those arising out of a breach of the agreement, would be solely and finally settled by arbitration. Even though there was only one Dealer Agreement, it was separately and independently enforceable for each of the vehicle brands.

Among several other inquiries related to the arbitrability of Champion's claim, the court considered whether Congress intended for Champion's claim to be nonarbitrable. Champion argued that Congress "explicitly carved out an exception" to the Federal Arbitration Act (FAA), 9 U.S.C. § 1 et seq., in passing the Motor Vehicle Franchise Contract Arbitration Fairness Act (Fairness Act), 15 U.S.C. § 1226. The Fairness Act "precludes the enforcement of pre-dispute arbitration clauses in 'motor vehicle franchise contracts.'" The court found that motor vehicles fall under the ambit of the Fairness Act when they are manufactured for the primary purpose of being used on public roads, streets, and highways. Thus, the court found that Champion's claims arising out of the snowmobile, ATV, Ranger, and LSV franchises were arbitrable, but not Champion's claim arising out of the Victory Motorcycle franchise.

Even though some of Champion's claims were arbitrable, the court denied Polaris' motion to compel, but granted Polaris' motion to stay. This was because the agreement compelled arbitration in Minnesota, which was outside of the court's jurisdiction. The court noted the unclear guidance for how courts should proceed in such situations. Some courts have held that a district court can compel arbitration outside of its own district when the location is specified in the arbitration agreement. Section 4 of the FAA simultaneously provides that a court can only compel arbitration in its own jurisdiction, but that a court should direct the parties to proceed to arbitration in accordance with the arbitration agreement. Finally, some circuit courts have held that a district court cannot compel arbitration in either district and should stay the proceeding pending resolution of the arbitration in the foreign district. Based on other district courts in the Second Circuit, the court followed the third approach and stayed the litigation so that the parties could arbitrate the arbitrable claims in Minnesota.

In *Jalee Consulting Group, Inc. v. XenoOne, Inc.*, No. 11-CV-4720, 2012 U.S. Dist. LEXIS 142056 (S.D. N.Y. Sept. 29, 2012), the court considered the enforceability of an arbitration provision requiring arbitration to take place in Seoul, South Korea. Jalee Consulting Group, Inc. (Jalee), a technology consulting and software development firm, entered into an agreement with XenoOne Korea to develop software for computers and mobile devices. The agreement contained an arbitration clause and forum selection clause that required arbitration in Seoul, South Korea according to the laws of the Republic of Korea. The dispute involved the amounts that XenoOne owed Jalee under the contract. Jalee sued XenoOne in New York and moved for an injunction requiring that any arbitration proceedings occur in New York rather than Seoul.   XenoOne moved to dismiss Jalee's complaint pursuant to Rule 12(b)(6).

Jalee sought to invalidate the forum selection clause based on the four grounds established by the Second Circuit in *Roby v. Corp. of Lloyd's*, 996 F.2d 1353, 1363 (2d Cir. 1993): 1) incorporation of the arbitral forum selection clause was the result of fraud or overreaching; (2) the complaining party will be deprived of his day in court due to the grave inconvenience or unfairness of the selected forum; (3) the fundamental unfairness of the chosen forum may deprive the plaintiff of a remedy; or (4) the clause contravenes a strong public policy.

Jalee attempted to support its fraud claim by alleging that it was forced to accept the forum selection clause because it was an agreement that represented a "significant injection of funding". Second, Jalee alleged that it would not receive a fair hearing in Seoul because board members of XenoOne were also associated with the Samsung Group, which exercises a "disproportionate and unfair influence" in Seoul. The court found that Jalee's allegations did not meet the Rule 9(b) pleading requirements because Jalee failed to identify any allegedly fraudulent statements, any speakers who allegedly made fraudulent statements, or when any allegedly fraudulent statement were made. Similarly, the court dismissed Jalee's claim of overreaching and found that the Agreement was an arm's-length, freely negotiated contract between two sophisticated parties.

The court also rejected Jalee's claims of grave inconvenience and unfairness. Jalee argued that, "not a single act. . . occurred outside of the New York State," and that's where all of the witnesses and evidence were located. However, Second Circuit case law is clear that "mere difficulty and inconvenience is insufficient to establish the unreasonableness of enforcing a forum selection clause." The court found that Jalee was a sophisticated entity that could have "perfectly foresee[n]" all of the alleged inconveniences it would face by arbitrating in Seoul. As such, the court held that Jalee could not "avoid honoring its contractual obligation simply because it would prefer not to."

Jalee did not fare any better with regard to its final two claims, fundamental unfairness and violation of strong public policy. The court held that Jalee failed to demonstrate that it would be deprived of all remedies, which is required for prevailing on fundamental unfairness grounds. Finally, Jalee's claim that the forum selection clause violated "New York's strong public policy to provide a protective local forum for local small businesses" was not supported by case law or the court. The court found that such a policy did not exist. Accordingly, the court held that the forum selection clause was enforceable and granted the XenoOne's motion to dismiss and compel arbitration.

In *Wallace v. Red Bull Distrib. Co.*, No. 12-CV-02431, 2013 U.S. Dist. LEXIS 102989 (E.D. Ohio July 23, 2013), the court granted the employer's motion to dismiss because all of the employee's claims were subject to a binding arbitration agreement. The plaintiff, Jeffrey Wallace, brought discrimination and defamation claims against Red Bull Distribution Company, which is a subsidiary of Red Bull GmbH. The plaintiff signed two arbitration agreements: one with his job application and one after the defendant offered him the job. The agreements differed slightly.

After Wallace brought his claims in federal court, the defendant made a motion to dismiss and compel arbitration, or in the alternative stay the proceedings and compel arbitration. Subject to the grounds at law or in equity that could revoke any contact, the Federal Arbitration Act (FAA) provides that courts shall enforce arbitration agreements. In *AT&T Mobility LLC v. Concepcion*, 131 S. Ct. 1740 (2011), the Supreme Court held that the FAA preempts state-law contract doctrines that only apply to arbitration agreements.

Without discussing *Concepcion*, plaintiff argued that the arbitration agreement was unconscionable. First the court discussed procedural unconscionability. At least before *Conception*, California courts held that adhesion contracts were procedurally unconscionable. The court held that even if *Conception* did not alter California's rules of procedural unconscionability, the fact that the plaintiff signed an adhesion contract creates only "minimal" unconscionably. In light of *Conception*, the court held that the defendant's failure to give the plaintiff a copy of the arbitration rules did not render the contract procedurally unconscionable.

Because the contract was only minimally procedurally unconscionable, only a high degree of substantive unconscionability would render the contract void. In light of *Conception* and other precedent, the court rejected plaintiff's claim that a contractual restriction on discovery and a unilateral modification provision made the agreement substantively unconscionable noting that the Supreme Court did not object to a similar modification provision in the contract at issue in *Conception*. Because the court found that the arbitration agreement was not unconscionable and that all the plaintiff's claims were subject to the arbitration agreement, the court dismissed the case.

B.   BINDING NON-SIGNATORIES

1.   Cases Enforcing Against Non-Signatories

In *Meena Enterprises v. Mail Boxes Etc., Inc.*, No. 12-1360, 2012 U.S. Dist. LEXIS 146406 (D. Md. Oct. 11, 2012), the court considered Defendant Mail Boxes, Etc.'s ("MBE") motion to stay proceedings and compel arbitration. Plaintiffs, Meena Enterprise, Inc. (Meena), and Sabathy Sengottuvelu, alleged that in 1997 College Park Enterprises, Inc. signed two franchise agreements ("Agreements") with MBE to operate two MBE franchises in Maryland. The Agreements contained arbitration clauses that mandated binding arbitration in the "locality in which the franchise is located."

In 2001 United Parcel Service ("UPS") purchased MBE. UPS announced that MBE would continue to offer choices among delivery carriers, but plaintiffs claimed that from the outset, UPS had "intended to convert the MBE stores to UPS stores." Plaintiffs entered into transfer agreements to purchase the two MBE franchises owned by College Park Enterprises, under which the plaintiffs assumed all of the rights and duties under the agreements. Plaintiffs also acknowledged that they had received copies of and were familiar with the terms of the agreements.

Plaintiffs purported to have entered into the Transfer Agreements based on "MBE's public representations that it would continue to operate its franchises as MBE stores." However, despite the representations of UPS and MBE, UPS required most of the MBE stores to change their names to "The UPS Store" and to "aggressively market UPS products and services." Though the stores could still offer competitors' products and services, they could do so only if specifically requested by customers. Further, Federal Express would "not allow its products or services to be offered by UPS Stores."

During the initial term of the agreements, Plaintiffs operated their store in the University of Maryland Student Union as an MBE store because "it was required to offer Federal Express shipping services" under its lease with the school. But when it came time to renew the agreements, MBE allegedly insisted that the University of Maryland location be converted to a UPS store. Plaintiffs explained why this was not possible, and requested that it be allowed to operate the location as an independent store after the Agreement expired. After not hearing from MBE, Plaintiffs sued MBE for breach of contract, fraudulent inducement, and negligent misrepresentation. MBE moved to compel arbitration.

Plaintiffs opposed MBE's motion to compel arbitration on two grounds: (1) that all of the parties to the action were non-signatories to the arbitration clause and never entered into an arbitration agreement; and (2) that the arbitration clause was procedurally and substantively unconscionable. The court held that the Plaintiffs were bound to the agreements by the doctrine of equitable estoppel because the Plaintiffs' claims arose out of, related directly to, and presumed the existence of the agreements. Therefore, the Plaintiffs were estopped from arguing that MBE could not enforce the arbitration clause. The court did not address Plaintiffs' unconscionability concerns because the arbitration clause contained a delegation provision that "unequivocally delegate[d] to the arbitrator all claims regarding the validity of the arbitration clause. . ." Accordingly, the court granted MBE's Motion to Stay Proceedings and Compel Arbitration.

In *Uptown Drug Co. v. CVS Caremark Corp.*, No. 12-CV-06559, 2013 U.S. Dist. LEXIS 102265 (N.D. Cal. July 22, 2013), the court granted in part the defendant's motion to compel arbitration. The court held that three of the plaintiff's claims were subject to arbitration. These claims were that the defendant violated: 1) California's Uniform Trade Secrets Act, 2) the "unlawful prong" of California's Unfair Competition Law (UCL), and 3) the common law prohibition against interfering with the plaintiff's prospective economic advantage. The court held that plaintiff's claims under the "unfair prong" of the UCL were not subject to arbitration.

The defendants were multiple entities including Caremark Rx, which is a "pharmacy benefit manager," affiliated with CVS pharmacies. The plaintiff, Uptown Drug, provided pharmacy services to individuals who participate in certain health plans. Caremark Rx provided prescription benefit plans to many of Uptown's customers. Uptown alleged that the defendants misappropriated information that Uptown provided to Caremark Rx so Caremark could reimburse Uptown for prescriptions it filled for customers in Caremark's benefit plans. Uptown claimed that Caremark used this information to compete directly with Uptown by marketing to its customers. Uptown sued Caremark and Caremark moved to compel arbitration.

A "provider agreement" between the plaintiff and a predecessor of Caremark contained an arbitration clause which required arbitration of all disputes. The plaintiff raised several arguments in opposition to the arbitration agreement, all of which the court rejected.

One of plaintiff's arguments was that some of the defendant entities could not enforce the arbitration agreement because they were not parties to the agreement. The court explained that non-signatories can enforce contracts under the doctrine of equitable estoppel in two situations. First, non-signatories can enforce an arbitration agreement when a signatory's claims rely on the terms of the agreement or its claims are intertwined with the underlying contract. Second, non-signatories can enforce arbitration agreements when a signatory alleges concerted misconduct by the non-signatory and a signatory and that misconduct is intimately connected with the underlying agreement. In this case, the court held that three of the plaintiff's claims—those under 1) California's Uniform Trade Secrets Act, 2) the "unlawful prong" of California's UCL, and 3) the common law of interference with prospective economic advantage—relied on the written agreement because the agreement governed the use, dissemination, and ownership of the data that the defendants allegedly misappropriated. Accordingly, the non-signatory defendants could enforce the arbitration clause regarding those claims. The plaintiff's fourth claim, which asserted violations of the unfair prong of the UCL, alleged that the defendants improperly excluded the plaintiff from certain networks. Because this claim did not rely on the written agreement, the non-signatories could not enforce the arbitration clause regarding this claim. The court stayed proceedings on this claim until after the arbitration of the other claims.

In *World Gym, Inc. v. Pla-Fit Franchise, LLC*, No. 12-11620, 2013 U.S. Dist. LEXIS 101978 (D. Mass. July 19, 2013), the court granted the defendant–franchisor's motion to compel arbitration. The plaintiffs were two fitness center franchisees. The defendants were the franchisor, Pla-Fit Franchise, LLC ("PFF"), and Twin Oaks Software Development ("Twin Oaks"). Twin Oaks is a software company that processed the plaintiffs' client membership fees and maintained a designated bank account.

Plaintiffs alleged that PFF breached oral promises that it would allow plaintiffs' to offer certain personal training services and that it would not allow competing franchisees to encroach upon the plaintiffs' locations. In addition, the franchise agreement granted PFF authority to allow Twin Oaks to remove funds from the plaintiffs' account for overdue royalty fees. However, the plaintiffs alleged that Twin Oaks allowed PFF to exceed its authority under the franchise agreement by allowing PFF to withdraw funds to cover expenses that did not relate to royalty fees and that the plaintiffs had no obligation to pay.

PFF argued that all of the plaintiffs' claims were subject to an arbitration clause in the franchise agreement. Although plaintiffs conceded that most of their claims fell within the arbitration clause, they argued that Twin Oaks could not enforce the arbitration agreement because it was not a party to agreement. The doctrine of equitable estoppel provides that a non-signatory can enforce an arbitration agreement when a signatory makes a claim against it that is intertwined with the agreement. In this case, plaintiffs alleged claims against Twin Oaks relating to the authority granted to Twin Oaks in the agreement containing the arbitration clause. Accordingly, the plaintiffs' claims against Twin Oaks were subject to arbitration.

In *Crazy Willy's Inc., v. Halloween Express, LLC.,* No. 12-CV-01496, 2013 U.S. Dist. LEXIS 36896 (D. Colo. Mar. 18, 2013), the court granted defendants' motion to dismiss for improper venue. Plaintiffs Crazy Willy's, Inc. ("Crazy Willy's") and Jack's Halloween, LLC ("Jack's") were Colorado franchisees of Defendant Halloween Express, LLC ("Halloween Express"). In 2011, Jack's agreed to buy rights to three Colorado stores from Crazy Willy's and Halloween Express approved the sale. Jack's also bought the inventory from Crazy Willy's. Crazy Willy's retained a security interest in the inventory. Jack's suffered losses in the three stores it purchased from Crazy Willy's and did not pay Crazy Willy's the full purchase price for the rights to the stores. Jack's claimed it was going to return the inventory to Crazy Willy's but it instead shipped it to Morris Costumes. Morris Costumes liquidated the inventory and the proceeds were paid to Morris Costumes and Halloween Express to satisfy amounts owed by Jack's. None was paid to Crazy Willy's. Crazy Willy's filed suit in Colorado alleging that Morris Costumes and Halloween Express took possession of property to which it held a security interest and the proceeds should have been paid to Crazy Willy's. Halloween Express moved to dismiss and compel arbitration.

The franchise agreements selected Ohio as the exclusive venue and arbitration as the manner to resolve any dispute. The court found that the arbitration clause covered the parties' dispute because it closely related to the agreements' terms. It also found that under the doctrine of *respondent superior* all defendants, including Morris Costumes (based on its security agreement), fell within the scope of the arbitration agreement. Thus, the court granted the motion to compel arbitration.

In *Tricon Energy Ltd. v. Vinmar International, Ltd..,* 718 F.3d 448 (5th Cir. 2013), the Fifth Circuit reviewed whether Tricon Energy and Vinmar formed a contract to resolve disputes by arbitration while forming a contract for the sale and purchase of mixed xylene. Working through brokers, Vimnar negotiated to purchase of 500 metric tons of mixed xylene from Tricon. Through a series of emails and sales contracts, the parties agreed on a price and other terms. However, neither party signed the signature page on the final sales agreement which contained an arbitration clause. Several months later when the price of mixed xylene fell, Vinmar tried to renege on the sale. Tricon initiated arbitration alleging breach of contract. A three-member arbitration panel concluded that the parties had entered into a binding contract when they negotiated the transaction through their broker and the terms of the contract were those summarized in the broker's last revised memorandum. The panel awarded Tricon over $1.3 million in damages plus pre-and post-award interest. Tricon petitioned to confirm the award and Vinmar moved to vacate the award. The district court confirmed the award. Vinmar appealed from the district court's ruling.

The Fifth Circuit ruled that while blank signature lines on the sales contract may be evidence that the parties did not intend to be bound by a contract unless they signed it, blank signature blocks alone are insufficient to raise a genuine dispute of material fact on appeal. Instead, the court looked to the parties' negotiations, past practices, common industry practice, and the parties binding decision to trade mixed xylene. After reviewing the series of emails and communications between the parties, the court found that Tricon and Vinmar intended to reach a binding agreement to arbitration, even if they did not sign the agreement to do so.

In *Awuah v. Coverall North America, Inc.*, 843 F. Supp. 2d 172 (D. Mass. 2012), the court considered whether certain individuals ("Transferees") were included in a class certification of Coverall franchisees who were non-signatories to an arbitration agreement with Coverall. Coverall franchises janitorial cleaning businesses. Coverall franchises can be obtained two ways: (1) signing a Janitorial Franchise Agreement with Coverall; or (2) signing a Consent to Transfer agreement. The Transferees who sought to be added to the class had acquired their Coverall franchisees by signing a three-party Consent to Transfer agreement in which a current franchisee agrees to sell his franchise, the transferee agrees to purchase the franchise, and Coverall consents to the sale.

The Consent to Transfer agreements did not contain arbitration clauses. However, the Consent to Transfer agreements referenced the underlying Janitorial Franchise Agreement, which did contain an arbitration clause, through a guaranty agreement stating that: "Transferee . . . shall succeed to all of Franchisee's rights and obligations under Franchisee's Janitorial Franchise Agreement." The Plaintiffs argued that the Transferees were not bound by the arbitration clause contained in the Janitorial Franchise Agreement because Coverall did not produce any evidence that the Transferees signed or were shown any arbitration clause. Coverall argued that the language of the Consent to Transfer agreements was sufficient to bind the Transferees.

The First Circuit has recognized that under certain circumstances, non-signatories can be bound by agreements signed by others. One such circumstance is when an arbitration agreement is incorporated by reference. Though the circuit courts are split on what is required for an effective incorporation, the "First Circuit has repeatedly held than an individual may not be bound to an arbitration clause if he does not have notice of it." Accordingly, the ultimate question was whether the Transferees have been given adequate notice of the claims that were subject to arbitration. The court found that there were two groups of Transferees: one that had been provided with the Franchise Offering Circular (Circular) containing a complete exemplar of Coverall's Franchise Agreement, and one that had not. The court found that the group that had been provided with the Circular had been put on notice of the arbitration agreement because the Circular contained the Janitorial Franchise Agreement that included the arbitration provision. Further, the court rejected the Plaintiffs argument that because Coverall did not call the Transferees attention to the contents of the Franchise Agreement, that it did not fulfill its obligation of providing minimal notice. Rather, the court ruled that by giving the Transferees the Circular, which called special attention to the terms of the Janitorial Franchise Agreement, that Coverall had met its burden and that those Transferees were bound by the arbitration clause. The court held that the second group of Transferees who had not received the Circular were not given adequate notice of the arbitration clause, and thus not bound by it because the guaranty agreement did not call attention to the arbitration clause in any way.

SCSJ Enterprises v. Hansen & Hansen Enterprises, 319 Ga. App. 210 (Ga. Ct. App. 2012), involved an appeal of an arbitration award confirmation in favor of Hansen & Hansen Enterprises, Inc., and Juden Enterprises, Inc. (collectively, Hansen) and against SCSJ Enterprises Inc., and Shandton Williams (collectively, SCSJ). The dispute arose after SCSJ purchased two UPS stores from Hansen. SCSJ executed two $250,000 promissory notes, one in favor of Hansen and one in favor of Juden Enterprises, which Williams personally guaranteed. The notes expressly provided that they were made subject to the terms and the conditions of the sales agreement, which included an arbitration provision. Following several appeals and remands concerning the arbitration and award, the trial court confirmed the arbitration award, which SCSJ appealed. SCSJ argued that the trial court erred in two principal ways: (1) confirming the award against Williams, who was not a party to the arbitration agreement, and (2) not recognizing SCSJ's right to terminate arbitration proceedings.

The court relied on the theory of equitable estoppel to dismiss SCSJ's argument that Williams, as a non-signatory, could not be compelled to arbitrate. As a general rule, only signatories to an arbitration agreement may be compelled to arbitrate under Georgia and federal law. However, in certain circumstances, equitable estoppel can be used to compel a non-signatory to arbitrate. The court reasoned that because (1) Williams signed personal guarantees for notes, and (2) Williams' guaranty on the notes was made subject to the terms of the agreement, applying the doctrine of equitable estoppel was appropriate.

As far as SCSJ's right to terminate arbitration proceedings, the court relied on the plain language of the agreement to render its decision. The agreement stated that a party could avoid arbitration and proceed to litigation if no final decision was rendered. The court held that "the mere fact that an award is vacated is not synonymous with the award never having been made," and dismissed SCSJ's argument, ultimately affirming the award.

See also *Cahill v. Alternative Wines, Inc.*, No. 12-CV-110, 2013 U.S. Dist. LEXIS 14588 (N.D. Iowa Feb. 4, 2013) (nonsignatory president of franchisor enforced arbitration clause in franchise agreement compelling arbitration of individual claims against him).

2.   *Cases Refusing To Enforce By Or Against Non-Signatories*

In *Marcus v. Florida Bagels, LLC*, No. 4D12-2971, 2013 Fla. App. LEXIS 6557 (Fla. Dist. Ct. App. April 24, 2013) the court affirmed an order denying the franchisor founder Ira Marcus's motion to stay and compel arbitration. The court found that because Marcus was not a party to the development agreement containing the arbitration clause, he could not rely on equitable estoppel to compel the signatories to arbitrate when they specifically repudiated the arbitration provision.

Plaintiffs sued Brooklyn Water Enterprises, the Brooklyn Water Bagel Franchise, Inc. ("BWB") and Marcus for making fraudulent representations. Marcus was the former officer and founder of BWB. Consistent with the language in the parties' contract, both BWB and plaintiffs chose not to arbitrate, but instead to litigate their claims. Marcus then filed a motion to stay and compel arbitration. Marcus was not a party to the development agreement, but argued that the doctrine of equitable estoppel applied and that the court should force the plaintiffs to arbitrate their claims against BWB and Marcus.

The court declined to apply equitable estoppel because Marcus was not a signatory and he could not enforce the arbitration provision. Applying the equitable estoppel doctrine would frustrate the agreement's performance and would nullify the choice made by the parties to the agreement to litigate.

Therefore, the court denied Marcus's motion and affirmed the parties' choice to proceed in court instead of arbitration.

Wells Enterprises, Inc. v. Olympic Ice Cream, No. 11-4109, 2012 U.S. Dist. LEXIS 151292 (N.D. Iowa 2012), involved alleged trademark violations by Olympic. Wells claimed that the name and trade dress used by Olympic with regards to its "FROZEN FRUIT" bar improperly infringed upon Wells' established rights for its "FROZFRUIT" bar. After Wells filed its claim, Olympic moved to dismiss, which was denied. Olympic then filed a motion to stay and compel arbitration.

The court first addressed whether it had personal jurisdiction over Olympic. The owners of Olympic, Frank and Michael Barone, had previously conducted businesses with Wells through another company they owned, Marina. Marina distributed Wells' products from 2005-2010 under agreements that established Wells' ownership of its trademarks. Wells argued that after the distributor agreement expired with Marina, the Barones, "'who through their ownership interest in [Marina] knew that [Marina] had acknowledged Wells' ownership in and to its trademarks and explicitly agreed not to adopt or use any confusingly similar marks or logos,' used Olympic 'to offer an infringing product on the market.'" Wells argued that Olympic "should not be able to hide behind corporate structure to avoid personal jurisdiction," and the court agreed.

The distributor agreements between Wells and Marina contained broad arbitration provisions that specifically included arbitrating the validity or enforceability of the arbitration provision itself. However, Olympic was never a party to the distributor agreements with Wells. Nevertheless, Olympic argued that Wells was required to arbitrate, based on Wells' prior agreements with Marina.

The court disagreed and denied Olympic's motion to compel arbitration. The court mainly relied on the Eighth Circuit's decision in *CD Partners, LLC v. Grizzle*, 424 F.3d 795 (8th Cir. 2005), where the court recognized two situations in which a non-signatory could compel a signatory to arbitrate under equitable estoppel. The first is when the relationship between the signatory and non-signatory defendants is sufficiently close that allowing the non-signatory to invoke arbitration prevents the arbitration agreement between the signatories from being avoided. The second is when the signatory must rely on the terms of the written agreement in asserting its claims against the non-signatory. In these situations, when a signatory's claims against a non-signatory "arise out of and relate directly to the written agreement, [] arbitration is appropriate."

The court found that neither situation was present, and that Olympic was factually distinguishable from *CD Partners*. In *CD Partners*, the individual defendants were officers of a bankrupt signatory and were sued as substitute defendants based on their direct involvement with the franchise agreements at issue. The court noted that had "Wells sought to hold Olympic liable for events that occurred during the Wells-Marina relationship on a theory that Olympic caused or is responsible for acts or omissions by Marina while Marina was a Wells distributor, the case would be somewhat analogous to *CD Partners*." However, Wells did not sue Olympic as a substitute defendant based on conduct that occurred while Wells and Marina had a contractual relationship. Rather, Wells' claims against Olympic arose after the contractual relationship between Wells and Marina was expired, and therefore compelling arbitration was not appropriate.

In *Everett v. Paul Davis Restoration, Inc.*, No. 10-CV-634, 2012 U.S. Dist. LEXIS 133682 (E.D. Wis. Sept. 18, 2012), the court considered whether Plaintiff could be bound as a non-signatory to a franchise agreement signed by her husband. Plaintiff's husband signed a Franchise Agreement (the "Agreement") with Paul Davis Restoration, Inc. ("PDRI") on behalf of EA Green Bay, LLC ("EAGB") as the Franchisee, and individually, as EAGB's 100% "Principal Owner." However, Mrs. Everett was a 50% co-owner of EAGB and held herself out as an owner of the Franchise. The Agreement required that all of the ownership interest of the Franchisee be held solely by the Principal Owner and that any transfer of shares be approved by PDRI. The Agreement also contained non-compete and arbitration provisions.

After the termination of the PDRI Agreement, Mr. Everett sold his ownership interest in the business to Mrs. Everett so that she could run it as an independent business. The Everetts announced via the business's website that the business's name would be changed to "Building Werks," after which PDRI sent the Everetts a cease and desist letter. Though the Everetts created a new LLC for Building Werks, the business continued to operate with the same employees and at the same location using EAGB's bank accounts and Federal Employer Identification Number.

PDRI initiated arbitration against the Everetts and EAGB, alleging that the Everetts and EAGB had breached the Agreement by "engaging in a sham transaction in an attempt to avoid," among other things, the non-compete provision. PDRI prevailed at arbitration and sought to have the award confirmed. PDRI argued that even though Mrs. Everett never signed the Agreement, she was bound to it, specifically the arbitration and non-compete provisions, under the doctrine of equitable estoppel. Mrs. Everett moved to vacate the award arguing that she was not bound by the Agreement because she never signed it and because PDRI had failed to establish that she directly benefitted from the Agreement.

In what seems like a hair-splitting decision, the court found that to bind Mrs. Everett to the Agreement as a non-signatory, PDRI needed to prove that she directly benefitted from the contract, not from the business that the contract made profitable. The court further explained that direct benefit on behalf of the non-signatory needed to be proven regardless of how closely the non-signatory was affiliated with another signing party. Thus, even though Mrs. Everett benefitted from the contractual relationship her husband and EAGB had with PDRI, the benefit was indirect because it derived from her ownership interest in EAGB and her marriage, not directly from the Agreement. As such, the court held that Mrs. Everett was not bound to the Agreement and vacated the award.

In *Hospira, Inc. v. Therabel Pharma N.V.*, No. 12-CV-8544, 2013 U.S. Dist. LEXIS 102196 (N.D. Ill. July 19, 2013) the court reviewed whether the doctrine of assumption could bind a party to an arbitration agreement that it did not sign. The court relied on state-law principles governing basic contract formation. By general rule, an arbitration agreement does not bind a party that does not sign it, and the agreement cannot compel a non-signatory to arbitrate.

Here, Therabel initiated a $19 million arbitration in Geneva Switzerland against Hospira over alleged fraud involving one of Hospira's wholly-owned subsidiaries, Javelin. However, Hospira never signed an arbitration agreement with Therabel. Hospira filed a declaratory judgment action seeking a declaration that it had no agreement to arbitrate with Therabel and an injunction preventing Therabel from proceeding with the arbitration.

Therabel argued that Hospira assumed Javelin's agreement to arbitrate when it took over Javelin's operations and acted as the licensor under the License Agreement with Therabel. The court ruled that a party must specifically manifest through subsequent action that it assumes an arbitration obligation. Further, although Javelin was a subsidiary of Hospira, Javelin operated as an independent legal identity, strengthening Hospira's argument that it did not assume Javelin's arbitration agreement.

The court also reviewed whether the doctrine of equitable estoppel could compel Hospira to arbitrate even if it did not sign the arbitration agreement. Therabel argued that Hospira was estopped from refusing to arbitrate because Hospira accepted the benefits under the license agreement, including Therabel's help to get approval from the Federal Drug Administration. Hospira denied it was estopped from refusing to arbitrate, arguing that any benefit provided by Therabel flowed to Javelin, its wholly-owned subsidiary. The court agreed with Hospira. The court found that Therabel failed to present evidence that the benefit to Hospira was direct, a key element to establishing equitable estoppel. The court denied the motion to compel arbitration against Hospira.

C.   WAIVER

In *Beaver v. Inkmart, LLC*, No. 12-66028 U.S. Dist. LEXIS 125050, 2012 (S.D. Fla. Sept. 4, 2012), the court held that the plaintiff–franchisee waived their right to stay proceedings and compel arbitration. Before the present dispute, the court dismissed the plaintiffs' original complaint without prejudice. After receiving a time extension, the plaintiffs filed an amended complaint. The defendant franchisor then filed motions to dismiss and for summary judgment. Thereafter, the plaintiffs filed a motion to stay proceedings and compel arbitration.

The court noted that while the Federal Arbitration Act broadly supports the enforcement of arbitration agreements, a party can unintentionally waive its right to compel arbitration. Courts use a two-part test to determine whether a party waived its right to arbitrate. The court considers 1) whether, under the totality of circumstances, the party acted inconsistently with the right to arbitration, and 2) whether the party's conduct prejudiced the other party.

In this case, the court held that given the totality of circumstances, the plaintiffs "substantially invoked the litigation machinery" inconsistent with the right to arbitrate by filing several motions and participating in discovery, deposing the franchisor's witness and serving document requests, interrogatories and requests for admission. The plaintiffs argued that they could not have sought arbitration until the court considered their request for equitable relief, which required discovery. The court rejected this argument noting that nothing in the franchise agreement prevented the arbitrator from granting equitable relief.

Next, the court held that the franchisor Inkmart would suffer prejudice if the court granted the motion to compel arbitration. While participating in discovery before a claim is arbitrable does not cause sufficient prejudice to constitute waiver, in this case the plaintiff could have sought arbitration from the start. Instead, it filed a complaint, an amended complaint, numerous motions and participated in discovery. The length of delay in demanding arbitration and expense incurred by Inkmart from participating in the litigation process could have been avoided had the plaintiff demanded arbitration early in the process. The court found that this prejudiced Inkmart. Accordingly, the court denied plaintiff's motion to compel arbitration.

D.   CHALLENGES TO ARBITRATION AWARDS

1.   Case Affirming Awards

In *Oxford Health Plans, LLC v. Sutter*, 133 S. Ct. 2064 (2013) the United States Supreme Court affirmed the lower courts' finding that an arbitrator did not exceed his powers under § 10(a)(4) of the Federal Arbitration Act when he ruled that an agreement authorized class action arbitration.

Sutter, a pediatrician, entered into a contract with Oxford Health Plan ("Oxford"), a health insurance company. Sutter brought a claim against Oxford on behalf of himself and a proposed class of other New Jersey doctors for failure to "make full and prompt payment to the doctors, in violation of their agreements." Oxford moved to compel arbitration under the agreement's arbitration clause, which was silent on the issue of class arbitration. The parties agreed that the arbitrator should decide whether their contract allowed for class action arbitration. The arbitrator reasoned that the clause sent to arbitration the same universal class of disputes that it barred the parties from bringing as civil actions in court. In other words, the intent of the clause was to vest in the arbitration process everything that was prohibited from the court process. The arbitrator found that a class action is plainly one of the possible forms of civil action that could be brought in a court absent an agreement to the contrary. Accordingly, the arbitrator concluded that "on its face, the arbitration clause ... expresses the parties intent that class arbitration can be maintained."

Oxford moved to vacate the arbitrators decision under § 10(a)(4) of the Federal Arbitration Act, claiming that the arbitrator's decision "exceeded [his] powers" under the Act. The district court denied the motion and the Third Circuit Court of Appeals affirmed. Oxford then asked the arbitrator to reconsider his decision in light of the Supreme Court's decision in *Stolt-Nielsen S.A. v. AnimalFeeds Int'l Corp.*, 559 US 662 (2010). In *Stolt-Nielsen,* the Court held "that 'a party may not be compelled under the FAA to submit to class arbitration unless there is a contractual basis for concluding that the party *agreed* to do so.'" (citing *Stolt-Nielsen*, 559 U.S. at 684) (emphasis in original). The arbitrator, however, found that *Stolt-Nielson* had no effect in the case before him. The parties in *Stolt-Nielson* stipulated that they had never reached an agreement on class arbitration. However, the parties in this case disputed the clause, which then required that the arbitrator construe the arbitration clause to glean the parties intent. Having performed that task, the arbitrator found that the arbitration clause unambiguously evinced an intent to allow class arbitration. Oxford again renewed its motion to vacate, the district court denied the motion, and the Third Circuit affirmed again.

The United States Supreme Court granted *certiorari* to resolve a circuit split over the application of § 10(a)(4). In its reasoning the Court emphasized the high burden required to vacate an arbitrator's order under § 10(a)(4) of the Act because '[i]t is not enough. . . to show that the [arbitrator] committed an error—or even a serious error.' *Id.* (citing *Stolt-Nielsen*, 559 U.S. at 671). A party must show not that the arbitrator interpreted the contract incorrectly or poorly but that he did not interpret it at all. Oxford had to show that the arbitrator lacked any contractual basis for his opinion. After examining the arbitrator's decision, the Court found that he had not abandoned his interpretative role, but twice did what the parties asked: he considered their contract and decided whether it reflected an agreement to permit class proceedings. That act itself sufficed to show that the arbitrator did not exceed his powers under § 10(a)(4). Thus, it rejected Oxford's arguments and affirmed the Court of Appeals.

In an interesting concurrence written by Justice Alito, he inferred that the outcome would have been different had the parties not consented to the arbitrator's authority to decide in the first instance whether the contract authorized class arbitration:

> "But unlike petitioner, absent members of the plaintiff class never conceded that the contract authorizes the arbitrator to decide whether to conduct class arbitration. It doesn't. If we were reviewing the arbitrator's interpretation of the contract *de novo*, we would have little trouble concluding that he improperly inferred "[a]n implicit agreement to authorize class action arbitration... from the fact of the parties agreement to arbitrate." *Stolt-Nielsen S. A.* v. *AnimalFeeds Int'l Corp.,* 559 U. S. 662, 685 (2010).

Indeed, the majority acknowledged in a footnote that they would have been in a position to review the arbitrator's determination *de novo* had Oxford argued below that the availability of class arbitration was a so-called gateway "question of arbitrability"-presumptively for the courts to decide. "*Stolt-Nielson* made clear that this court has not yet decided whether the availability of class arbitration is a question of arbitrability." Id. at n.2 citing *Green Tree Financial Corp. v Bazzle*, 539 U.S. 444, 452 (2003). The lesson to be learned from Oxford is to challenge the arbitrator's authority to determine whether the arbitration clause allows for class arbitration.

In *Choice Hotels Int'l, Inc. v. Special Spaces, Inc.*, No. 12-733, 2012 U.S. Dist. LEXIS 153005 (D. Md. Oct. 23, 2012), Choice Hotels successfully confirmed an arbitration award against a franchisee that had been terminated for failure to construct a hotel. The franchise agreement contained a liquidated damages clause that applied if the agreement was terminated for cause. The terminated franchisee failed to participate in the underlying arbitration, but sought to vacate the award in the confirmation proceeding because Choice had not acted in good faith in terminating the agreement. The former franchisee argued that the arbitration award lacked a "reasonable basis."

In granting Choice's motion for summary judgment confirming the award, the court noted that its power to vacate under the FAA is limited to specific statutory reasons, such as when the award was procured by corruption, fraud, or undue means, or where the award was the product of some misconduct or partiality, or if the arbitrator exceeded the scope of his or her powers. Since the former franchisee failed to establish any of these limited grounds, the court granted Choice's motion for summary judgment and confirmed the arbitration award.

In *Budget Blinds Inc. v. LeClair,* No. 12-1101, 2013 U.S. Dist. LEXIS 7463 (C.D. Cal. Jan. 16, 2013), the court upheld an arbitrator's finding that the franchisor Budget Blinds constructively terminated a franchise agreement in violation of the Wisconsin Fair Dealership Law (WFDL). The dispute arose when a franchisee complained to Budget Blinds that a neighboring franchisee (LeClair) was making sales in its territory. Budget Blinds confirmed the extraterritorial activity and then initiated arbitration against LeClair, allegedly without contacting LeClair to discuss the dispute or providing any notice or opportunity to cure. Budget Blinds also cut off LeClair's access to the Budget Blinds' record-keeping and management web portal and its external website.

The arbitrator found that by cutting off LeClair's access to the portal and the external website, initiating arbitration, and referring internet and telephone leads to other franchisees, Budge Blinds constructively terminated LeClair's franchise agreement. In doing so, Budget Blinds violated the WFDL by failing to provide notice and the required 60-day cure period. Budget Blinds appealed the arbitrator's decision to the district court.

Budget Blinds argued that its initiation of arbitration to seek a declaration that it was permitted to terminate the franchise agreement meant that it had not terminated the franchise agreement, constructively or otherwise. The court disagreed, finding that by taking the actions it did, Budget Blinds constructively terminated the franchise agreement in violation of the WFDL without formally terminating it. The court affirmed the arbitration award.

In *Real Living Real Estate, LLC v. Chicago Agent Partners, LLC,* No. 12-CV-9262, 2013 U.S. Dist. LEXIS 55467 (N.D. Ill. Apr. 18, 2013), the franchisor Real Living filed a motion to confirm an arbitration award against Chicago Agent Partners and seven other parties (collectively, herein, the "Respondents"). The Respondents each renewed a Franchise Agreement with Real Living which included a promissory note. However, shortly after executing the Agreements, the Respondents informed Real Living that they were going to cease doing business as Real Living and refuse to pay their respective promissory notes.

Real Living initiated arbitration and claimed that the Respondents breached their obligations by terminating the franchises and failing to pay the promissory notes. The arbitrator found in favor of Real Living. The Respondents argued that the award should be vacated because it was procured through fraudulent and undue means. Specifically, the Respondents claimed that Real Living had failed to disclose civil actions involving the franchise system in accordance with the Federal Trade Commission's disclosure requirement. *See* 16 C.F.R. § 436. The Respondents' presented evidence of four undisclosed civil actions against Real Living prior to the execution of the Agreements. Due to Real Living's omission, the Respondents argued that they were prevented from making a fully informed decision when entering into the Agreements.

Per the Seventh Circuit, for a movant to vacate an arbitration award due to fraud or undue means, the movant must establish that the fraud was: (1) not discoverable upon the exercise of due diligence prior to the arbitration; (2) materially related to an issue in the arbitration; and (3) established by clear and convincing evidence.

The Respondents admitted that their attorney knew of the four undisclosed lawsuits prior to the arbitration. Indeed, Respondents raised the issue at the arbitration and presented evidence regarding how the omission affected their decision not to renew the franchise agreements. As a result, they could not prove the first element to establish fraud or undue means. Accordingly, the court affirmed the arbitration award in favor of Real Living.

In *Saleemi v. Doctor's Associates, Inc.*, 292 P.3d 108, 176 Wash.2d 368 (2013), the court considered whether the franchisor waived its right to challenge an interlocutory order compelling arbitration by not immediately seeking discretionary review. Doctor's Associates, Inc. (DAI), was the Subway franchisor for Saleemi and Saryar (Respondents), who collectively owned three Subway franchises in Washington state. The Franchise Agreement included a forum selection clause, but not a choice of law clause.

The Agreement limited damages to compensatory damages not exceeding $100,000 or the amount of royalties and fees paid to DAI during the preceding three years and contained an in-term noncompete provision preventing the Respondents from owning, operating, or assisting another to own or operate a business which was identical with or similar to the Subway restaurant.

After receiving a tip that the Respondents had opened a new restaurant named Puccini's, DAI researched the tip and found what it believed was evidence that the one of the Respondents was working there. DAI did not follow its normal procedures for following up on the matter. Typically with violations of non-compete provisions, DAI would refer the matter to the internal legal team, who would in turn send a default letter describing the nature of the violation and providing an opportunity to cure. However, in this instance, DAI sent a termination letter that did not describe the violation or offer an opportunity to cure. The Respondents' attorney pressed DAI's attorney and DAI sent a follow up letter that described the violation and allowed 60 days to cure. The Respondents attempted to cure within the 60 day window, but stopped the process when DAI filed a demand for arbitration before the 60 day window had expired.

The Respondents filed suit alleging that DAI's conduct violated the franchise agreements, Washington's Franchise Investment Protection Act and Washington's Consumer Protection Act. The trial court found the Connecticut forum selection clause unconscionable and unenforceable and ordered the disputes to be arbitrated in Washington under Washington law, with no limitation on remedies. DAI did not seek discretionary review of the trial court's order and proceeded to arbitration where the arbitrator denied DAI's claims and ruled for the Respondents. DAI moved to vacate the arbitration award, primarily arguing that the order compelling arbitration directed the arbitrator to disregard the damage limitation provisions of the franchise agreement. When asked by the trial court why DAI had not sought discretionary review, counsel responded that the cost and expense of taking an appeal would not be a wise allocation and suggested that subsequent case law provided additional support for upholding the Connecticut forum selection clause. The trial court noted that in order to vacate the arbitration award, there needed to be clear error on the face of the award. Having found none, the trial court concluded that "it is clear that the defense is unhappy with the result, so you're trying to get a second bite at the apple and it's not going to happen on my watch." DAI appealed.

On appeal, the Supreme Court of Washington held that a party who fails to seek discretionary review of an order compelling arbitration must show prejudice based on the order before an appellate court will review the merits of the challenge. The court reasoned that such an approach promotes the purposes of arbitration, speed and convenience, while still allowing aggrieved parties to obtain relief. Further, the court explained that in civil cases, errors that are not prejudicial are rarely grounds for relief, and that this principle has been applied to arbitration by other courts.

The court found that, notwithstanding the trial judge's order striking the damage limitations provision as unenforceable, the face of the arbitration award showed that the arbitrator was keenly aware of the damage limitation provisions and the award was "carefully limited" to comply with the provisions in the franchise agreement. With respect to the choice of venue provision, the court observed that the arbitration was conducted in Washington by the same arbitration group and under the same rules as required by the franchise agreements. For these reasons, the court held that DAI failed to show any prejudice. Accordingly, the court affirmed the appellate court's decision and denied DAI's motion to vacate the arbitration award.

2. Cases Vacating Awards

In a rare decision to vacate an arbitration award, in *Thomas Kinkade Company fka Media Arts Group, Inc. v. White*, 711 F.3d 719 (6th Cir. 2013) the Court of Appeals affirmed a district court's decision to vacate an arbitration award because of the arbitrator's lack of impartiality. Thomas Kinkade Company ("Kinkade") entered into several contracts with Nancy and David White (the "Whites") to sell Kinkade's artwork. The contracts included a clause requiring that the parties arbitrate disputes under the Rules of the American Arbitration Association ("AAA"). Kinkade initiated arbitration against the Whites for not paying for artwork and the Whites counterclaimed for fraudulent inducement. Each party nominated an arbitrator and the two nominated arbitrators selected a "neutral" third arbitrator.

Nearly five years after the arbitration was commenced and after 50 days of hearings, the supposedly "neutral" arbitrator announced to Kinkade that the Whites and their hand-picked arbitrator had each hired the neutral arbitrator's firm for engagements that were likely to be "substantial." Kinkade's objections fell on deaf ears. Thereafter, a series of irregularities occurred at the arbitration, all in the Whites' favor. Eventually the neutral arbitrator entered a $1.4 million award in the Whites' favor. Kinkade moved to vacate the award on the grounds of "evident partiality." The district court granted Kinkade's motion and vacated the arbitration award. The Whites appealed and the Sixth Circuit affirmed.

The Sixth Circuit found that the arbitration had been "a model of how not to conduct one." The first attorney for the Whites sent a surreptitious live feed of the hearing to a nearby hotel where a disgruntled former Kinkade employee sent back cross-examination questions via instant message. The White's second attorney departed the case after being convicted of tax fraud. The Whites then failed to respond to multiple discovery requests and denied the existence of critical financial documents. The Whites also began bringing new business to the neutral arbitrator's law firm. The arbitrator assured the parties that he would not participate in this business, but did not separate himself from the financial benefits of it. After this new business came to his firm, there were additional irregularities in the arbitration that all favored the Whites. For instance, the neutral arbitrator gave the Whites two additional chances, post-hearing, to produce 8,800 pages of financial documents supporting their damage claims – even though they denied the documents existed in discovery and failed to introduce them at the arbitration hearing. In addition, the neutral arbitrator denied Kinkade a virtually uncontested, straightforward breach of contract claim against the Whites and did not respond to any of Kinkade's written objections. Kinkade filed a motion to the AAA and to the arbitrators directly seeking disqualification of the neutral arbitrator. Both demands were denied. After all of this, the neutral arbitrator awarded damages to the Whites exceeding $1.4 million.

The Federal Arbitration Act authorizes vacation of awards when there is "evident partiality" or corruption by the arbitrators. To demonstrate partiality the challenging party must establish specific facts that indicate that the arbitrator was partial and had an improper motive. In this case, the Sixth Circuit found that Kinkade established a "convergence of undisputed facts that, considered together, show a motive for (the neutral arbitrator) to favor the Whites and multiple, concrete actions in which he appeared to actually favor them." This included both the Whites and their attorney hiring the neutral arbitrator's law firm for engagements that by all appearances seemed substantial and the neutral's action in allowing the Whites to rely upon 8,800 pages of documents they deliberately and wrongfully withheld for more than four years. The neutral arbitrator also awarded the Whites nearly $500,000 in attorney's fees after the plain terms of interim award indicated that the Whites' request for fees had been denied. The court found that these actions, when combined with the dealings between the Whites and the neutral arbitrator's firm, were more than sufficient to show evident partiality. The Sixth Circuit affirmed the district court's order vacating the arbitration award.

V.   Other Procedural Issues

A.   WAIVER OF JURY TRIALS

In *Novus Franchising, Inc. v. Superior Entrance Systems, Inc.*, No. 12-CV-204, 2012 U.S.Dist. LEXIS 115640 (W.D. Wis. Aug.16, 2012) a Wisconsin-based franchisee challenged a jury waiver provision in a franchise agreement that contained a Minnesota choice of law provision.   Significantly, the Minnesota Franchise Act prohibits jury waiver clauses in franchise agreements.   However, the Minnesota choice of law provision in the franchise agreement also stated that if the franchisee was not located in Minnesota, the Minnesota Franchise Act would not apply. This is consistent with established Minnesota case law finding that the Minnesota Franchise Act does not apply to nonresidents or those who operate in a franchise territory located entirely outside Minnesota. The court determined that the Wisconsin Fair Dealership law applied to the franchisee defendants. Because the Wisconsin Fair Dealership law does not contain a prohibition against jury waivers, the court found that all parties waived their right to a jury trial, including a nonsignatory corporation that operated as the nominal franchisee.

See also, *Dunkin' Donuts Franchising, LLC v. SAI Food & Hospitality, LLC*, No. 11-CV-01484, 2013 U.S. Dist. LEXIS 35942 (E.D. Mo. Mar. 15, 2013) (court enforced a jury waiver provision in franchise agreement where language of the waiver was unambiguous, clearly readable, there was no allegation of exploitation and the franchisee was represented by counsel in its contractual dealings with franchisor).

B.   COLLATERAL ESTOPPEL AND RES JUDICATA

In *Fullington v. Equilon Enterprises, LLC*, 2012 Cal. App. LEXIS 1116 (Cal. Ct. App. Oct. 25, 2012) the court reversed the trial court's grant of summary adjudication in favor of a franchisor on a former franchisee's claims of fraud and violation of Bus. & Prof. Code § 21148.

Fullington and other lessee-dealers ("Fullington") filed action against Equilon and four individuals ("Equilon") alleging violation of Business and Professional Code § 21148 for intentional interference with Fullington's attempts to sell his Shell gas station franchise. Fullington also alleged fraud, claiming an Equilon sales consultant misrepresented the existence of the Interim Rent Challenge ("IRC"), by which a lessee-dealer could challenge the amount of rent using an appraisal of the dealer's land, equipment, and improvements. Equilon moved for summary adjudication of the § 21148 claim, asserting the claim was barred by res judicata because it arose from the same "transaction" as previously litigated claims. In *HRN, Inc. v. Shell Oil Co.* (Harris County Tex., 234th Jud. Dist. No. 1999-28202) ("*HRN*"), Fullington and other independent Shell lessee-dealers alleged that the manner in which Shell set wholesale gasoline prices and gas station rent resulted in a breach of contract and constituted a variety of torts. The court granted summary judgment for the defendants and the Texas Supreme Court affirmed the grant of summary judgment. Based on the HRN case, the court granted summary adjudication for Equilon, finding that Fullington's § 21148 claim was related in time, space, origin, and motivation to the claims and allegations in *HRN*, and therefore arose from the same transaction.

Fullington appealed and the California Court of Appeals reversed the summary adjudication dismissing the § 21148 and fraud claims, finding that Fullington's prior and current claims did not arise from the same facts. The court found that: (1) there was no factual overlap between the relevant causes of action in the two actions; (2) the relevant events to the two suits are separated in time; and; (3) the claims alleged in *HRN* and the present claims would not form a convenient trial unit because the *HRN* case involved hundreds of plaintiffs and corporate conduct, where the § 21148 claim only involved Fullington as plaintiff. Equilon also failed to establish that the § 21148 claim was ripe when the Texas court entered judgment in *HRN*. Under § 21140.4 of the Bus. & Prof. Code , a § 21148 violation is not actionable unless a franchisee "is *injured* in his business or property by reason of a violation of this chapter." Equilon failed to submit any evidence establishing Fullington's date of injury.

The court also found that Fullington's prior and current claims were not barred by res judicata merely because they were based on actions taken "for the same reason." The court reversed the summary adjudication in favor of Equilon.

C.   STATUTE OF LIMITATIONS

1.   Contractual Limitations Provisions

In *Creative Playthings Franchising, Corp. v. Reiser*, 978 N.E.2d 765 (Mass. 2012), the Supreme Judicial Court of Massachusetts received a certified question from the United States District Court for the District of Massachusetts. At issue was whether a franchise agreement governed by Massachusetts law could include a limitations period that shortened the time within which claims must be brought.

The Massachusetts general laws set forth a six-year limitations period for contract claims. In this case, the parties agreed to a limitations period shorter than six years. The court noted that Federal law allows parties to contractually agree to a shorter term, and it saw no reason why a blanket limitation should prohibit parties from agreeing to shorten the statutorily prescribed period of limitations. Placing emphasis on how parties arrive at such an agreement, the court explained that if a claim arises under the contract, the agreed-upon limitations period was subject to negotiation, was not otherwise limited by controlling statute, was reasonable, was not a statute of repose, and was not contrary to public policy, the shortened limitations period could be enforceable. Accordingly, the court answered the certified question in the affirmative.

The certified question was narrowly defined and did not address the specific language in the parties' franchise agreement. Therefore, the court did not reach the question of whether the particular limitations provision in the Creative Playthings franchise agreement was enforceable.

In *Progressive Foods, LLC v. Dunkin' Donuts, Inc.*, Nos. 11-3296, 11-3335, 2012 U.S. App. LEXIS 16815 (6th Cir. Aug. 9, 2012), Progressive Foods, LLC ("Progressive Foods") brought suit against defendant Dunkin' Donuts, Inc. ("Dunkin' Donuts") and its affiliates over the development of Dunkin' Donuts' franchises in the Cleveland, Ohio area. Dunkin' Donuts filed a counterclaim and motion for summary judgment, which the district court denied. Following a bench trial, the district court awarded Progressive Foods $336,000 in damages, concluded that Dunkin' Donuts was entitled to $100,000 in franchise fees, and denied Dunkin' Donuts' request for declaratory and injunctive relief, as well as interest, costs, and attorneys' fees. The parties cross-appealed that judgment.

Dunkin' Donuts argued that Progressive Foods' award should be reversed because the claims were barred by the contractual limitations period in the franchise agreements. The agreement specified that claims must be brought within two years after discovery of the facts giving rise to the claim. Progressive Foods filed suit on October 3, 2007. In its initial complaint, Progressive Foods alleged that it had timely notified Dunkin' Donuts on August 3, 2005, which was more than two years prior to the date it brought suit. Thus, the statement was a binding admission as to when it discovered the basis for its claims against Dunkin' Donuts. Alternatively, Progressive Foods argued that even if its admission was binding, it was not dispositive because the district court granted judgment jointly and severally against all defendants and the limitations period did not apply to a Dunkin'

Donuts affiliate, Third Dunkin' and its successors, who did not sign the franchise agreements.

Not persuaded by Progressive Foods' argument, the court found that the limitations language in the franchise agreements applied to all of Dunkin's successors and "controlled affiliated entities", including Third Dunkin'. The court found that the district court's grant of joint and several liability to Progressive Foods on its claims against Dunkin' Donuts was irrelevant. Accordingly, the court reversed the award of damages to Progressive Foods, finding that Progressive Foods' claims were untimely, and Dunkin' Donuts was entitled to judgment as a matter of law on its counterclaim.

In *Massey, Inc. v. Moe's Southwestern Grill, LLC*, No. 07-CV-741, 2012 U.S. Dist. LEXIS 109081 (N.D. Ga. Aug. 3, 2012), franchisees David Titshaw, Taylor Investment Partners II, LLC, Rounding third, LLC, and 3M Restaurants, LLC (collectively "franchisees") brought a motion to reconsider after the court granted defendant franchisor Moe's Southwest Grill, LLC's motion for summary judgment dismissing the franchisee's claims based on a one year contractual limitations term..

Franchisees brought suit against the franchisor, claiming it had failed to properly disclose that its owner held an interest in a designated supplier. Although the owner held an interest in the supplier as early as 2001, the franchisor failed to disclose that interest until its 2004 Uniform Franchise Offering Circular ("UFOC"). The franchisor argued that its franchisees received notice of the ownership interest through the franchisor's UFOC more than one year before they brought legal action. The franchisees argued that because they were under no legal duty to read the UFOC provided to them, they should not be assumed to have read the information in the UFOC.

The district court granted Moe's motion after finding that the franchisees' claims were barred by the one-year contractual-limitations term in the franchise agreements. Rejecting the franchisees' argument, the court found that a reasonably prudent franchisee would have read the UFOC, even if it was under no legal duty to read the UFOC. Based on this finding, the court charged the franchisees with notice of UFOC's terms more than one year prior to the time initiated litigation. Because the summary motion was properly granted, the court denied the franchisees' motion for reconsideration.

In *A Love of Food I, LLC v. Maoz Vegetarian USA, Inc.*, No. 12-CV-1117, 2013 U.S. Dist. LEXIS 102184 (D. D.C. July 22, 2013) the court denied Defendant Maoz Vegetarian USA's ("Maoz") motion for leave to amend its answer to include an affirmative defense based on a one-year statute of limitations provision in the parties' franchise agreement.

Maoz filed a motion to amend its answer based on a provision in its 2007 franchise agreement. The motion was filed after the close of discovery, almost two years after the court's deadline for filing an amended answer, after motions to dismiss and motions for summary judgment were adjudicated in part, after a judge in the District of Maryland transferred the case to the District of Columbia, and after this Court inquired whether the parties sought to renew their previously-filed, still-pending motions for summary judgment.

The Court found that the "good cause" standard of Fed. R. Civ. P. 16 applied, rather than the looser standard under Fed. R. Civ. P. 15, as Maoz asserted. District court case law makes clear that once the court enters a scheduling order, that schedule can only be modified with the court's consent and with good cause shown. Although motions to amend pleadings within the time set by the scheduling order are subject to review under the Rule 15 standard, motions to amend filed *after* a scheduling order deadline are subject to the more stringent "good cause" standard of Rule 16. The primary factor in determining whether the "good cause" standard has been met is the diligence of the moving party. This inquiry is focused on the reasons the moving party gives for the delay. Here, the sole explanation provided by Maoz was oversight. The court noted that the defendant mentioned the affirmative defense in a summary judgment brief a year earlier, but did not seek to amend its answer at that time. In responding to defendant's invocation of the statute of limitations argument at the summary judgment stage, plaintiff clearly stated that Fed. R. Civ. P. 8(c)(1) required that affirmative defenses be raised in the responsive pleadings. Yet even after being put on notice, defendant let another full year pass before moving to amend the answer. The Court held that Maoz's contention that it should be given leave to amend pleadings to include a forgotten affirmative defense did not constitute good cause and denied the motion.

2.   *Statutory Limitations Provisions*

In *Stocco v. Gemological Institute of America, Inc.*, No. 12-CV-1291, 2013 U.S. Dist. LEXIS 1603 (S.D. Cal. Jan. 3, 2013), franchisees Fredrick and Kathleen Stocco filed suit against franchisor Gemological Institute of America, Inc., claiming that the franchisor violated California's franchise disclosure laws by not providing the franchisees with a franchise offering circular or registering the franchise in violation of the California Corporations Code. The franchisees alleged that the breach caused them to suffer damages and was grounds for the rescission of their franchise agreement. The franchisor contended that the claim should be dismissed because the California Corporations Code did not apply and the claim was time-barred under Cal. Corp. Code §31303, which gave the franchisees four years from the date of act or transgression constituting the violation in which to file a claim. The agreement was signed in 2007 and constituted the act or transgression allegedly in violation of the California Franchise Act.

Finding that the License Agreement was effective when signed on December 20, 2007, more than four years and five months before the franchisees filed suit on May 29, 2012, the court concluded that the claim was barred by the statute of limitations. Accordingly, the court dismissed the franchisee's claim.

In *JoLyssa Educ. Dev., LLC v. Banco Popular N. Am.*, No. 11- CV-1503, 2012 U.S. Dist. LEXIS 136400 (D. Conn. Sept. 19, 2012), the United States District Court for the District of Connecticut held that Plaintiff's negligence, fraud, and unfair trade practices claims were barred by several Connecticut statutes of limitation.

Robert Spada, sole member of JoLyssa Educational Development, LLC ("Plaintiff"), became a Huntington Learning Center ("Huntington") franchisee in June 2006. At Huntington's encouragement, Plaintiff used The Business Resource Store as a loan consultant to help obtain an SBA loan. Plaintiff's loan consultant increased sales him projections on the pro forma required by Defendant Banco Popular in order to satisfy the bank's financing requirements. In 2007, Plaintiff received an SBA loan for the build-out and operating capital for the Huntington franchise. Plaintiff constructed, opened and operated the center. However, after losing a significant amount of money, Plaintiff failed in the operation of the franchise. Plaintiff closed the franchise on October 30, 2008, and made loan payments to Defendant through 2008. Defendant continued to send monthly statements to Plaintiff into 2011. Plaintiff filed for bankruptcy on December 29, 2009.

Plaintiff sued Defendant Banco for negligence, breach of contract, fraud, and violation of the Connecticut Unfair Trade Practices Act ("CUTPA"). Banco moved to dismiss each of the counts based on statute of limitation defenses and for failure to state a claim. In Connecticut, negligence claims are subject to a two-year statute of limitations. Conn. Gen. Stat. §§ 52-584. Common law fraud is subject to a three-year statute of limitations. Conn. Gen. Stat. § 52-577. CUPTA claims, like tort claims, are subject to a three-year statute of limitations. On all three counts, Plaintiff's complaint was based on Defendant's loan approval and closing on April 30, 2007, almost four and one-half years before Plaintiff initiated the lawsuit on September 29, 2011. The Court rejected Plaintiff's argument that the continued loan payments to Defendant tolled the statute of limitations, constituting a continued breach of duty. The Court held that the negligence, fraud, and unfair trade practices (CUTPA) claims were barred by the statute of limitations and dismissed Plaintiff's Complaint with leave to replead the breach of contract claim.

In *Bayit Care Corp. v. Tender Loving Care Health Care Services*, 843 F.Supp.2d 381 (E.D.N.Y. 2012), plaintiff Bayit Care Corp. ("Bayit") claimed that defendant Tender Loving Health Care Services ("Tender Loving") violated New York's Franchise Sales Act by failing to provide certain disclosure documentation prior to entering into an amendment to the parties franchise agreement. Tender Loving brought a motion to dismiss, alleging that Bayit's claim was time-barred by the three-year statute of limitations.

At issue in this case was whether the statute of limitations began to run when the original franchise agreement was signed in 1992 or whether an amendment to the franchise agreement in 2010 triggered the disclosure requirements of New York's Franchise Sales Act and effectively restarted the three year statute of limitations period under the Act. Bayit claimed the 2010 amendment altered the financial structure of the franchise relationship and constituted an offer of a new franchise, thereby triggering disclosure requirements and restarting the clock for purposes of the statute of limitations. Tender Loving claimed the amendment was simply a renewal or extension of the 1992 agreement and did not trigger disclosure obligations. As such, Bayit's claim was time-barred.

The court concluded that Bayit did not provide evidence to show the 2010 amendment "fundamentally altered the financial structure of the agreement," or interrupted the operation of the business and re-triggered the disclosure requirements. Moreover, Bayit did not cite any case law to support the proposition that changes to a financial structure of a franchise relationship would remake the franchise relationship entirely, thereby re-triggering the disclosure requirements. Accordingly, the 2010 amendment did not restart the statute of limitations and Bayit's claim was time-barred.

D.   CLASS ACTIONS

1.   Certification Granted, or Granted in Part

In *Agne v. Papa John's International*, 286 F.R.D. 559 (W.D. Wash. 2012), the court considered Plaintiff's motion for class certification. Plaintiff alleged that Defendants Papa John's International, Papa John's USA, OnTime4U, LLC, and certain Papa John's franchisees, violated the Telephone Consumer Protection Act ("TCPA"), the Washington Consumer

Protection Act, and the common law negligence doctrine by sending her and thousands of others unsolicited text messages advertising Papa John's Pizza.

Defendant OnTime4U, a marketing company, offered to increase the profits of Papa John's by sending text message advertisements to Papa John's customers. OnTime4U told Papa John's franchises "that it was legal to send texts without express customer consent because there was an existing business relationship between the customers and the Papa John's restaurants." Certain Papa John's franchisees provided OnTime4U with the telephone numbers of customers who had purchased pizza, and OnTime4U sent text advertisements soliciting customers to purchase Papa John's products.

Plaintiff received three messages from OnTime4U despite never giving express consent to Papa John's to send her text messages. Other customers had the same experience, and a former OnTime4U partner testified that to her knowledge, none of the Papa John's franchisees had ever received prior consent from customers to send them text message advertisements. There was no evidence that any customer has ever provided consent to receiving the text advertisements.

Papa John's International and Papa John's USA (collectively "Papa John's"), argued that franchisees must comply with certain standards pursuant to the franchise agreements, but generally maintain control over the day-to-day operations of their restaurants. Further, Papa John's asserted that "franchisees make their own local marketing decisions." Plaintiff, however, argued that even though there was no evidence that Papa John's directly contracted with OnTime4U to send the text messages, Papa John's nevertheless "directed, encouraged, and authorized its franchisees to use OnTime4U's services."

Plaintiff moved for certification of two classes, both of which were opposed by the Defendants for lack of standing and failing to meet the requirements for class certification set out in Rule 23 of the Federal Rules of Civil Procedure. The court first addressed the issue of standing. Papa John's argued that the Plaintiff lacked Article III standing to sue anyone other than the Papa John's franchisee that worked with OnTime4U because the injury was not fairly traceable to Papa John's. The court did not agree and found that Plaintiff had satisfied the "fairly traceable" standard because she alleged that Papa John's was both directly and vicariously liable for the text messages. The court also found that Plaintiff had statutory standing despite the fact that she was not the primary account holder, nor did she pay the bill on her cell phone plan, because she was the intended recipient of the messages.

Rule 23(a) of the Federal Rules of Civil Procedure sets out four requirements that must be met for a court to certify a class: (1) ascertainability; (2) numerosity; (3) commonality; and (4) typicality. The court found that the ascertainability requirement was met because the class definitions, "All persons in the United States of America who were sent, to their cellular telephone numbers, at least one unsolicited text message that marketed a Papa John's branded product, good, or service through OnTime4U," and "All persons in Washington State who were sent, to their cellular telephone numbers, at least one unsolicited text message that marketed a Papa John's branded product, good, or service through OnTime4U," provided "sufficiently precise and objective criteria to determine class membership." Next, the court found that the numerosity requirement was met because Plaintiff asserted that the Papa John's franchisees that had provided OnTime4U with customer phone numbers had provided over 68,000 numbers. Third, the court found that the commonality requirement was satisfied because Plaintiff's allegation was not "merely that all class members suffered a violation of the TCPA, but rather that all class members were sent substantially similar unsolicited text messages by the same defendants, using the same automatic dialing technology." And finally, the court found that the typicality requirement was met because Plaintiff's claims, like all class members' claims, arose from the text marketing campaigns commissioned by Papa John's franchisees and executed by OnTime4U.

The court next considered whether Plaintiff had met the predominance and superiority requirements for certifying a class under Rule 23(b)(3). The court found that Plaintiff had met the predominance requirement because individual inquiries would not overwhelm common issues. The court also found that the superiority requirement was met because, among other things, the $500 statutory damages provision of the TCPA would not sufficiently "compensate the average consumer for the time and effort that would be involved in bringing a small claims action against a national corporation like Papa John's." Accordingly, the court granted Plaintiff's motion for class certification.

In *White v. 14051 Manchester, Inc.*, No. 12-CV-469, 2012 U.S. Dist. LEXIS 170052 (E.D. Mo. Nov. 30, 2012) the court considered Plaintiffs' motion to conditionally certify a class of employees who claimed violations of the Fair Labor Standards Act. ("FSLA") Plaintiffs White and Carroll ("Plaintiffs") were employed by Defendant Hotshots Sports Bar & Grill ("Hotshots") as servers and/or bartenders. As tipped employees, Plaintiffs were paid an hourly rate, as well as a portion of the tips paid by customers. Plaintiffs alleged that they were required to participate in a "tip pool" where tipped employees shared tips with other non-tipped employees, including the doormen, cooks and dishwashers. Plaintiffs claimed that this policy applied uniformly to all Hotshots locations. Plaintiffs alleged claims for violation of the FLSA, 29 U.S.C. § 201 et seq, and Missouri Minimum Wage Law, § 290.500 et seq.

Plaintiffs defined the putative class as "Hotshots employees who have worked as tipped employees or participated in a tip pool at any of the Hotshots locations at any time during the last three years." Hotshots opposed the certification on the ground that they did not control the employment practices at Hotshots franchise locations.

Under Section 7 of the FLSA, "an employer cannot subject non-exempt employees to a work week in excess of forty hours unless the employee is compensated for his or her overtime with additional pay of at least one one-half times his or her regular hourly wage." Further, a collective action under the FLSA to recover overtime compensation can be maintained "by one or more employees for and in behalf of himself or themselves and other employees similarly situated." Like other district courts in the Eighth Circuit, the court conducted a two-step analysis to determine whether the Hotshots employees were similarly situated. First, the court engaged in a lenient evaluation considering whether the plaintiff could make a "modest factual showing sufficient to demonstrate that they and potential plaintiffs together were victims of a common policy or plan that violated the law." Second, after the close of discovery, the defendant moves to decertify the class and the court applies a stricter standard to the similarly situated question that can be met by "detailed allegations supported by affidavits."

The court found that Plaintiffs met the "modest factual showing" burden. First, because Hotshots' purported policy violated the FLSA and Plaintiffs specifically alleged that they, and other similarly situated employees, were denied compensation as a result of Hotshots' policy. And second, the Supreme Court has advised that "whether a relationship is covered by the FLSA turns on the economic realities of the working relationship rather than technical definitions relating to employment." Thus, the court found that even though the potential class members were employed by different Hotshots franchisees, the employees were subject to the same tip-pool policy and worked and acted directly or indirectly in the interest of Hotshots, therefore meeting the FLSA's definition of employee. Accordingly, the court granted the Plaintiffs' motion to conditionally certify the class.

Following the conditional certification, in *White v. 14051 Manchester, Inc.*, No. 12-CV-469, 2012 U.S. Dist. LEXIS 178621 (E.D. Mo. Dec. 18,

2012), Hotshots moved to modify the order of conditional class certification. Hotshots argued that the franchisee locations should not be a part of the conditionally certified class. In response, Plaintiffs argued that Hotshots was basically asking for a "do over" of the conditional class certification order. The court agreed with the Plaintiffs and refused to modify the order to exclude the Hotshots franchisee's employees from the conditional class.

In *Brewer v. General Nutrition Corporation*, No. 11-CV-03587, 2013 U.S. Dist. LEXIS 2948 (N.D. Cal. Jan. 7, 2013), the court considered Plaintiff's Motion for Conditional Certification of a Fair Labor Standards Act ("FLSA") Opt-in Class. Plaintiff brought the collective action against his former employer, General Nutrition Corporation ("GNC") for alleged wage and hour violations. Plaintiff worked for a corporate-owned GNC as a Sales Associate and later as an Assistant Manager. Plaintiff routinely worked the closing shift, in which he would clock out and then continue to perform an array of mandatory closing duties, including off-site bank deposits. Plaintiff was not compensated for time spent performing the bank deposits and other closing duties. Further, Plaintiff was typically scheduled to work 35-40 hours per week, but usually worked over 40 hour per week without receiving overtime pay.

Plaintiff alleged that as a matter of corporate policy and practice, GNC did not compensate its employees for time spent making bank deposits and performing other closing duties. GNC had a written policy that required employees working the closing shift to deposit cash collected during business hours at an off-site bank on a nightly basis after clocking out for the day. However, GNC did not have a documented system in place for compensating its employees for the time spent performing closing duties. GNC trained employees who worked the closing shift to estimate how much time would be spent performing closing duties. However, the timekeeping system allowed only one half-hour to perform the closing duties. GNC argued that the closing duties took far less than one half-hour to perform and that employees were able to amend time sheets if the closing duties took longer. However, GNC did not offer any documentation of its policies regarding estimating how long closing activities would take or amending incorrect timesheets.

Plaintiff sought a collective action under the FLSA of all current and former employees who worked the closing shift and/or worked shifts alone as a Sales Associate or Manager. The FLSA provides a private right of action for violations of the FLSA, including a suit on behalf of other "similarly situated" employees. Certification of a collective action typically proceeds in two stages, and the court engaged in the analysis required for the first stage. In the first stage, known as the "notice" stage, plaintiffs carry the burden of providing "substantial allegations, supported by declarations of or discovery, to establish that" the putative class members are similarly situated and "were together the victims of a single decision, policy, or plan."

The court found that Plaintiff had met the "modest factual showing" standard for GNC Sales Associates and Assistant Managers, but not for senior-level Managers. Plaintiff's allegations that GNC imposed a policy requiring its Sales Associates and Assistant Managers to perform work after clocking out was supported by job descriptions, Declarations of the Plaintiff himself, Putative FLSA Class members from GNC locations around the United States and excerpts from deposition transcripts of GNC officials. All of the evidence confirmed that GNC had "no written policy setting forth the procedure for an employee to be paid for time spent performing post-closing duties; no written policy on estimating hours worked; and no written policy on adjusting hours to account for time spent performing post-closing duties if an employee exceed[ed] the time estimate." Because Plaintiff's allegations did not include senior-level Managers, the court granted in part Plaintiff's motion for conditional certification of a FLSA opt-in class.

In *Villa v. United Site Services of California, Inc.*, No. 12-CV-00318, 2012 U.S. Dist. LEXIS 162922 (N.D. Cal. Nov. 13, 2012), the court considered Plaintiff's motion to certify a class and several sub-classes for alleged Fair Labor Standard Act ("FLSA") claims pursuant to 29 U.S.C. § 216(b) as well as a conditional certification of a FLSA collective action. Plaintiff worked as a service technician and pickup and delivery driver for the Defendant, who rents and services portable toilets, restroom trailers, portable sinks, and temporary fencing. Service technicians drive on pre-determined daily routes where they service, sanitize, and restock restroom units.

Plaintiff alleged that Defendant: (1) failed to provide adequate meal and rest breaks; and (2) shifted hours between pay periods to avoid paying overtime. Plaintiff claimed that Defendant had a policy of requiring workers to work through their meal breaks, while still counting the time as unpaid meal break time; required employees to remain with their vehicles and answer phone or radio calls during breaks that, under California law, were supposed to be completely free from work responsibilities; scheduled work days too tightly to allow for off-duty breaks; and failed to pay overtime compensation due as a result of shifts longer than eight hours during which breaks were not provided. Further, Plaintiff claimed that he was instructed by his supervisor to "record hours worked in excess of 12 hours in a day in future pay periods."

The court first considered Plaintiff's class for the meal and rest break class. Per Rule 23(a) of the Federal Rules of Civil Procedure, four requirements must be met for a court to certify a class: (1) ascertainability; (2) numerosity; (3) commonality; and (4) typicality. Defendant did not contest that Plaintiff satisfied the first two requirements. Accordingly, the court focused its analysis on the final two requirements. The court found that commonality existed because there was a common question that could be answered on a class-wide basis: "whether the Defendant had an illegal policy or practice from deducting time from its workers' shifts for off-duty meal breaks whether or not those meal breaks were taken." The court also found that the typicality requirement was satisfied because Plaintiff "alleged that all class members suffered the same injury" of being "required to remain on duty during meal breaks without being paid for that time, and being deprived of overtime compensation."

The court next considered whether Plaintiff had met the predominance and superiority requirements for certifying a class under Rule 23(b)(3). The court found that Plaintiff did not satisfy the predominance requirement because the evidence he presented, which included language from the Associate Handbook, as well as depositions of the Defendant's Operations Manager and Vice President, could not "show that there was a uniform policy or practice" with regard to meal and rest breaks. The court further found that Plaintiff could not meet the superiority requirement because individual proof would be "necessary to establish for each employee whether meal breaks were taken or permitted, and what restrictions were placed on those meal breaks." Accordingly, the court denied Plaintiff's motion to certify the meal and rest break class, and ultimately denied the hour-shifting sub-class for the same reason.

The court then considered Plaintiff's motion for conditional certification of a FLSA collective action based on Defendant's failure to pay overtime compensation. Under the FLSA, employees may bring a collective action on behalf of other "similarly situated" employees based on alleged violations of the FLSA. The court conducted the first of a two-step analysis to determine whether the employees were similarly situated. Under the first step, the court determined whether Plaintiff had shown "that some identifiable factual or legal nexus b[ound] together the various claims of the class members in a way that hearing the claims together promote[d] judicial efficiency. . . " The court found that Plaintiff's allegation that he and other class members were similarly situated "because they were subject to [the] Defendant's alleged common policy of deducting time from employees' pay without confirming whether they had indeed taken their off-duty breaks," was sufficient for conditional certification of the FSLA collective action.

In *Gessele v. Jack in the Box, Inc.*, No. 10-CV-00960, 2013 U.S. Dist. LEXIS 46758 (D. Or. Apr. 1, 2013), the court reviewed a magistrate judge's findings and recommendation ("F&R") relating to a possible class certification under the Fair Labor Standards Act ("FLSA"). The putative class action was brought by employees of Jack in the Box restaurants for alleged violations of the minimum wage and overtime provisions of the FLSA. Plaintiffs were all employed by Jack in the Box and started at minimum wage positions. However, some of the plaintiffs were promoted to "team leader" positions that, though hourly positions, had management responsibilities such as ensuring that employees took their statutory breaks. Some of the plaintiffs were also promoted to salaried management positions.

Plaintiffs alleged three categories of violations that caused them to be "paid less than minimum wage or to not receive overtime wages: (1) wrongful deductions for the Workers' Benefit Fund ("WBF") assessment; (2) wrongful deductions for shoes; and (3) failing to pay for certain break periods." Plaintiffs' WBF claims arose when the assessment rate, which was paid evenly by employers and employees to provide benefits to injured workers, decreased. After the decrease, Jack in the Box did not alter the amount that it took from its employees, thereby deducting a disproportional amount from them. Plaintiffs' shoe claims arose from the fact that Jack in the Box required Plaintiffs to wear slip-resistant shoes purchased from a specific vendor, and encouraged employees to do so through a payroll deduction. Finally, Plaintiffs' meal break claims were based in the fact that Jack in the Box allegedly failed to pay for breaks that lasted more than twenty minutes but less than thirty minutes. The magistrate recommended that the court certify the WBF and shoe claims, but not the break claims, and the court accepted the magistrate's recommendation in full.

As opposed to the traditional two-step approach utilized by courts considering whether employees are similarly situated within the meaning of the FLSA, the court took an intermediate approach. Under the intermediate approach, the court determined whether conditional certification was appropriate under the lenient notice standard, and then used the more stringent decertification standard to account for all of the discovery that had been conducted. The magistrate initially found that all three claims met the first burden, but that the meal break claims did not meet the second-stage burden. Plaintiffs objected to the magistrate's decision to use the second-stage criteria on the basis that discovery had not been completed. The court found that Plaintiffs had conducted "exhaustive discovery," and that therefore, using the intermediate standard was appropriate.

The court then addressed Jack in the Box's argument that certification was improper for the shoe claims because it had not violated the FLSA. The court noted that Jack in the Box was raising the same claims it had raised before the magistrate; including arguing that the shoes were not required uniform, but "other facilities" under the FLSA. The court found that although the court's ultimate decision on the topic would determine whether or not the class won, "the possibility of individualized issues regarding whether the employees signed authorization forms for the payroll deductions for the cost of shoes d[id] not overwhelm the common factual and legal questions of the proposed class." Thus, the court certified the shoe claims.

Finally, the court addressed the meal break claims. The magistrate found, and the court supported, that certification of the claims was precluded for several reasons, including the fact that individual inquiries would be necessary to determine if Jack in the Box was in violation of the FLSA. Under the FLSA, workers who are on "bona fide" meal breaks, typically at least thirty minutes and not counted as hours worked, must be "completely relieved" from work duties. However, the FLSA does not require an employer to provide meal breaks. Thus, the court concluded that to determine whether a specific employee was owed overtime for a meal break, the court would have to conduct individual inquiries into whether an employee's break between twenty and thirty minutes was a bona fide meal break, whether the shortened break was long enough to count as a bona fide meal break, and why the employee did not take the full meal break. Because individual issues predominated, the court denied certification of the meal break claim.

2. Certification Denied

In *Martin v. JTH Tax, Inc.*, No. 10-CV-03016, 2013 U.S. Dist. LEXIS 15512 (D. S.C. Feb. 5, 2013) plaintiffs sought to certify a class against franchisor Liberty Tax Service and its owners John and Danny Hewitt. The plaintiffs alleged that Liberty Tax and two of its franchisees in South Carolina concocted a scheme to defraud federal and state taxing authorities by soliciting and/or submitting false information on tax returns in order to increase profits. Plaintiffs alleged that Liberty Tax taught its franchisees and their employees to sell unnecessary forms and schedules and complete tax returns so that the franchisees could charge greater fees, on a per form basis, to customers. In turn, customers would receive a greater tax refund, out of which the franchisees' were paid. Ultimately, many of the customers were audited and incurred additional tax liability, interest and penalties. The plaintiffs alleged claims for breach of contract, breach of fiduciary duty and unjust enrichment. Plaintiffs also alleged RICO claims against any John and Danny Hewitt personally. The plaintiffs sought to certify a class consisting of all customers of the South Carolina Liberty Tax franchisees who prepared returns and charged additional fees for preparing schedules or forms that accompanied the basic tax return.

In deciding the class certification issue, the court relied heavily on the decision in *Wal-Mart Stores, Inc. v. Dukes*, 131 S. Ct. 2541, 180 L. Ed. 2d 374 (2011). Under Rule 23(a)(2), plaintiffs must show common questions of law or fact to the class. The Supreme Court in *Wal-Mart* held that "certification is proper only if the trial court is satisfied, after rigorous analysis, that the prerequisites for the 23(a) have been satisfied." The "rigorous analysis" test often requires determinations that overlap with the merits of the case. The *Wal-Mart* decision also clarified that under Rule 23(a)(2), commonality is not satisfied by simply raising common questions, but instead showing that the class members "have suffered the same injury." *Wal-Mart*, 131 S. Ct. at 2551. After conducting the rigorous analysis, the court determined that the plaintiff failed to carry its burden of demonstrating commonality. Each of the class members had their taxes done at two different Liberty Tax locations, submitted tax information for different years of income, paid for different numbers of forms or schedules, claimed different deductions, and had different auditing experiences in terms of deductions being allowed or disallowed. As a result, the court observed "in no way could the named plaintiffs present "common" questions for the court to resolve. Instead, a fact intensive analysis must be made into each class representative's alleged injury. This conclusion also prevented plaintiffs from meeting the predominance requirement under Rule 23(b)(3) because individualized damage determinations cut against class certification under Rule 23(b)(3). The court denied class certification.

In *MP Vista, Inc. v. Motiva Enterprises,* LLC, 286 F.R.D. 299 (E.D. La. 2012), the court considered Plaintiffs MP Vista, Inc., Habib Petroleum Corp., and Bay Point Oil Corp.'s (collectively "Plaintiffs") Motion for Class Certification. Plaintiffs were gas station owners and operators who were franchisees of Defendants Motiva Enterprises, LLC (Motiva) and/or Shell Oil Company (Shell) (collectively "Defendants"). Though the gas station franchisees independently operated their gas stations, they purchased gasoline from Motiva pursuant to sales agreements. In May 2004, Motiva learned that some of the fuel that it refined was contaminated. However, by the time Motiva learned of the contamination, the gasoline had already been distributed to certain dealers and franchisees. Motiva ordered dealers that may have received the contaminated fuel to cease gasoline sales until the gasoline had been tested and cleared by Motiva. As a result, the length of time that each station was close varied. The stations continued to offer ancillary items such as convenience store items and car washes during the period of closure.

Plaintiffs sought to represent a class of gas station franchisees who purchased and received contaminated gasoline in May 2004. Plaintiffs contended that "each franchisee's gas station suffered direct economic damages as a result of following Defendants' instructions to shut down," which resulted in diminished consumer confidence in the Shell branded stations. Defendants opposed the certification on the basis that Plaintiffs could not satisfy the typicality, adequacy, and predominance factors required for class certification pursuant to Rules of Civil Procedure 23(a) and 23(b)(3). The court limited its discussion to predominance.

Plaintiffs argued that predominance existed because there was a central issue of "whether the subject motor fuel was contaminated, whether the contaminated gasoline was sold and delivered to various franchisees across the effected states, whether Defendants issued instructions to cease and desist the sale of the contaminated motor fuel and the economic damages arising there from . . ." Further, Plaintiffs argued that their expert witness, Dr. Olson, utilizing "easily verifiable business records" and industry average information, developed a formulaic method for calculating damages that offered "a reliable, verifiable and easily reproducible" formula for calculating each putative class member's damages.

Defendants argued that "determining what (if any) losses were caused by the incident would require a station-by-station assessment of each dealer's experience and economic circumstances." Further, Defendants opposed Dr. Olson's formula for several reasons, including the fact that it did not account for other possible causes of lower sales besides the fuel contamination and that it assumed that each dealer's ancillary sales would decrease by the same percentage as the station's fuel sales, even though some stations' ancillary sales increased. Further, Defendants argued that predominance could not be proven because the Plaintiffs and Dr. Olson admitted that the issue of proximate cause would be a highly individualized inquiry. Plaintiffs responded that "the common question of Motiva's liability for manufacturing and distributing sub-standard fuel overr[ode] any individual damage calculation."

The court agreed with Defendants and found that Dr. Olson's formula was inadequate for several reasons. First, the formula failed to account for factors outside of the fuel contamination that may have led to decreased sales and it solely attributed the loss to the fuel contamination. Second, the model failed to demonstrate a way of establishing that decreased sales were proximately caused by the fuel contamination incident. And finally, the court found that assessing the losses would require an individualized assessment of each station's day-to-day operations. The court denied Plaintiff's motion for class certification.

In *Doe v. Southern Gyms, LLC*, No. 12-CV-1566, 2013 LEXIS 576 (La. Mar. 19, 2013), the Louisiana Supreme Court reviewed the lower court's decision granting Plaintiff's motion for class certification. Plaintiff was a member of Anytime Fitness, a franchised fitness center owned by Southern Gyms, LLC in Baton Rouge Louisiana. Southern Gyms purchased a franchise for the fitness center from franchisor Anytime Fitness, Inc. An assistant manager and trainer at the fitness center, Telschow, secretly videotaped Plaintiff, along with other women, in the women's locker room. Telschow placed a pen camera in the locker room on 10 to15 occasions, recording the locker room for 1 to 2 hours. Telschow admitted that he videotaped at least 5 other women in various stages of undress and about 20 women doing non-intimate things such as washing their hands or combing their hair. Telschow claimed that he erased the images after he viewed them and that he never downloaded or shared the images. The only images that remained at the time of the Plaintiff's suit were the images of her and three other women that had never been seen by Telschow.

Plaintiff filed an action called "Class Action Petition for Damages " and alleged negligence against Southern Gyms, Anytime Fitness and its employees for failing to properly supervise its employees and protect its patrons from criminal acts. Plaintiff also alleged invasion of privacy and intentional infliction of emotional distress against Telschow, individually. Plaintiff moved for class certification and although the district judge expressed doubt as to whether it should be granted, he granted the motion. Defendants appealed and argued that Plaintiff had failed to prove the numerosity requirement. The court of appeals affirmed the district court's ruling, and the Supreme Court of Louisiana then reviewed the lower court's decisions.

The Louisiana class action procedure parallels Federal Rule of Civil Procedure 23, requiring a party to prove numerosity, commonality, typicality, adequacy of representative parties, and objectively definable class. The court focused on the numerosity requirement. Plaintiff argued that the fact that Telschow deleted or erased the videotapes he had taken of women in the locker room did not prohibit proceeding as a class action. However, there were multiple barriers to Plaintiff's efforts to proceed on a class basis: 1) The potential class members did not know whether or not they were videotaped; 2) Plaintiff did not know whether every other woman who entered the gym utilized the locker room; 3) Plaintiff had no knowledge of any other women captured on videotape; 4) Plaintiff did not know how many days or on which days Telschow videotaped, and 5) Plaintiff had no evidence of any damage or injury suffered by others and no evidence of a causal link between Telschow's actions and any purported damages. Further, Telschow only knew one of the women he videotaped and was not able to identify or recognize the others. Based on the evidence presented, the court held that the plaintiff failed to carry her burden of proof that there were a sufficient number of aggrieved parties to meet the numerosity requirement for class certification. Accordingly, the court reversed the appellate court's judgment affirming and the district court's order granting class certification.

3. Discovery in Class Actions

In *Russell v. Happy's Pizza Franchise*, No. 12-CV-323, 2013 U.S. Dist. LEXIS 6390 (W.D. Mich. Jan. 16, 2013), the court considered Plaintiff's motion for leave to conduct additional discovery required to respond to the Defendants', Happy's Pizza Franchise, LLC (collectively "Franchisor"), motion for summary judgment. Plaintiff was part of a class action against the Franchisor for failing to pay overtime wages in violation of the Fair Labor Standards Act ("FLSA"). Plaintiff claimed that more discovery was necessary to show that the Franchisor was the "employer" within the scope of the FLSA. Franchisor objected to the motion on the grounds that Plaintiff had all of the information he needed, that Plaintiff sought irrelevant information and Plaintiff's motion was deficient.

Franchisor first argued that the Plaintiff was in possession of over 16,000 pages of documents and that was all of the information that he needed. Specifically, Franchisor argued that because Plaintiff possessed the Happy's Pizza Franchise Agreement, which "explicitly prohibited the Franchisor from exerting control over the wages and hours of franchisee employees," that they were not "employers" within the meaning of the FLSA. The court however found that while the Franchisor was not the employer within the meaning of the FLSA on paper, Plaintiff was nevertheless "entitled to test whether the prohibition of control espoused in the Franchise Agreement existed in reality," because "[i]n deciding whether a party is an employer, 'economic reality' controls rather than common law concepts of agency." The court found that because no discovery had taken place as to the economic realities of the relationship between Franchisor and the franchisee's employees, Plaintiff did not have all of the information that he needed. For the same reason, the court dismissed the Franchisor's claim that the information sought by the Plaintiff was irrelevant.

Finally, the Franchisor argued that Plaintiff's Rule 56(d) motion was deficient because it was untimely and failed to state what material facts could have been uncovered in discovery. The court concluded that the motion was not untimely and that Plaintiff was only required to specify what information he would seek through discovery, which he did. Accordingly, the court granted Plaintiff's motion for additional discovery.

E.   CLASS ACTION SETTLEMENTS

In *Reid v. SuperShuttle International, Inc.*, No. 08-CV-4854, 2012 U.S. Dist. LEXIS 113117 (E.D. N.Y. Aug. 10, 2012), the court considered Plaintiffs' motion for final approval of a proposed settlement of a class action. Plaintiffs were current and former franchisees of SuperShuttle International, Inc. that asserted various wage and unpaid overtime claims under the New York Labor Law and the Fair Labor Standards Act. The settlement consisted primarily of monetary relief of $100 for class members who did not currently have a SuperShuttle franchise and a new SuperShuttle program that would allow current franchisees to sell a new ten-year franchise through financing provided by SuperShuttle.

The court concluded that the settlement was "fair, adequate, and reasonable." First, the court found that the settlement was a "product of arm's length negotiations conducted by experienced counsel knowledgeable in complex class litigation." Second, the court found that the likely duration and expense of the case favored settlement because absent settlement, the case would likely have taken "substantial time and resources to resolve. Further, the court found that Plaintiffs would have faced "significant risks" in establishing that SuperShuttle was liable. The court noted that Plaintiffs would have faced "a real and substantial risk of obtaining nothing" if the case proceeded. Thus, even though the court questioned the adequacy of the "modest" settlement and 38% of the class members opted out of the settlement, the court approved it.

In *Spillman v. RPM Pizza, LLC*, No. 10-349, 2013 U.S. Dist. LEXIS 72947 (M.D. La. May 23, 2013), the court conducted a fairness hearing pursuant to Federal Rule of Civil Procedure 23(e) to determine whether a class action settlement was "fair, reasonable, adequate, and in the best interest of the class." Plaintiff filed a class action complaint against Domino's franchisee RPM Pizza, LLC and Domino's Pizza LLC for alleged violations of the Telephone Consumer Protection Act ("TCPA"). The class consisted of individuals who had received automated telephone calls from or on behalf of RPM or one of Domino's other franchised stores. The Settlement Agreement created a common fund totaling $9,750,000. As a result, the settlement was subject to the Class Action Fairness Act ("CAFA") and had to comply with 28 U.S.C §§ 1714-15.

Under the Settlement Agreement, the members of the largest sub-class were to receive a fully transferable, single-use voucher for a large one-topping pizza that could only be redeemed for pick-up at RPM-owned Domino's stores in the states of Louisiana, Alabama, and Mississippi. Under section 1714, a proposed settlement cannot provide a greater payment to particular class members solely on the basis of being geographically closer to the court. The court found that the settlement agreement did not violate section 1714 because the basis for geographic location had "nothing to do with geographic proximity to the court." Rather, the court found that the provision was the result of the fact that RPM operated in those three states, and that the majority of class members had phone numbers within area codes originating in Louisiana, Alabama, and Mississippi. The court found that the appropriate Notice of Compliance had been filed without objection, satisfying section 1715. Accordingly, the court found that the settlement agreement complied with the CAFA requirements.

After the court found that the requirements of Federal Rule of Civil Procedure 23(a) and (b)(3) were satisfied, the court utilized the factors identified in *Reed v. General Motor. Corp.*, 703 F.2d 170, 172 (5th Cir. 1983), to determine whether the settlement agreement was fair, reasonable, and adequate. The court found that the parties would benefit from settlement for several reasons, including: that the history of the litigation showed that it had been long, complex, and expensive; the fact that each side would face substantial obstacles if there were no settlement and litigation continued; and that the settlement had been achieved only after two unsuccessful mediation sessions and returning to litigation. The court then found that there was no evidence to suggest fraud or collusion, and that continuing litigation would not likely bring any greater benefits. Finally, after considering the opinions of class counsel and the class representative, who supported the settlement, the court found that the settlement was fair, reasonable, adequate, and in the best interest of the class.

F.   SERVICE OF PROCESS

In *Gates v. Crescent Hotels & Resorts,* No. 13-00149, U.S. Dist. LEXIS 88346 (S.D. Ala. June 6, 2013) the magistrate judge issued a report and recommendation granting plaintiff Tamela Gates' motion to remand to the Circuit Court of Mobile County, Alabama. The report and recommendation was adopted by the District Court on June 24, 2013. Gates filed a personal injury action in the Circuit Court of Mobile County, Alabama against Marriott International, Inc. on December 27, 2012. She claimed that Marriott was negligent for failing to operate and maintain its hotel after she slipped and fell at the Marriott hotel in Mobile Alabama. Marriott International, Inc. accepted service on December 31, 2012. On January 24, 2013, Marriott filed a motion to dismiss claiming it, as the franchisor, was the incorrect party, but failed to identify the franchisee operating the hotel in mobile. Gates then served the summons and complaint on the hotel located in Mobile in January 28, 2013. On February 23, 2013 Marriott identified its franchisee, Crescent Hotels & Resorts, LLC ("Crescent"), as the correct defendant.

On February 27, 2013 Gates amended her complaint, substituting Crescent as the defendant instead of Marriott International, Inc. On March 28, 2013, Crescent filed a notice of removal based on diversity jurisdiction. Gates moved to remand alleging that the removal was untimely because Crescent filed 88 days after Marriott International was served and 60 days after Gates served the hotel manager at the hotel. Defendant, however, argued that they had 30 days after receipt of service and that they were not served with the amended complaint until February 28, 2013.

To resolve this dispute, the court considered when Crescent became a defendant and had standing to remove. Under existing Supreme Court precedent, the removal window is triggered by simultaneous service of the summons and complaint, but not by mere receipt of the complaint unattended by any formal service. The court found that when the hotel manager was personally served on the hotel premises where the injury allegedly occurred, service was complete on Crescent, the owner of the hotel. Even though the wrong defendant was designated in the complaint, it identified that specific Marriott hotel location as the location where the incident occurred. Therefore, the 30-day clock began with the service on the hotel manager on January 28, 2013, and the defendant's removal on March 28, 2013 was untimely.

In *Hurtado v. 7-Eleven, Inc.*, No. 13-1043, 2013 U.S. App. Unpub. LEXIS 7883 (7th Cir. 2013) the appellate court affirmed a district court finding that the franchisor 7-Eleven was not served with process. Hurtado, a former employee of a 7-Eleven store in Des Plaines, Illinois filed suit against 7-Eleven, alleging he was discriminated against because of his age and national origin. The district court appointed a federal marshal to serve 7-Eleven, but the marshal was unsuccessful. Hurtado then mailed the complaint to the Des Plaines Store address and Bassyto, Inc., an independent franchisee that owned the store, appeared in court. Hurtado moved to dismiss Bassyto and requested a default judgment against 7-Eleven for failing to defend the suit. 7-Eleven asserted that Bassyto was not its registered agent, it had not been properly served, and the suit should be dismissed under Fed. R. Civ. P. 12(b)(5) because the time for service had expired (pursuant to Fed. R. Civ. P. 4(m)). The district court dismissed Bassyto without prejudice, finding that 7-Eleven had not been served, and extended the deadline for Hurtado to serve process. Hurtado failed to serve 7-Eleven or move for another extension before the new deadline and the district court dismissed the suit without prejudice. On appeal, the Seventh Circuit Court held that because Hurtado failed to take advantage of the extension granted by the district court, the district court did not abuse its discretion by dismissing his suit. The court also stated that Hurtado's pro se status did not excuse him from exercising diligence and timely complying with service of process rules.

G.   MOOTNESS

In *Gossett Motor Cars v. Hyundai Motor America, Inc.*, No. M2011-01769, 2012 Tenn. App. LEXIS 542 (Tenn. Ct. App. Aug. 2, 2012), a dispute arose when Gossett Motor Cars, a Hyundai dealer in the Memphis area ("Gossett"), received a letter from Hyundai Motor America, Inc. ("Hyundai") notifying Gossett of Hyundai's intent to grant a Hyundai franchise to Skelton ("Skelton"), another dealer in Gossett's market area. Gossett filed a letter of protest with the Tennessee Motor Vehicle Commission ("TMVC"), and a TMVC attorney filed a petition for a contested case proceeding with the Administrative Procedures Division of the Secretary of State's Office. Hyundai filed a motion to dismiss based on Gossett's failure to serve Hyundai with the protest letter within 30 days of receiving notification of Hyundai's intent to grant another dealership. An administrative law judge ("ALJ") granted the motion. Following the dismissal, the TMVC granted the Hyundai franchise to Skelton. Gossett then filed a motion for reconsideration of the ALJ's order, which the ALJ denied. Gossett then filed a petition for appeal of the ALJ's order, and the ALJ denied the motion on its merits. Gossett then filed a petition for writ of certiorari in the Davidson County Chancery Court. The chancery court concluded that Gossett's letter of protest was enough to commence a contested case proceeding and that Gossett was not required to serve Hyundai within 30 days of receiving notice of the proposed dealership. Nevertheless, the chancery court found that the case was moot and dismissed the petition for review. On appeal, Gossett argued that the chancery court erred in dismissing his petition for review.

The appellate court held that the action was moot, as the TMVC had granted the franchise to Skelton and Gossett did not want any of the possible damages available. Thus, since there was no relief possible, the court found that the case was moot.

In *JOC Inc. v. ExxonMobil Oil Corp.*, 507 Fed. Unpub. Appx. 208 (3rd Cir. Dec. 18, 2012), the court dismissed Appellants ExxonMobil Oil Corporation ("Exxon") and Sung Eel Chang Auto, t/a Ashwood Exxon ("Ashwood") cross-appeal from a district court preliminary injunction as moot.

The court consolidated three appeals that all concerned the former Ashwood Exxon gas station. As a franchisee, Ashwood leased its property from Exxon and was obligated to purchase gasoline from Exxon. In 2008, Ashwood filed suit against Exxon, claiming that it charged Ashwood higher rates for gasoline than it did other competing stations in violation of New Jersey law. Exxon argued that its pricing was lawful and that Ashwood's own business practices were the cause of any financial distress. The suit was removed to federal court for diversity of citizenship. In 2009, Ashwood stopped paying rent. Exxon then commenced proceedings to terminate the franchise, and Ashwood moved for a preliminary injunction to bar termination while the lawsuit was ongoing.

In 2010, the district court issued three orders that barred Exxon from terminating the franchise for Ashwood's prior contractual violations. However, the court refused to bar Exxon from terminating the franchise for any future violations. Exxon appealed the partial bar, and Ashwood cross-appealed the denial of a broader injunction. After the appeals were filed, Exxon terminated the Ashwood franchise on the basis of Ashwood's new violations of the contracts. Ashwood was evicted from the station in January 2012.

The court recognized that it had jurisdiction to review the preliminary injunction. However, the court lost jurisdiction due to an event that occurred while the case was pending on appeal. In appealing the partial preliminary injunction, Exxon sought the right to terminate the Ashwood franchise, and Ashwood sought to prevent termination. The franchise no longer existed, so there was no longer a franchise to terminate or save. Accordingly, the court could no longer grant either party effective relief, and it dismissed the case as moot.

H.   NAMING THE PROPER PARTY

In *Paul Davis Restoration of S.E. Wisconsin, Inc. v. Paul Davis Restoration of Northeast Wisconsin*, 831 N.W.2d 413 (Wis. 2013), the Wisconsin Supreme Court was asked to decide "whether an otherwise valid judgment can be enforced against a legal entity when the judgment is entered against the name under which the legal entity does business." Holding that such a valid judgment can and should be enforced, the court reversed the court of appeals' decision and remanded for further proceedings.

This case arose from a territory-related dispute between two franchisees, Paul Davis Restoration of S.E. Wisconsin, Inc. (Southeast) and Paul Davis Restoration of Northeast Wisconsin (Northeast). Pursuant to the franchise agreement, binding arbitration was required to resolve the dispute. As a result of the arbitration process, Southeast was awarded $101,693 against Northeast, which is the name under which EA Green Bay, LLC did business. Southeast then sought to enforce the judgment via a garnishment action under Wisconsin Statute Section 812.01.

EA Green Bay, LLC opposed the garnishment action at the circuit court on the grounds that the judgment was entered only against Northeast, the name under which it did business, and thus not enforceable. Relying on two Wisconsin cases, the circuit court held that Northeast had "no independent legal significance apart from [EA Green Bay, LLC]," and the names "refer to the same legal entity." It thus held that the valid judgment was enforceable against Northeast and EA Green Bay, LLC. Citing the same cases as the circuit court, the court of appeals reversed. The court determined that where a company does business under a name different from the legal entity, the name is "merely descriptive of" and "not . . . distinct from" the corporation operating the business and is "a legal nonentity." The court reasoned that the judgment against such a name was unenforceable and could not serve as the basis for a garnishment action.

Agreeing with the circuit court and the majority of courts from other jurisdictions, the Wisconsin Supreme Court determined that "the name under which a legal entity does business 'does not create or constitute an entity distinct from the [corporation] operating the business.'" Thus, there was no basis for holding that a judgment against such a name, indistinct from the legal entity to which it is attached, cannot be enforced against that entity. The court reversed and remanded for further proceedings consistent with its opinion.

In a case with a similar situation, but a different outcome, in *Verhoogen vs. United Parcel Service, Inc.*, No. 12-CA-104, 2013 Ohio App. Lexis 2233 (Ct. App. Ohio June 4, 2013), a consumer sued the franchisor UPS and its franchisee identified as "the UPS store 3832" for damage to property that occurred when the UBS store shipped a stovetop for the customer. The customer won at trial, and judgment was entered against UPS and the franchisee for over $4,000. On appeal, the franchisee argued that the customer sued the wrong party. The Franchise Agreement, admitted into evidence, clearly indicated that the name of the franchisee was "XFD, Inc."

and that "the UPS store 3832" was merely a name given to it by UPS to identify it as a franchisee. When this became clear at trial, the proper avenue should have been to amend the pleadings to conform to the evidence. However, because the customer acted *pro se*, this was not done and as the court put it, the consumer was "left with a hollow victory." Although the plaintiff won a judgment, there is no one to levy against to fulfill the judgment. The court reversed the judgment.

In *The Business Store, Inc. v. Mail Boxes, Etc.*, No. 11-3662, 2012 U.S. Dist. LEXIS 128330 (D.N.J. Sept. 7, 2012), Defendant Mail Boxes, Etc. ("MBE") sought leave to file a Third-Party Complaint against F. Dana Harris and Jennifer D. Harris ("Harrises"). The dispute involved former MBE franchisee, The Business Store, Inc.'s ("TBS") claims of breach of contract and improper termination. MBE filed an Answer and Counterclaim seeking damages for TBS's alleged material breaches of certain franchise agreements and a $65,000 promissory note. The Harrises were the owners of TBS and the guarantors of TBS's obligations under several agreements between the parties and allegedly provided MBE with a continuing guaranty of TBS's obligations. Thus, MBE argued that the Harrises were directly and independently liable to MBE for TBS's material breach of and obligations under the franchise agreements and promissory note. As such, MBE sought leave of the court to bring the Harrises into the matter as third-party defendants.

Under Federal Rule of Civil Procedure 14(a), defendants may implead a third-party within 10 days after serving their original answer. MBE filed the motion 11 days beyond the deadline, but argued that delay, which was inadvertent and caused by a change of counsel, would not prejudice TBS because discovery was still in its infancy. Further, MBE asserted that any delay of the final resolution would be "far outweighed by the benefits of judicial economy in consolidating [the] matters." TBS argued that MBE had previously taken no action to join the Harrises even though MBE had ample time to do so. TBS further alleged that joining the Harrises would completely change the character of the litigation by increasing the amount of discovery required, increasing overall costs, increasing use of judicial resources, and decreasing the likelihood of settlement.

In considering whether to grant the motion, the court considered the timeliness of the motion, the potential for complicating issues at trial, the probability of delaying the trial, and whether TBS would be prejudiced. The court first found that the parties had been aware of the Harrises existence and the fact that they may be joined as third-party defendants since early in the litigation. Next, the court found that even though the motion was filed

11 days late, it was not filed "so far beyond the deadline as to cause significant delay in the flow of the litigation." Further, the court found that since discovery was still in its infancy, adding the Harrises would have a minimal impact and would not significantly delay the trial. Additionally, the court found that because the Harrises were potentially liable under MBE's counterclaims, any delay would be outweighed by the benefits of consolidating the matter. Finally, the court found that while it was possible that the character of the litigation would change and that costs would increase, the change ultimately promoted judicial economy and that any increases would offset the potential costs to the parties if MBE filed a completely separate suit to recover from the Harrises. The court granted MBE leave to file a third-party complaint.

I.   ADMISSIBILITY OF EXPERT TESTIMONY

In *BP West Coast Products, LLC v. Shalabi*, No. 11-1341, 2013 U.S. Dist. LEXIS 56069 (W.D. Wash. Apr. 18, 2013), the court considered Plaintiff BP's motion to strike expert witnesses pursuant to Federal Rule of Civil Procedure 37(c)(1). BP moved to exclude Defendants' expert witnesses because they were not properly disclosed under Federal Rule of Civil Procedure 26(a)(2)(C)(ii), which requires a party to disclose a summary and supporting facts of each unretained expert's opinions. There were three expert witnesses that BP sought to strike: Cuneo, Pennington, and Schiller. Cuneo and Pennington, whose testimony description were one sentence each, were expected to give expert opinions "regarding the field of franchise relationships, in particular ARCO franchise relationships; zone pricing and gasoline delivery." Schiller, the Defendants' lawyer, was expected to testify about attorney's fees.

Defendants argued that any failure to disclose was harmless and that the opinions offered would be "substantially similar" to what had been expressed in the experts' declarations. Defendants further argued that BP could not "claim surprise, prejudice or other harm by Defense counsel serving as an expert on attorney's fees" because such practice was customary. BP argued that the "substantially similar" description of the experts' testimony was vague and left the door open for discussing matters that had not been disclosed.

The court ultimately granted the motion in part. The court found that Defendants' "failure to provide more than a one sentence description of Cuneo or Pennington's testimony" was unjustified and harmful because the descriptions did not allow BP a basis for preparing to oppose the witnesses. As a result, Cueno and Pennington were excluded as experts. With respect to attorney Schiller, the Washington Rules of Professional Conduct state that a lawyer shall not act as an advocate at a trial in which the lawyer is likely to be a necessary witness unless, the testimony relates to the "nature and value legal services rendered" in the case. Schiller's declaration stated that he intended to testify as an expert that the attorney's fees incurred in the case were "reasonable and necessary". To the extent that he intended to argue that his fees were reasonable or necessary, he was prohibited from doing so by rule 3.7 of the Washington Rules of Professional Conduct. As a result, the court held that Schiller could testify, but his testimony would be limited to the nature and value of the legal services rendered and not whether the attorney's fees incurred were reasonable and necessary.

In *Jack Tyler Engineering Company v. Colfax Corporation*, No. 10-02373, 2013 U.S. Dist. LEXIS 51603 (W.D. Tenn. Apr. 10, 2013), the court considered motions from both parties to exclude expert testimony. The dispute arose when Defendant Colfax Corporation, an industrial and construction products manufacturer ("Colfax"), unilaterally terminated an exclusive distributorship agreement with Plaintiff Jack Tyler Engineering Company ("JTE"). JTE retained Dr. Ralph Scott ("Scott") to calculate its alleged lost profit damages from the termination and Colfax retained Z. Christopher Mercer ("Mercer") to rebut Scott's testimony. Neither side contested the qualifications of the opposing expert. Colfax argued that Scott's testimony was unreliable under Federal Rule of Evidence 702, and JTE argued that Mercer's testimony was unreliable and irrelevant under Federal Rules of Evidence 702 and 703.

The court noted that reliability under Rule 702 is focused on the principles and methodology used by the expert as opposed to the conclusions they reach. Thus, the court held that because Colfax merely argued that Scott's analysis did not account for all of the relevant factors, as opposed to contesting the methodology used by Scott, exclusion was not warranted. Rather, the court found that such concerns should be addressed at trial. Similarly, the court denied JTE's motion to exclude Mercer's testimony. JTE argued that Mercer's testimony should be excluded under Rule 702 because he should have used the "ex-post" methodology instead of the "ex-ante" methodology, which was unreliable and outdated. The court found that Mercer could have reliably used either methodology and deciding which was better depended on the facts of the case. Thus, just because JTE did not agree that the facts of the case warranted using the ex-post method over the ex-ante method did not make the ex-post method unreliable. Finally, JTE argued that Mercer's testimony was irrelevant because it supported Colfax's anticipated defense as opposed to rebutting Scott's opinion. The court first noted that the standard for relevance was "extremely liberal," and then found that it was acceptable for Mercer to discuss factors that were not in Scott's testimony because the factors were relevant to Mercer's critique and what he saw as important considerations that Scott did not make. The court denied both motions.

J.   SCOPE OF DISCOVERY

This case provides a cautionary tale when attempting to protect documents from production in discovery by asserting the attorney-client privilege. In *Campero USA Corp. v. ADS Foodservice, LLC*, No. 12-20571, 2012 U.S. Dist. LEXIS 184497 (S.D. Fla. Dec. 13, 2012), the court was asked to reconsider a motion it granted to compel the Franchisor to produce allegedly privileged emails. The motion was filed by franchisee Defendants, ADS Foodservice, LLC and its principal, Spencer, (collectively "Defendants") for production of certain emails that franchisor Campero USA Corp. ("Plaintiff") refused to produce due to the attorney-client and/or work product privileges. In refusing to reverse its prior order compelling production, the court found that even after directing Plaintiff to support its claim of privilege and reminding Plaintiff of the correct standard to use, Plaintiff failed to produce sufficient evidence to support the alleged privilege and, as such, had failed to meet its burden to establish that the emails were protected.

The court offered a reminder of how future litigants should proceed when asserting a privilege: "(1) Bates stamp each document or otherwise specifically identify each communication; (2) start with Rule of Evidence 501, and, if necessary, proceed to case law to determine what law of privilege governs the communication and identify the elements of that privilege; (3) for each document or communication, identify the rule that establishes that each element of the privilege applies to that communication; (4) prepare a privilege log that has enough information about the communication so that the opposing party or the Court can determine, at minimum, that the claimed privilege might apply; and (5) engage in a meaningful give-and-take conferral with opposing counsel, where both parties have before them the privilege log, the elements of the applicable privilege law, and the party asserting the privilege has before him or her the allegedly privileged communication and the evidence that establishes each element of the privilege, so that questions can be answered." The court further advised that if at that point the dispute was still not resolved, the parties should then involve the court. The court affirmed its prior order compelling production of the emails.

In *Meltzer/Austin Restaurant Corporation v. Benihana National Corporation*, No. 11-CV-542, 2013 U.S. Dist. LEXIS 41838 (W.D. Tex. Mar. 26, 2013), the court considered the scope of discovery under New York law. The dispute arose from "the deteriorating relationship" between franchisee Plaintiff Meltzer ("Meltzer"), and franchisor Benihana National Corporation ("Benihana"), following the death of Benihana's founder. Specifically, Meltzer alleged that in the summer and fall of 2009, he began receiving franchise-violation notices from Benihana for changes that had previously been approved.

Meltzer and Benihana disagreed as to "whether information related to Benihana's treatment of other franchisees and corporate stores [wa]s discoverable under New York law." Meltzer argued that because all contracts under New York law contain an implied covenant of good faith and fair dealing, "information concerning Benihana's enforcement of its standards and treatment of other franchisees [wa]s discoverable." Further, Meltzer argued that Benihana's alleged unfair treatment of him could "only be shown through evidence on how Benihana treated its other restaurants." Benihana, however, argued that the implied covenant of good faith and fair dealing was limited to the terms of the contract and that it did "not create an obligation on the part of the franchisor to treat all franchisees equally." Therefore, Benihana argued that information regarding how it treated other franchisees was irrelevant and undiscoverable as long as it was enforcing rights under its franchise agreement with Meltzer.

The court concluded that Meltzer was entitled to "limited discovery of information related to other Benihana franchisees and corporate stores." The court, aided by case law, concluded that the implied covenant of good faith and fair dealing can be breached even where the contract permits the alleged conduct and where the express terms of the contract are not breached. Further, under New York law, when a contract requires the exercise of discretion, it is accompanied by "a promise not to act arbitrarily or irrationally in exercising that discretion." The court found that because the franchise agreement between Melzer and Benihana required Benihana to exercise discretion in judging whether or not Melzer maintained high-quality standards, Benihana had a duty to exercise that discretion in good faith. Accordingly, the court allowed limited discovery for the purpose of gathering evidence that other franchises were treated differently.

K.   SANCTIONS

Repeatedly lying and violating court orders was found to be an insufficient reason to grant a default judgment against a McDonalds' franchisee in *Syed*

Ali Husain v. The Superior Court of Marin County, No. A136692, 2013 Cal. App. Unpub. LEXIS 2321 (Ct. App. Cal. Mar. 28, 2013). The Husains owned McDonald's franchises in the San Francisco area. The parties disputed whether McDonald's promised to provide a new 20-year franchise agreement to the Husains. The Husains sued to enforce this promise and McDonald's cross-complained to compel the Husain's to restore three disputed restaurants.

During the initial trial, Mr. Husain presented evidence that he mailed an acceptance of the new franchise agreement in the form of a certificate of mailing with a January 21, 2006 postmark stamp. McDonald's presented evidence that Mr. Husain lied because the post office was closed on that day and it would have been impossible to get that date stamp. Despite the evidence of fabrication, the court denied McDonald's motion for terminating sanctions because the Husains agreed to dismiss the contract claim.

After the Husains completed their case-in-chief, McDonald's renewed its motion for terminating sanctions, contending that Mr. Husain had 1) presented falsified invoices and used them to substantiate an overstated investment amount and testified untruthfully about the documents; 2) falsified the certificate of mailing; and 3) violated a court order on a motion *in limine* not to refer to Mrs. Husain's breast cancer. The court found that the Husains committed perjury, provided false evidence, and willfully and repeatedly violated the court's orders. Therefore, it held that no lesser sanctions would be appropriate and granted terminating sanctions dismissing the Husain's third amended complaint with prejudice, striking the Husain's answer to McDonald's amended cross-complaint and scheduling a prove up hearing regarding McDonald's damages. Husain's appealed.

The appellate court, while not approving the Husains' conduct, reversed these sanctions. The court emphasized that terminating sanctions are "a drastic measure that denies a party the right to a trial on the merits" and their use should limited. Furthermore, it found that this case was not the type of rare case in which "any remedy short of dismissal [is] inadequate to preserve the fairness of the trial." *Id*. at *7.

In reversing the sanction, the court's reasoning focused on the Civil Discovery Act and the court's inherent power. First, the court found that terminating sanctions were not authorized for discovery abuse under the Civil Discovery Act. The only situation under the Act that allows for such action is failure to obey an order compelling document production. The court found that the Husains' actions could not be characterized as failing to produce documents and, therefore, terminating sanctions were not appropriate. Second, the court found that terminating sanctions can be justified as an exercise of the court's inherent supervisory power. However, it did not exercise this power because McDonald's made no showing that "the Husains' misconduct deprived it of a fair adversary trial in any sense." *Id.* at *15.

For these reasons, the court held that lesser sanctions would fully protect McDonald's right to a fair trial. The court granted the petition for a writ of mandate to Plaintiffs, directing the district court to vacate its order granting terminating sanctions. The court ordered the district court to reinstate the Husains' pleadings and set the matter for a new trial.

Guy Blume, a Dairy Queen franchisee, had a very litigious 2011, 2012 and early 2013, ending with his loss by default judgment as ordered in *American Dairy Queen Corp. v. Blume*, No. 11-358, 2013 U.S. Dist. LEXIS 59394 (D. Minn. Jan. 11, 2013). After Blume's franchise was terminated for non-payment of royalties and other fees, he was sued by ADQ in Minnesota in 2011. Blume's motion to dismiss or transfer to Iowa was denied. Blume also contacted Judge Richard Kyle's chambers numerous times by telephone, asking to be heard on a number of matters.

The court did not care for these contacts and issued an Order directing Blume to obtain hearing dates by mailing an undated Notice of Hearing to the court and allowing the court to set the hearing. Blume violated this Order more than once, and he was informed by the court that future failure to comply could result in sanctions, including default judgment.

On February 29, 2012, Blume became upset with the court when it allowed ADQ to file a proposed order in connection with a motion to amend. Blume sent an email to chambers stating that the Minnesota case "stinks of impropriety" and ended with the statement "WTF Man?" Blume later sent another e-mail which ended with "this is a joke and cover up in Minnesota." Blume was ordered to appear and show cause why he should not be sanctioned for this misconduct and for alleging that ADQ had subjected him to death threats. Blume did not appear. Blume also refused to be deposed by ADQ. After being compelled by the court to appear at deposition, Blume stated that he would not answer any questions and would be invoking his 6th (*sic*) and 14th Amendment rights not to answer questions.

Blume then filed numerous motions without complying with the court's previous instructions. ADQ moved to strike the motions and for sanctions. While ADQ's motion was pending, Blume filed two appeals to the Eighth Circuit, three motions, and several other documents. After Blume's appeals were dismissed, the court ruled on ADQ's motions to dismiss and for sanctions.

The court found that, since Blume had been warned and sanctioned on several occasions and yet showed no evidence he intended to comply with the court's orders, default judgment was the only proper sanction.

Another case where the franchisor sought and received default judgment as a sanction was *Howard Johnson International, Inc. v. Kim*, No. 11-3438, 2012 U.S. Dist. LEXIS 178026 (D.N.J. Dec. 17, 2012). Mr. Kim was not nearly as colorful as Mr. Blume. Mr. Kim filed an Answer and Counterclaim but simply refused to participate in the litigation process thereafter.

Despite numerous efforts by the court and HJI to contact Mr. Kim, he failed to provide a joint discovery plan, failed to provide Rule 26 disclosures, and failed to appear for a pre-trial conference. The court found this misconduct "willful" and found it could not be remedied by any other sanction. While Mr. Kim may have had a defense on the merits, this fact did not preclude default judgment where Mr. Kim simply refused to participate in the litigation process. Default judgment was entered against Mr. Kim.

The litigation misconduct of the franchisee in *Precision Franchising, LLC v. Gatej*, No. 12-CV-158, 2012 U.S. Dist. LEXIS 175450 (E.D. Va. Dec. 11, 2012), was even less egregious. Gatej simply failed to answer Rule 36 requests for admissions for several months, eventually answering them on October 24, 2012. The discovery deadline was set for December 14, 2012. Rather than extending the discovery period or issuing some other lesser sanction, the Court deemed all of the requests for admissions admitted. Once the requests were deemed admitted, the court found that Precision Franchising was entitled to summary judgment.

In *Days Inn Worldwide, Inc. v. May & Young Hotel – New Orleans, LLC*, No. 11-CV-01546, 2012 U.S. Dist. LEXIS 179344 (D. N.J. Dec. 19, 2012) the defendant franchisee was "unable to present any evidence" at a bench trial in light of the failure of the franchisee's president's failure to appear as a witness. Defendant's counsel appeared, but did not seek a continuance of the case because "it appeared likely" that the president "would never appear for trial." The court heard Days Inns' evidence and ruled for Days Inns on its breach of contract claims.

Carpet Cops, Inc. v. Carpet Cops, LLC, No. 11-CV-00561, 2012 U.S. Dist. LEXIS 127239 (D. Nev. Sept. 6, 2012) involved a former franchisee's failure to appear in a Lanham Act action alleged continued use of the franchisor's marks post-termination. The Court ordered oral argument and found that, while their might be meritorious defenses to be had, defendants had failed to appear and default judgment was proper. However, the court significantly reduced the amount claimed by Carpet Cops, and even denied default judgment on one claim *sua sponte*.

In *PSP Franchising v. Dubois*, No. 12-CV-11693, 2013 U.S. Dist. LEXIS 28048 (E.D. Mich. Feb. 28, 2013), the Dunkin' Donuts franchisor terminated a franchisee and then sued for injunctive relief enforcing a non-compete and for under $100,000 in damages, plus attorneys' fees. Dubois failed to appear. The Magistrate recommended injunctive relief, but felt an evidentiary hearing was necessary on claimed past and future royalties and unpaid invoices for merchandise. PSP asked the federal judge to grant all relief requested.

The judge determined that all relief could be granted without a hearing since all damages were either (1) supported by admissible evidence or (2) readily discernible from figures submitted in affidavits. Since future damages of $42,000 could be calculated just by looking at the liquidated damages provision of the Franchise Agreement, no hearing was necessary.

In *Bletas v. Deluca*, No. 11-CV-1777, 2013 U.S. Dist. LEXIS 103592 (S.D. N.Y. July 18, 2013), the count granted the defendants' motion for sanctions and attorneys' fees and denied one plaintiff's motion to withdraw. The plaintiffs were Greek residents who operated Subway franchisees increase and an attorney who represented the franchisees in an arbitration proceeding. The plaintiffs raised constitutional, human rights, tax, fraud, libel, corruption antitrust and various other criminal offenses and sought over $1 billion in damages. In the current case, the franchisees were ostensibly pro se and the attorney asserted her own claims against the defendants. The defendants included several individuals, including a U.S. District Court Judge, Subway International B.V., Doctor's Associates, Inc., Subway' founder, Fred Deluca and Subway's attorneys of record.

In November 2011, the court granted the defendants' motion to dismiss the plaintiff's complaint, granted defendants' motion for sanctions and ordered the plaintiffs to pay defendants' attorneys' fees and costs. The plaintiffs appealed. While the appeal was pending, the defendants filed an amended motion in the district court that corrected an inadvertent omission and added one of the plaintiffs to the motion for sanctions. The district court stayed consideration of the defendants' amended motion until after the appeal. The Second Circuit affirmed the district court's first order and remanded to the district court to determine the proper amount of attorneys' fees in connection with the appeal. The defendants then renewed their amended motion for sanctions in the district court.

The plaintiffs argued that the court should further defer consideration of the defendants' renewed motion for sanctions until after the Second Circuit addressed the plaintiffs' petition for rehearing en banc. However, the Second Circuit had already denied the plaintiffs' petition. Accordingly, the district court granted the defendants' renewed motion for sanctions and ordered the plaintiffs to pay the defendants' attorneys' fees.

Finally, the court denied one plaintiff's motion to withdraw from the case. The court found strong evidence that the attorney–plaintiff filed the motion without the named plaintiff's authorization. In addition, the court held it would be inappropriate to allow a plaintiff to withdraw from the case when the only remaining aspect of the case was to pay to defendants' the sanctions the court imposed against all the plaintiffs.

CHAPTER ❖ 10

International

I.   Introduction

It has been a relatively active year for franchise developments in several significant markets outside the United States. These include Canada, Australia and Indonesia. As reported in last year's Annual Developments, the Manitoba Franchise Statute became effective on October 1, 2012. This made Manitoba the fifth Canadian province to enact legislation regulating franchising. Also summarized are new franchise regulations proposed by British Columbia.

Australia is also on the cusp of a major revision to its Franchising Code of Conduct. On June 17, 2013, the Australian government issued a Consultation Paper suggesting 18 separate recommended changes, which are summarized below. Although the proposed revisions to the Australian Franchise Code are in the comment phase and have not become law, it is very likely that most of the recommendations will be adopted.

Finally, as franchising continues to expand in Asian markets, the Indonesian government recently issued new regulations that became effective August 31, 2012.

II. Canada

A. LEGISLATIVE DEVELOPMENTS

1. Manitoba's Franchises Act

Manitoba's *Franchises Act*, SM 2010, c 13 became effective on October 1, 2012. This made Manitoba the fifth Canadian province to enact franchise legislation. The *Franchises Act* applies to franchise agreements entered into on or after October 1, 2012 as long as the franchised business operates partly or wholly in Manitoba. It also applies to renewals or extensions of franchise agreements that were entered into either before or after October 1, 2012, and certain provisions apply to franchise agreements entered into before October 1, 2012. The *Franchises Act* requires the duty of fair dealing in the performance and enforcement of franchise agreements. It stipulates that franchisors must give every prospective franchisee a copy of the franchisor's disclosure document (the "FDD") and specifies the requirements surrounding the delivery and contents of the FDD. Its provisions also encompass such matters as the interpretation of franchise agreements, rescission, damages and defenses.

2. British Columbia's Proposed Franchise Legislation

On April 2, 2013, the British Columbia Law Institute (the "BCLI") issued the *Consultation Paper on a Franchise Act for British Columbia* (the "Consultation Paper"). The purpose of the Consultation Paper is to assess whether BC should enact franchise legislation. As part of the discussion, the BCLI is currently seeking feedback from franchisors, franchisees, business and consumer organizations and the general public regarding the proposed legislation. Interested parties have until September 30, 2013 to provide input on the Consultation Paper that will be considered by the BCLI as it prepares a final report. Both the Canadian Franchise Association and the Canadian Bar Association are presently reviewing the Consultation Paper and will be submitting comments to the BCLI as part of this process.

B. CASE LAW

In the *1250264 Ontario Inc. v. Pet Valu Canada Inc.*, 2013 ONCA 279 (CanLII) decision, the Ontario Court of Appeal determined the validity of the opt-out process in a certified class proceeding brought on behalf of franchisees against the franchisor, Pet Valu Canada Inc. Near the end of the opt-out period, a group of franchisees who opposed the class action campaigned to persuade other class members to opt out. The campaign was successful. More than half of the proposed class submitted opt-out notices by the end of the opt-out period. The representative plaintiff moved for an order to invalidate these opt-out notices, alleging that the class members had been coerced into submitting them. The Ontario Superior Court of Justice granted the order. He referenced the standard from *1176560 Ontario Ltd. v. Great Atlantic & Pacific Co. of Canada ("A&P")* that involvement in a class action must occur on an informed and voluntary basis that is free from undue influence. The franchisor appealed and the Court of Appeal reversed, finding that the opt-out notices were valid. It upheld the use of the *A&P* standard, but held that a finding of coercion was unsupported by the evidence. With respect to the number of individuals that had opted out, the Court of Appeal held that the number of opt-outs is very rarely a basis for decertification and that certified class proceedings may continue despite the diminished size of the class. The Court of Appeal noted that if parties become aware that class members are engaging in improper conduct, representative plaintiffs must promptly seek court intervention and defendants should not "sit idly by in the face of such conduct without running the risk that a court will invalidate opt-outs" (para 44). The Court of Appeal demonstrated a concern for protecting the fairness of the opt-out process and maintaining close judicial scrutiny of both the franchisor's and the franchisees' actions.

In *2189205 Ontario Inc. et al. v. Springdale Pizza Depot Ltd et al.*, 2013 ONSC 1232 (CanLII), the plaintiffs were former franchisees of the Pizza Depot franchise system. They rescinded their franchise agreements with the defendant franchisor, Springdale Pizza Depot Ltd. ("Springdale"), pursuant to § 6 of the *Arthur Wishart Act (Franchise Disclosure), 2000* (the "Act") for Springdale's failure to provide a required disclosure document. A Special Master conducted a hearing to determine the damages owed to the franchisees pursuant to § 6(6)(a) – (d) of the Act. Subsections (a) – (c) require the franchisor to refund any money received from the franchisee and to purchase back any inventory, supplies and equipment bought by the franchisee pursuant to the franchise agreement. Subsection (d) of the Act requires the franchisor to compensate the franchisee for any losses it incurs less the amounts in subsections (a) – (c). The Master awarded the franchisees damages under subsections (a) – (c), but not under subsection (d) as he found the franchisees had earned a net profit of $8,314.48 while in operation. Springdale brought a motion to oppose confirmation of the Master's reference report on a number of grounds. In particular, Springdale argued that it was entitled to set off any profits earned by the franchisees during the operation of their franchise against any amounts claimed due by the franchisor under § 6(6)(a) – (c) of the Act. Springdale argued that a set-off would place the former franchisees in the same position they were in before signing the franchise agreement, which is consistent with the restitutionary nature of the rescission remedy. The Ontario Superior Court of Justice dismissed Springdale's motion. It held that a rescinding franchisee is entitled to recover all amounts under § (6)(a) – (c) of the Act even if it suffers no loss under subsection (d) and even if it has otherwise made a profit while in operation.

In *3574423 Canada Inc. v. Baton Rouge Restaurants Inc.*, 2013 ONCA 39 (CanLII), 3574423 Canada Inc. (the "Franchisee"), a franchisee of the Baton Rouge restaurant franchise with a location in the City of Toronto, had a contractual right of first refusal for the next franchise location in the Greater Toronto Area. Over the years, the Franchisee turned down the franchisor's offers regarding a number of franchise locations. The Franchisee was given two opportunities by the franchisor to acquire a franchise location in Thornhill, both of which it turned down. The Franchisee commenced an action for damages based on breach of a contractual duty of good faith and breach of the duty of fair dealing pursuant to the *Arthur Wishart Act (Franchise Disclosure), 2000* (the "Act"), alleging that the franchisor withheld critical information regarding the Thornhill property. This critical information related to the terms of the lease for the Thornhill property and the size of the territory for that location. The Franchisee alleged that had it known that information, it would have purchased the Thornhill property. The action was dismissed by the trial judge and the Franchisee appealed. The Ontario Court of Appeal dismissed the appeal. It held that the duty of fair dealing in § 3 of the Act "calls for a balancing of the rights of both franchisees and franchisors" (para 18). The Court of Appeal noted that the Franchisee could have requested further details regarding the lease, but instead turned down the offer without seeking further information. The Court of Appeal also noted that the Franchisee's principals were sophisticated and practical businessmen with considerable experience in managing an existing franchise. Further, the terms of the lease were not materially different from those in the offer. With respect to the size of the territory, the Court of Appeal found that this had not been a significant factor in the Franchisee's decision to turn down the opportunity to purchase the Thornhill location. The Franchisee's failure to seek more information in this regard led the Court of Appeal to find the argument without merit.

In *Fairview Donut Inc. v. TDL Group Corp.*, 2012 ONCA 867 (CanLII), the franchisees of TDL Group Corp. and Tim Hortons Inc. ("Tim Hortons") commenced a proposed class action for various causes of action including breach of contract, misrepresentation, unjust enrichment, violations of the *Competition Act* and breach of the duty of good faith. The motion judge held that while certification of a class action would be appropriate for a number of issues, none of the proposed claims had any chance of success. Consequently, the action was dismissed. The franchisees appealed, alleging that Tim Hortons breached the franchise agreement in two ways: 1) by requiring franchisees to purchase donuts at commercially unreasonable prices when Tim Hortons transitioned to a new donut production system; and 2) by requiring franchisees to sell items on the Lunch Menu at unprofitable prices. The language in the franchise agreement stated that "[t]he franchisor is entitled to consider the profitability and prosperity of the system as a whole." Based on the motion judge's comprehensive review of Tim Hortons' procedure for considering the franchisees' position regarding the new donut production system, the Court of Appeal agreed that Tim Hortons had made a rational business decision that would benefit the franchisees in the long-term. The Court of Appeal dismissed the franchisees' appeal. The franchisees' application for leave to appeal to the Supreme Court of Canada was dismissed with costs.

III. Australia

On January 14, 2013 the Federal Government announced the review of the Franchising Code of Conduct by Mr. Alan Wein, an experienced franchising practitioner and mediator. On June 17, 2013 the Government issued a consultation paper giving background for the review, and seeking submissions. After reviewing submissions and engaging in extensive consultation with key stakeholders, the Wein Report was presented to the Government on 30 April, 2013. On June 17, 2013 the Government welcomed the recommendations and announced a consultation process with key stakeholders to assess the regulatory impact of the proposed amendments to the Code. That process is continuing notwithstanding the Federal election to be held on September 7, 2013, but legislation can be introduced during this period as the Government is in caretaker mode.

Although a change of Government is the likely outcome of the election, the Shadow Minister for Small Business has signaled his in principle support for the Wein Report recommendations. The recommendations also have general support from the Australian Competition and Consumer Commission ("ACCC"), which is the regulator charged with enforcing the Code, and the peak industry body, the Franchise Council of Australia. Although the general thrust of the amendments appears to have bi-partisan support, some additional uncertainty exists due to the fact that the Federal Opposition has also indicated its intention to legislate to prohibit unfair contractual provisions in "standard form" business contracts. If introduced, such legislation could well catch franchise agreements unless they are specifically exempted.

The Franchise Council of Australia is discussing the implementation of the Wein Report recommendations with the Federal Government, and has also approached the Federal Opposition seeking an exemption from the unfair contracts legislation for franchise agreements that are covered by the Code. Those discussions are likely to continue throughout 2013, and possibly beyond.

If implemented, the Wein Report recommendations will significantly strengthen the Code and give the ACCC enhanced enforcement powers. The recommendations are also designed to improve disclosure and reduce compliance cost, including compliance costs for foreign franchise systems.

The Wein Report makes 18 recommendations, which are summarized below. Those most relevant to U.S. based franchise systems are starred.-

1. A franchisor must provide a disclosure document with the franchisor's notice of intention to renew, which must be provided at least 6 months prior to the end of the franchise term. This is in addition to the normal disclosure obligation prior to signing a franchise agreement;

*2. A foreign franchisor is to have reduced disclosure obligations in certain circumstances. It is proposed that a foreign franchisor be relieved of its obligation to update its disclosure document annually, but perhaps be required to provide written responses to any queries in relation to a franchise agreement to which it is a party on matters that would be contained in a disclosure document;

3. A franchisor must disclose its right to conduct on-line sales in the disclosure document;

4. The short form disclosure document in Annexure 2 of the Code is to be removed;

5. Franchisors are to provide a generic risk statement to prospective franchisees. The statement is not intended to address specific risks related to that particular franchise, but rather generic risks;

*6. Franchisees have a right to terminate a franchise agreement in the event of insolvency, and franchisees become secured creditors in any liquidation for an amount calculated as the unexpired portion of the initial franchise fee;

*7. Franchisors are prohibited from imposing unreasonable capital expenditure requirements on franchisees;

8. The requirements for administration of marketing funds are to be strengthened;

*9. The common law duty of good faith is to be expressly included in all franchise agreements and in relation to the franchise relationship;

10. A franchisee must initiate any request that the franchisee's details be excluded from a disclosure document;

11. A franchisee must provide all reasonable information to a franchisor before triggering the 42 day notice period;

*12. If a franchisor does not grant a franchisee an extension of a franchise agreement upon expiration and the franchisee is not in breach and other conditions are satisfied, any post-term non-compete provisions shall not apply to the franchisee;

13. The Code mediation process applies to all mediations including court mediations;

*14. A franchisor cannot pass on to a franchisee the costs of dispute resolution, and cannot be required to litigate outside the Australian State where the franchise is located. (This recommendation is contentious, and is contrary to the generally accepted principle that the parties to a business contract should be free to choose the law and jurisdiction that are to apply to the contract.);

*15. The ACCC is given stronger enforcement powers including the ability to issue infringement notices and levy new pecuniary penalties for breach of the Code, conduct random audits, disqualify individuals from managing a company and request a court to order royalty free periods and payment of money into marketing funds;

16. Minimum term agreements and standard term contracts in the motor vehicle sector should be subject to further scrutiny and analysis;

17. There should be no further review of the Code for at least 5 years; and

18. Various drafting improvements set out in the annexure to the Wein Report should be made in consultation with representatives of the franchise sector.

Although most of the recommendations seem relatively innocuous at first glance, there are numerous implementation challenges. There are also concerns in relation to recommendations 6, 9, 12, 14 and 15, and discussions are still continuing with Government in relation to these issues.

The Franchise Council of Australia is currently working closely with the Federal Government to develop amendments to the Code that give effect to the intent of the recommendations without imposing additional compliance costs or having unintended consequences. In the background interest groups unhappy that the Wein Report did not recommend changes such as automatic extension of franchise agreement term or compensation at end of term and a new statutory duty of good faith (that was essentially unfair contracts legislation in another guise) continue to lobby for additional changes. The South Australian State Government has not yet confirmed whether it will abandon its stated intent of enacting State based legislation governing franchising, although the inclusion of the good faith duty and enhanced penalties for the ACCC make it hard for that State to justify further legislation.

From the foregoing one can see that franchise regulation in Australia remains in a state of flux, although the core elements of the regulatory framework remain unchanged.

IV. Indonesia

Although franchising in Indonesia has been regulated since 1997, the Indonesian government has recently issued Regulation of the Minister of Trade ("MOT") No. 53/M-DAG/PER/8/2012 regarding the Implementation of Franchising ("Regulation 53"). The new regulations replace Minister of Trade Regulation No. 31/M-DAG/PER/2008 and contain some controversial and new protectionist rules which may have an adverse impact on foreign brands wishing to do business in Indonesia. Regulation 53 became effective at the end of August 2012. The new regulation provides a more comprehensive regulatory framework, as well as placing new limitations and requirements on franchisors and franchisees. A summary of some of the more salient regulations includes:

Restrictions on appointment: A franchisor is not allowed to appoint a business enterprise with whom it has a controlling relationship as a franchisee. "Having a controlling relationship" means an ownership relationship or having management decisions made by the same personnel. Consequently, franchise owners may not appoint its subsidiary as a franchisee.

Minimum 80% local products/services requirement: Regulation 53 requires franchisors and franchisees to use at least 80% local content for raw materials and machinery used in their franchise businesses. Although there are waivers of this requirement available if products and services required by the franchise business are not available locally, the waiver is only available from a yet-to-be formed "Assessment Team." Additionally, there are no clear guidelines as to what is included in the 80% requirement or what is required to obtain a waiver.

Business license restrictions: Franchisors and franchisees are limited to engaging in business activities provided for in their business licenses. Although they may sell other goods related to their main business, this is limited to a maximum of 10% of total sales.

Clean break: In the event the franchisor unilaterally terminates a franchise agreement prior to its natural expiration date, it may not appoint a new franchisee in the same territory unless and until it settles all issues resulting from the termination of the franchise agreement in a written settlement agreement containing a "clean break joint statement" or it obtains a "permanent legally binding court decision".

Compliance with applicable laws: Both the franchisee and the franchisor are obligated to comply with all of the laws or regulations that relate to their specific business activities, including consumer protection, health, environmental, space planning, labor and intellectual property laws.

Presentation to the Assessment Team: a franchisor may be required to give a presentation on the franchise business to the Assessment Team as part of the registration process.

Additional regulations issued by the Indonesian MOT since Regulation 53 limit the number of franchise outlets that may be owned by franchisors and franchisees for minimarkets, supermarkets, department stores and hypermarkets. Additional regulations limit the number of outlets for food and beverage service businesses, including restaurants, bistros, bars and taverns, and cafés. Additional regulations limit the number of outlets to be owned and managed by the franchisor and the franchisee. Commentary from the Indonesian government indicates that these new rules are intended to end monopolies by franchisors and support local businesses.

TABLE OF CASES

Cases

TABLE OF CASES

TABLE OF CASES

INDEX

INDEX